Agnes

I'm far too young to look this hot.

by
TONY COCHRAN

Andrews McMeel
Publishing

Kansas City

Agnes is syndicated by Creators Syndicate. For information, write Creators Syndicate, 5777 W. Century Blvd., Suite 700, Los Angeles, CA 90045.

04 05 06 07 08 BBG 10 9 8 7 6 5 4 3 2 1

ISBN: 0-7407-4135-7

Library of Congress Control Number: 2003111159

For Vickie, without whom my heart would not sing
and Agnes could not speak.

As I always say, when the limelight finally shines, you better be ready to dance like a frantic monkey or they will just point that bad boy at someone who has done their homework in a more timely and conscientious manner. So I would like to take this opportunity to point myself out. Pointing yourself out is the quickest and most efficient way to up the wattage of limelights. If you wait for other people to point you out, you may find that you are generally unpointoutable and may very well be a no one in particular, and most no one in particulars end up bemoaning their fates to other no one in particulars, in less than desirable gathering places like coin laundromats and church basements. I, however, am well versed on the subject of me and can speak at length about it with many words and much confidence. Unlike a lot of people who talk at length about themselves, I am a very interesting topic. If people think I am full of myself, it's only because I can't bear to throw any of me away. It's taken a long time to gather it all up, and I have no outside of me luggage space, unless you count that collapsable vinyl shoe storage unit my granma bought for me but I have no idea where it is. I hope you enjoy me, for I know I do at times. I may sound selfish but remember... the only difference between selfish and selfless is several letters.

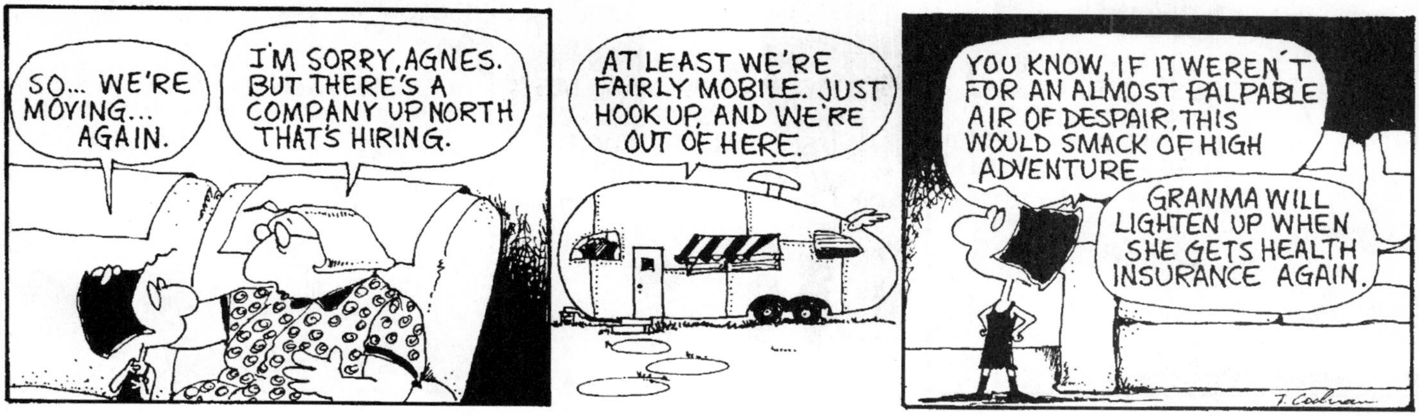
SO... WE'RE MOVING... AGAIN.
I'M SORRY, AGNES. BUT THERE'S A COMPANY UP NORTH THAT'S HIRING.
AT LEAST WE'RE FAIRLY MOBILE. JUST HOOK UP, AND WE'RE OUT OF HERE.
YOU KNOW, IF IT WEREN'T FOR AN ALMOST PALPABLE AIR OF DESPAIR, THIS WOULD SMACK OF HIGH ADVENTURE.
GRANMA WILL LIGHTEN UP WHEN SHE GETS HEALTH INSURANCE AGAIN.

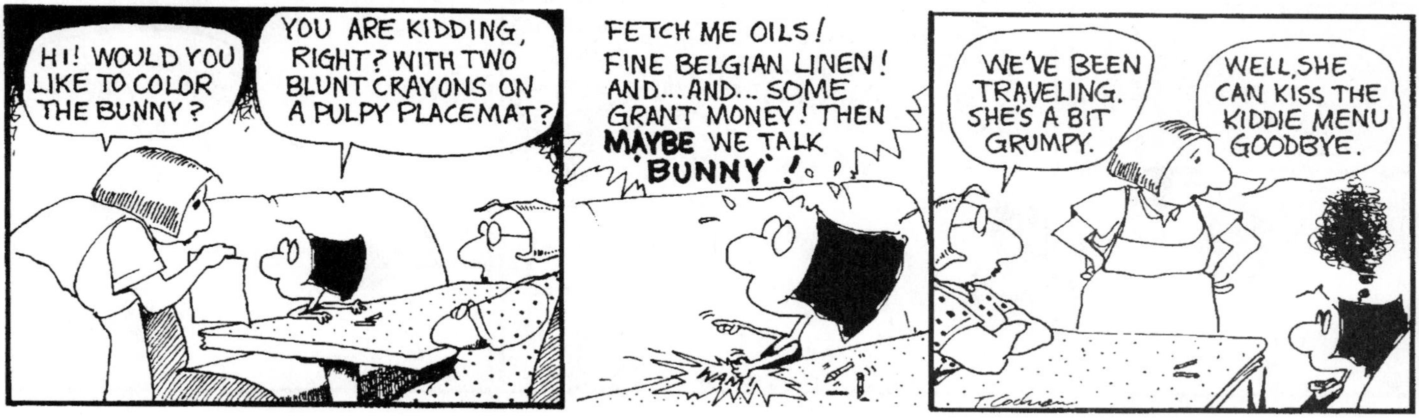
HI! WOULD YOU LIKE TO COLOR THE BUNNY?
YOU ARE KIDDING, RIGHT? WITH TWO BLUNT CRAYONS ON A PULPY PLACEMAT?
FETCH ME OILS! FINE BELGIAN LINEN! AND... AND... SOME GRANT MONEY! THEN MAYBE WE TALK "BUNNY"!
WE'VE BEEN TRAVELING. SHE'S A BIT GRUMPY.
WELL, SHE CAN KISS THE KIDDIE MENU GOODBYE.

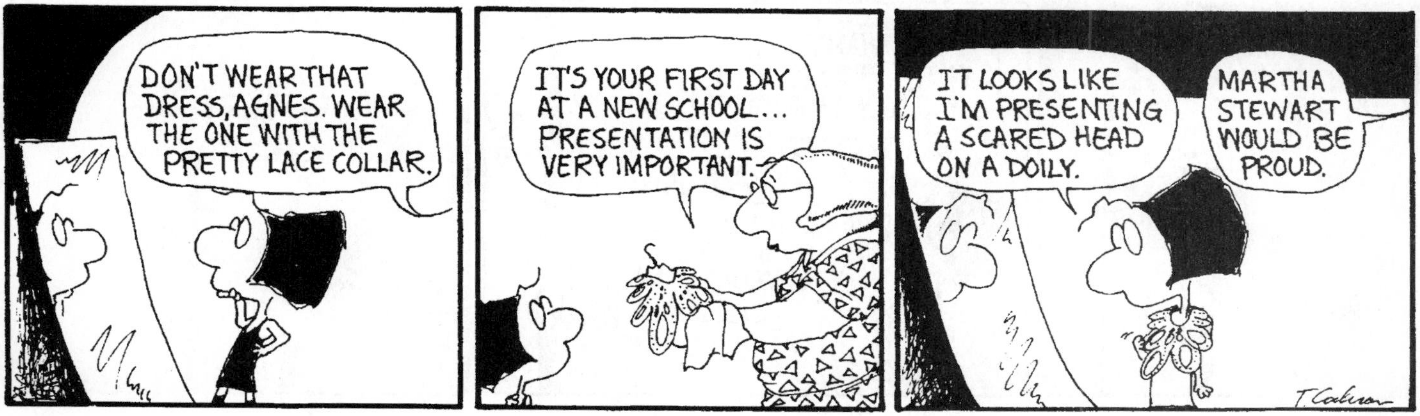
DON'T WEAR THAT DRESS, AGNES. WEAR THE ONE WITH THE PRETTY LACE COLLAR.
IT'S YOUR FIRST DAY AT A NEW SCHOOL... PRESENTATION IS VERY IMPORTANT.
IT LOOKS LIKE I'M PRESENTING A SCARED HEAD ON A DOILY.
MARTHA STEWART WOULD BE PROUD.

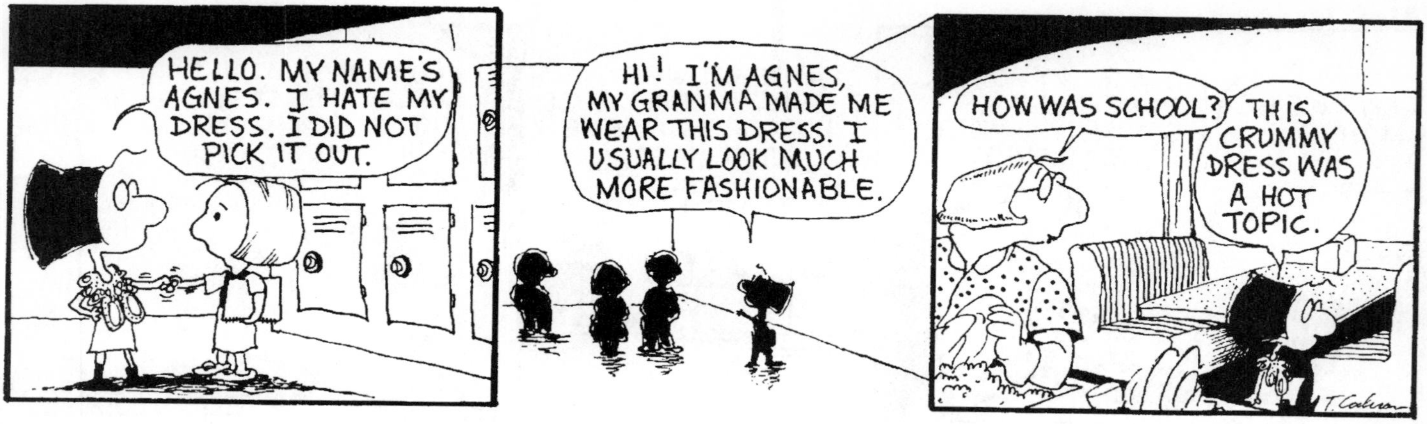
HELLO. MY NAME'S AGNES. I HATE MY DRESS. I DID NOT PICK IT OUT.
HI! I'M AGNES, MY GRANMA MADE ME WEAR THIS DRESS. I USUALLY LOOK MUCH MORE FASHIONABLE.
HOW WAS SCHOOL?
THIS CRUMMY DRESS WAS A HOT TOPIC.

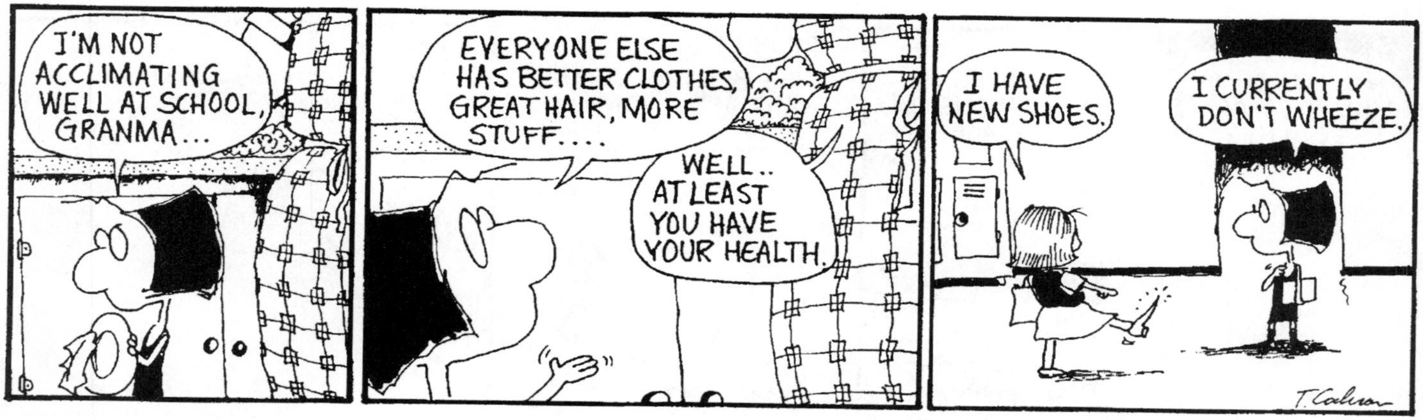
I'M NOT ACCLIMATING WELL AT SCHOOL, GRANMA...
EVERYONE ELSE HAS BETTER CLOTHES, GREAT HAIR, MORE STUFF....
WELL.. AT LEAST YOU HAVE YOUR HEALTH.
I HAVE NEW SHOES.
I CURRENTLY DON'T WHEEZE.

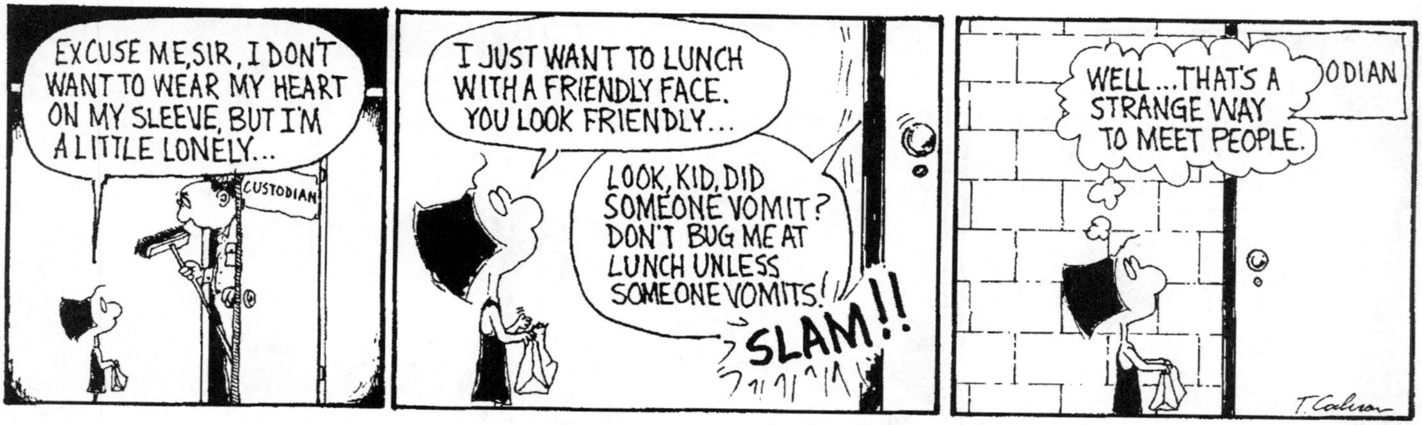
EXCUSE ME, SIR, I DON'T WANT TO WEAR MY HEART ON MY SLEEVE, BUT I'M A LITTLE LONELY...
CUSTODIAN
I JUST WANT TO LUNCH WITH A FRIENDLY FACE. YOU LOOK FRIENDLY...
LOOK, KID, DID SOMEONE VOMIT? DON'T BUG ME AT LUNCH UNLESS SOMEONE VOMITS!
SLAM!!
WELL...THAT'S A STRANGE WAY TO MEET PEOPLE.
ODIAN

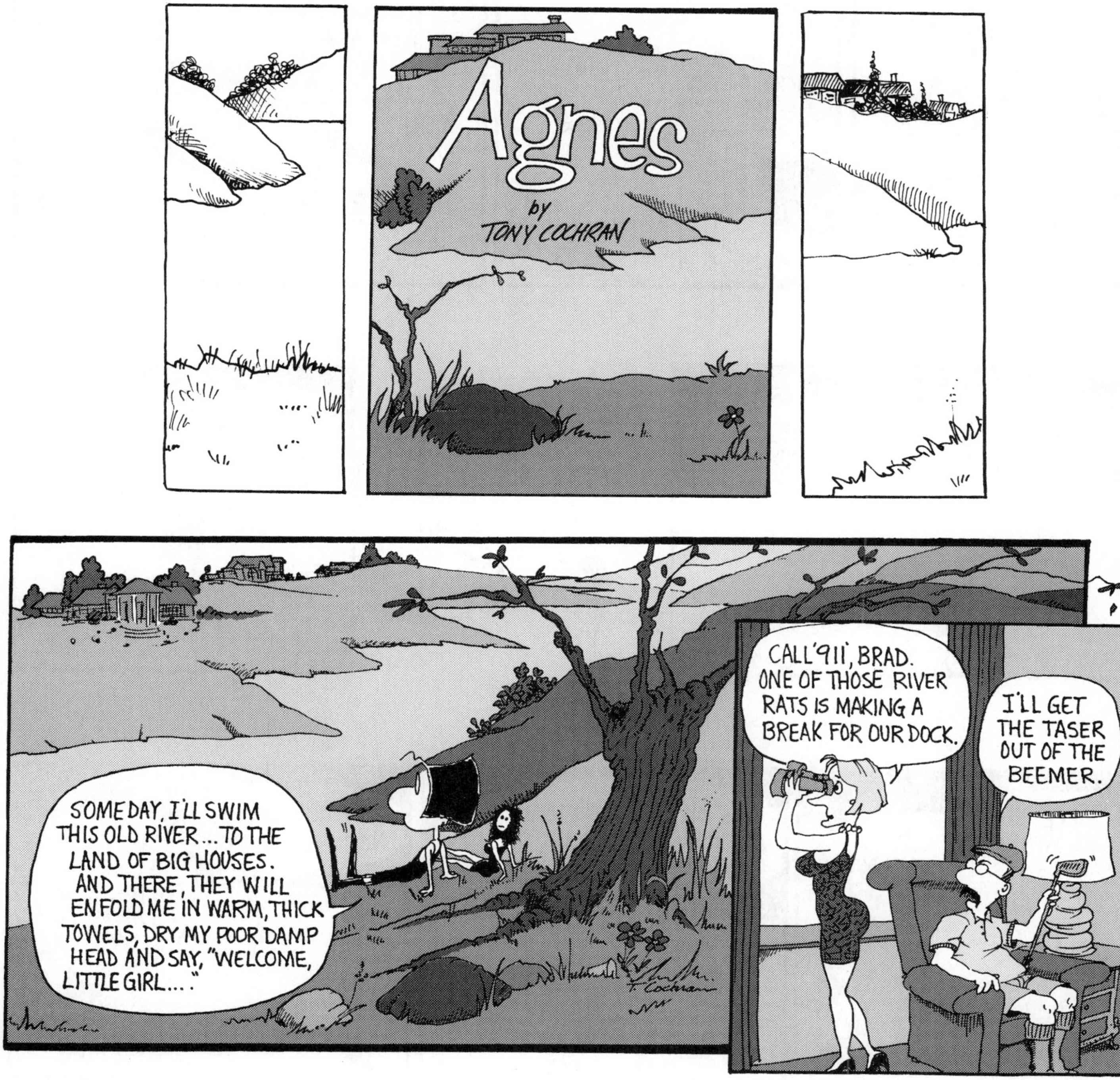
Agnes
by TONY COCHRAN
SOMEDAY, I'LL SWIM THIS OLD RIVER... TO THE LAND OF BIG HOUSES. AND THERE, THEY WILL ENFOLD ME IN WARM, THICK TOWELS, DRY MY POOR DAMP HEAD AND SAY, "WELCOME, LITTLE GIRL...."
CALL '911', BRAD. ONE OF THOSE RIVER RATS IS MAKING A BREAK FOR OUR DOCK.
I'LL GET THE TASER OUT OF THE BEEMER.
T. Cochran

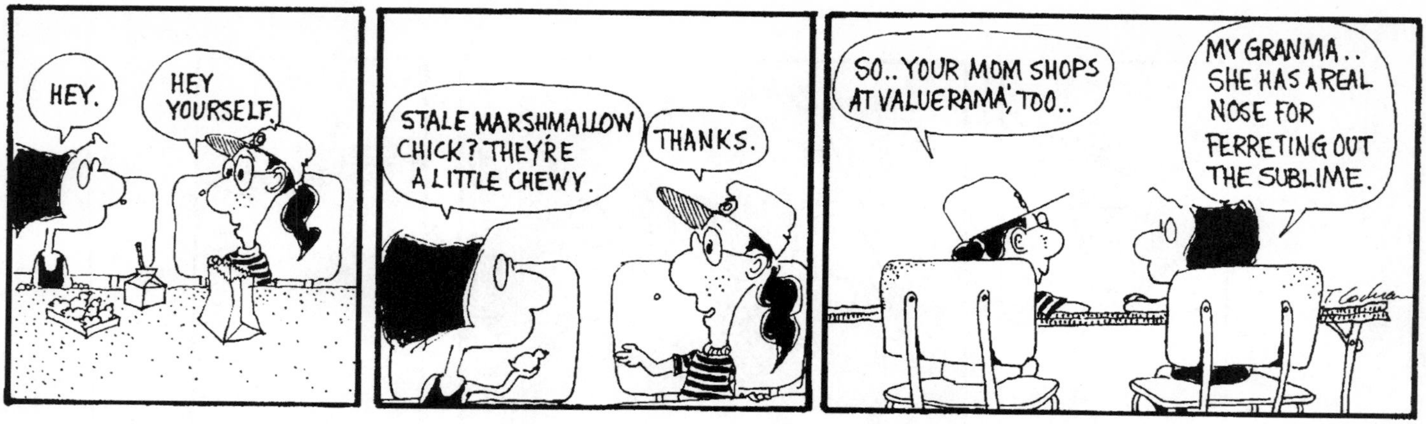
HEY.
HEY YOURSELF.
STALE MARSHMALLOW CHICK? THEY'RE A LITTLE CHEWY.
THANKS.
SO.. YOUR MOM SHOPS AT VALUE RAMA, TOO..
MY GRANMA.. SHE HAS A REAL NOSE FOR FERRETING OUT THE SUBLIME.

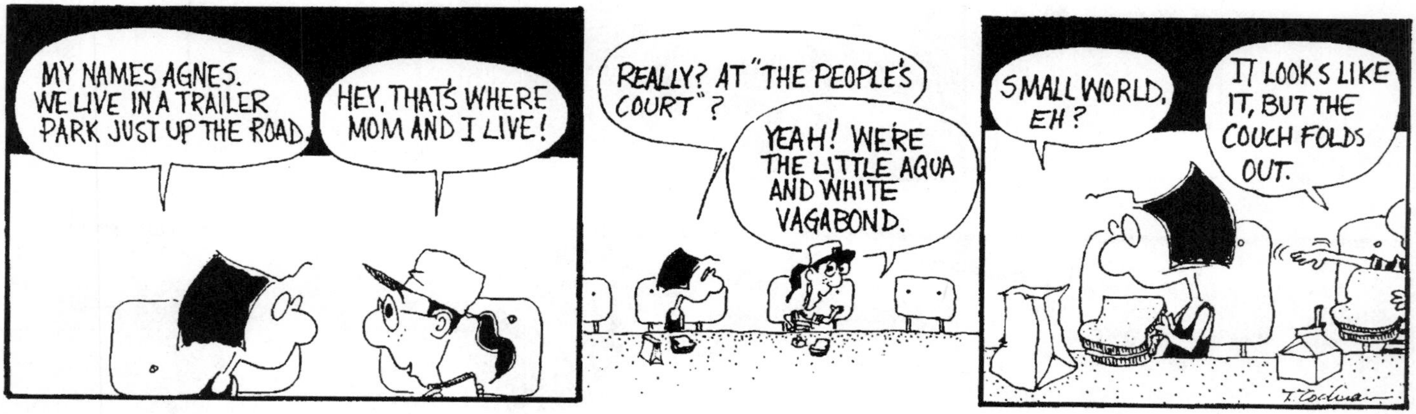
MY NAMES AGNES. WE LIVE IN A TRAILER PARK JUST UP THE ROAD.
HEY, THAT'S WHERE MOM AND I LIVE!
REALLY? AT "THE PEOPLE'S COURT"?
YEAH! WE'RE THE LITTLE AQUA AND WHITE VAGABOND.
SMALL WORLD, EH?
IT LOOKS LIKE IT, BUT THE COUCH FOLDS OUT.

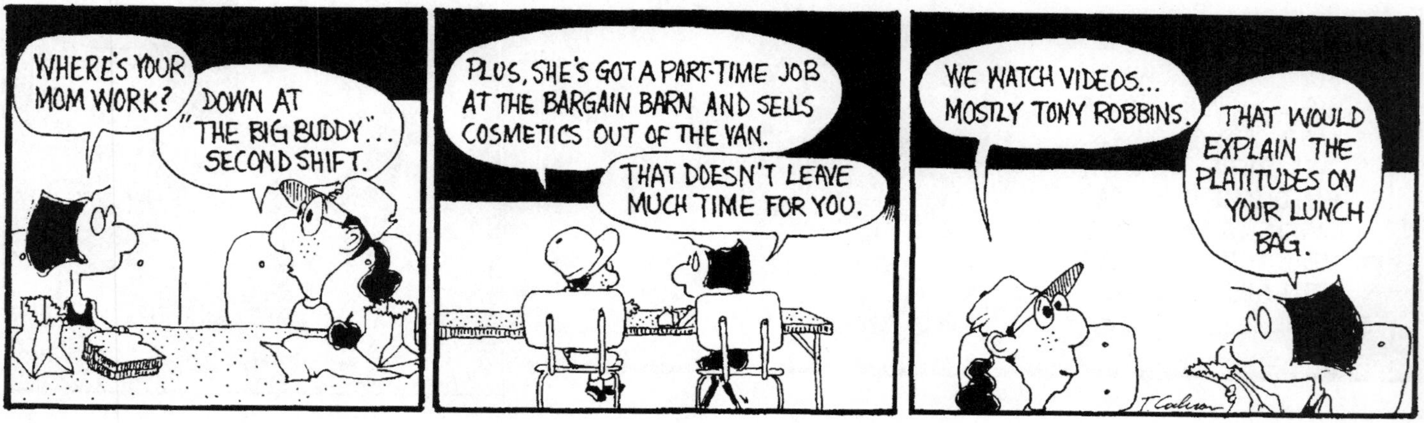
WHERE'S YOUR MOM WORK?
DOWN AT "THE BIG BUDDY"... SECOND SHIFT.
PLUS, SHE'S GOT A PART-TIME JOB AT THE BARGAIN BARN AND SELLS COSMETICS OUT OF THE VAN.
THAT DOESN'T LEAVE MUCH TIME FOR YOU.
WE WATCH VIDEOS... MOSTLY TONY ROBBINS.
THAT WOULD EXPLAIN THE PLATITUDES ON YOUR LUNCH BAG.

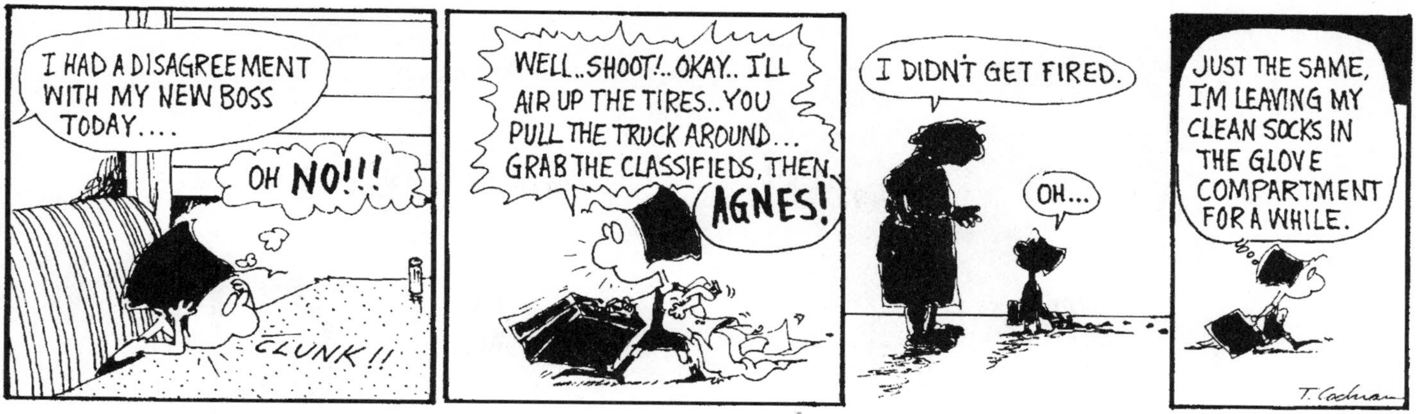
I HAD A DISAGREEMENT WITH MY NEW BOSS TODAY....
OH NO!!!
CLUNK!!
WELL..SHOOT!..OKAY.. I'LL AIR UP THE TIRES..YOU PULL THE TRUCK AROUND... GRAB THE CLASSIFIEDS, THEN...
AGNES!
I DIDN'T GET FIRED.
OH...
JUST THE SAME, I'M LEAVING MY CLEAN SOCKS IN THE GLOVE COMPARTMENT FOR A WHILE.
T. Cochran

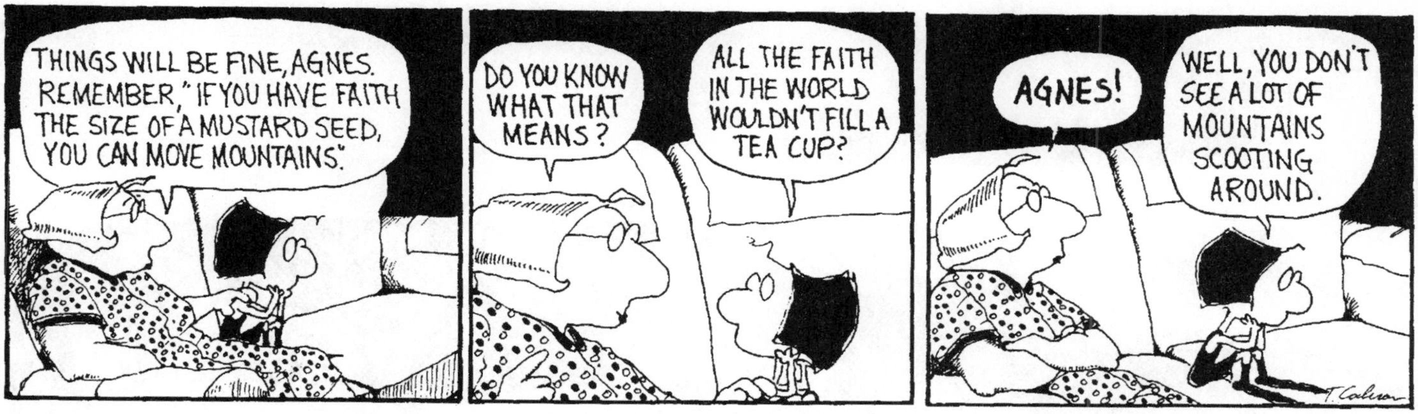
THINGS WILL BE FINE, AGNES. REMEMBER, "IF YOU HAVE FAITH THE SIZE OF A MUSTARD SEED, YOU CAN MOVE MOUNTAINS."
DO YOU KNOW WHAT THAT MEANS?
ALL THE FAITH IN THE WORLD WOULDN'T FILL A TEA CUP?
AGNES!
WELL, YOU DON'T SEE A LOT OF MOUNTAINS SCOOTING AROUND.
T. Cochran

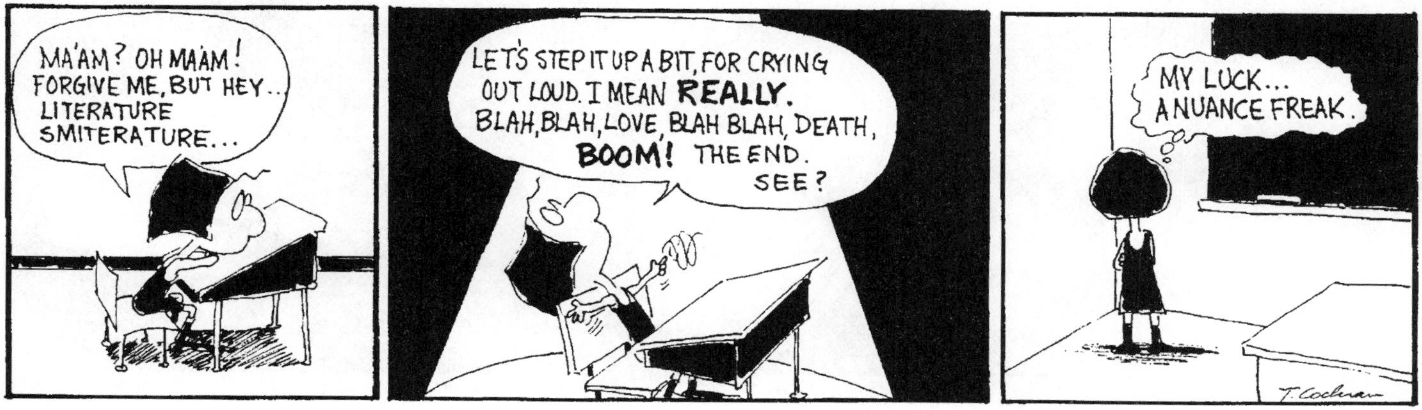
MA'AM? OH MA'AM! FORGIVE ME, BUT HEY.. LITERATURE SMITERATURE...
LET'S STEP IT UP A BIT, FOR CRYING OUT LOUD. I MEAN REALLY. BLAH, BLAH, LOVE, BLAH BLAH, DEATH, BOOM! THE END. SEE?
MY LUCK... A NUANCE FREAK.
T. Cochran

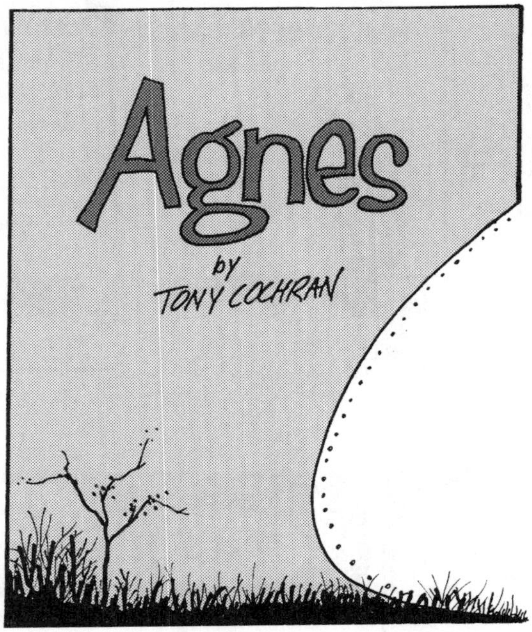
Agnes
by
TONY COCHRAN

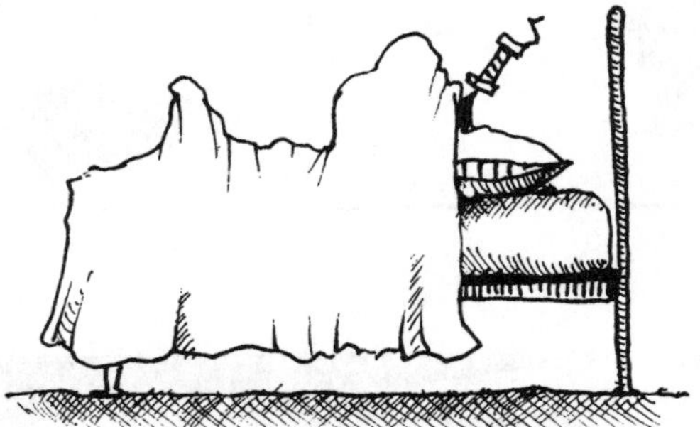

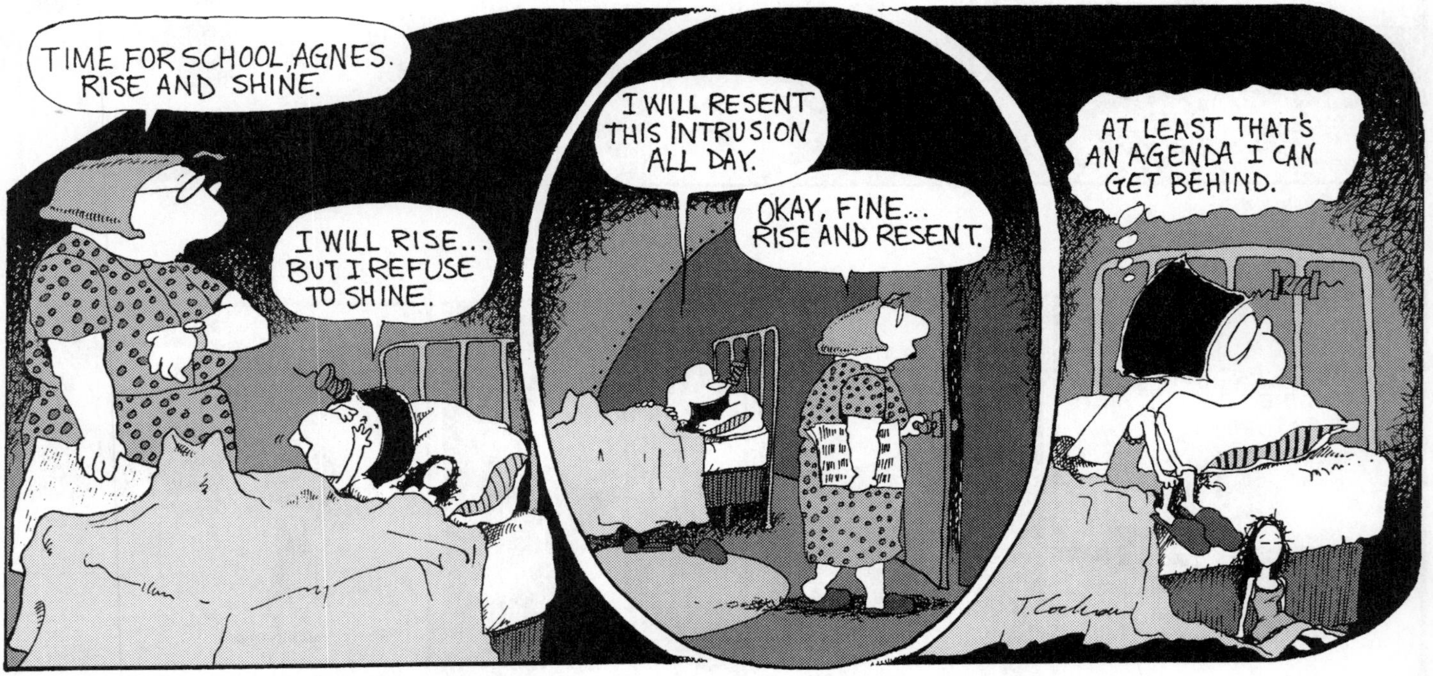
TIME FOR SCHOOL, AGNES. RISE AND SHINE.
I WILL RISE... BUT I REFUSE TO SHINE.
I WILL RESENT THIS INTRUSION ALL DAY.
OKAY, FINE... RISE AND RESENT.
AT LEAST THAT'S AN AGENDA I CAN GET BEHIND.
T. Cochran

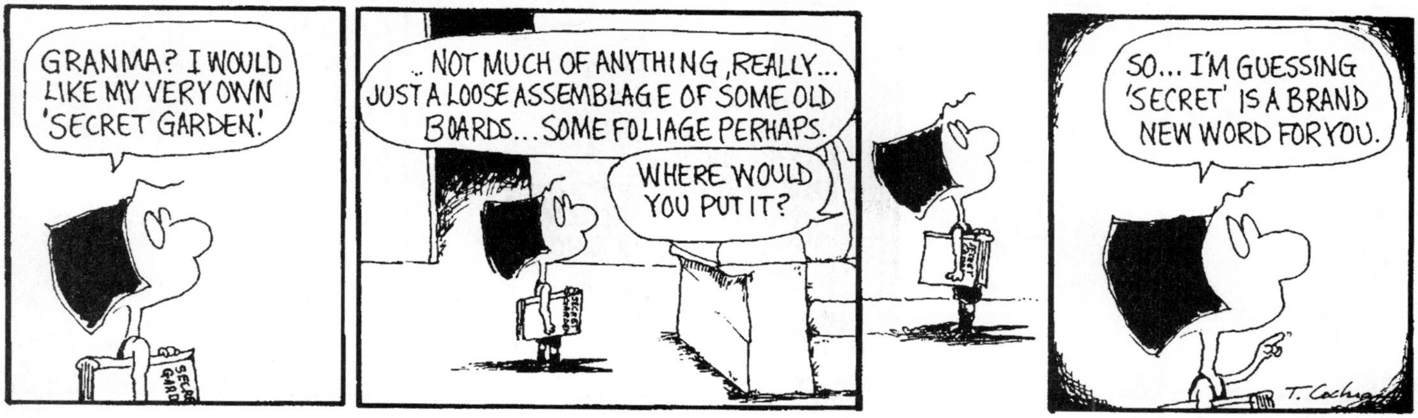
GRANMA? I WOULD LIKE MY VERY OWN 'SECRET GARDEN.'
... NOT MUCH OF ANYTHING, REALLY... JUST A LOOSE ASSEMBLAGE OF SOME OLD BOARDS... SOME FOLIAGE PERHAPS.
WHERE WOULD YOU PUT IT?
SO... I'M GUESSING 'SECRET' IS A BRAND NEW WORD FOR YOU.

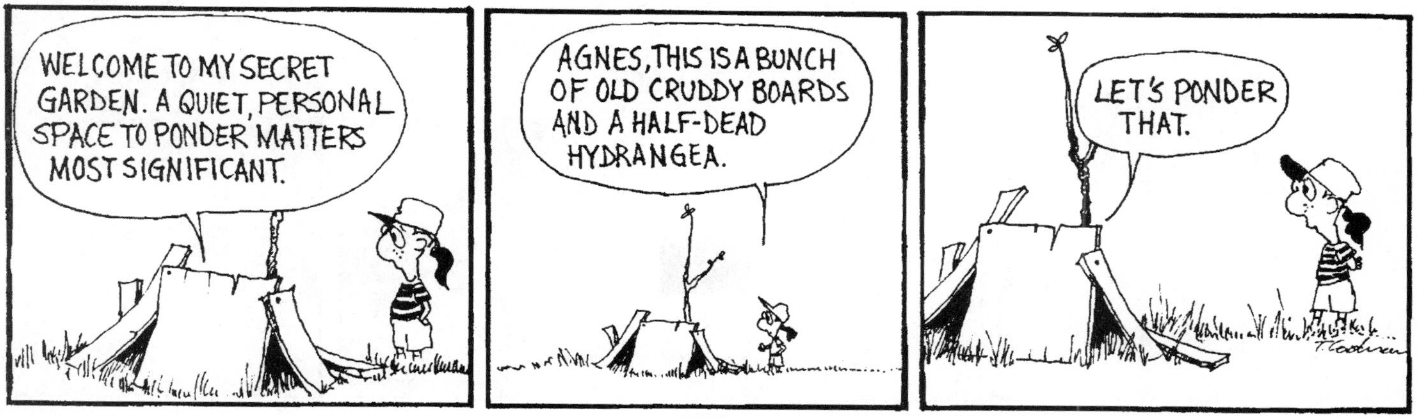
WELCOME TO MY SECRET GARDEN. A QUIET, PERSONAL SPACE TO PONDER MATTERS MOST SIGNIFICANT.
AGNES, THIS IS A BUNCH OF OLD CRUDDY BOARDS AND A HALF-DEAD HYDRANGEA.
LET'S PONDER THAT.

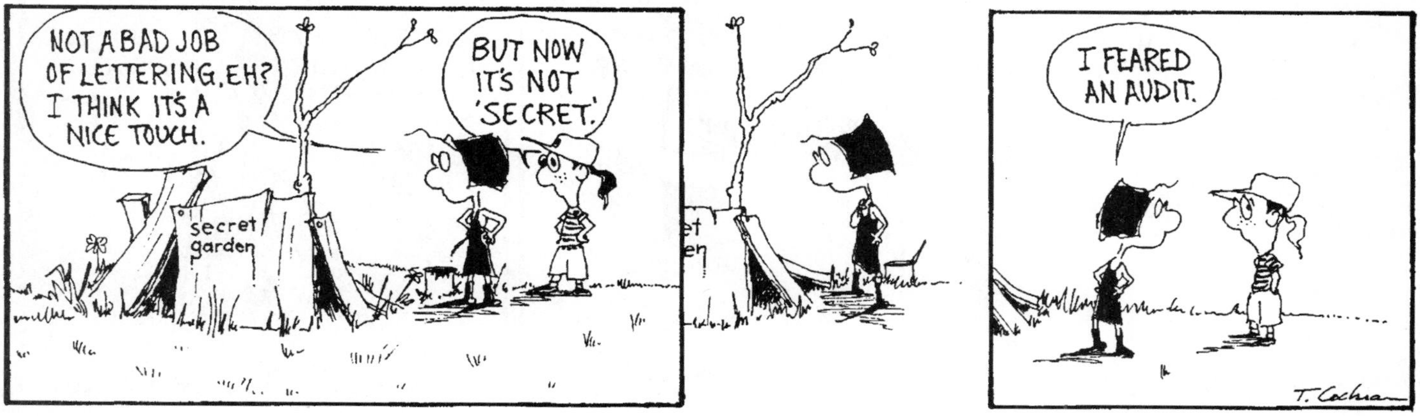
NOT A BAD JOB OF LETTERING, EH? I THINK IT'S A NICE TOUCH.
secret garden
BUT NOW IT'S NOT 'SECRET.'
I FEARED AN AUDIT.

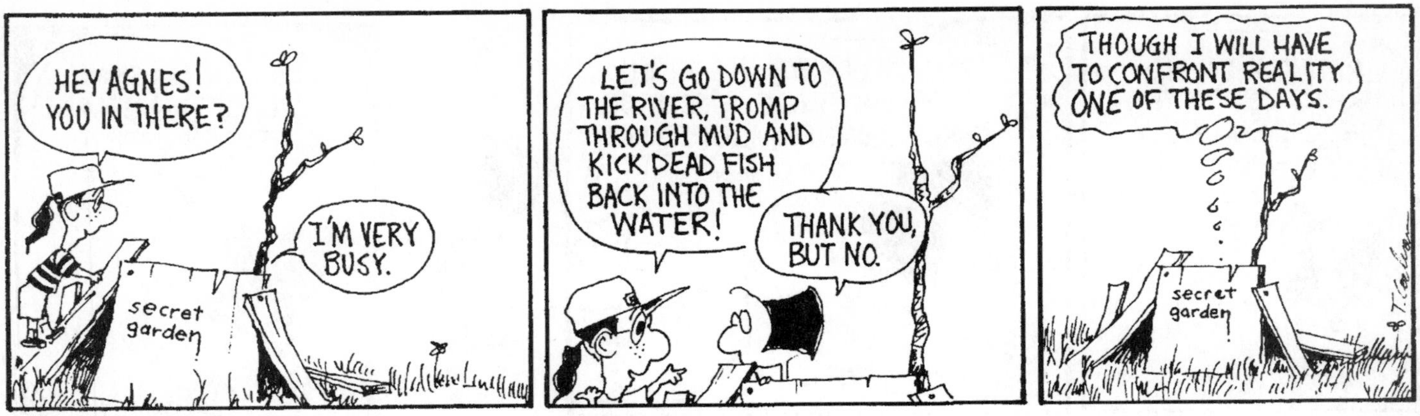
HEY AGNES! YOU IN THERE?
I'M VERY BUSY.
secret garden
LET'S GO DOWN TO THE RIVER, TROMP THROUGH MUD AND KICK DEAD FISH BACK INTO THE WATER!
THANK YOU, BUT NO.
THOUGH I WILL HAVE TO CONFRONT REALITY ONE OF THESE DAYS.
secret garden

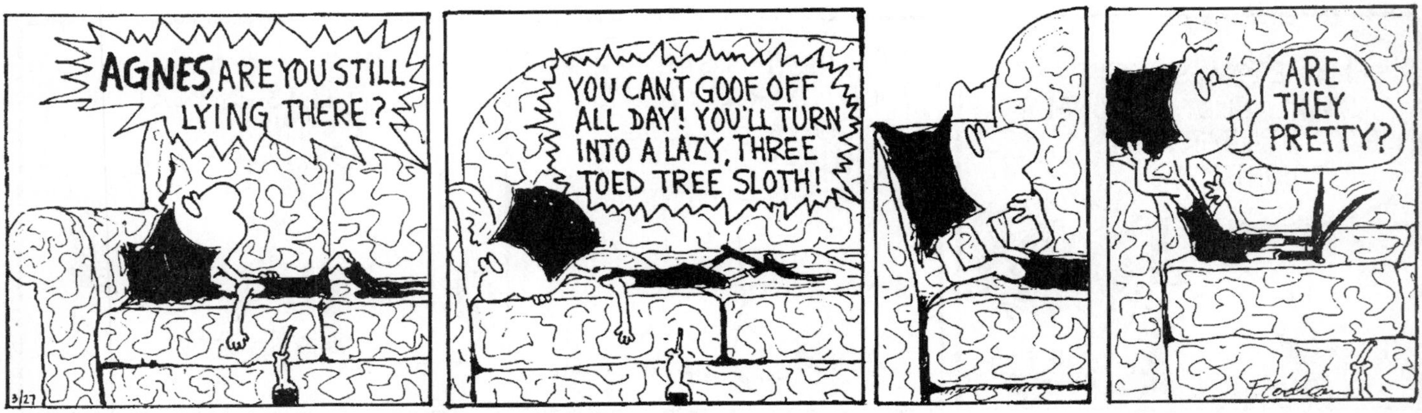
AGNES, ARE YOU STILL LYING THERE?
YOU CAN'T GOOF OFF ALL DAY! YOU'LL TURN INTO A LAZY, THREE TOED TREE SLOTH!
ARE THEY PRETTY?
3/27

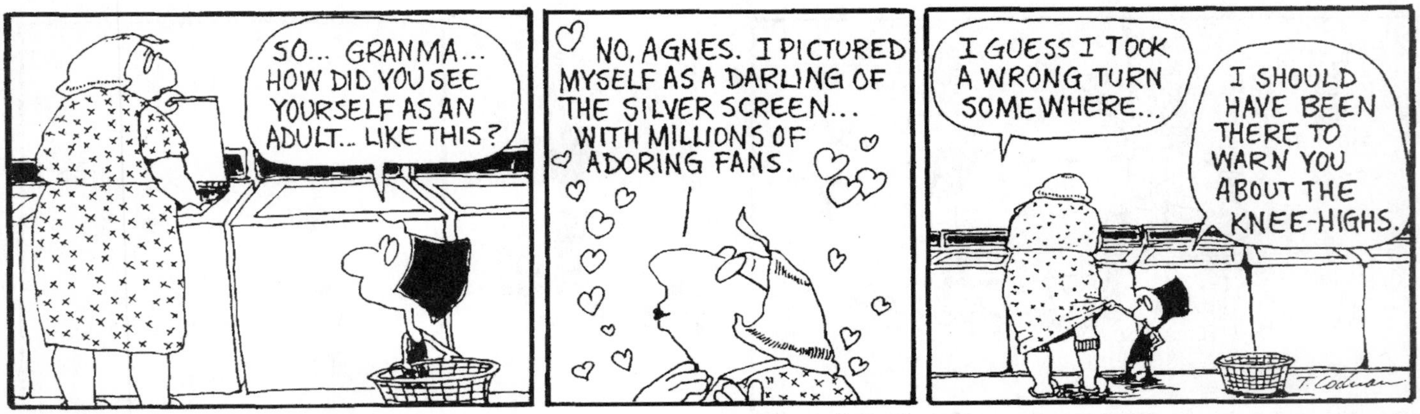
SO... GRANMA... HOW DID YOU SEE YOURSELF AS AN ADULT... LIKE THIS?
NO, AGNES. I PICTURED MYSELF AS A DARLING OF THE SILVER SCREEN... WITH MILLIONS OF ADORING FANS.
I GUESS I TOOK A WRONG TURN SOMEWHERE...
I SHOULD HAVE BEEN THERE TO WARN YOU ABOUT THE KNEE-HIGHS.

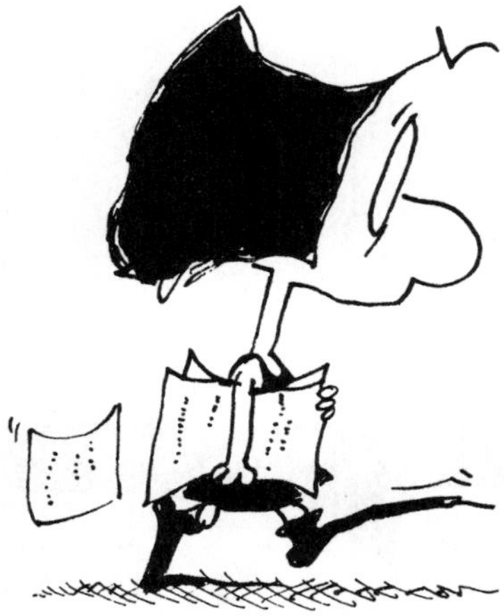

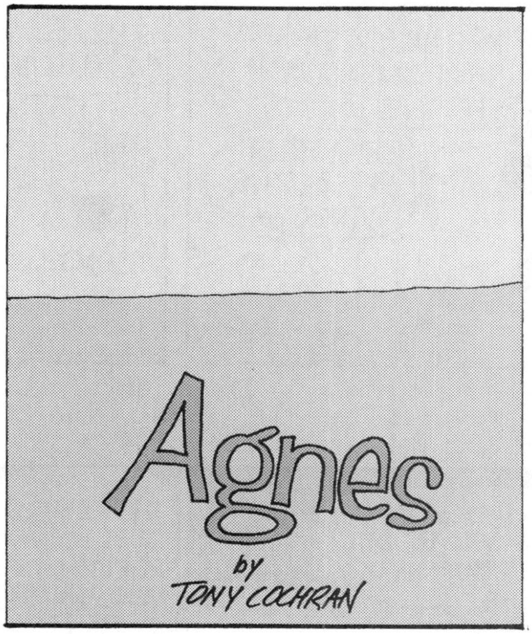

Agnes
by
TONY COCHRAN

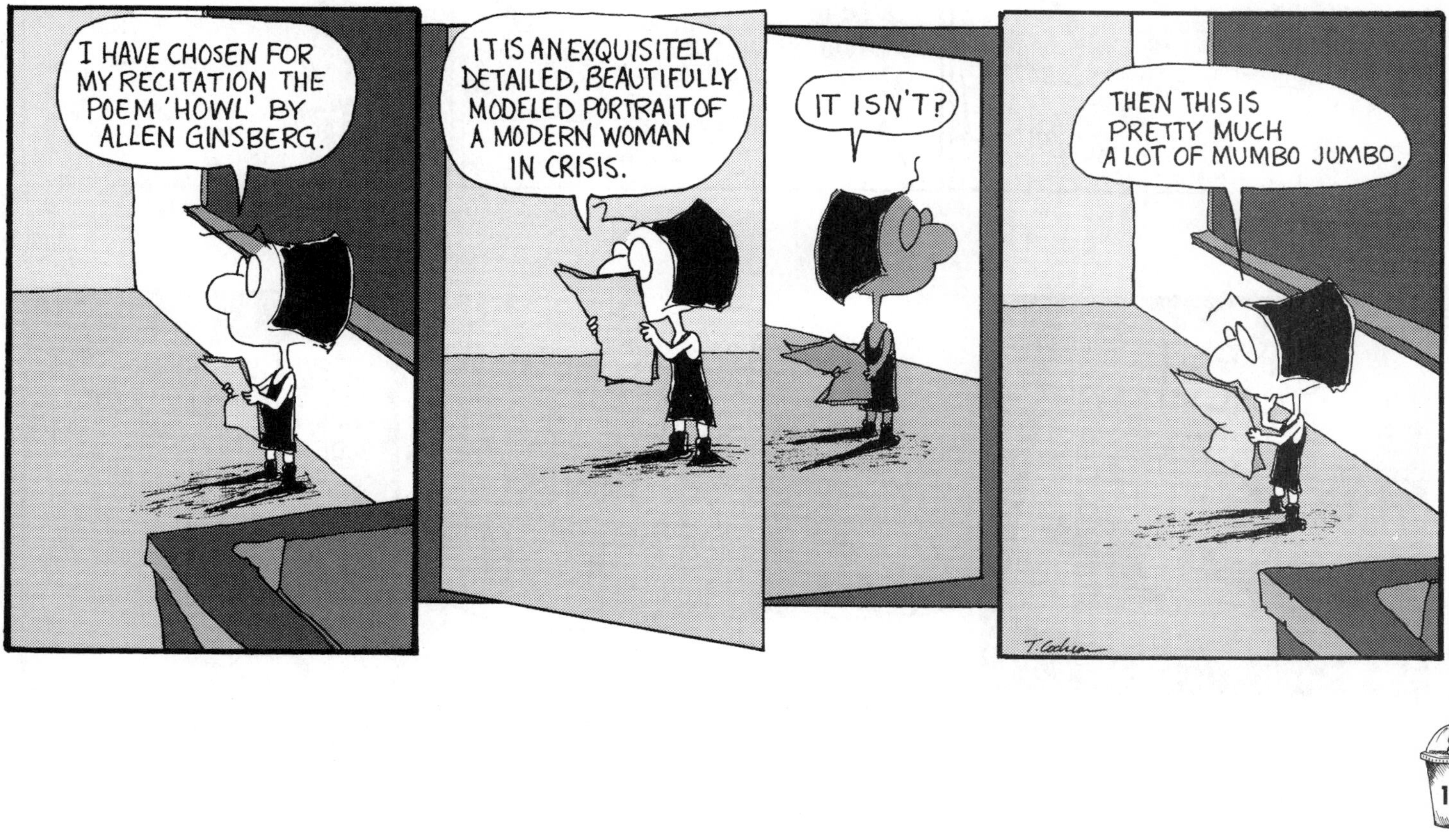

I HAVE CHOSEN FOR MY RECITATION THE POEM 'HOWL' BY ALLEN GINSBERG.
IT IS AN EXQUISITELY DETAILED, BEAUTIFULLY MODELED PORTRAIT OF A MODERN WOMAN IN CRISIS.
IT ISN'T?
THEN THIS IS PRETTY MUCH A LOT OF MUMBO JUMBO.

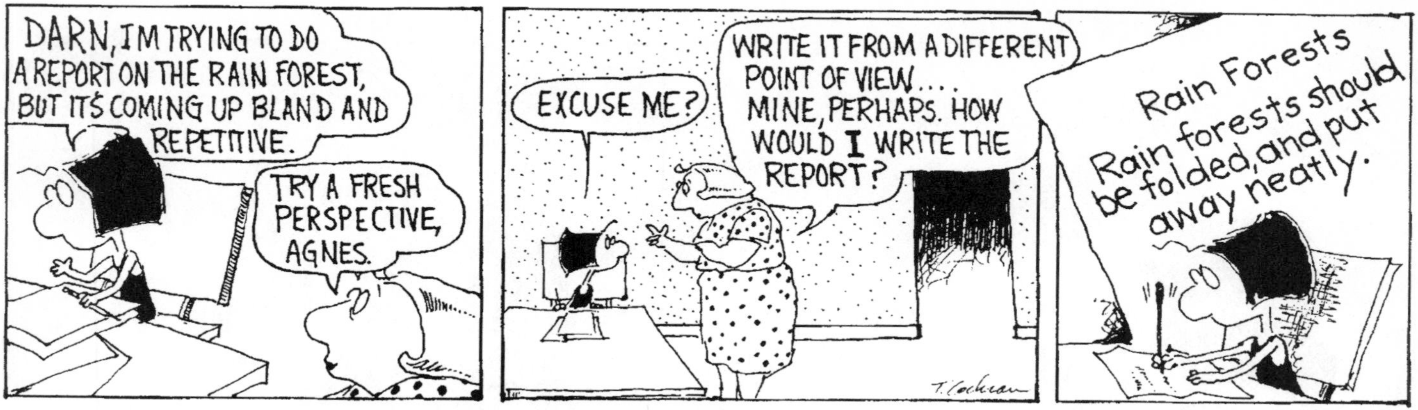
DARN, IM TRYING TO DO A REPORT ON THE RAIN FOREST, BUT IT'S COMING UP BLAND AND REPETITIVE.
TRY A FRESH PERSPECTIVE, AGNES.
EXCUSE ME?
WRITE IT FROM A DIFFERENT POINT OF VIEW.... MINE, PERHAPS. HOW WOULD I WRITE THE REPORT?
Rain Forests
Rain forests should be folded, and put away neatly.

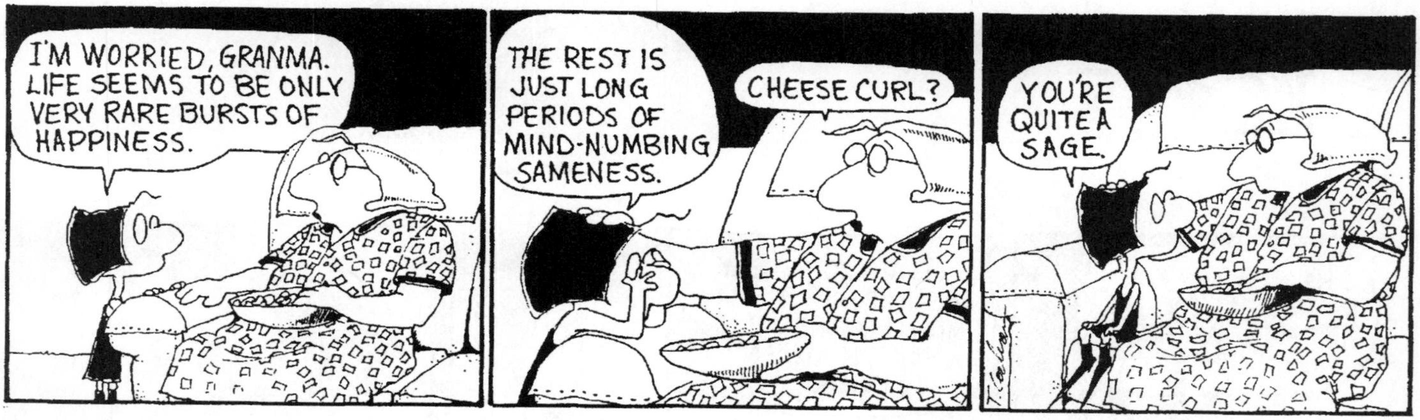
I'M WORRIED, GRANMA. LIFE SEEMS TO BE ONLY VERY RARE BURSTS OF HAPPINESS.
THE REST IS JUST LONG PERIODS OF MIND-NUMBING SAMENESS.
CHEESE CURL?
YOU'RE QUITE A SAGE.

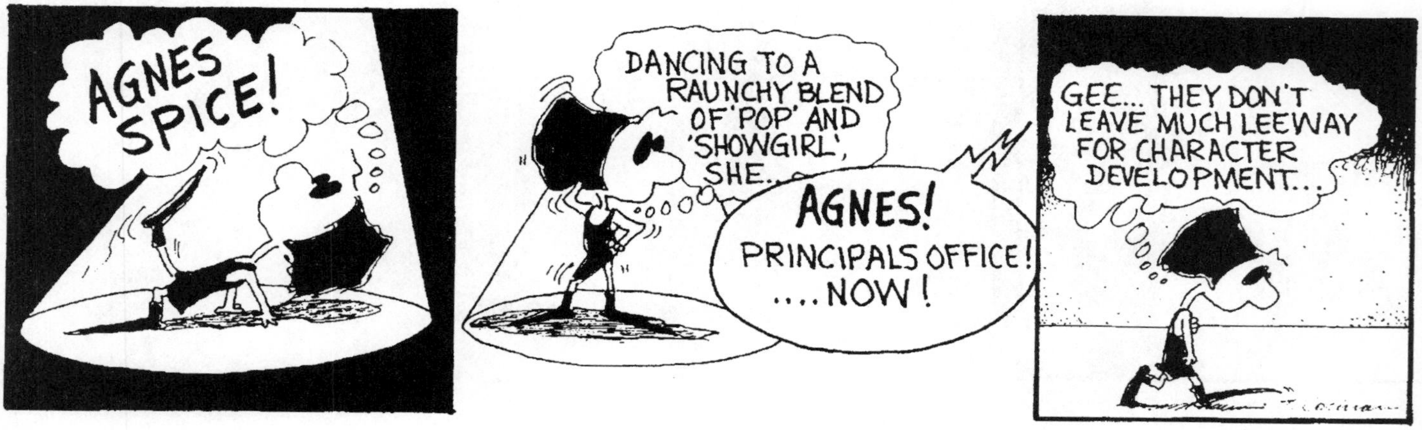
AGNES SPICE!
DANCING TO A RAUNCHY BLEND OF 'POP' AND 'SHOWGIRL', SHE...
AGNES! PRINCIPALS OFFICE! ....NOW!
GEE... THEY DON'T LEAVE MUCH LEEWAY FOR CHARACTER DEVELOPMENT...

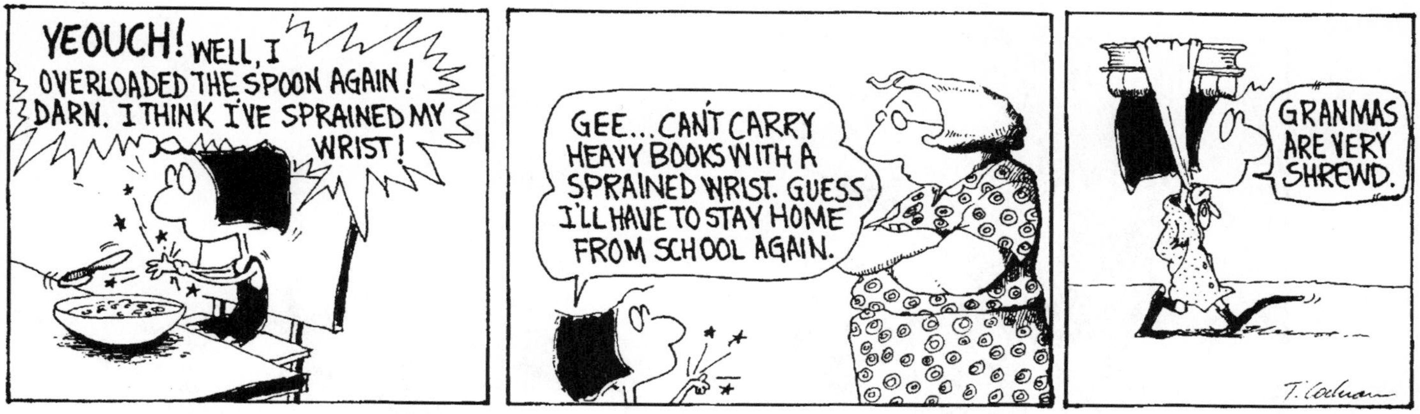
YEOUCH! WELL, I OVERLOADED THE SPOON AGAIN! DARN. I THINK I'VE SPRAINED MY WRIST!
GEE... CAN'T CARRY HEAVY BOOKS WITH A SPRAINED WRIST. GUESS I'LL HAVE TO STAY HOME FROM SCHOOL AGAIN.
GRANMAS ARE VERY SHREWD.
T. Cochran

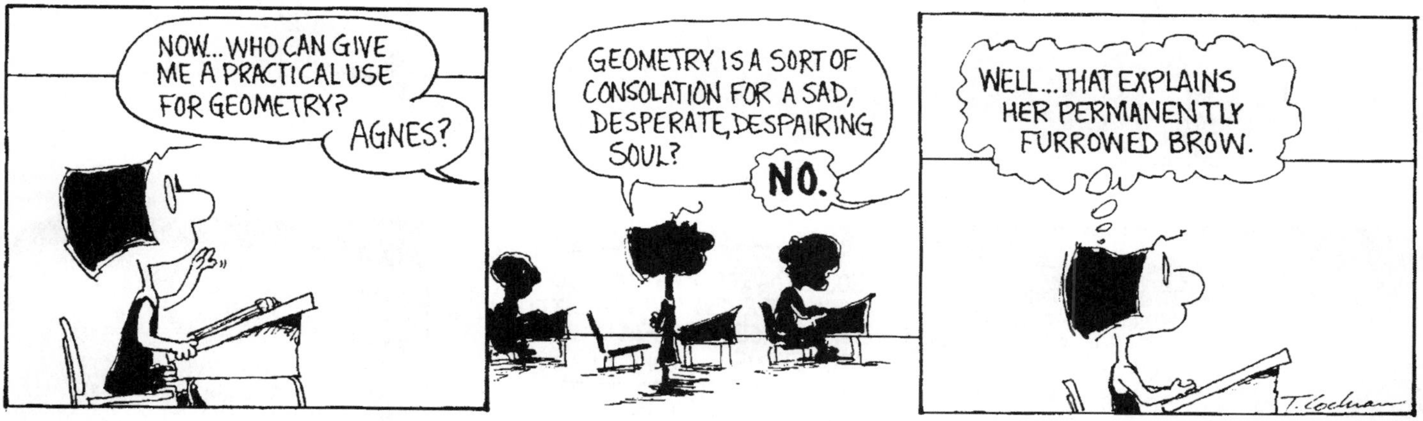
NOW... WHO CAN GIVE ME A PRACTICAL USE FOR GEOMETRY? AGNES?
GEOMETRY IS A SORT OF CONSOLATION FOR A SAD, DESPERATE, DESPAIRING SOUL?
NO.
WELL... THAT EXPLAINS HER PERMANENTLY FURROWED BROW.
T. Cochran

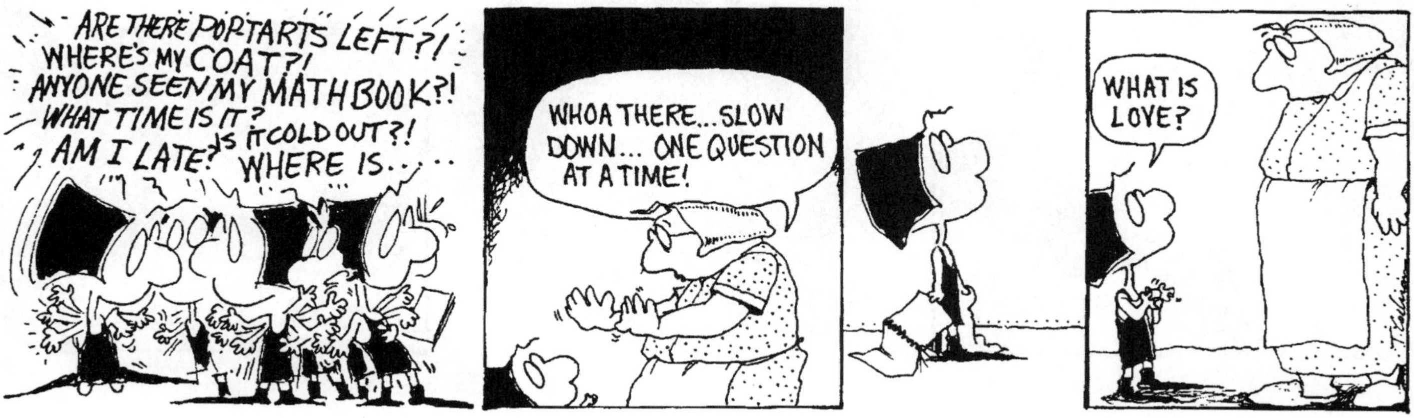
ARE THERE POPTARTS LEFT?!
WHERE'S MY COAT?!
ANYONE SEEN MY MATH BOOK?!
WHAT TIME IS IT?
IS IT COLD OUT?!
AM I LATE?
WHERE IS...
WHOA THERE... SLOW DOWN... ONE QUESTION AT A TIME!
WHAT IS LOVE?
T. Cochran

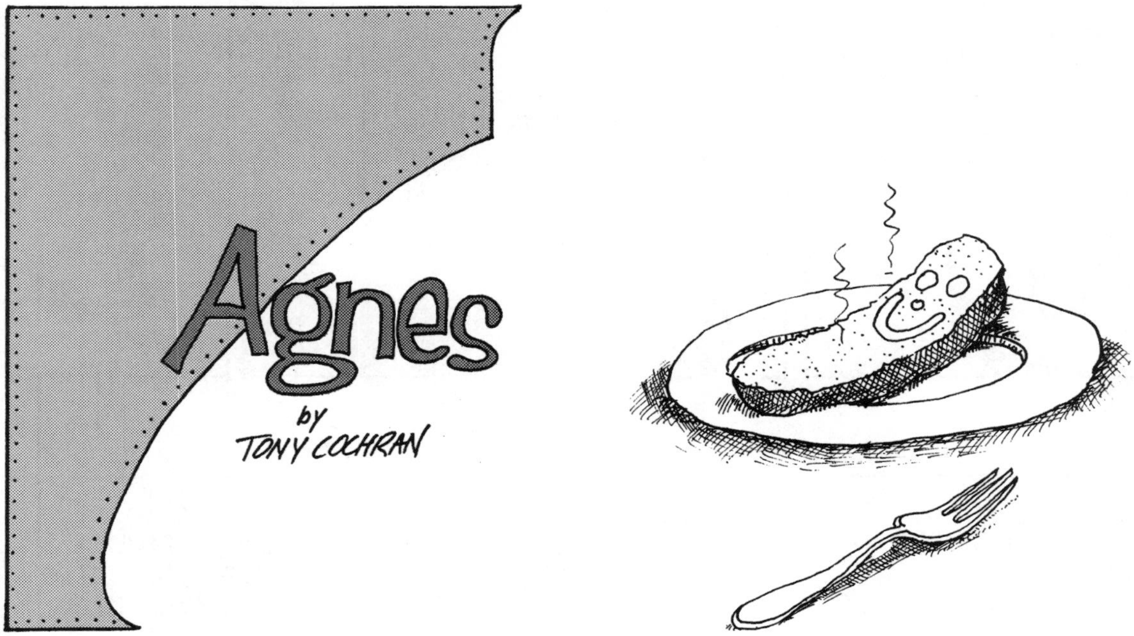
Agnes
by
TONY COCHRAN

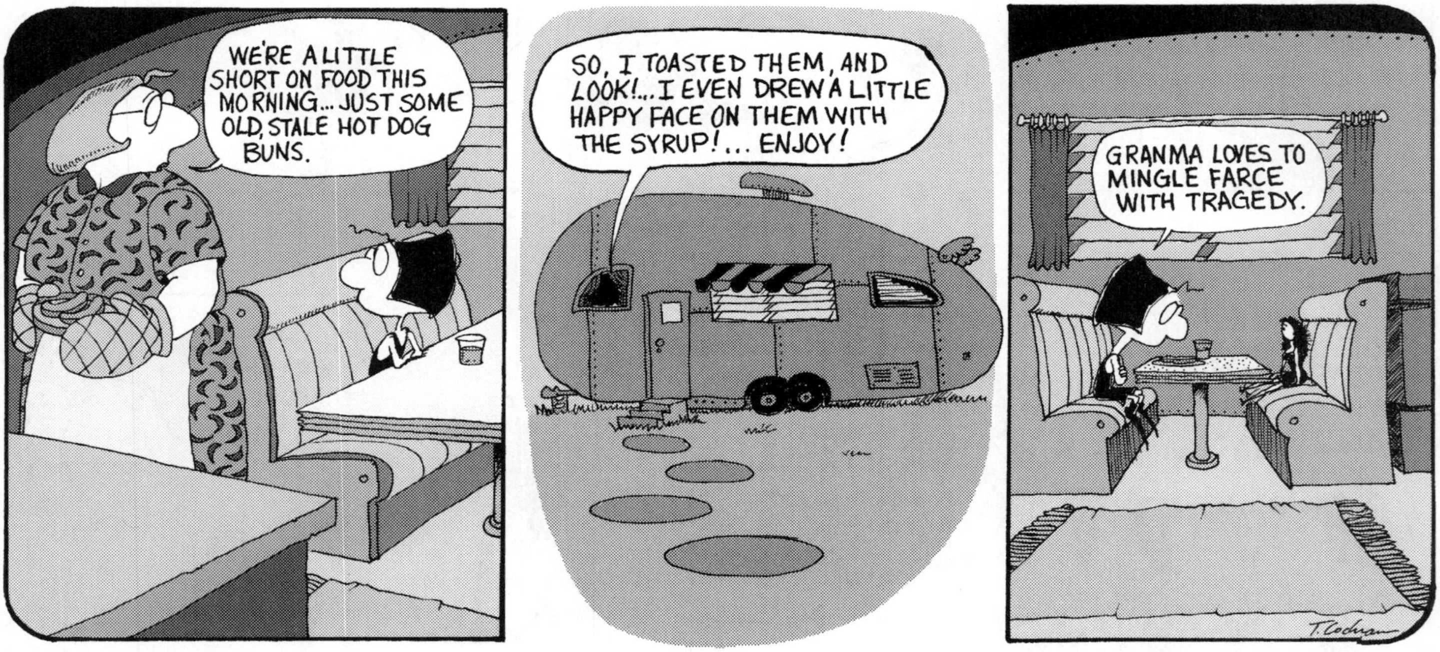
WE'RE A LITTLE SHORT ON FOOD THIS MORNING... JUST SOME OLD, STALE HOT DOG BUNS.
SO, I TOASTED THEM, AND LOOK!... I EVEN DREW A LITTLE HAPPY FACE ON THEM WITH THE SYRUP!... ENJOY!
GRANMA LOVES TO MINGLE FARCE WITH TRAGEDY.
T. Cochran

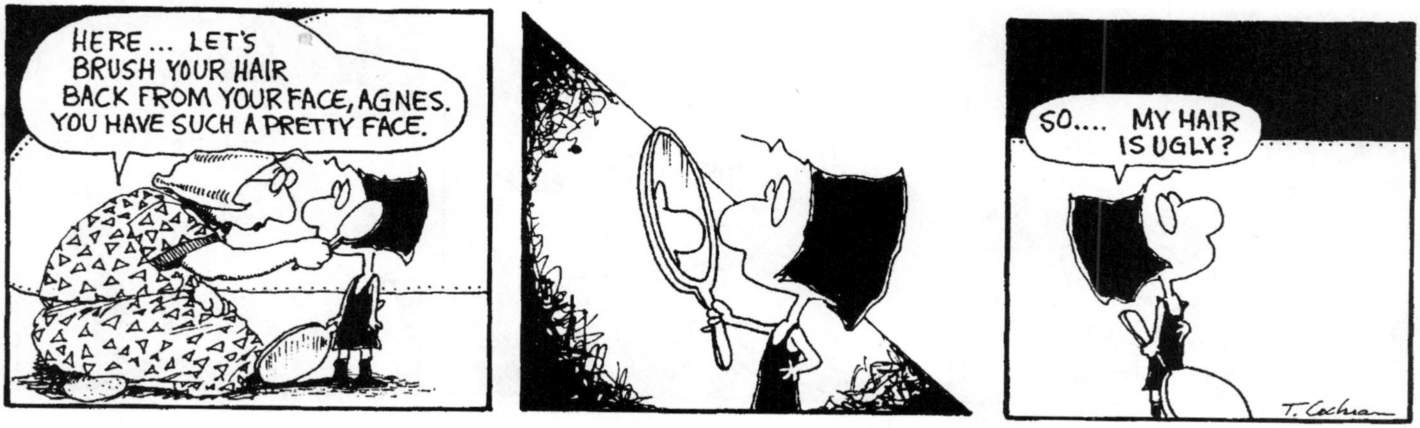
HERE... LET'S BRUSH YOUR HAIR BACK FROM YOUR FACE, AGNES. YOU HAVE SUCH A PRETTY FACE.
SO.... MY HAIR IS UGLY?

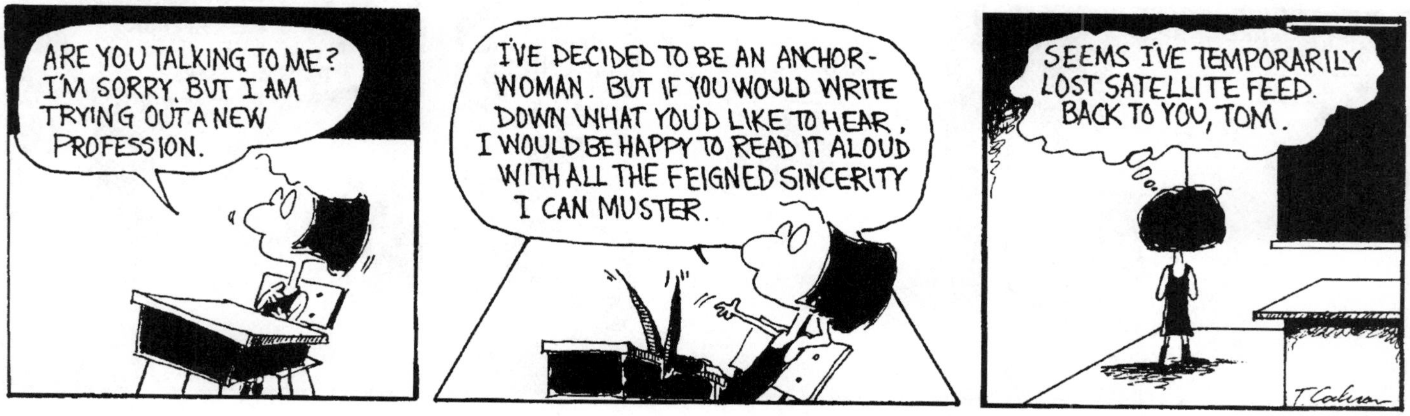
ARE YOU TALKING TO ME? I'M SORRY, BUT I AM TRYING OUT A NEW PROFESSION.
I'VE DECIDED TO BE AN ANCHOR-WOMAN. BUT IF YOU WOULD WRITE DOWN WHAT YOU'D LIKE TO HEAR, I WOULD BE HAPPY TO READ IT ALOUD WITH ALL THE FEIGNED SINCERITY I CAN MUSTER.
SEEMS I'VE TEMPORARILY LOST SATELLITE FEED. BACK TO YOU, TOM.

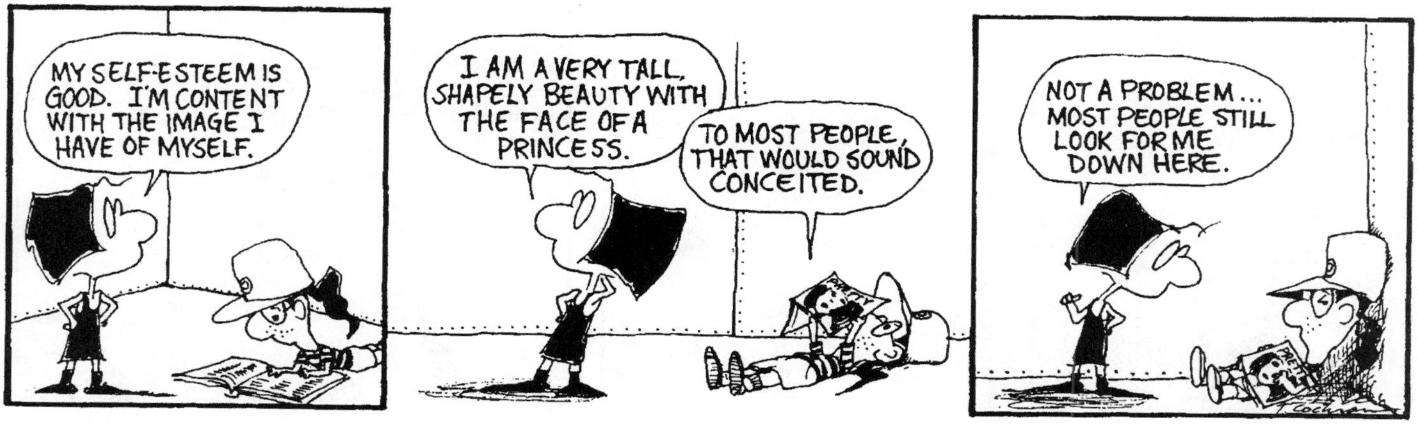
MY SELF-ESTEEM IS GOOD. I'M CONTENT WITH THE IMAGE I HAVE OF MYSELF.
I AM A VERY TALL, SHAPELY BEAUTY WITH THE FACE OF A PRINCESS.
TO MOST PEOPLE, THAT WOULD SOUND CONCEITED.
NOT A PROBLEM... MOST PEOPLE STILL LOOK FOR ME DOWN HERE.

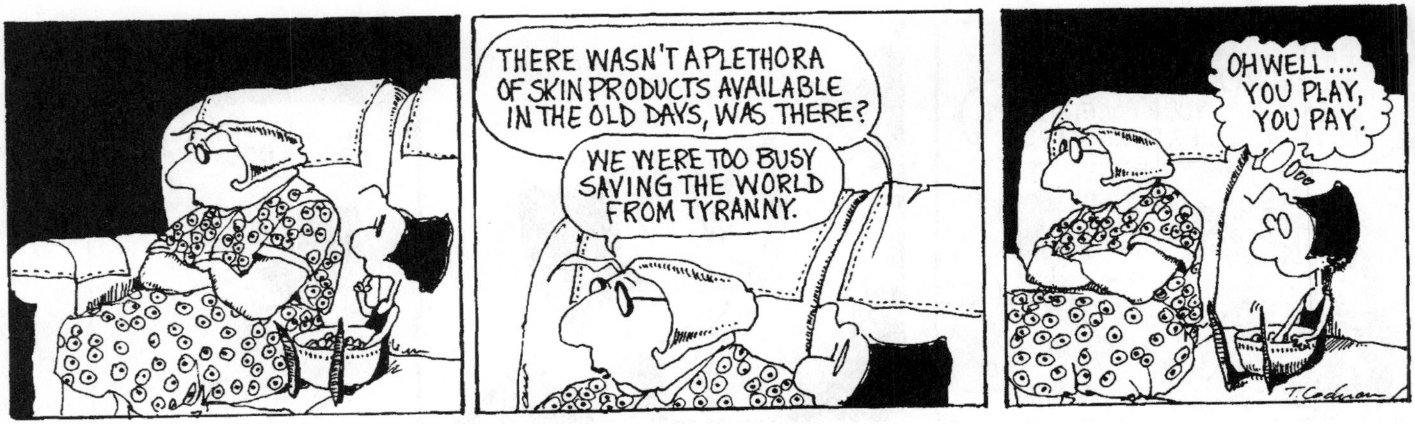
THERE WASN'T A PLETHORA OF SKIN PRODUCTS AVAILABLE IN THE OLD DAYS, WAS THERE?
WE WERE TOO BUSY SAVING THE WORLD FROM TYRANNY.
OH WELL.... YOU PLAY, YOU PAY.
T. Cochran

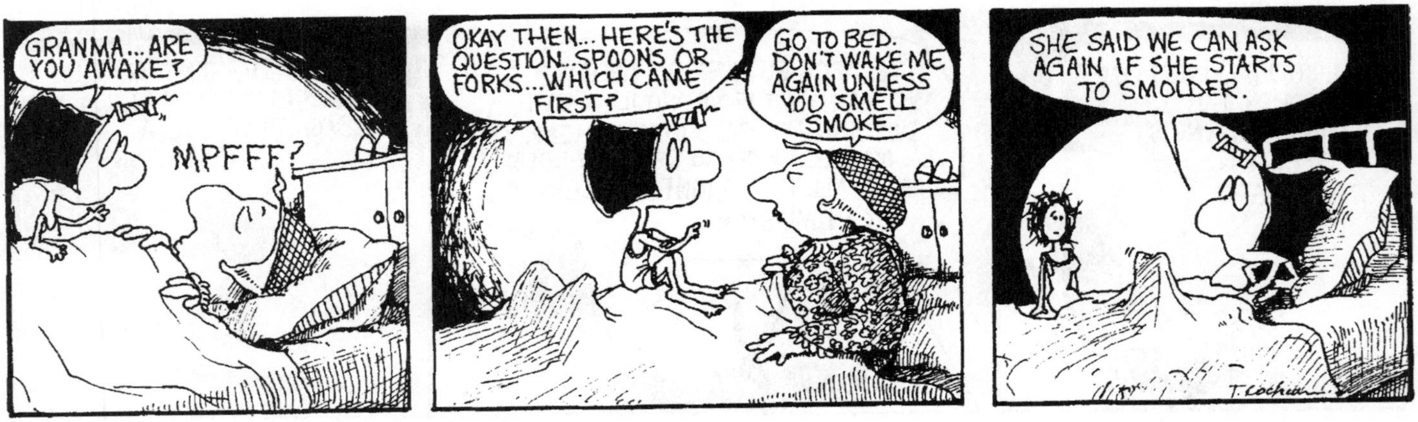
GRANMA... ARE YOU AWAKE?
MPFFF?
OKAY THEN... HERE'S THE QUESTION...SPOONS OR FORKS...WHICH CAME FIRST?
GO TO BED. DON'T WAKE ME AGAIN UNLESS YOU SMELL SMOKE.
SHE SAID WE CAN ASK AGAIN IF SHE STARTS TO SMOLDER.
T. Cochran

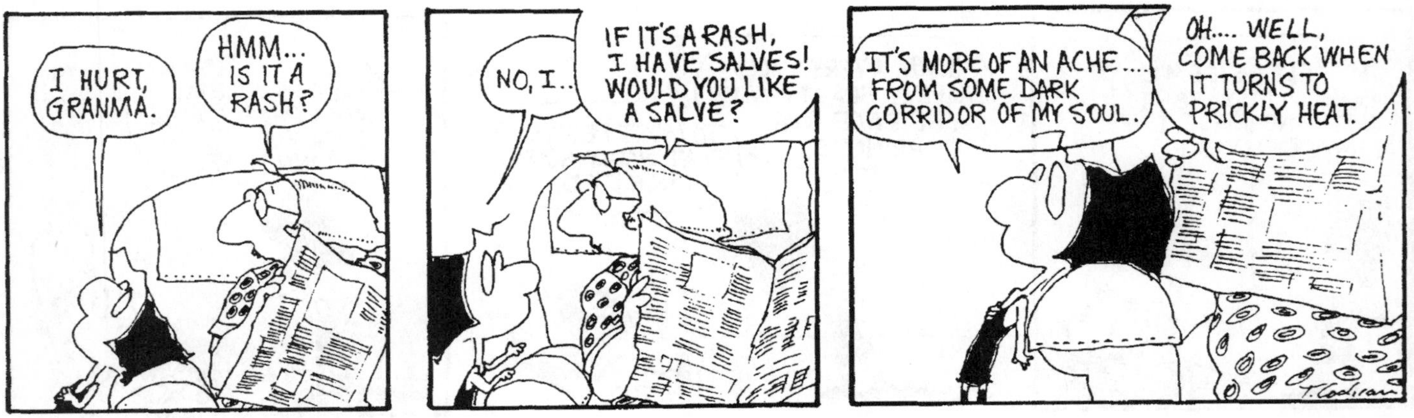
I HURT, GRANMA.
HMM... IS IT A RASH?
NO, I..
IF IT'S A RASH, I HAVE SALVES! WOULD YOU LIKE A SALVE?
IT'S MORE OF AN ACHE.... FROM SOME DARK CORRIDOR OF MY SOUL.
OH.... WELL, COME BACK WHEN IT TURNS TO PRICKLY HEAT.
T. Cochran

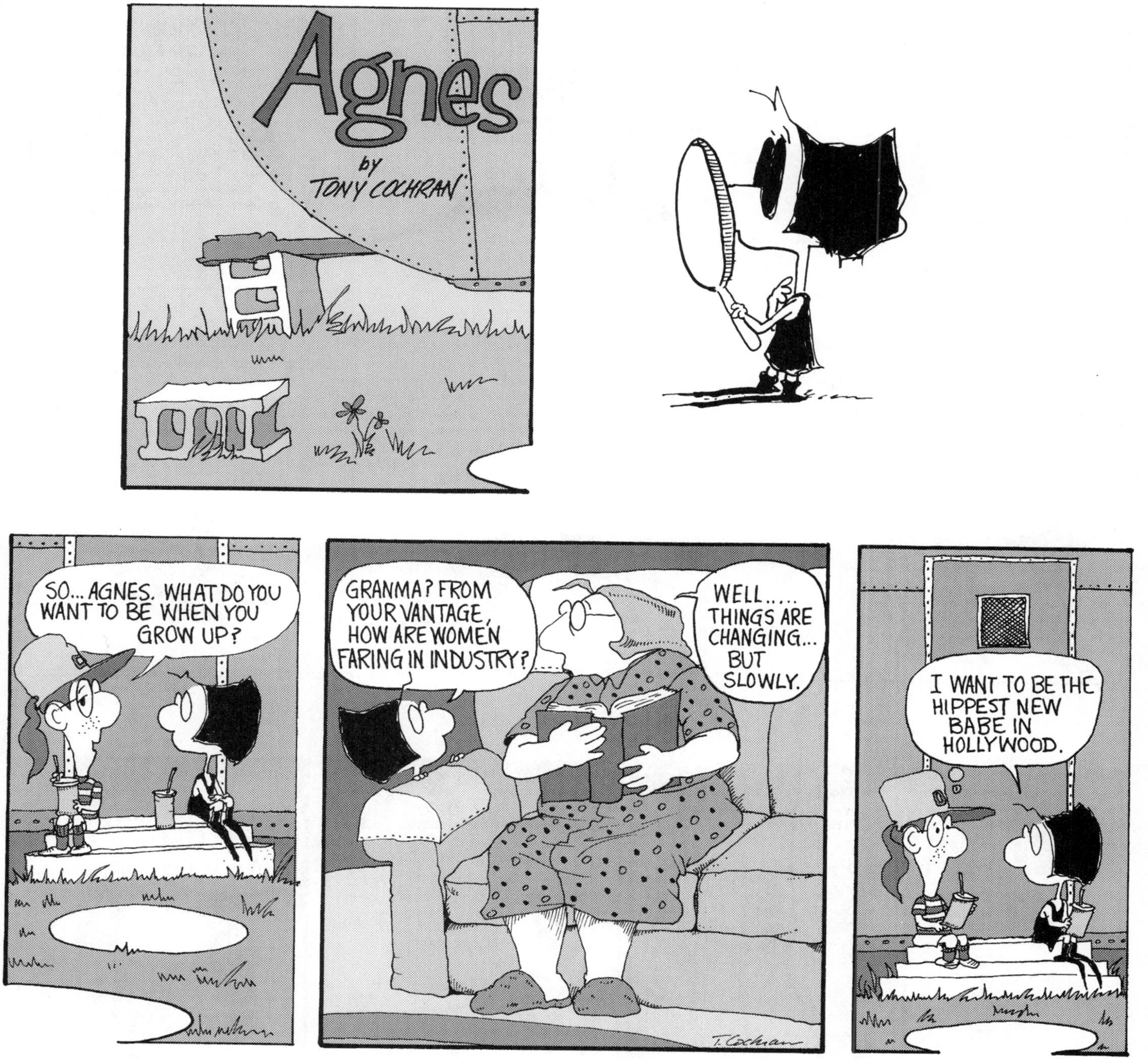
Agnes
by TONY COCHRAN
SO... AGNES. WHAT DO YOU WANT TO BE WHEN YOU GROW UP?
GRANMA? FROM YOUR VANTAGE, HOW ARE WOMEN FARING IN INDUSTRY?
WELL..... THINGS ARE CHANGING... BUT SLOWLY.
T. Cochran
I WANT TO BE THE HIPPEST NEW BABE IN HOLLYWOOD.

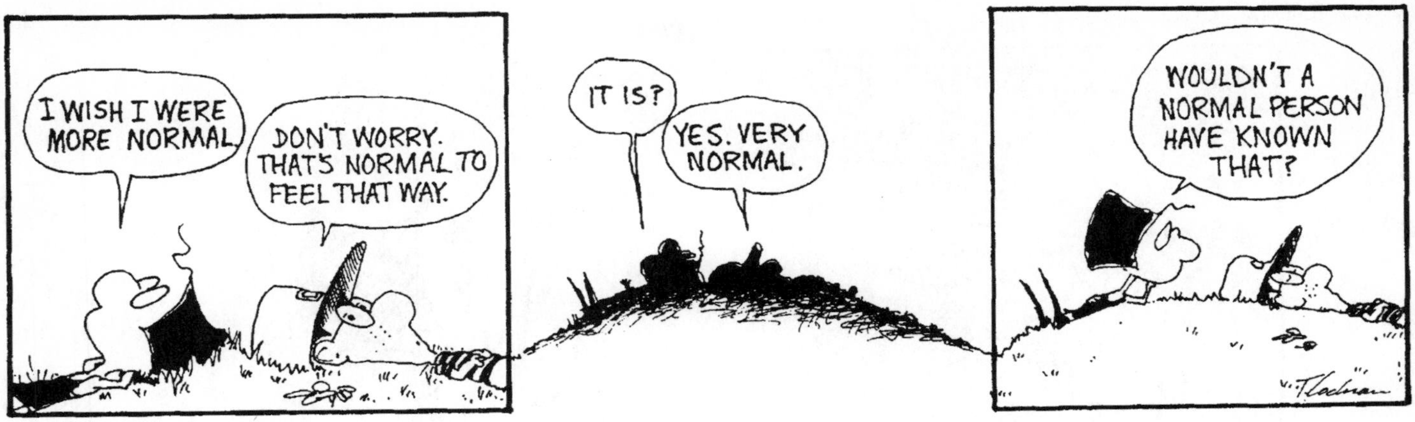
I WISH I WERE MORE NORMAL.
DON'T WORRY. THAT'S NORMAL TO FEEL THAT WAY.
IT IS?
YES. VERY NORMAL.
WOULDN'T A NORMAL PERSON HAVE KNOWN THAT?
T. Cochran

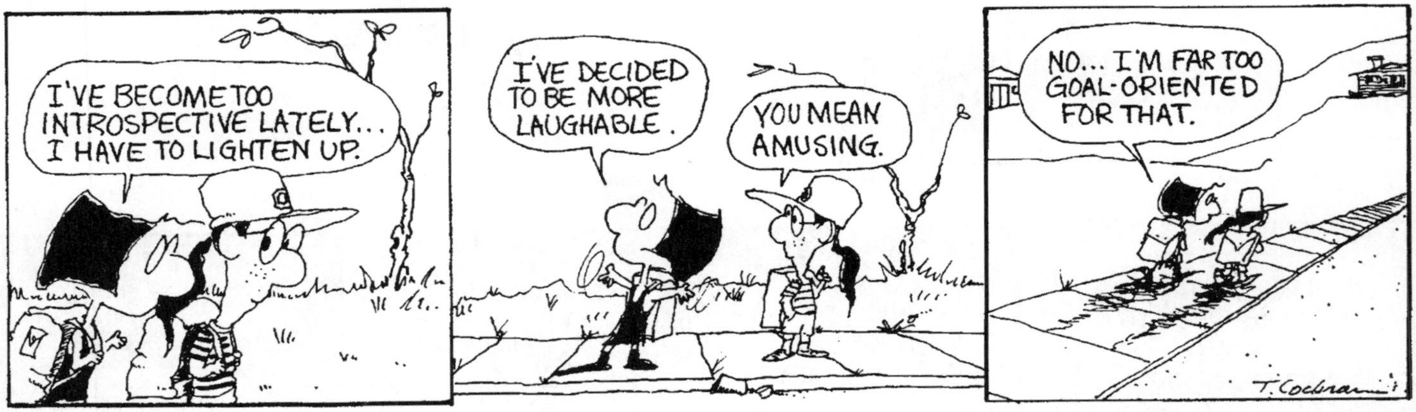
I'VE BECOME TOO INTROSPECTIVE LATELY... I HAVE TO LIGHTEN UP.
I'VE DECIDED TO BE MORE LAUGHABLE.
YOU MEAN AMUSING.
NO... I'M FAR TOO GOAL-ORIENTED FOR THAT.
T. Cochran

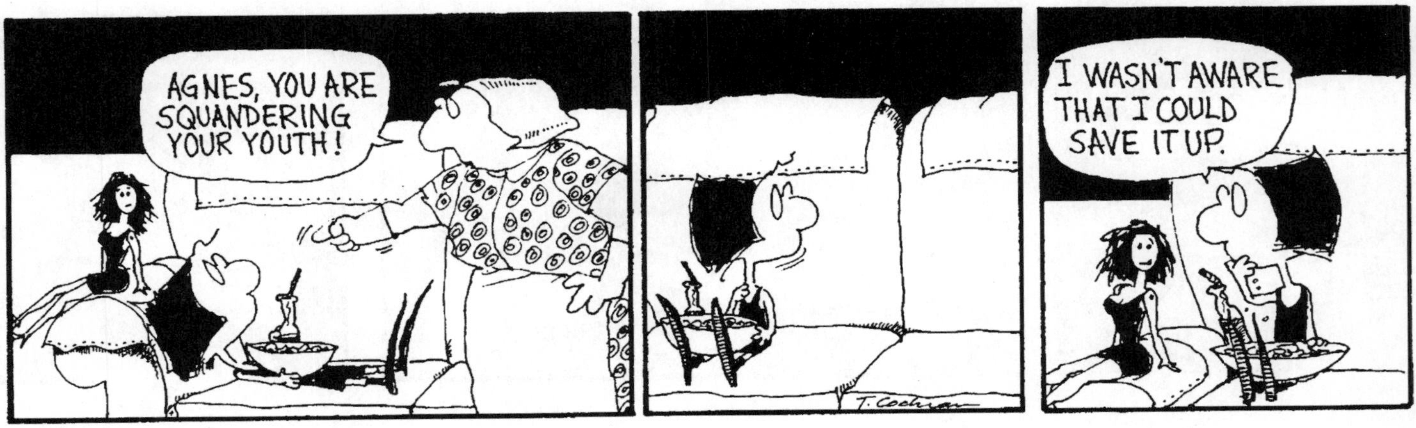
AGNES, YOU ARE SQUANDERING YOUR YOUTH!
T. Cochran
I WASN'T AWARE THAT I COULD SAVE IT UP.

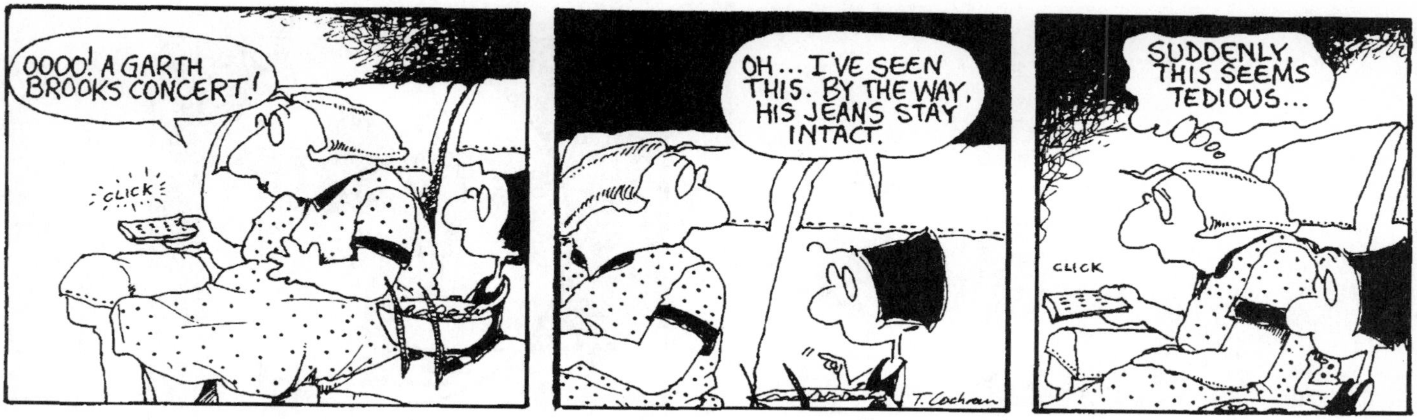
OOOO! A GARTH BROOKS CONCERT!
CLICK
OH... I'VE SEEN THIS. BY THE WAY, HIS JEANS STAY INTACT.
SUDDENLY, THIS SEEMS TEDIOUS...
CLICK

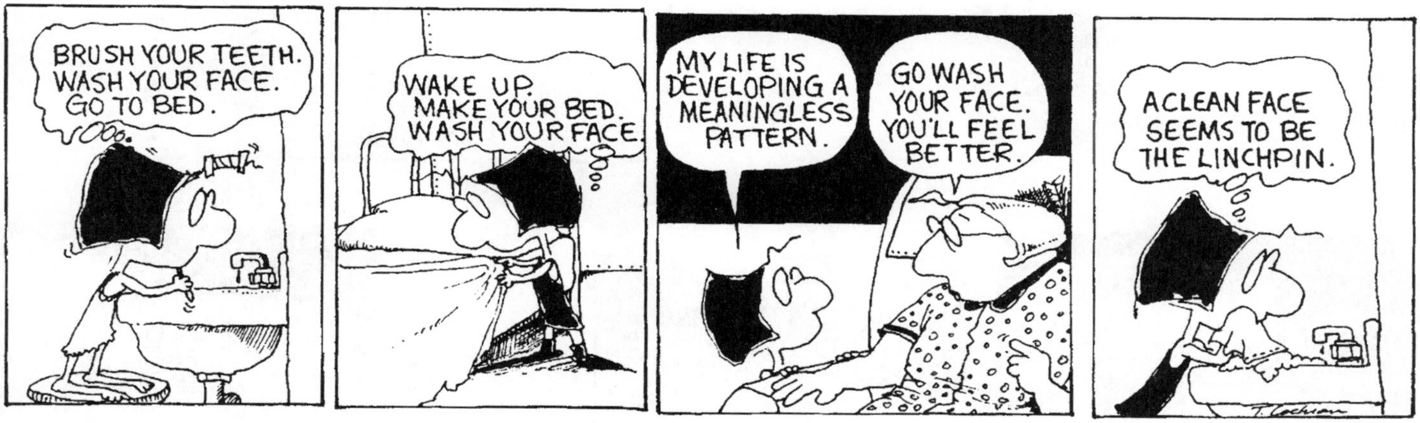
BRUSH YOUR TEETH. WASH YOUR FACE. GO TO BED.
WAKE UP. MAKE YOUR BED. WASH YOUR FACE.
MY LIFE IS DEVELOPING A MEANINGLESS PATTERN.
GO WASH YOUR FACE. YOU'LL FEEL BETTER.
A CLEAN FACE SEEMS TO BE THE LINCHPIN.

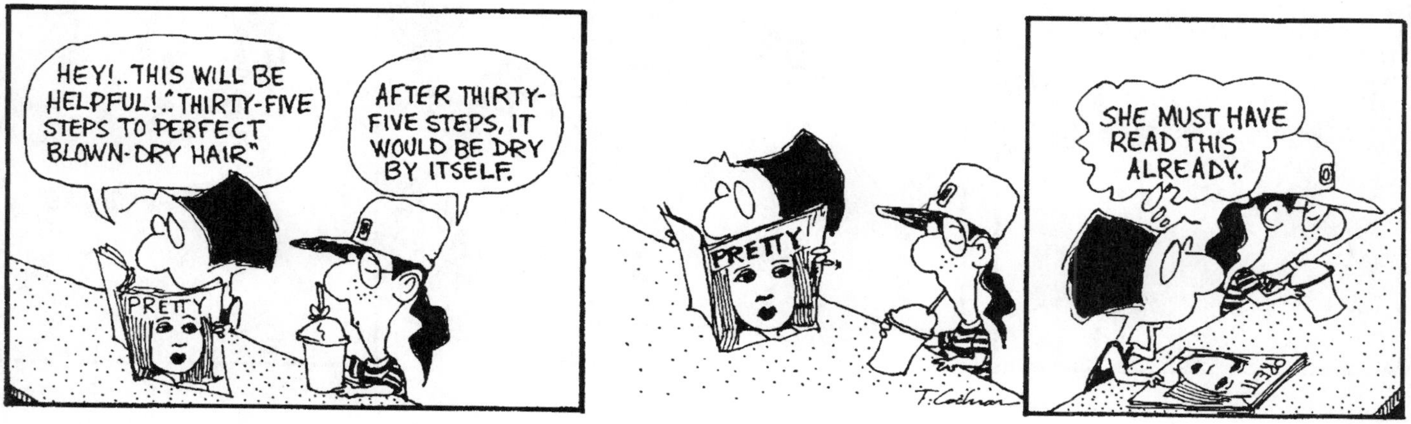
HEY!..THIS WILL BE HELPFUL!.."THIRTY-FIVE STEPS TO PERFECT BLOWN-DRY HAIR."
AFTER THIRTY-FIVE STEPS, IT WOULD BE DRY BY ITSELF.
PRETTY
PRETTY
SHE MUST HAVE READ THIS ALREADY.

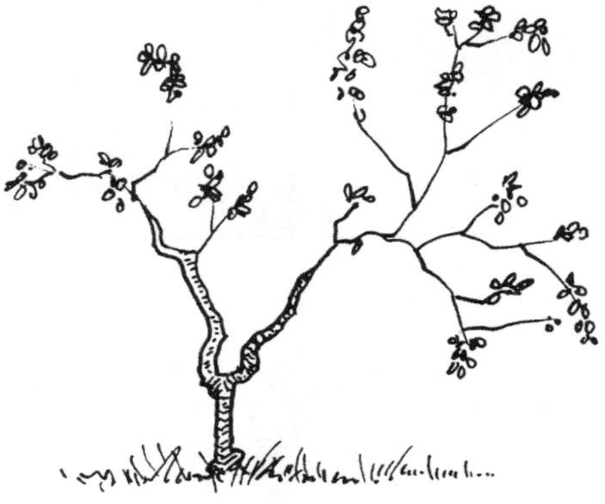

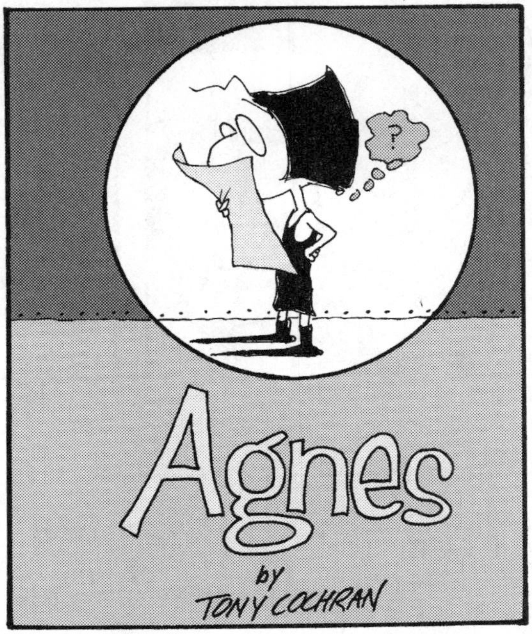
?
Agnes
by
TONY COCHRAN

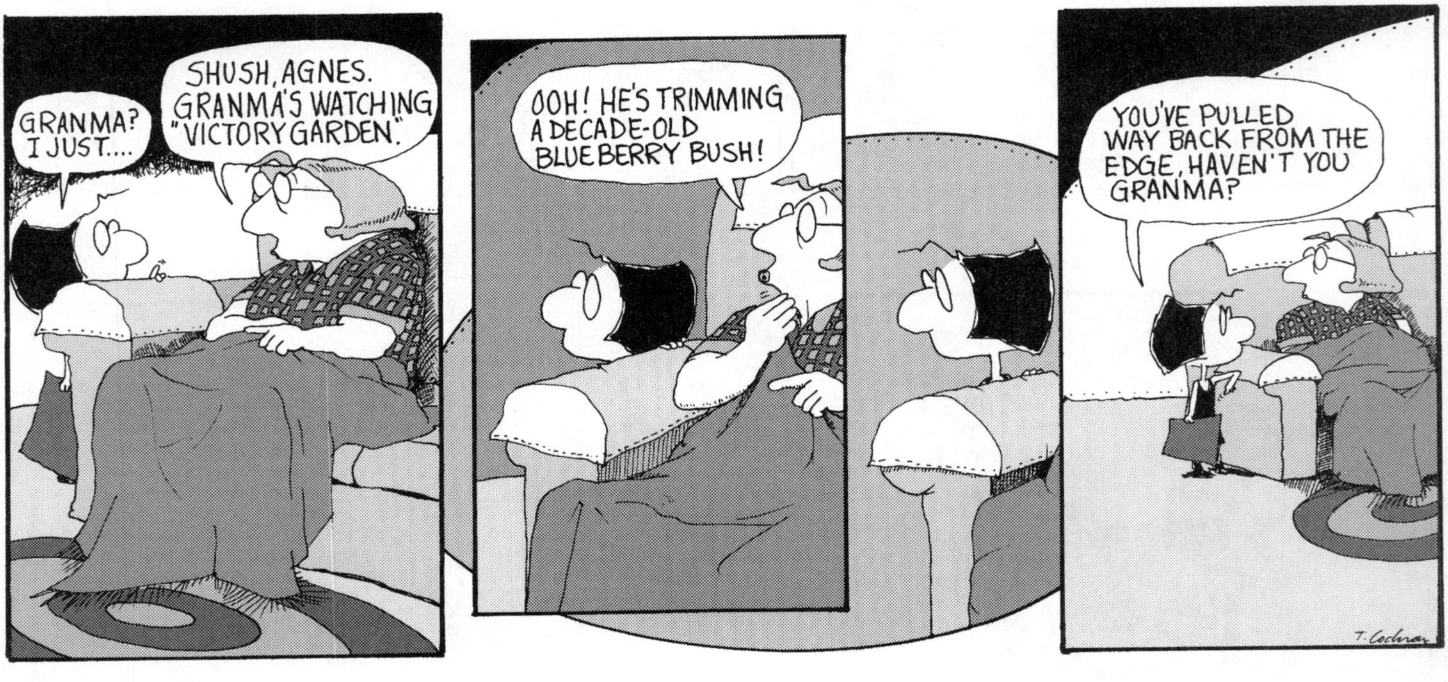
GRANMA? I JUST....
SHUSH, AGNES. GRANMA'S WATCHING "VICTORY GARDEN."
OOH! HE'S TRIMMING A DECADE-OLD BLUEBERRY BUSH!
YOU'VE PULLED WAY BACK FROM THE EDGE, HAVEN'T YOU GRANMA?
T. Cochran

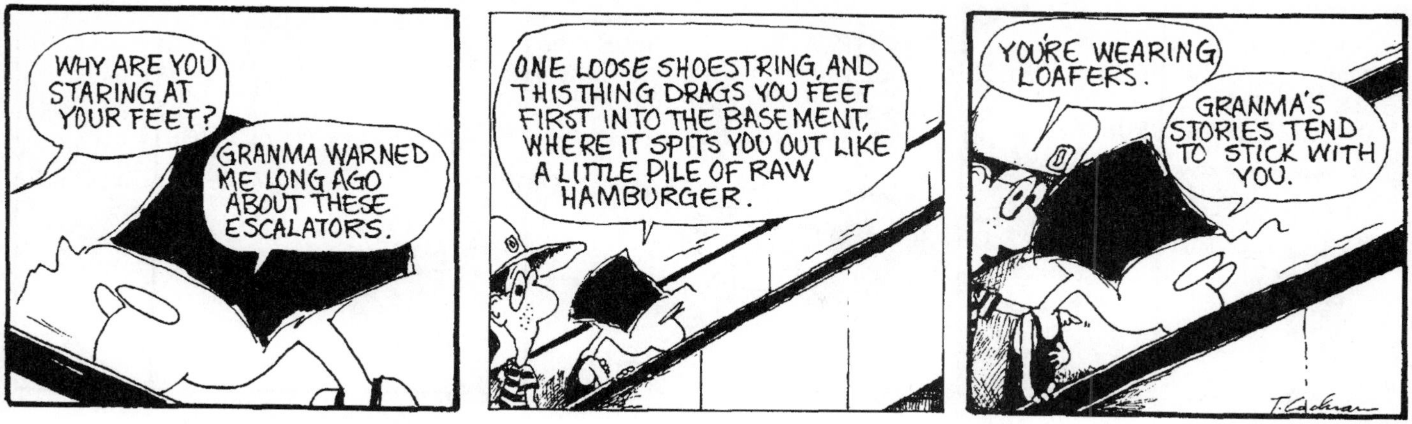
WHY ARE YOU STARING AT YOUR FEET?
GRANMA WARNED ME LONG AGO ABOUT THESE ESCALATORS.
ONE LOOSE SHOESTRING, AND THIS THING DRAGS YOU FEET FIRST INTO THE BASEMENT, WHERE IT SPITS YOU OUT LIKE A LITTLE PILE OF RAW HAMBURGER.
YOU'RE WEARING LOAFERS.
GRANMA'S STORIES TEND TO STICK WITH YOU.

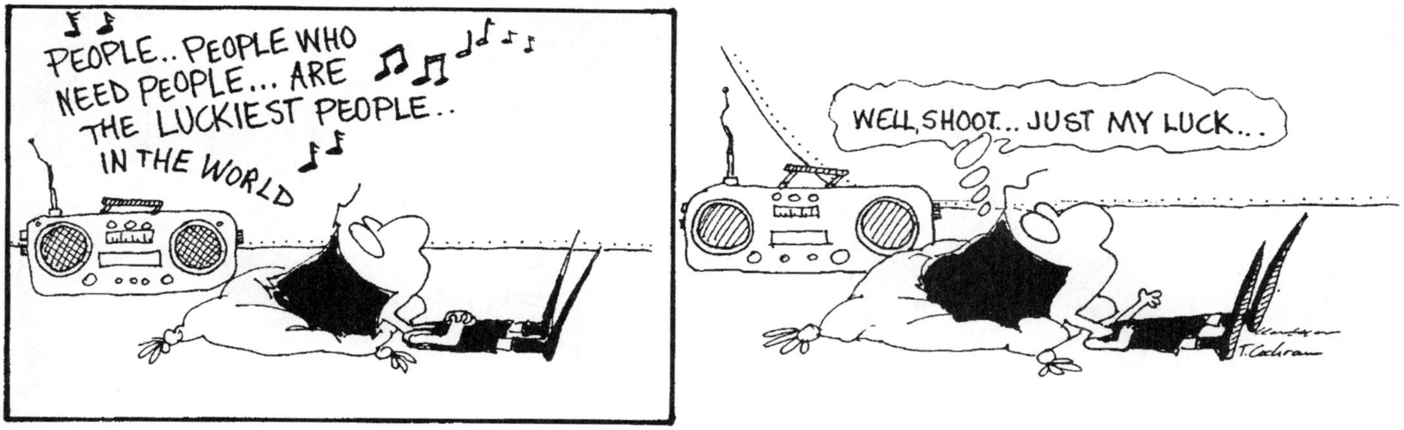
PEOPLE.. PEOPLE WHO NEED PEOPLE... ARE THE LUCKIEST PEOPLE.. IN THE WORLD
WELL, SHOOT... JUST MY LUCK...

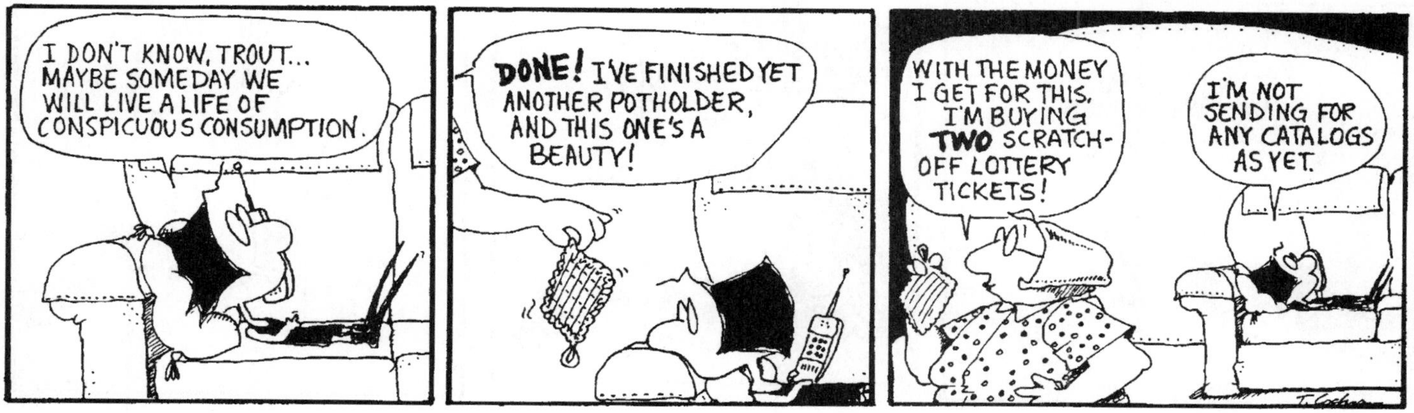
I DON'T KNOW, TROUT... MAYBE SOMEDAY WE WILL LIVE A LIFE OF CONSPICUOUS CONSUMPTION.
DONE! I'VE FINISHED YET ANOTHER POTHOLDER, AND THIS ONE'S A BEAUTY!
WITH THE MONEY I GET FOR THIS, I'M BUYING TWO SCRATCH-OFF LOTTERY TICKETS!
I'M NOT SENDING FOR ANY CATALOGS AS YET.

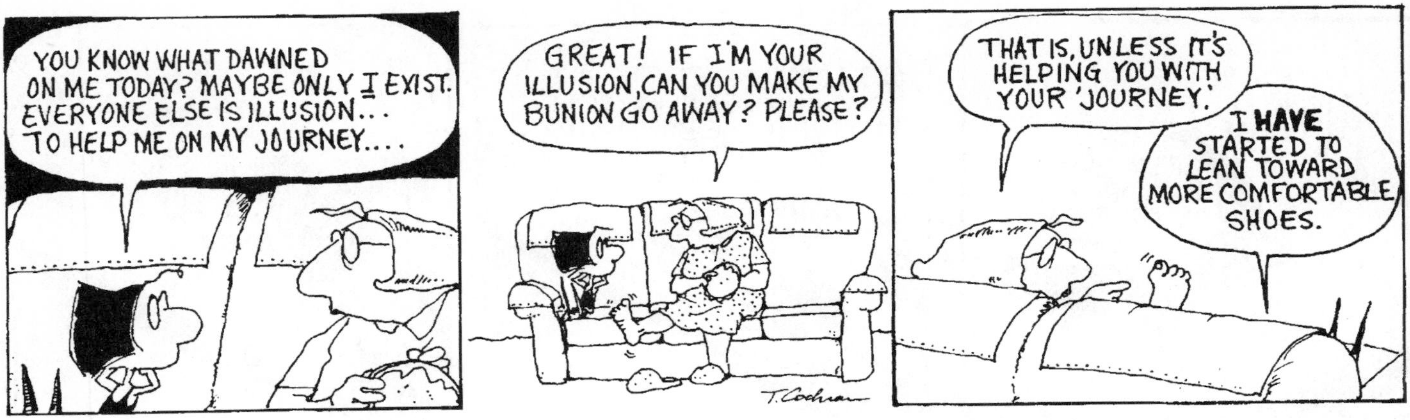
YOU KNOW WHAT DAWNED ON ME TODAY? MAYBE ONLY I EXIST. EVERYONE ELSE IS ILLUSION... TO HELP ME ON MY JOURNEY....
GREAT! IF I'M YOUR ILLUSION, CAN YOU MAKE MY BUNION GO AWAY? PLEASE?
T. Cochran
THAT IS, UNLESS IT'S HELPING YOU WITH YOUR 'JOURNEY.'
I HAVE STARTED TO LEAN TOWARD MORE COMFORTABLE SHOES.

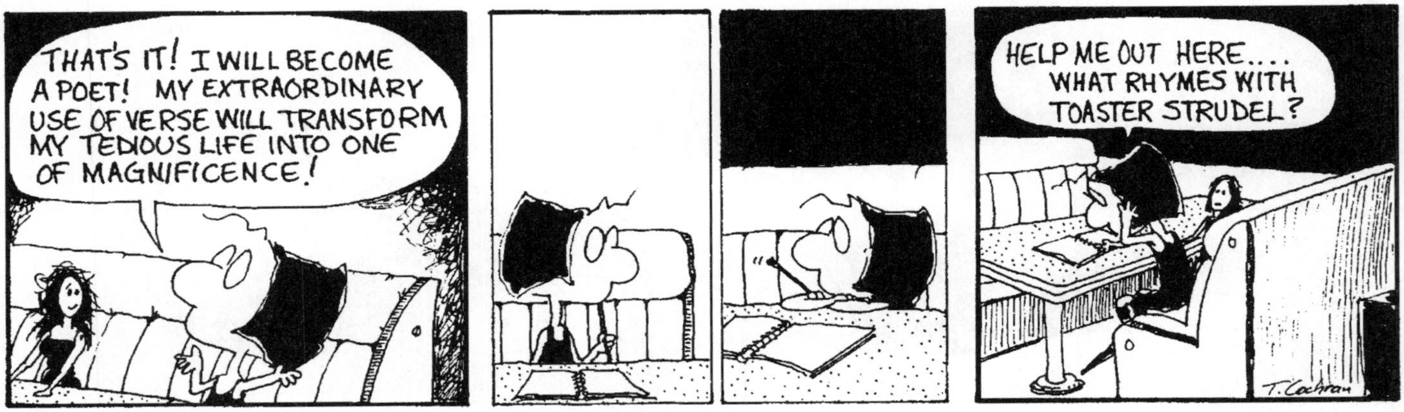
THAT'S IT! I WILL BECOME A POET! MY EXTRAORDINARY USE OF VERSE WILL TRANSFORM MY TEDIOUS LIFE INTO ONE OF MAGNIFICENCE!
HELP ME OUT HERE.... WHAT RHYMES WITH TOASTER STRUDEL?
T. Cochran

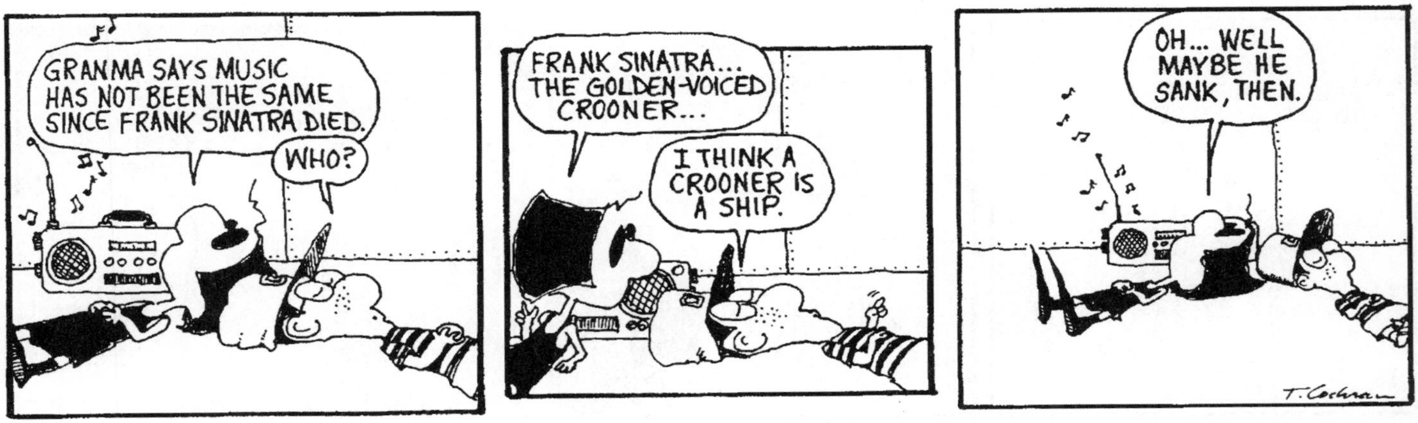
GRANMA SAYS MUSIC HAS NOT BEEN THE SAME SINCE FRANK SINATRA DIED.
WHO?
FRANK SINATRA... THE GOLDEN-VOICED CROONER...
I THINK A CROONER IS A SHIP.
OH... WELL MAYBE HE SANK, THEN.
T. Cochran

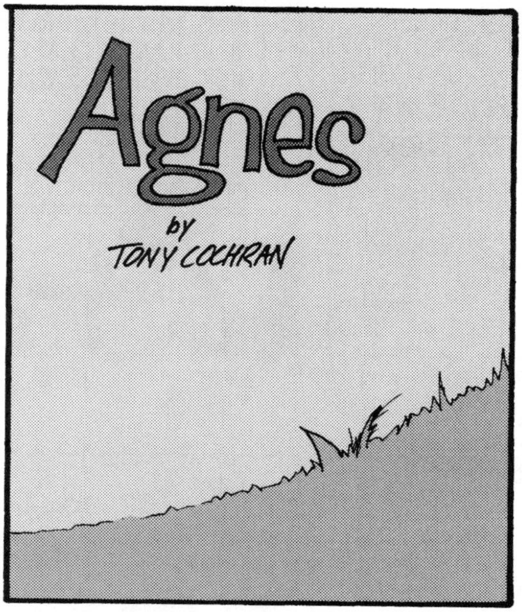
Agnes
by
TONY COCHRAN

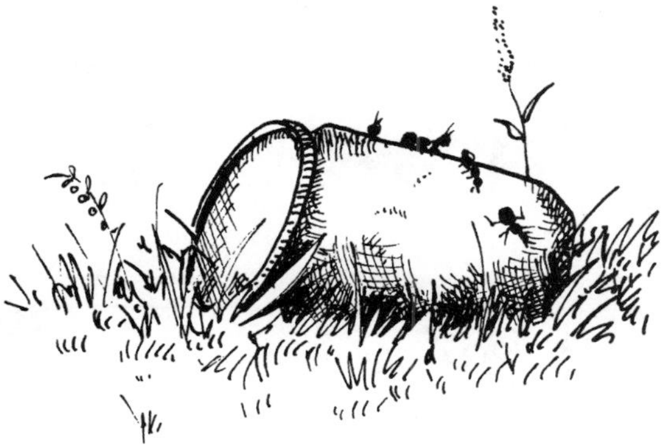

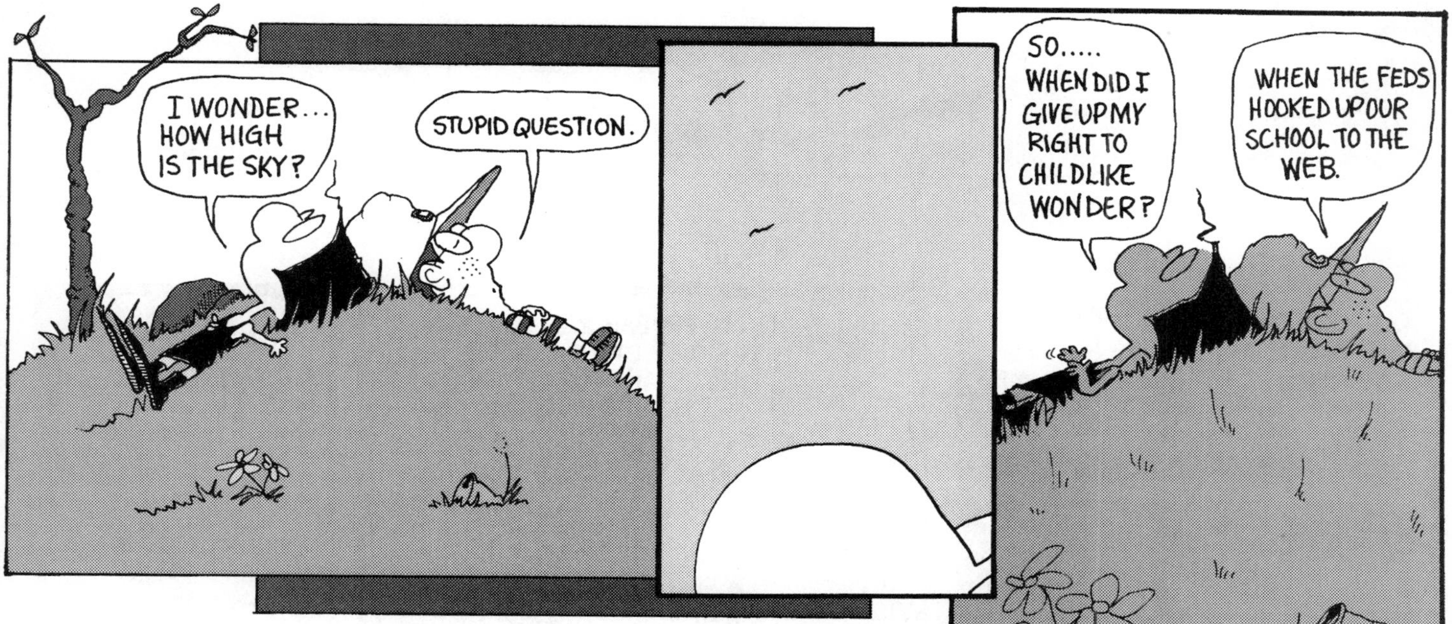
I WONDER... HOW HIGH IS THE SKY?
STUPID QUESTION.
SO..... WHEN DID I GIVE UP MY RIGHT TO CHILDLIKE WONDER?
WHEN THE FEDS HOOKED UP OUR SCHOOL TO THE WEB.

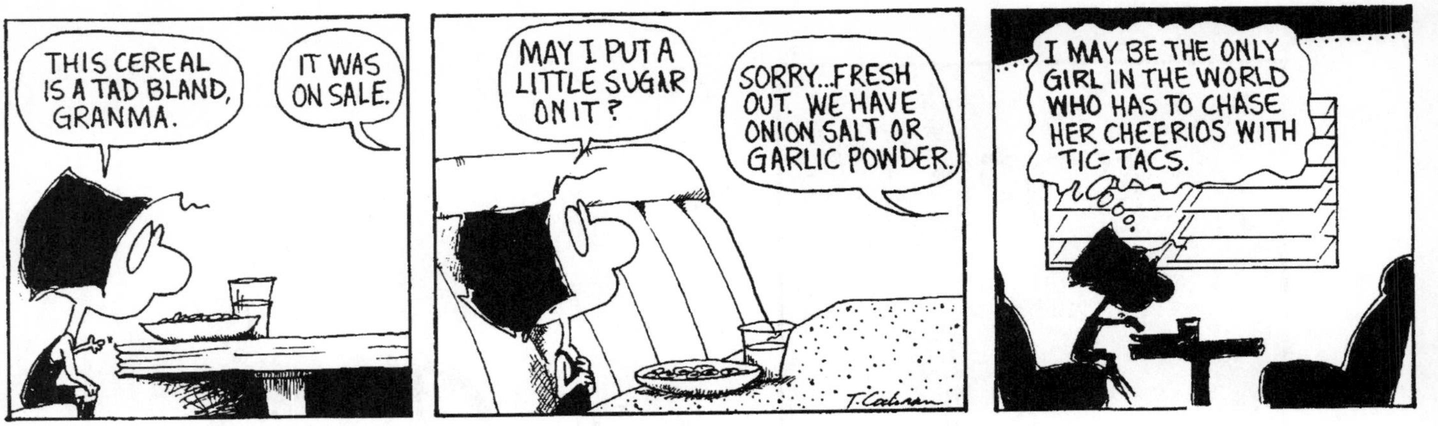
THIS CEREAL IS A TAD BLAND, GRANMA.
IT WAS ON SALE.
MAY I PUT A LITTLE SUGAR ON IT?
SORRY...FRESH OUT. WE HAVE ONION SALT OR GARLIC POWDER.
I MAY BE THE ONLY GIRL IN THE WORLD WHO HAS TO CHASE HER CHEERIOS WITH TIC-TACS.
T. Cochran

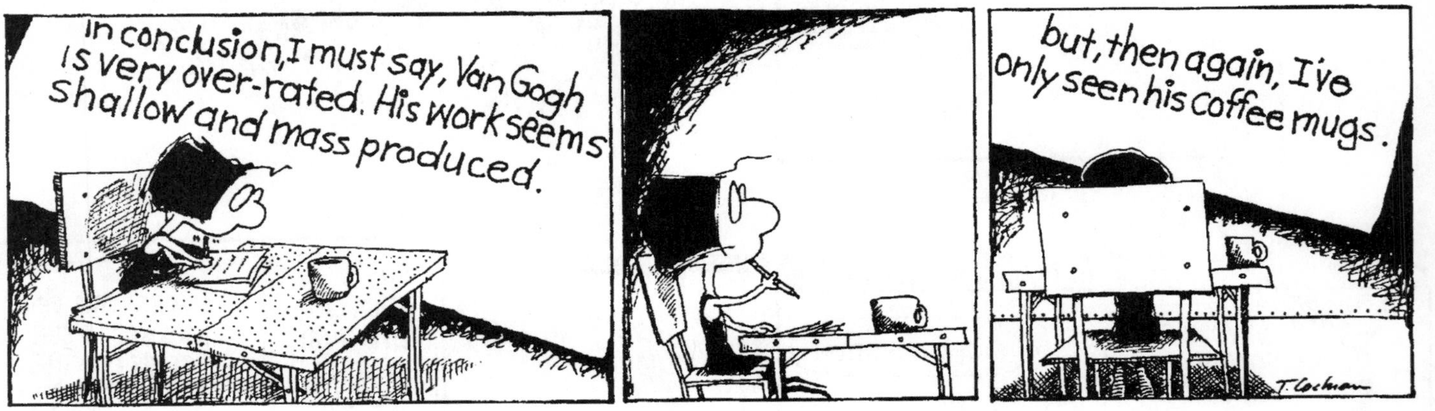
in conclusion, I must say, Van Gogh is very over-rated. His work seems shallow and mass produced.
but, then again, I've only seen his coffee mugs.
T. Cochran

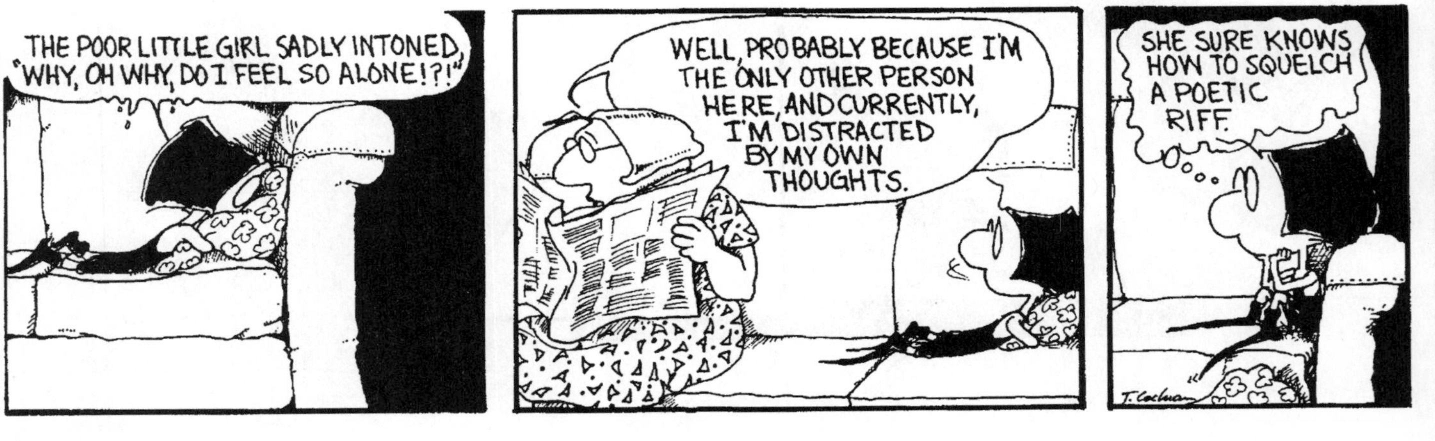
THE POOR LITTLE GIRL SADLY INTONED, "WHY, OH WHY, DO I FEEL SO ALONE!?!"
WELL, PROBABLY BECAUSE I'M THE ONLY OTHER PERSON HERE, AND CURRENTLY, I'M DISTRACTED BY MY OWN THOUGHTS.
SHE SURE KNOWS HOW TO SQUELCH A POETIC RIFF.
T. Cochran

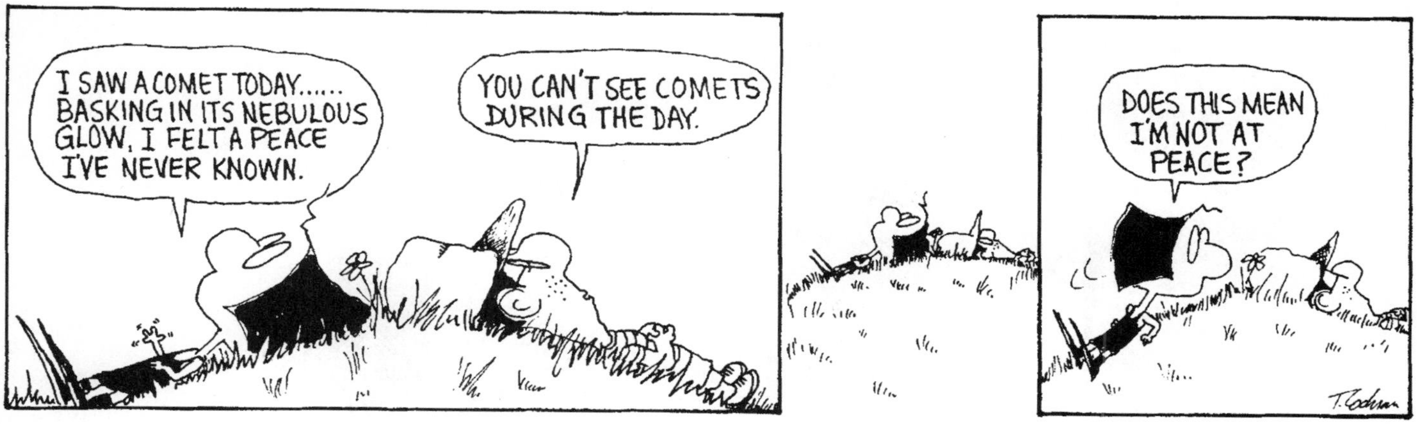
I SAW A COMET TODAY...... BASKING IN ITS NEBULOUS GLOW, I FELT A PEACE I'VE NEVER KNOWN.
YOU CAN'T SEE COMETS DURING THE DAY.
DOES THIS MEAN I'M NOT AT PEACE?
T. Cochran

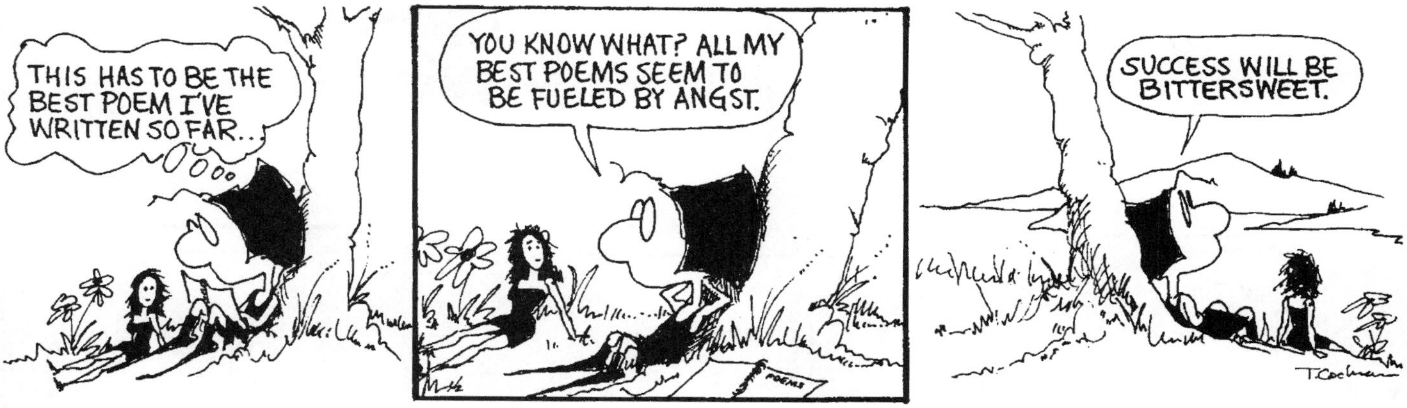
THIS HAS TO BE THE BEST POEM I'VE WRITTEN SO FAR...
YOU KNOW WHAT? ALL MY BEST POEMS SEEM TO BE FUELED BY ANGST.
SUCCESS WILL BE BITTERSWEET.
T. Cochran

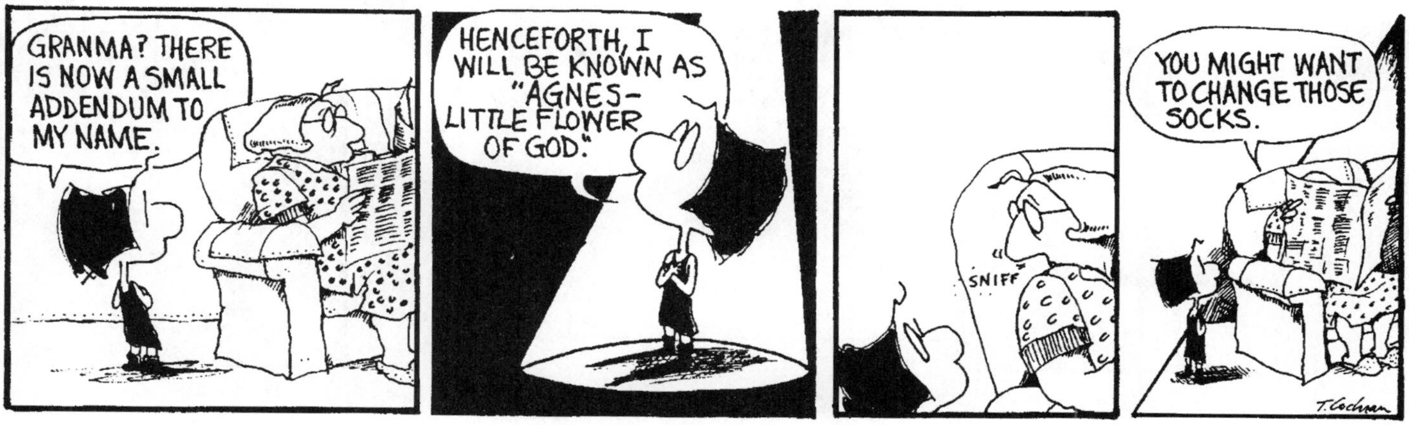
GRANMA? THERE IS NOW A SMALL ADDENDUM TO MY NAME.
HENCEFORTH, I WILL BE KNOWN AS "AGNES-LITTLE FLOWER OF GOD."
SNIFF
YOU MIGHT WANT TO CHANGE THOSE SOCKS.
T. Cochran

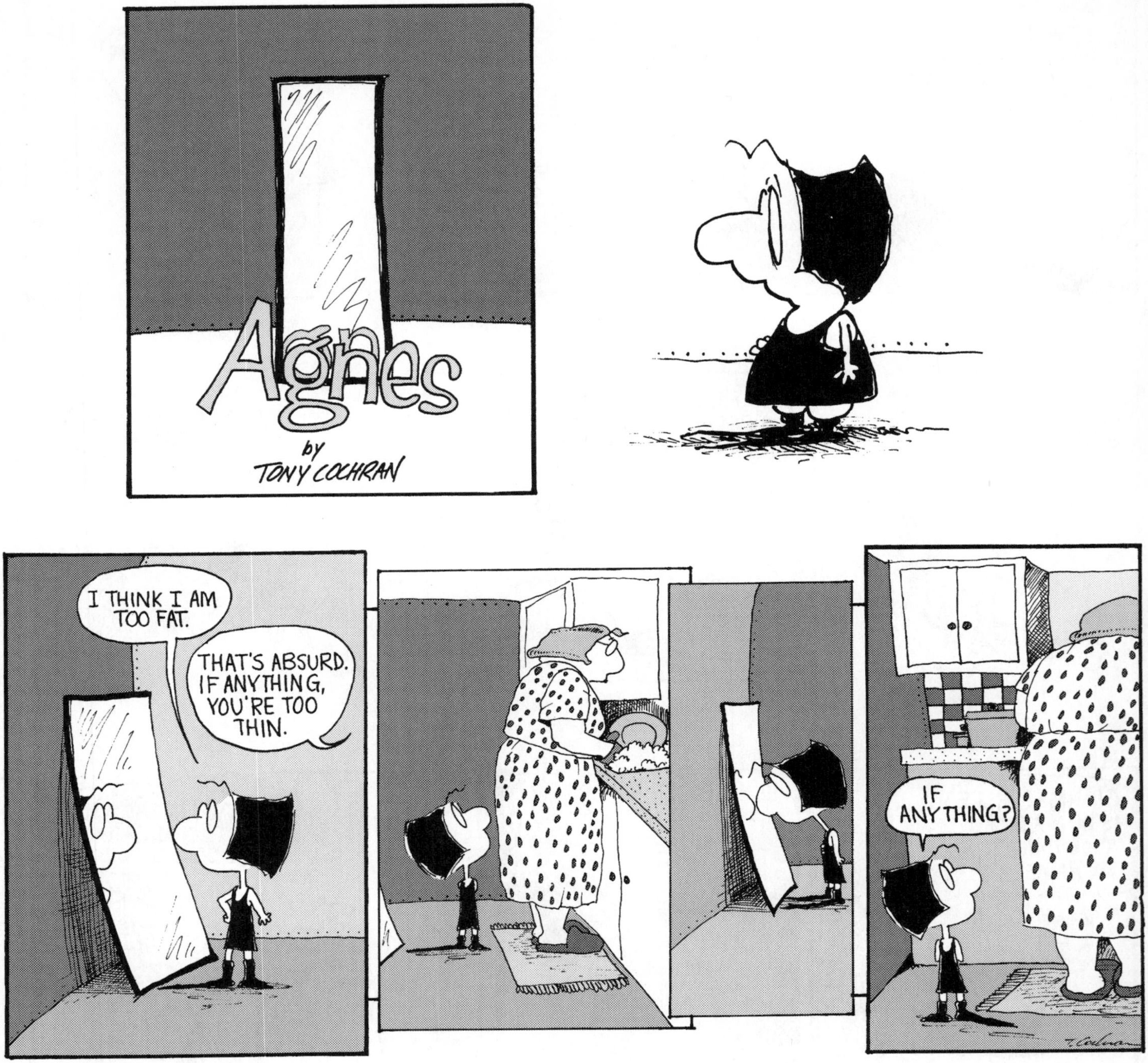
Agnes
by
TONY COCHRAN
I THINK I AM TOO FAT.
THAT'S ABSURD. IF ANYTHING, YOU'RE TOO THIN.
IF ANYTHING?

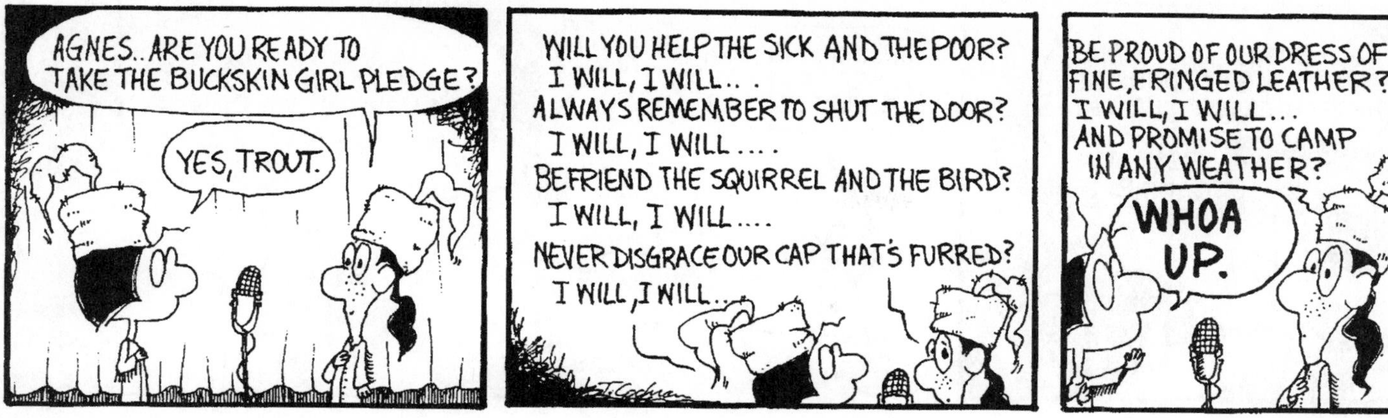

AGNES.. ARE YOU READY TO TAKE THE BUCKSKIN GIRL PLEDGE?
YES, TROUT.
WILL YOU HELP THE SICK AND THE POOR?
I WILL, I WILL.. .
ALWAYS REMEMBER TO SHUT THE DOOR?
I WILL, I WILL....
BEFRIEND THE SQUIRREL AND THE BIRD?
I WILL, I WILL....
NEVER DISGRACE OUR CAP THAT'S FURRED?
I WILL, I WILL..
BE PROUD OF OUR DRESS OF FINE, FRINGED LEATHER?
I WILL, I WILL...
AND PROMISE TO CAMP IN ANY WEATHER?
WHOA UP.

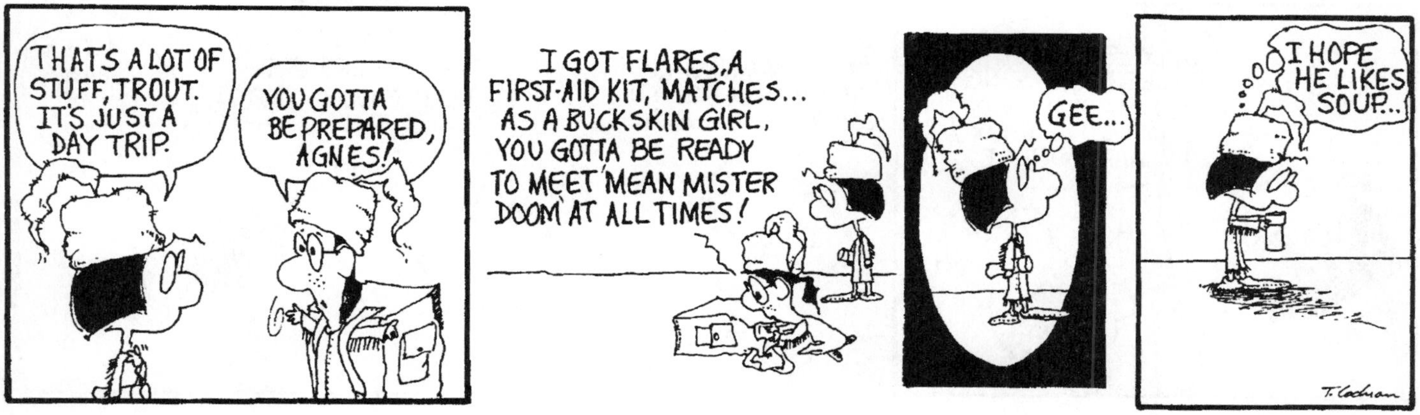

THAT'S A LOT OF STUFF, TROUT. IT'S JUST A DAY TRIP.
YOU GOTTA BE PREPARED, AGNES!
I GOT FLARES, A FIRST-AID KIT, MATCHES... AS A BUCKSKIN GIRL, YOU GOTTA BE READY TO MEET 'MEAN MISTER DOOM' AT ALL TIMES!
GEE...
I HOPE HE LIKES SOUP...

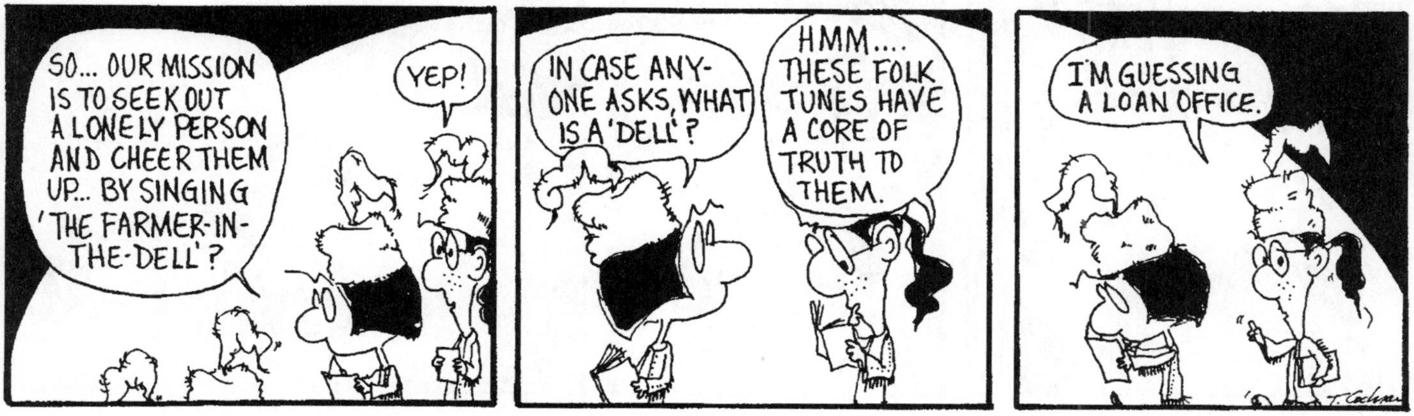

SO... OUR MISSION IS TO SEEK OUT A LONELY PERSON AND CHEER THEM UP... BY SINGING 'THE FARMER-IN-THE-DELL'?
YEP!
IN CASE ANY-ONE ASKS, WHAT IS A 'DELL'?
HMM.... THESE FOLK TUNES HAVE A CORE OF TRUTH TO THEM.
I'M GUESSING A LOAN OFFICE.

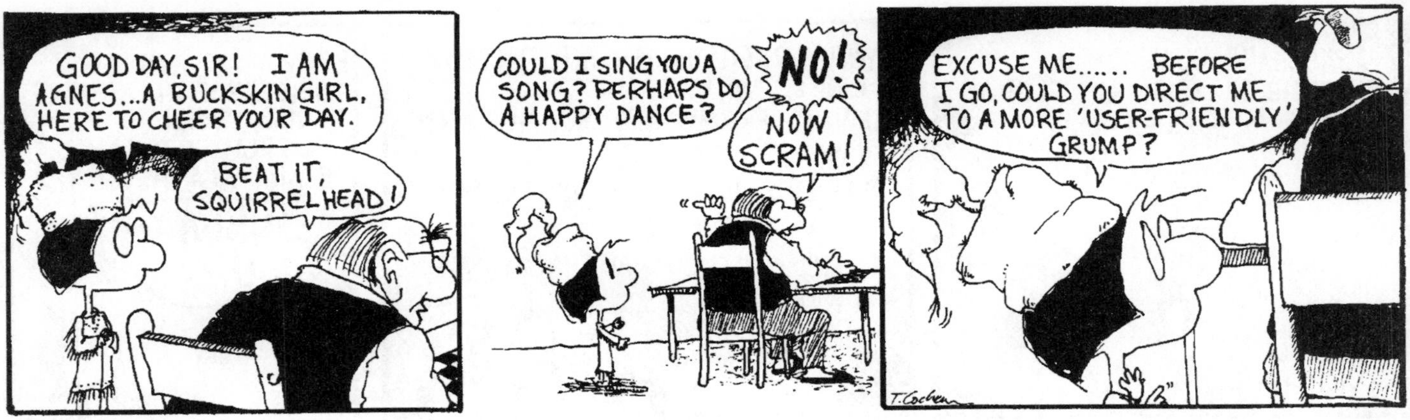
GOOD DAY, SIR! I AM AGNES...A BUCKSKIN GIRL, HERE TO CHEER YOUR DAY.
BEAT IT, SQUIRREL HEAD!
COULD I SING YOU A SONG? PERHAPS DO A HAPPY DANCE?
NO!
NOW SCRAM!
EXCUSE ME...... BEFORE I GO, COULD YOU DIRECT ME TO A MORE 'USER-FRIENDLY' GRUMP?
T. Cochran

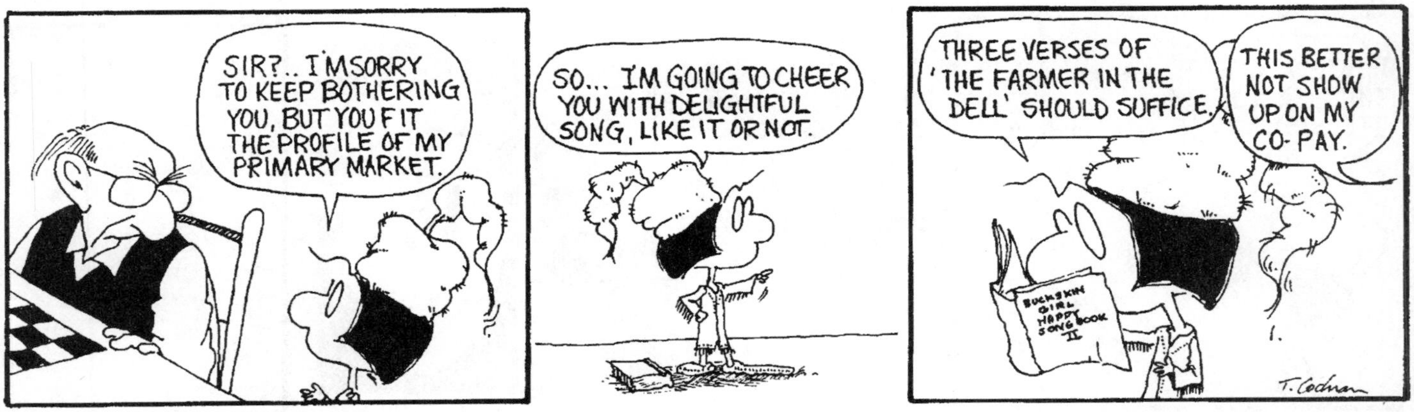
SIR?.. I'M SORRY TO KEEP BOTHERING YOU, BUT YOU FIT THE PROFILE OF MY PRIMARY MARKET.
SO... I'M GOING TO CHEER YOU WITH DELIGHTFUL SONG, LIKE IT OR NOT.
THREE VERSES OF 'THE FARMER IN THE DELL' SHOULD SUFFICE.
THIS BETTER NOT SHOW UP ON MY CO-PAY.
BUCKSKIN GIRL HAPPY SONG BOOK II
T. Cochran

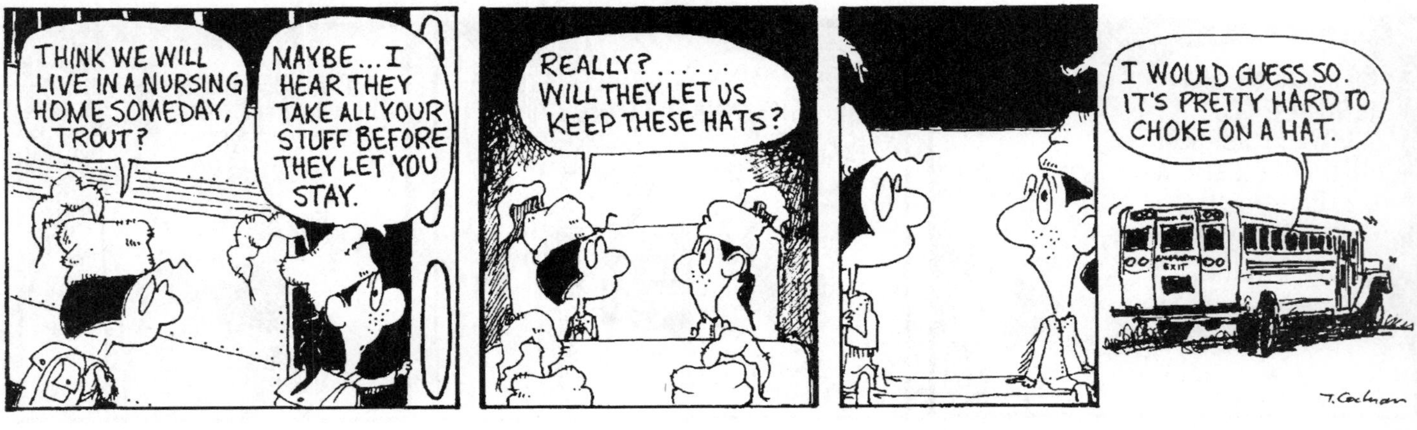
THINK WE WILL LIVE IN A NURSING HOME SOMEDAY, TROUT?
MAYBE... I HEAR THEY TAKE ALL YOUR STUFF BEFORE THEY LET YOU STAY.
REALLY?...... WILL THEY LET US KEEP THESE HATS?
I WOULD GUESS SO. IT'S PRETTY HARD TO CHOKE ON A HAT.
T. Cochran

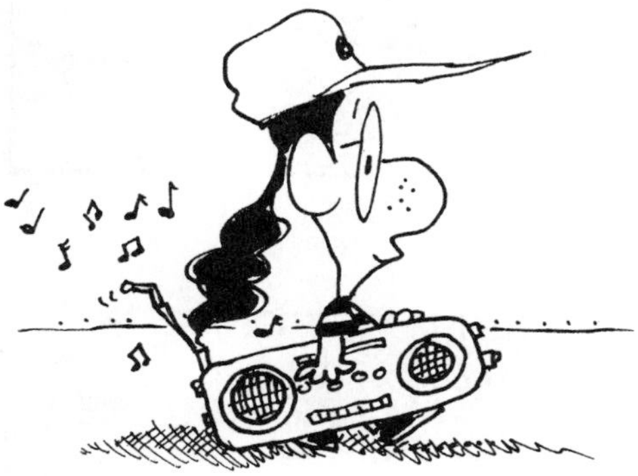

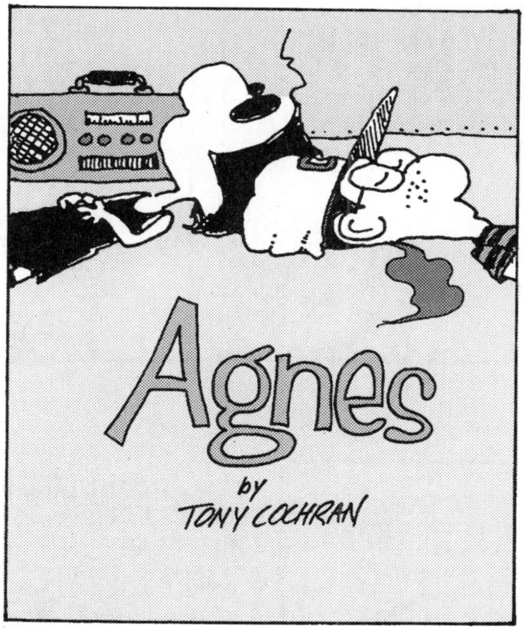
Agnes
by TONY COCHRAN

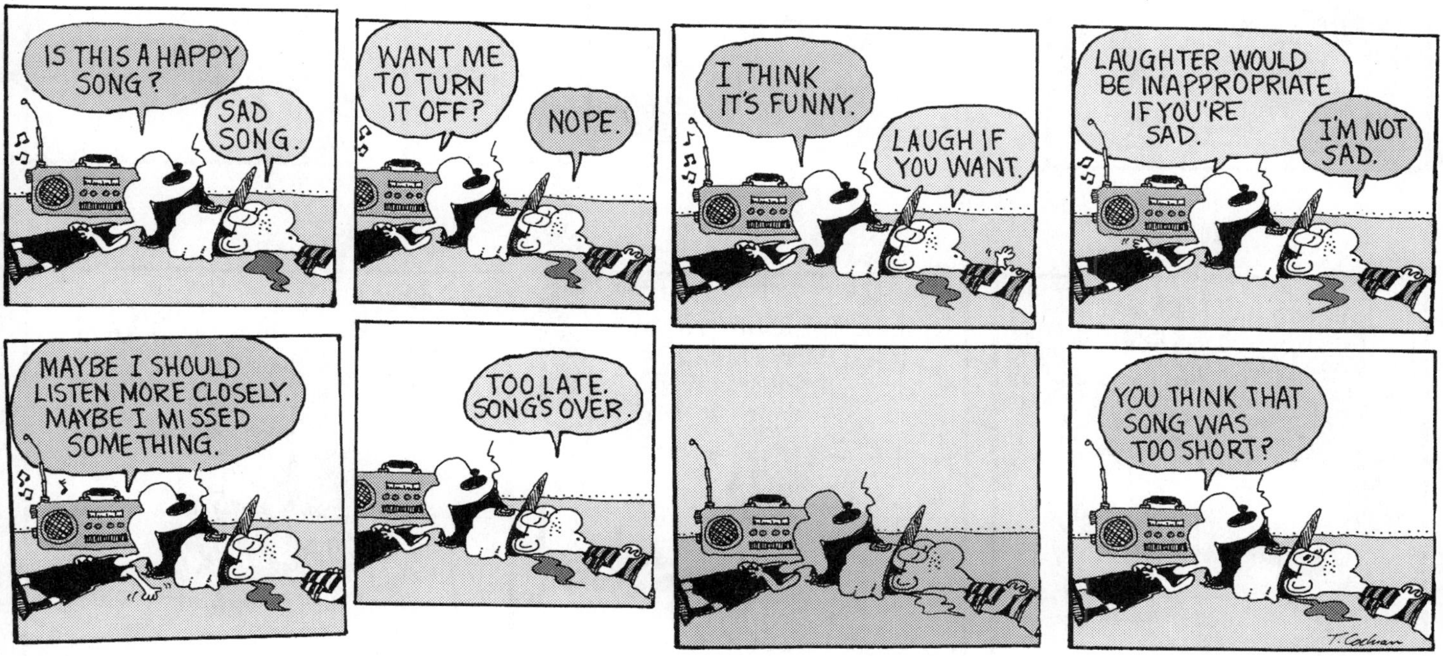
IS THIS A HAPPY SONG?
SAD SONG.
WANT ME TO TURN IT OFF?
NOPE.
I THINK IT'S FUNNY.
LAUGH IF YOU WANT.
LAUGHTER WOULD BE INAPPROPRIATE IF YOU'RE SAD.
I'M NOT SAD.
MAYBE I SHOULD LISTEN MORE CLOSELY. MAYBE I MISSED SOMETHING.
TOO LATE. SONG'S OVER.
YOU THINK THAT SONG WAS TOO SHORT?
T. Cochran

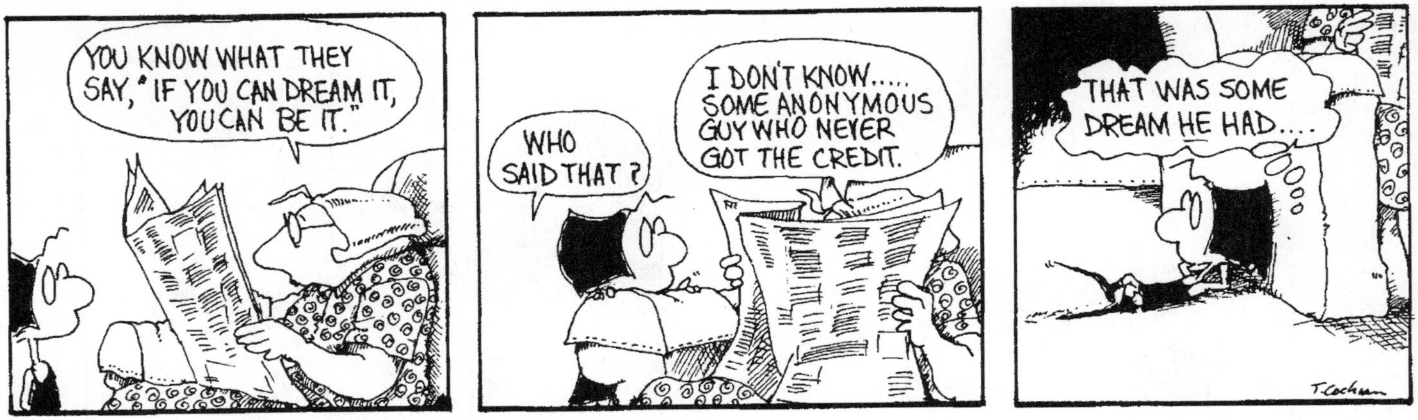
YOU KNOW WHAT THEY SAY, "IF YOU CAN DREAM IT, YOU CAN BE IT."
WHO SAID THAT?
I DON'T KNOW..... SOME ANONYMOUS GUY WHO NEVER GOT THE CREDIT.
THAT WAS SOME DREAM HE HAD....

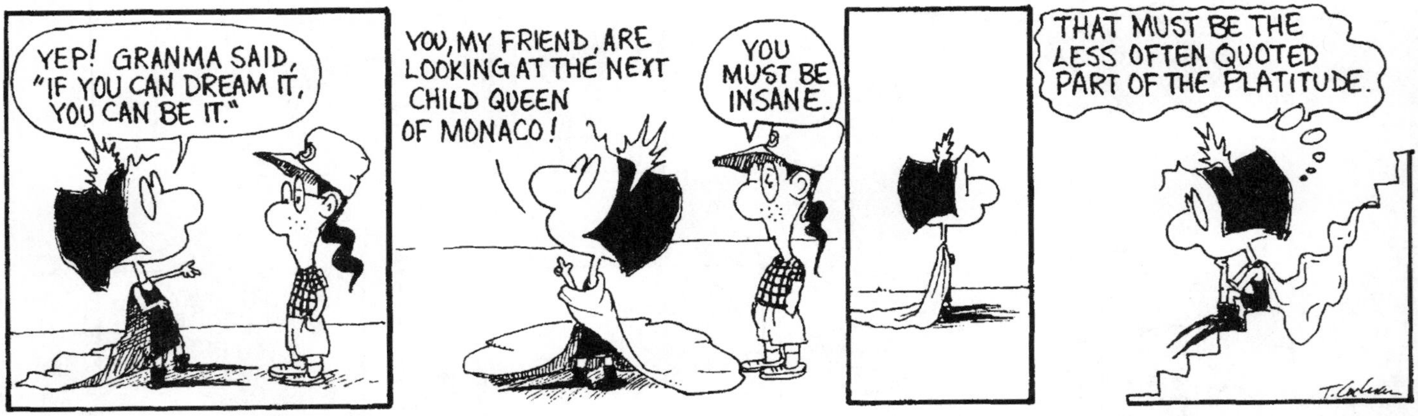
YEP! GRANMA SAID, "IF YOU CAN DREAM IT, YOU CAN BE IT."
YOU, MY FRIEND, ARE LOOKING AT THE NEXT CHILD QUEEN OF MONACO!
YOU MUST BE INSANE.
THAT MUST BE THE LESS OFTEN QUOTED PART OF THE PLATITUDE.

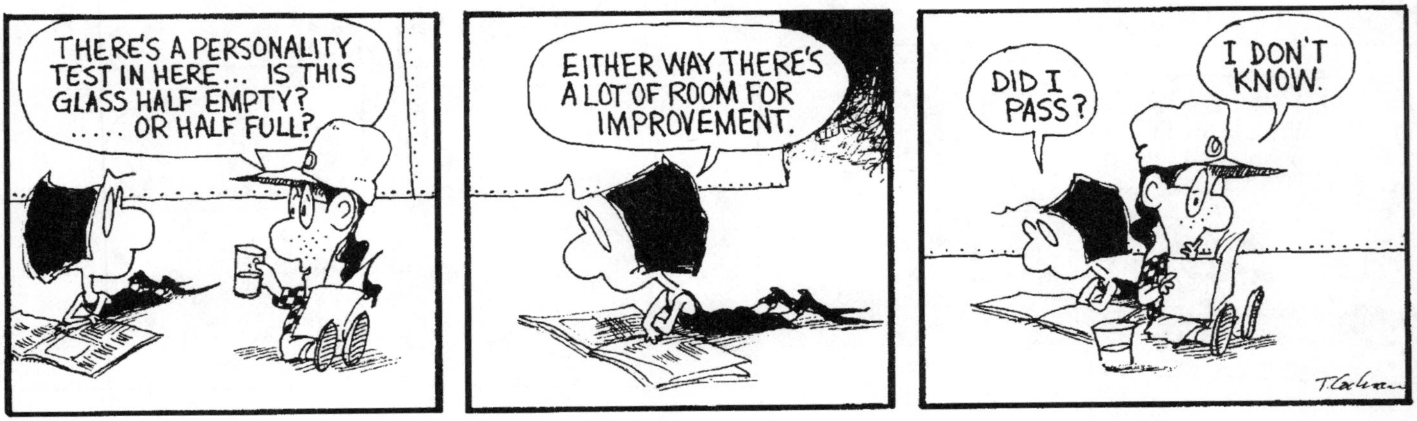
THERE'S A PERSONALITY TEST IN HERE... IS THIS GLASS HALF EMPTY? ..... OR HALF FULL?
EITHER WAY, THERE'S A LOT OF ROOM FOR IMPROVEMENT.
DID I PASS?
I DON'T KNOW.

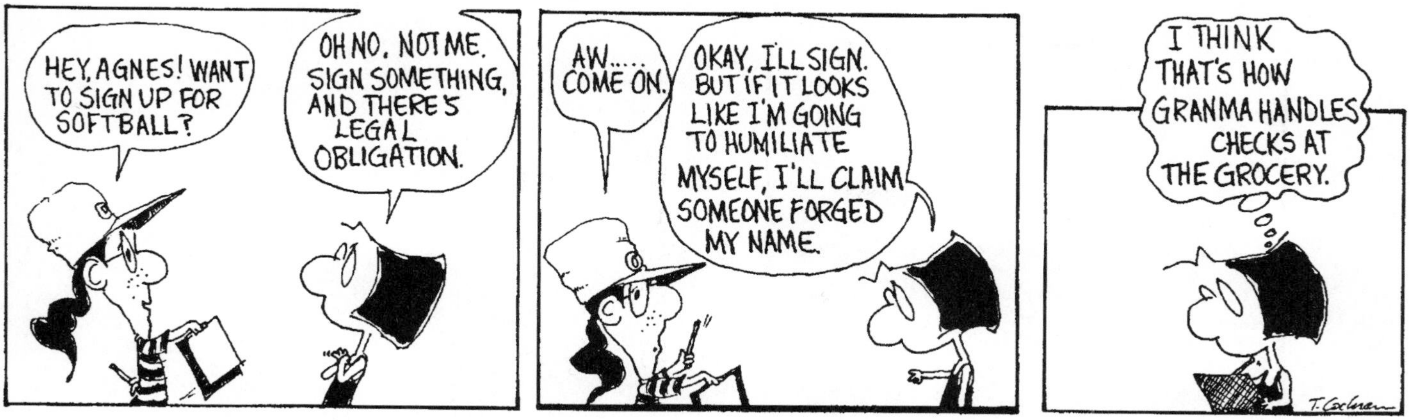
HEY, AGNES! WANT TO SIGN UP FOR SOFTBALL?
OH NO. NOT ME. SIGN SOMETHING, AND THERE'S LEGAL OBLIGATION.
AW..... COME ON.
OKAY, I'LL SIGN. BUT IF IT LOOKS LIKE I'M GOING TO HUMILIATE MYSELF, I'LL CLAIM SOMEONE FORGED MY NAME.
I THINK THAT'S HOW GRANMA HANDLES CHECKS AT THE GROCERY.
T. Cochran

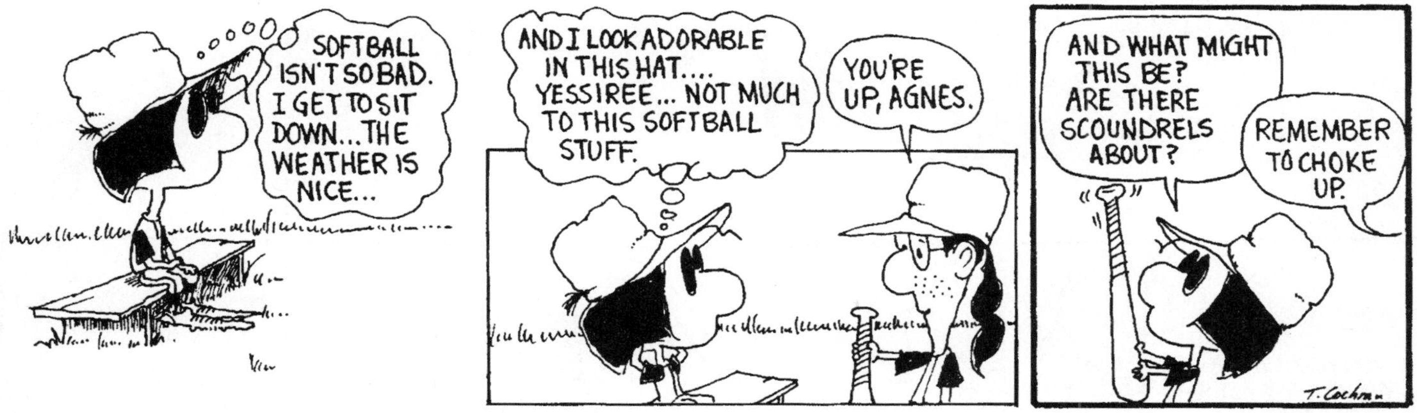
SOFTBALL ISN'T SO BAD. I GET TO SIT DOWN... THE WEATHER IS NICE...
AND I LOOK ADORABLE IN THIS HAT.... YESSIREE... NOT MUCH TO THIS SOFTBALL STUFF.
YOU'RE UP, AGNES.
AND WHAT MIGHT THIS BE? ARE THERE SCOUNDRELS ABOUT?
REMEMBER TO CHOKE UP.
T. Cochran

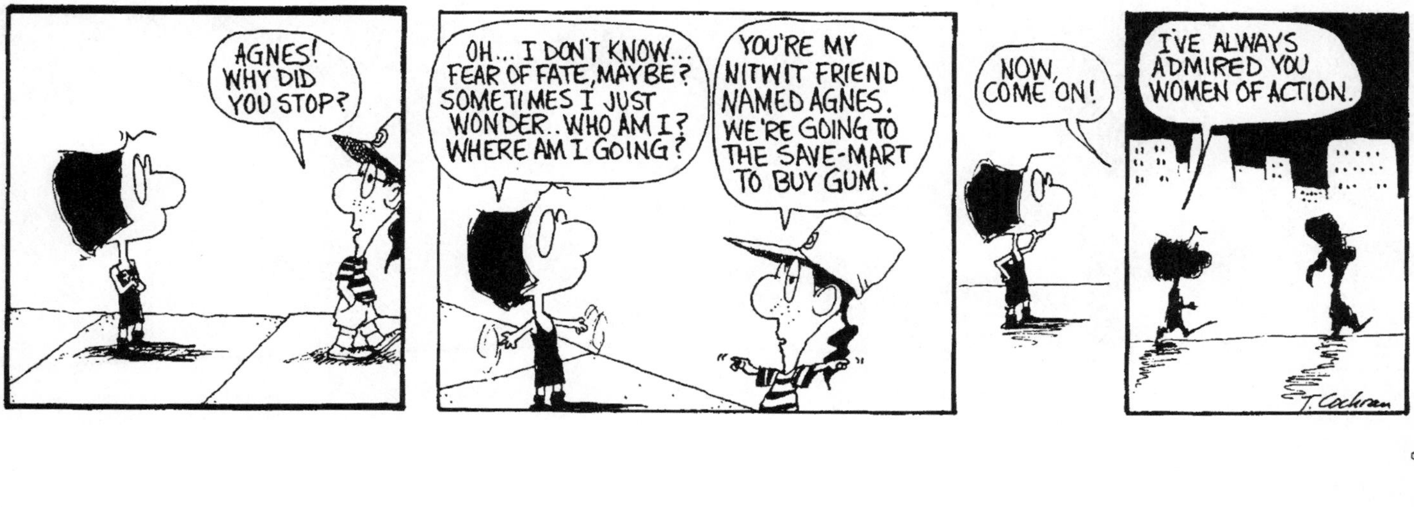
AGNES! WHY DID YOU STOP?
OH... I DON'T KNOW... FEAR OF FATE, MAYBE? SOMETIMES I JUST WONDER.. WHO AM I? WHERE AM I GOING?
YOU'RE MY NITWIT FRIEND NAMED AGNES. WE'RE GOING TO THE SAVE-MART TO BUY GUM.
NOW, COME ON!
I'VE ALWAYS ADMIRED YOU WOMEN OF ACTION.
T. Cochran

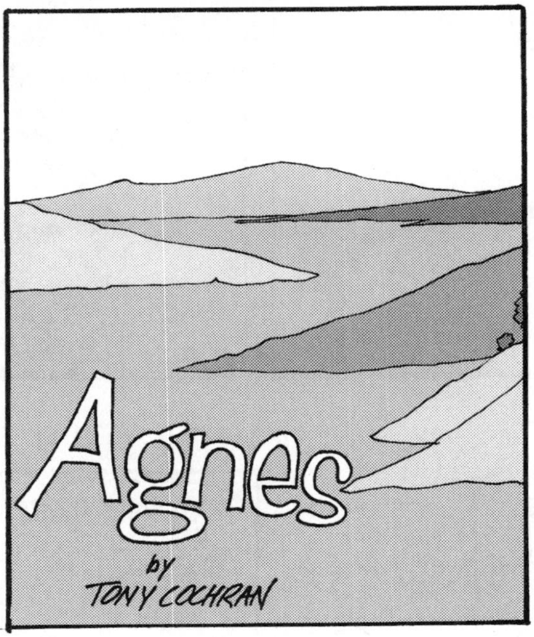
Agnes
by
TONY COCHRAN

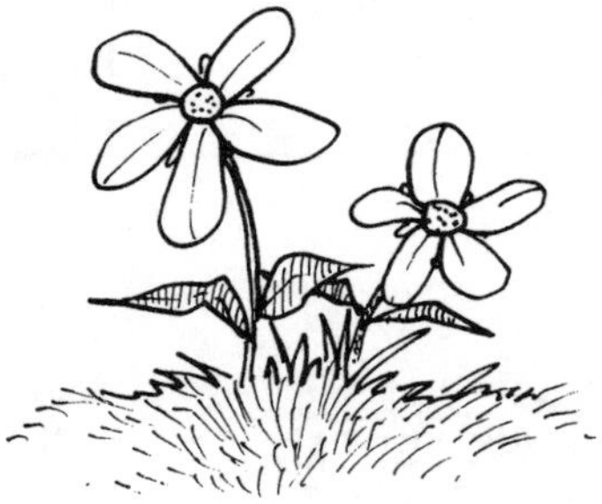

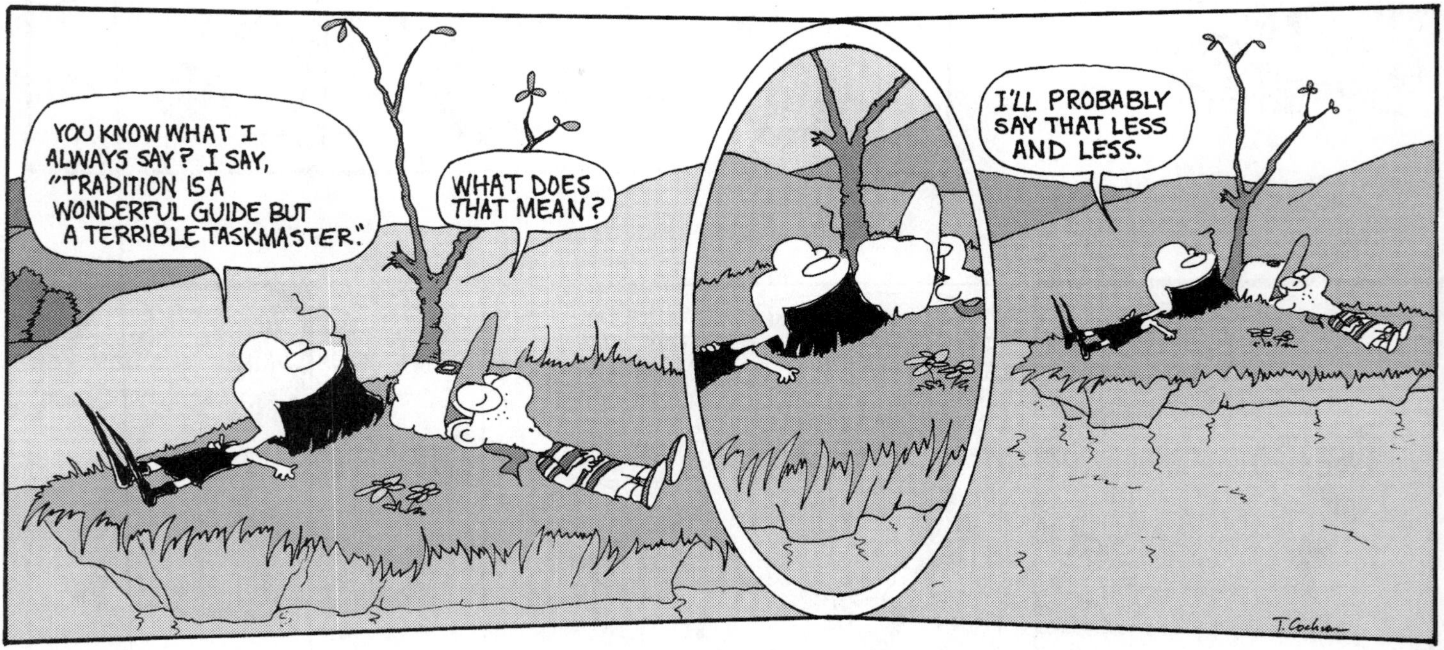
YOU KNOW WHAT I ALWAYS SAY? I SAY, "TRADITION IS A WONDERFUL GUIDE BUT A TERRIBLE TASKMASTER."
WHAT DOES THAT MEAN?
I'LL PROBABLY SAY THAT LESS AND LESS.
T. Cochran

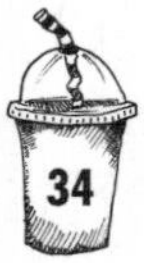

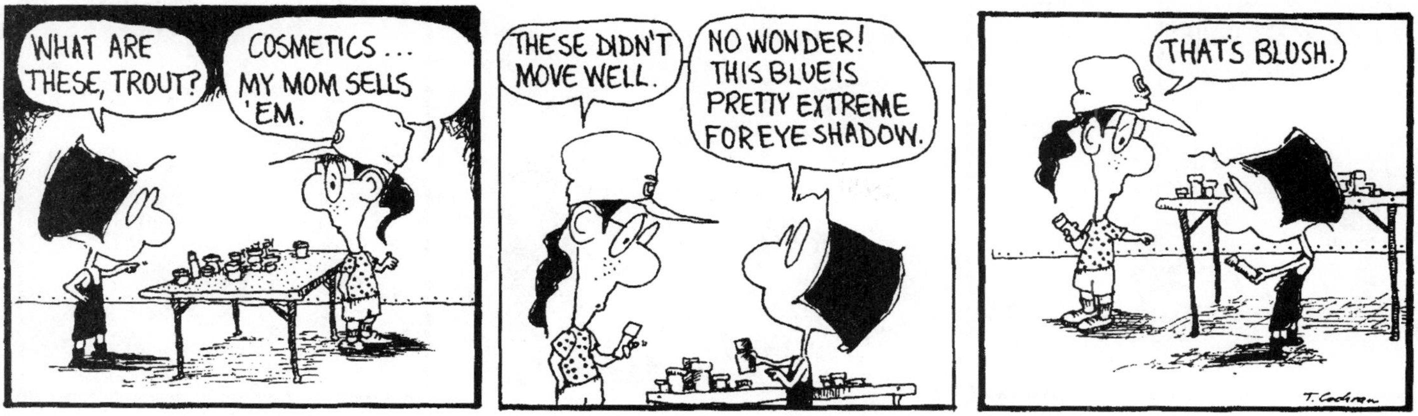
WHAT ARE THESE, TROUT?
COSMETICS... MY MOM SELLS 'EM.
THESE DIDN'T MOVE WELL.
NO WONDER! THIS BLUE IS PRETTY EXTREME FOR EYE SHADOW.
THAT'S BLUSH.
T. Cochran

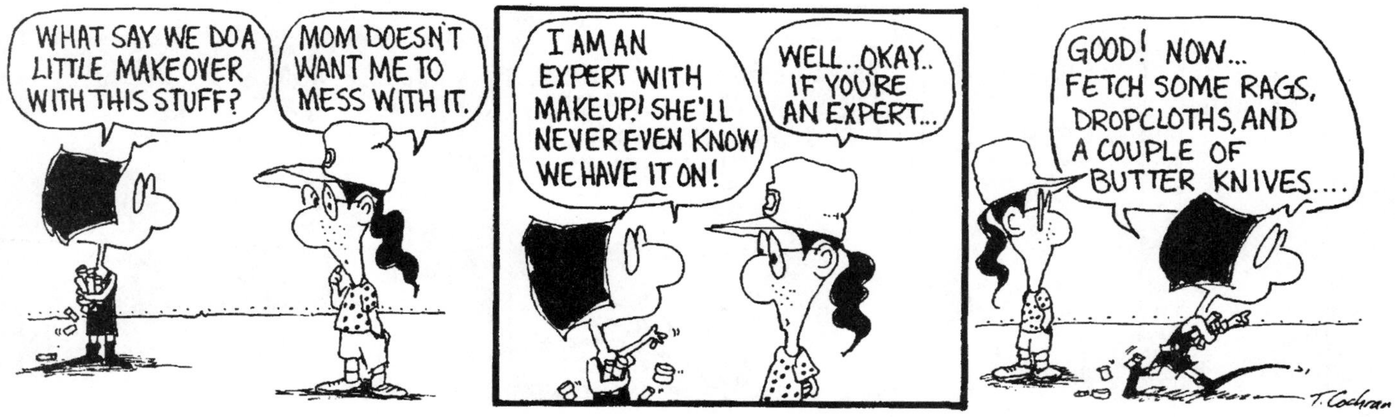
WHAT SAY WE DO A LITTLE MAKEOVER WITH THIS STUFF?
MOM DOESN'T WANT ME TO MESS WITH IT.
I AM AN EXPERT WITH MAKEUP! SHE'LL NEVER EVEN KNOW WE HAVE IT ON!
WELL..OKAY.. IF YOU'RE AN EXPERT...
GOOD! NOW... FETCH SOME RAGS, DROPCLOTHS, AND A COUPLE OF BUTTER KNIVES....
T. Cochran

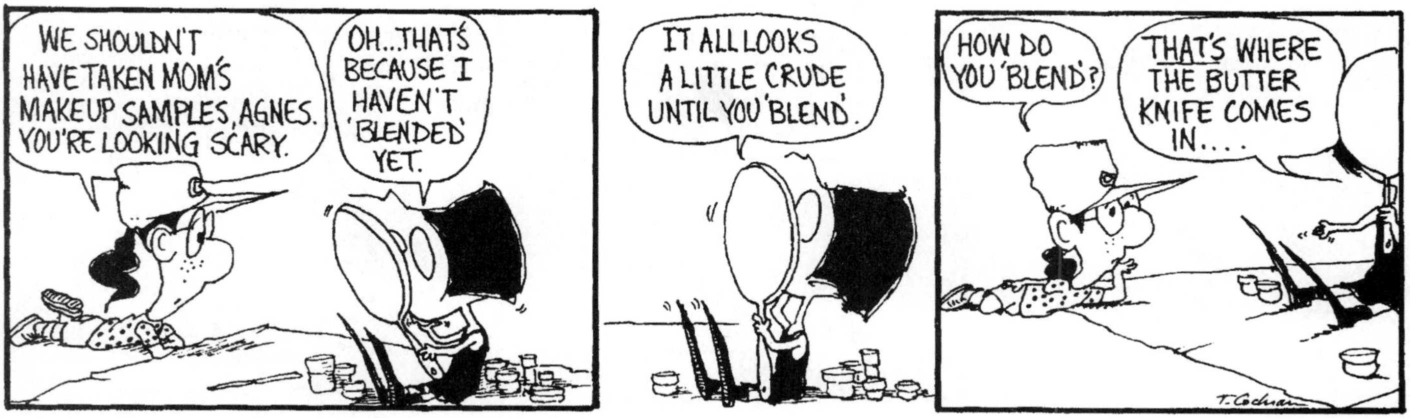
WE SHOULDN'T HAVE TAKEN MOM'S MAKEUP SAMPLES, AGNES. YOU'RE LOOKING SCARY.
OH...THAT'S BECAUSE I HAVEN'T 'BLENDED' YET.
IT ALL LOOKS A LITTLE CRUDE UNTIL YOU 'BLEND'.
HOW DO YOU 'BLEND'?
THAT'S WHERE THE BUTTER KNIFE COMES IN....
T. Cochran

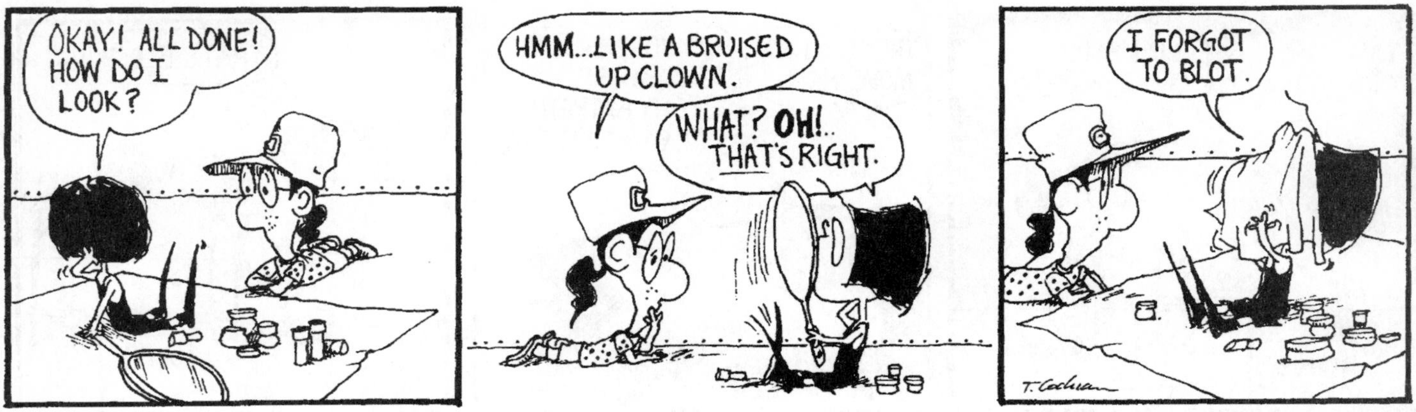
OKAY! ALL DONE! HOW DO I LOOK?
HMM...LIKE A BRUISED UP CLOWN.
WHAT? OH!.. THAT'S RIGHT.
I FORGOT TO BLOT.
T. Cochran

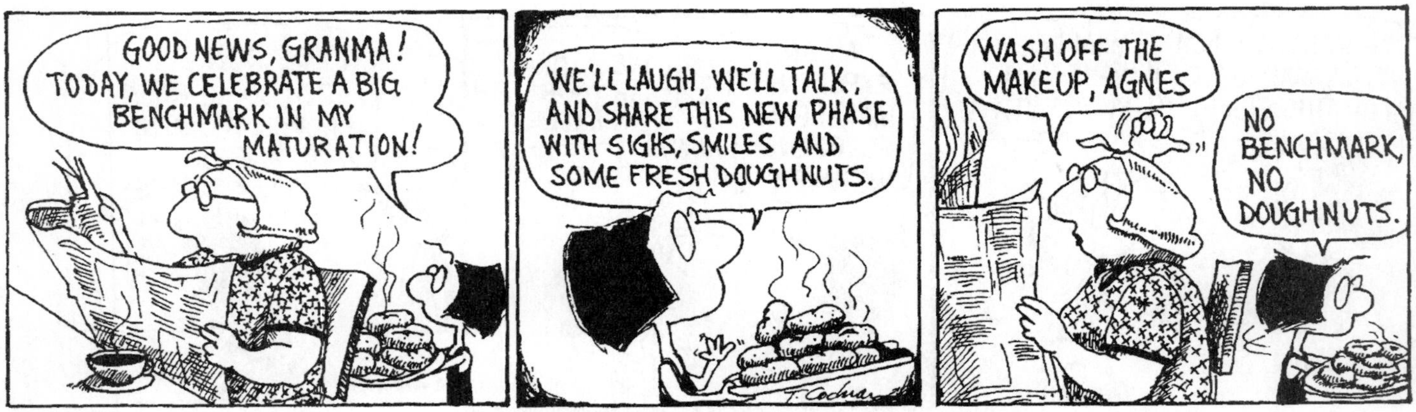
GOOD NEWS, GRANMA! TODAY, WE CELEBRATE A BIG BENCHMARK IN MY MATURATION!
WE'LL LAUGH, WE'LL TALK, AND SHARE THIS NEW PHASE WITH SIGHS, SMILES AND SOME FRESH DOUGHNUTS.
T. Cochran
WASH OFF THE MAKEUP, AGNES
NO BENCHMARK, NO DOUGHNUTS.

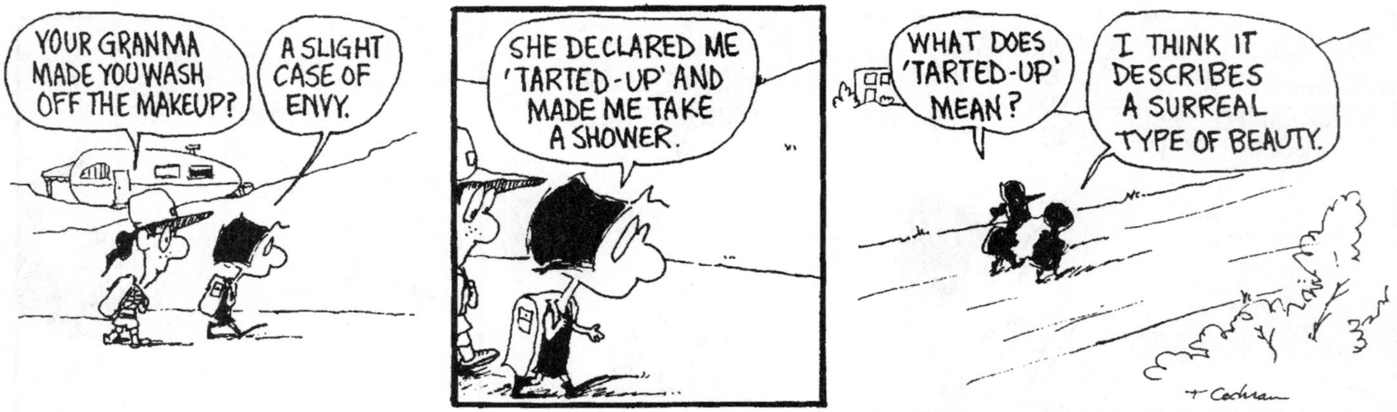
YOUR GRANMA MADE YOU WASH OFF THE MAKEUP?
A SLIGHT CASE OF ENVY.
SHE DECLARED ME 'TARTED-UP' AND MADE ME TAKE A SHOWER.
WHAT DOES 'TARTED-UP' MEAN?
I THINK IT DESCRIBES A SURREAL TYPE OF BEAUTY.
T. Cochran

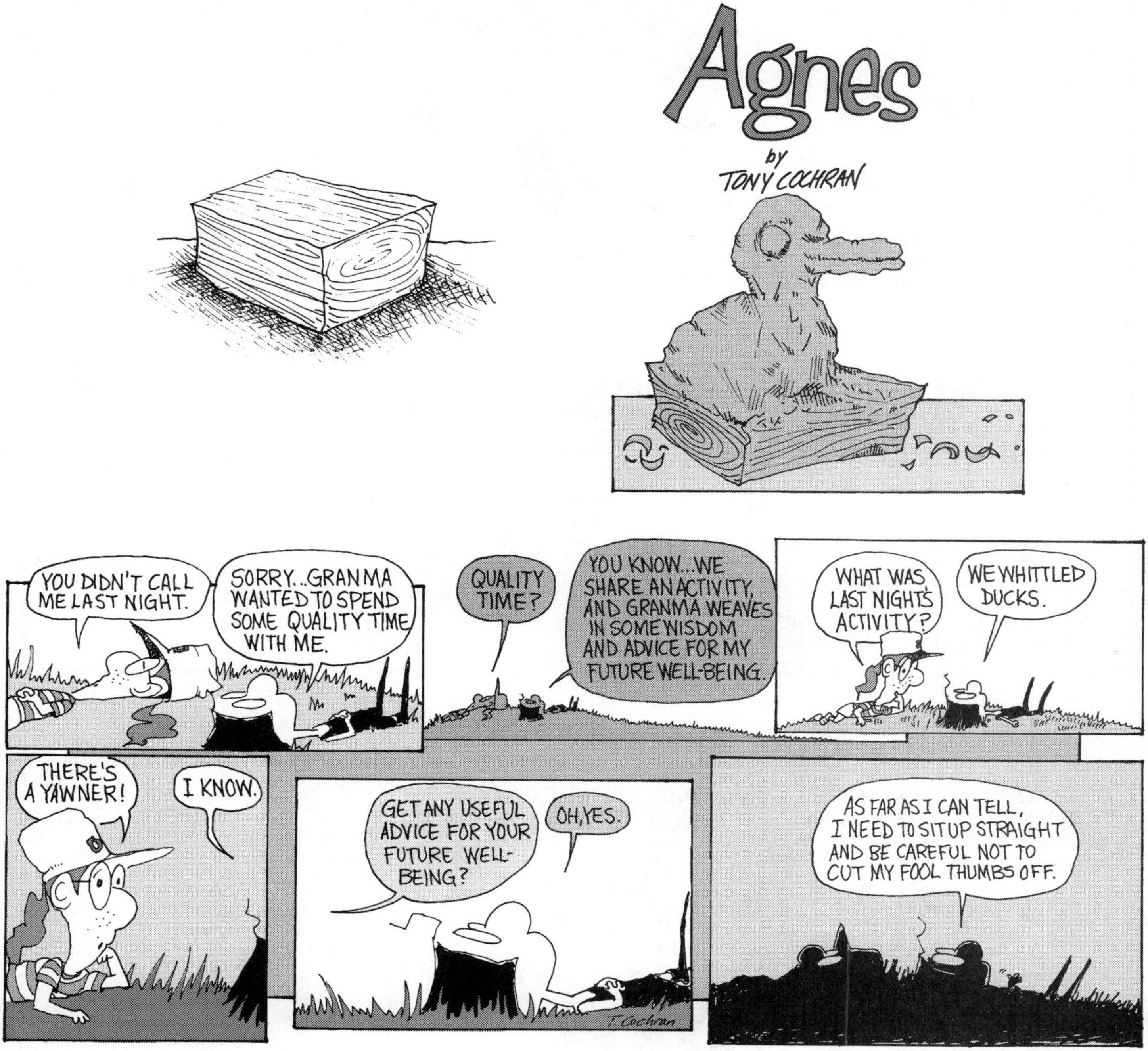
Agnes
by
TONY COCHRAN
YOU DIDN'T CALL ME LAST NIGHT.
SORRY...GRANMA WANTED TO SPEND SOME QUALITY TIME WITH ME.
QUALITY TIME?
YOU KNOW...WE SHARE AN ACTIVITY, AND GRANMA WEAVES IN SOME WISDOM AND ADVICE FOR MY FUTURE WELL-BEING.
WHAT WAS LAST NIGHT'S ACTIVITY?
WE WHITTLED DUCKS.
THERE'S A YAWNER!
I KNOW.
GET ANY USEFUL ADVICE FOR YOUR FUTURE WELL-BEING?
OH, YES.
AS FAR AS I CAN TELL, I NEED TO SIT UP STRAIGHT AND BE CAREFUL NOT TO CUT MY FOOL THUMBS OFF.
T. Cochran

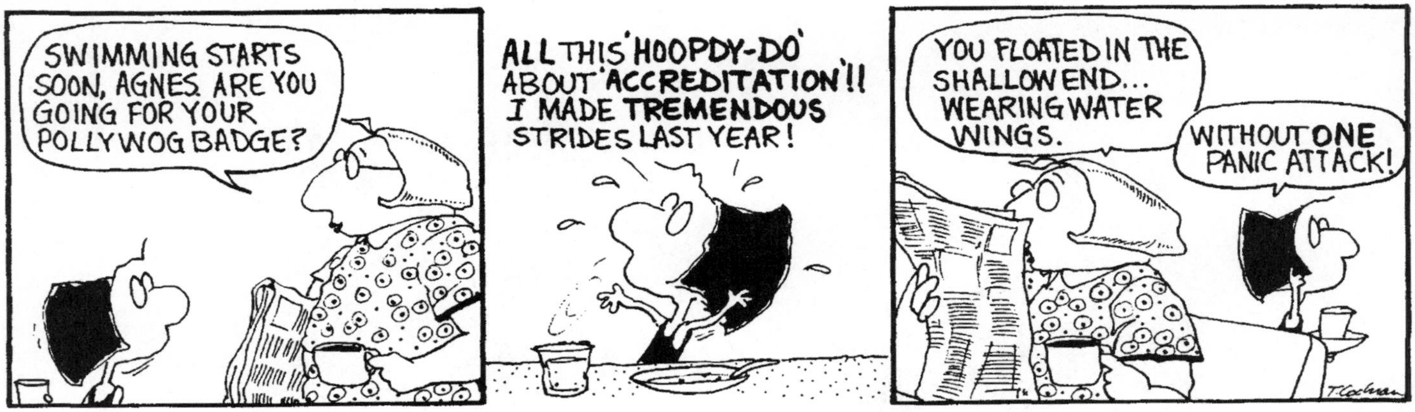
SWIMMING STARTS SOON, AGNES. ARE YOU GOING FOR YOUR POLLYWOG BADGE?
ALL THIS 'HOOPDY-DO' ABOUT 'ACCREDITATION'!! I MADE TREMENDOUS STRIDES LAST YEAR!
YOU FLOATED IN THE SHALLOW END... WEARING WATER WINGS.
WITHOUT ONE PANIC ATTACK!
T. Cochran

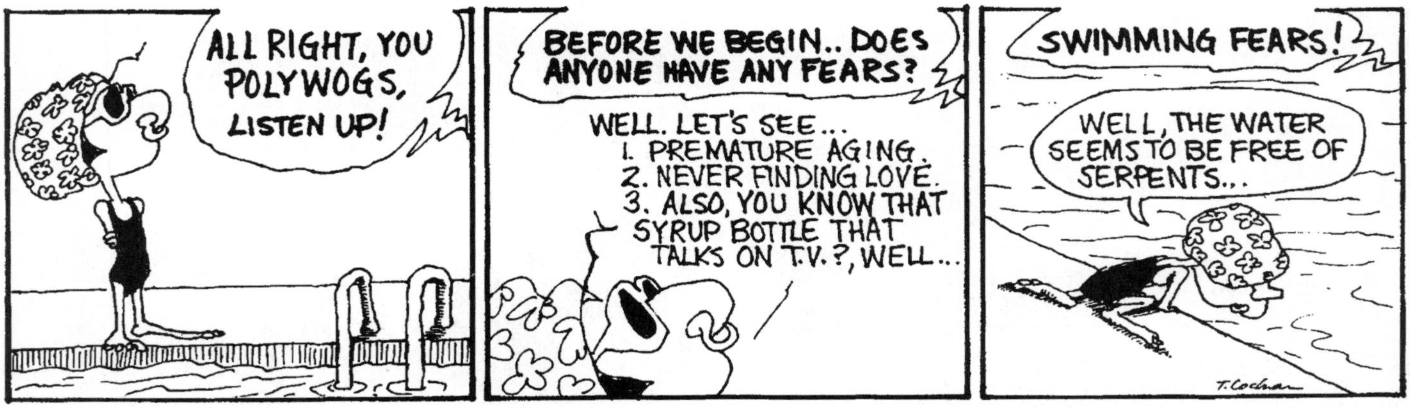
ALL RIGHT, YOU POLYWOGS, LISTEN UP!
BEFORE WE BEGIN.. DOES ANYONE HAVE ANY FEARS?
WELL. LET'S SEE...
1. PREMATURE AGING.
2. NEVER FINDING LOVE.
3. ALSO, YOU KNOW THAT SYRUP BOTTLE THAT TALKS ON T.V.?, WELL...
SWIMMING FEARS!
WELL, THE WATER SEEMS TO BE FREE OF SERPENTS...
T. Cochran

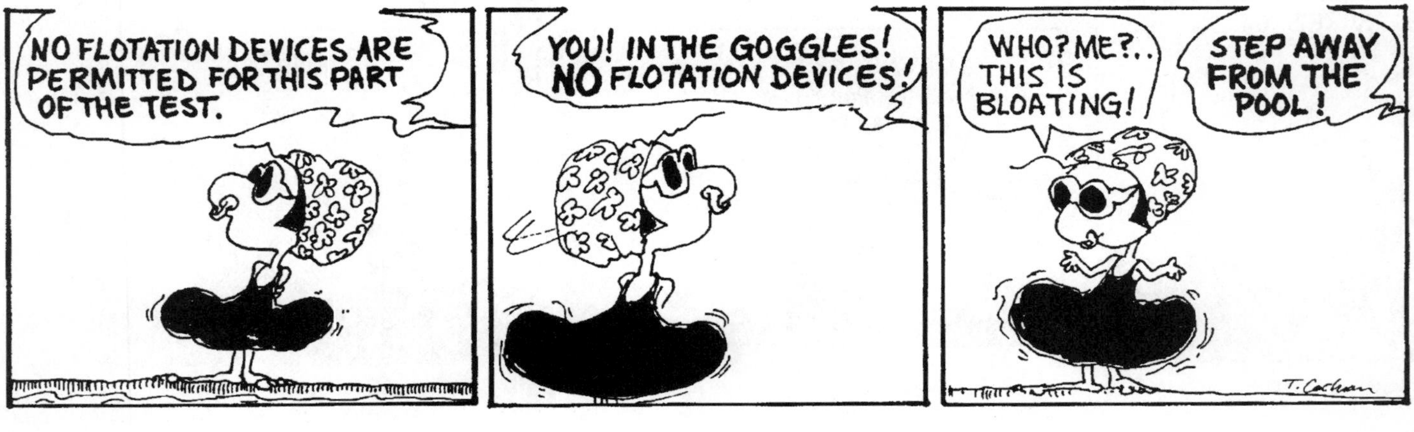
NO FLOTATION DEVICES ARE PERMITTED FOR THIS PART OF THE TEST.
YOU! IN THE GOGGLES! NO FLOTATION DEVICES!
WHO? ME?.. THIS IS BLOATING!
STEP AWAY FROM THE POOL!
T. Cochran

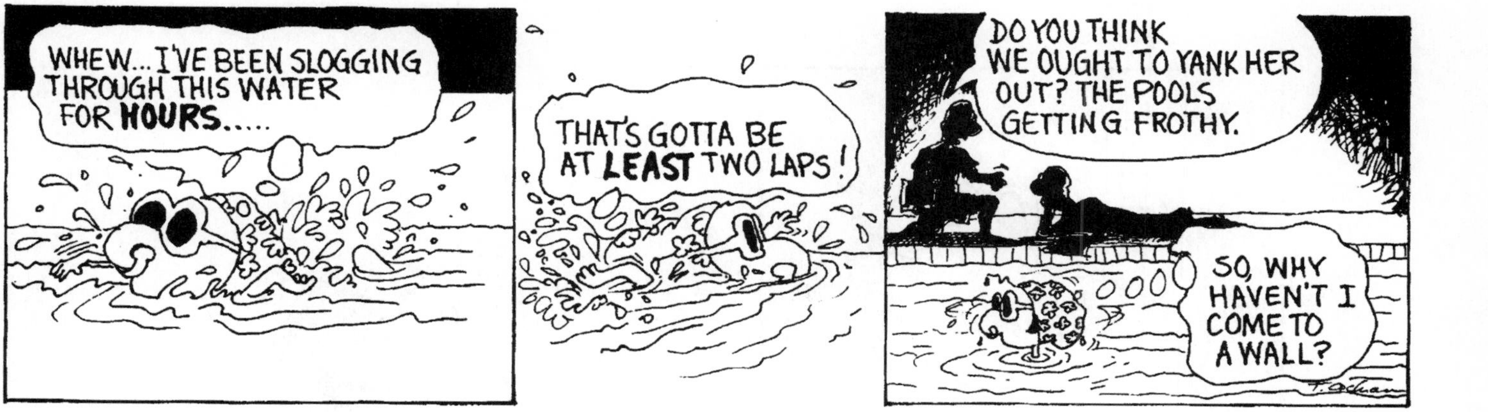
WHEW... I'VE BEEN SLOGGING THROUGH THIS WATER FOR **HOURS**.....
THAT'S GOTTA BE AT **LEAST** TWO LAPS!
DO YOU THINK WE OUGHT TO YANK HER OUT? THE POOLS GETTING FROTHY.
SO, WHY HAVEN'T I COME TO A WALL?
T. Cochran

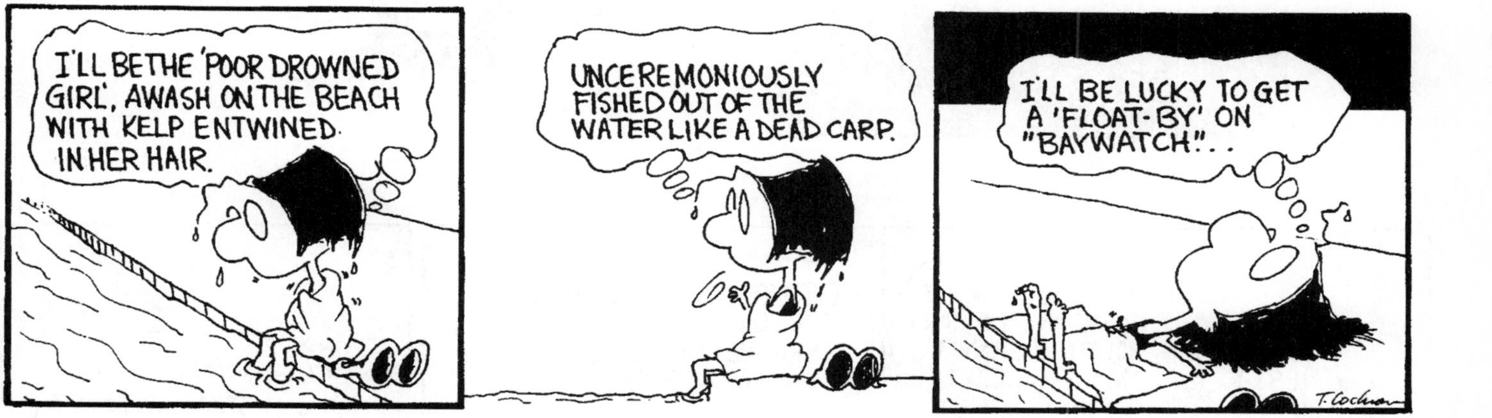
I'LL BE THE 'POOR DROWNED GIRL', AWASH ON THE BEACH WITH KELP ENTWINED IN HER HAIR.
UNCEREMONIOUSLY FISHED OUT OF THE WATER LIKE A DEAD CARP.
I'LL BE LUCKY TO GET A 'FLOAT-BY' ON "BAYWATCH"..
T. Cochran

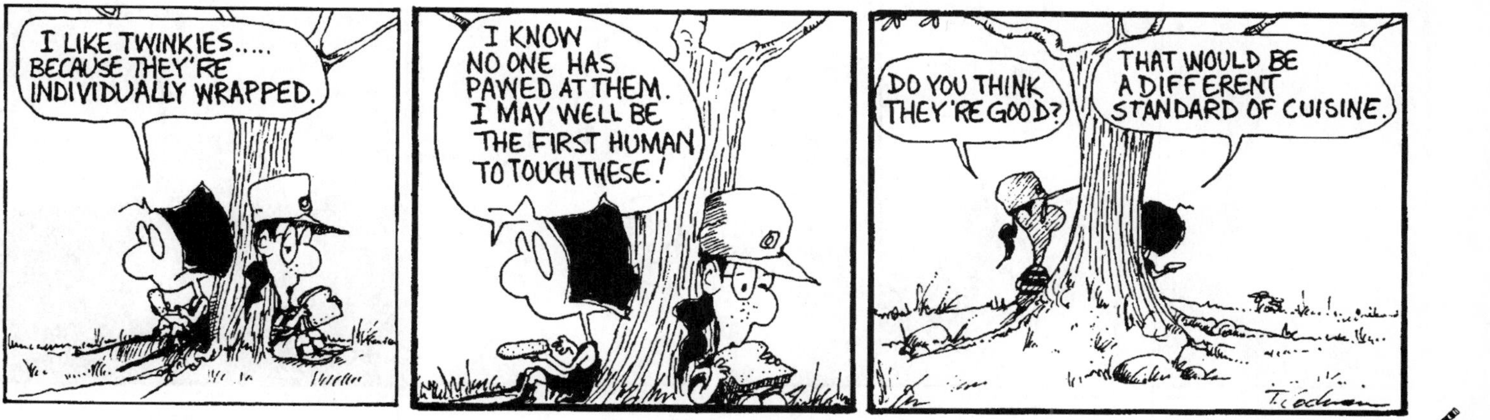
I LIKE TWINKIES..... BECAUSE THEY'RE INDIVIDUALLY WRAPPED.
I KNOW NO ONE HAS PAWED AT THEM. I MAY WELL BE THE FIRST HUMAN TO TOUCH THESE!
DO YOU THINK THEY'RE GOOD?
THAT WOULD BE A DIFFERENT STANDARD OF CUISINE.
T. Cochran

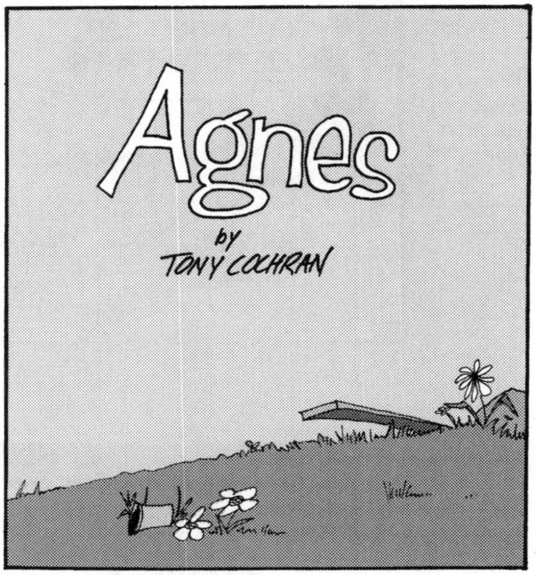
Agnes
by
TONY COCHRAN

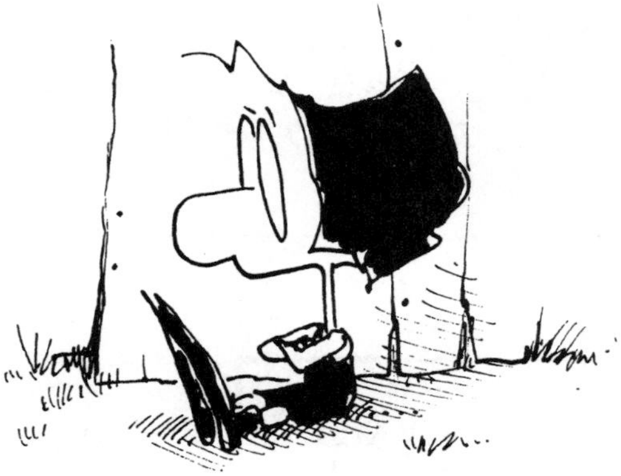

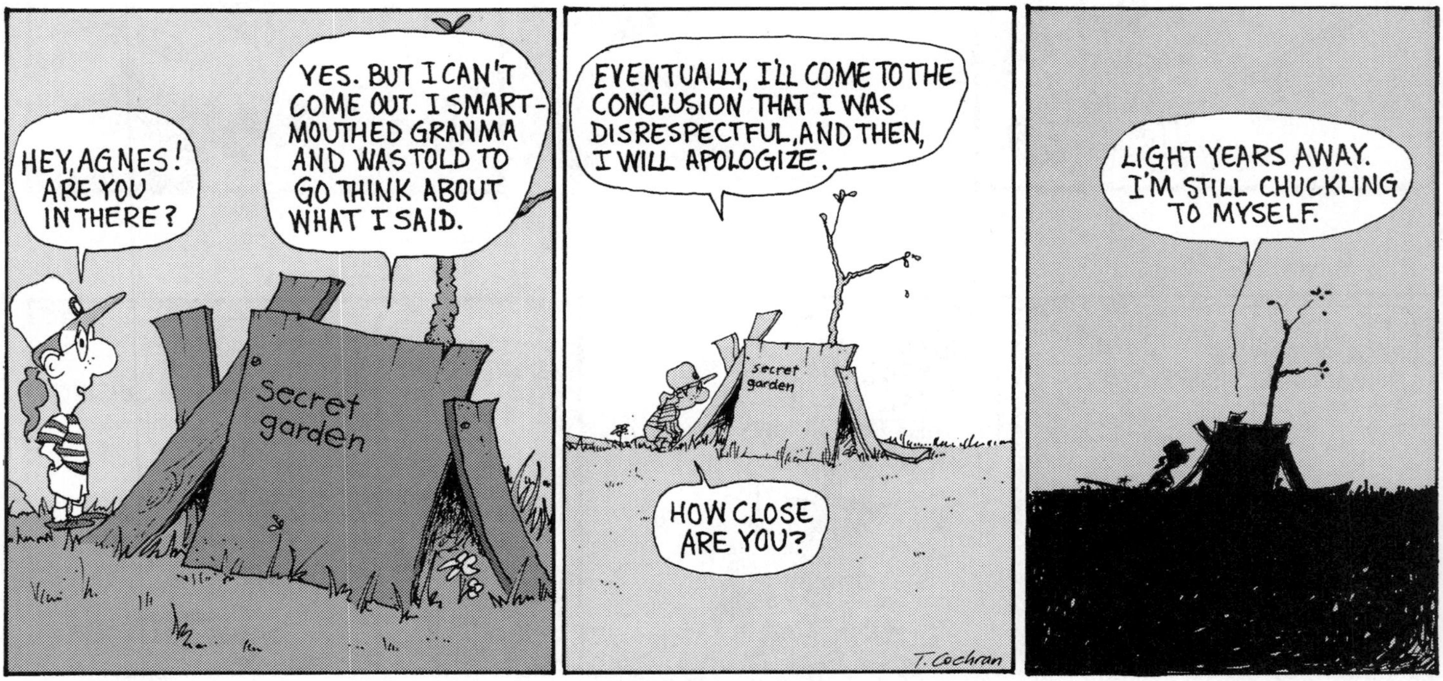
HEY, AGNES! ARE YOU IN THERE?
YES. BUT I CAN'T COME OUT. I SMART-MOUTHED GRANMA AND WAS TOLD TO GO THINK ABOUT WHAT I SAID.
secret garden
EVENTUALLY, I'LL COME TO THE CONCLUSION THAT I WAS DISRESPECTFUL, AND THEN, I WILL APOLOGIZE.
HOW CLOSE ARE YOU?
T. Cochran
LIGHT YEARS AWAY. I'M STILL CHUCKLING TO MYSELF.

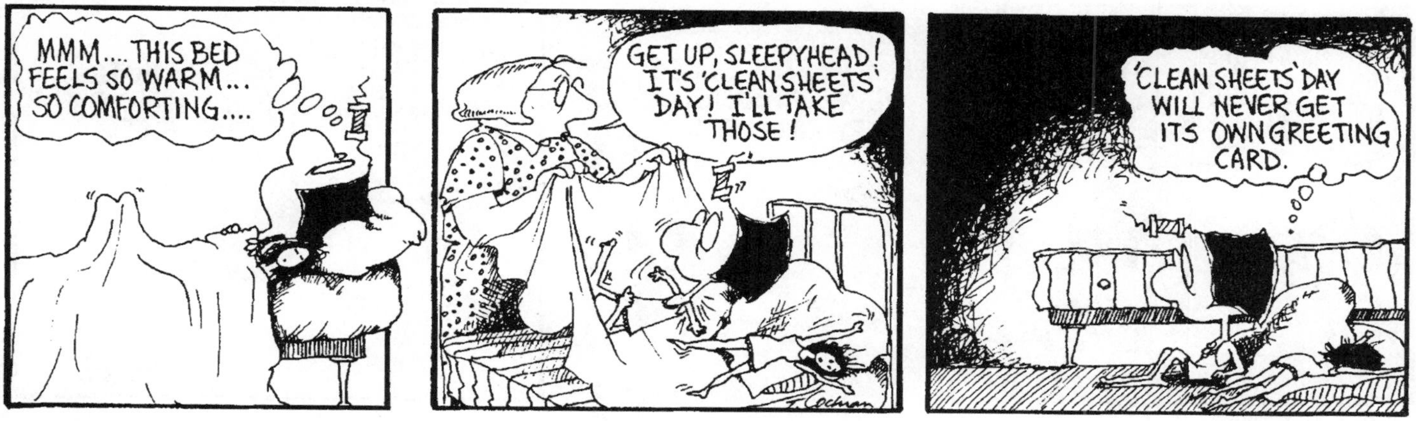
MMM.... THIS BED FEELS SO WARM... SO COMFORTING....
GET UP, SLEEPYHEAD! IT'S 'CLEAN SHEETS' DAY! I'LL TAKE THOSE!
'CLEAN SHEETS' DAY WILL NEVER GET ITS OWN GREETING CARD.
T. Cochran

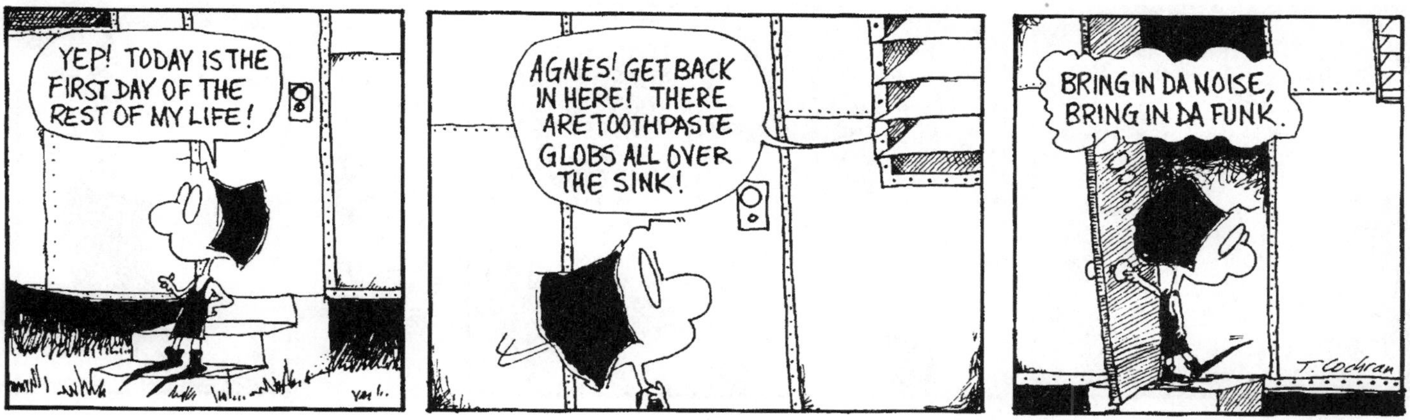
YEP! TODAY IS THE FIRST DAY OF THE REST OF MY LIFE!
AGNES! GET BACK IN HERE! THERE ARE TOOTHPASTE GLOBS ALL OVER THE SINK!
BRING IN DA NOISE, BRING IN DA FUNK.
T. Cochran

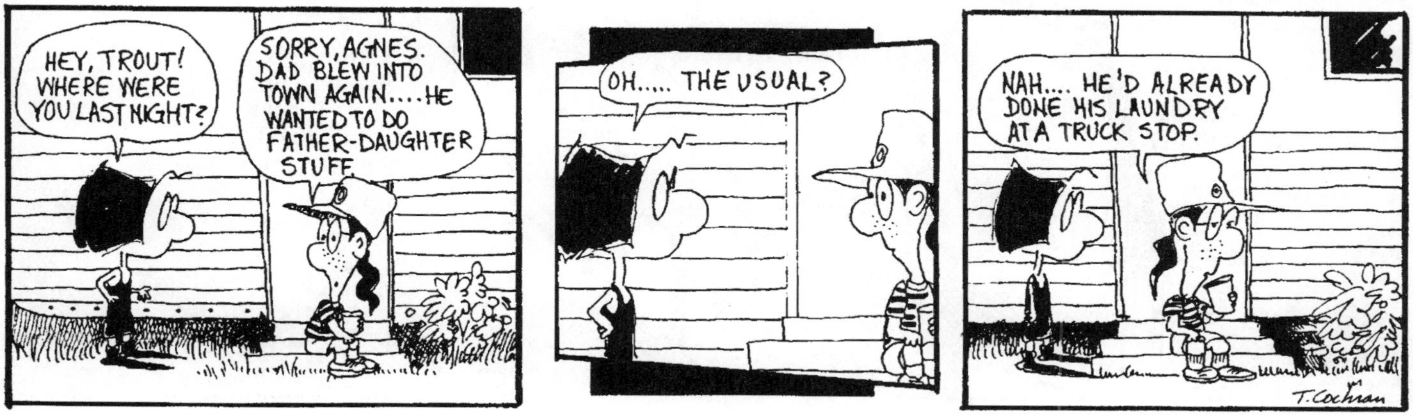
HEY, TROUT! WHERE WERE YOU LAST NIGHT?
SORRY, AGNES. DAD BLEW INTO TOWN AGAIN.... HE WANTED TO DO FATHER-DAUGHTER STUFF.
OH..... THE USUAL?
NAH.... HE'D ALREADY DONE HIS LAUNDRY AT A TRUCK STOP.
T. Cochran

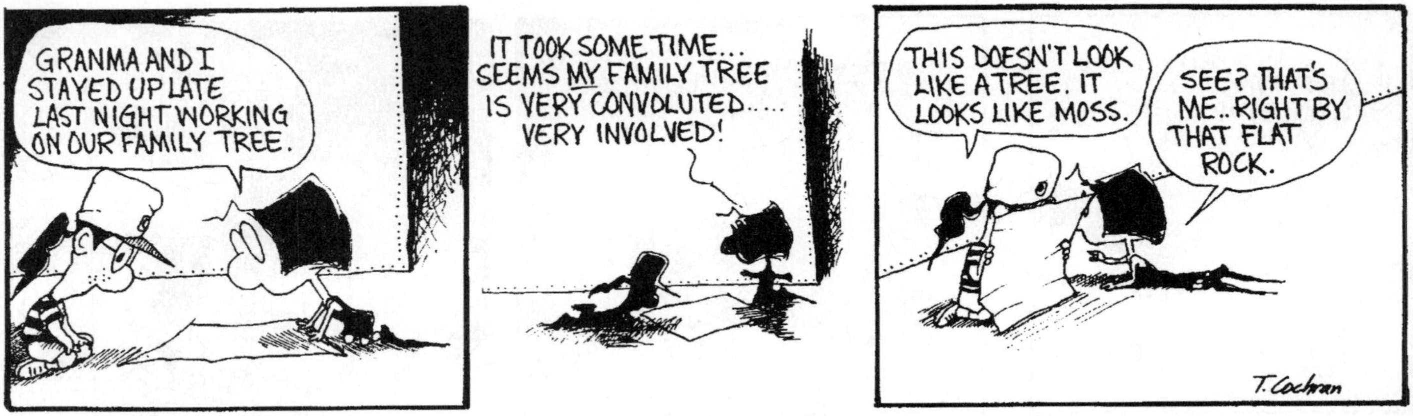
GRANMA AND I STAYED UP LATE LAST NIGHT WORKING ON OUR FAMILY TREE.
IT TOOK SOME TIME... SEEMS MY FAMILY TREE IS VERY CONVOLUTED.... VERY INVOLVED!
THIS DOESN'T LOOK LIKE A TREE. IT LOOKS LIKE MOSS.
SEE? THAT'S ME.. RIGHT BY THAT FLAT ROCK.
T. Cochran

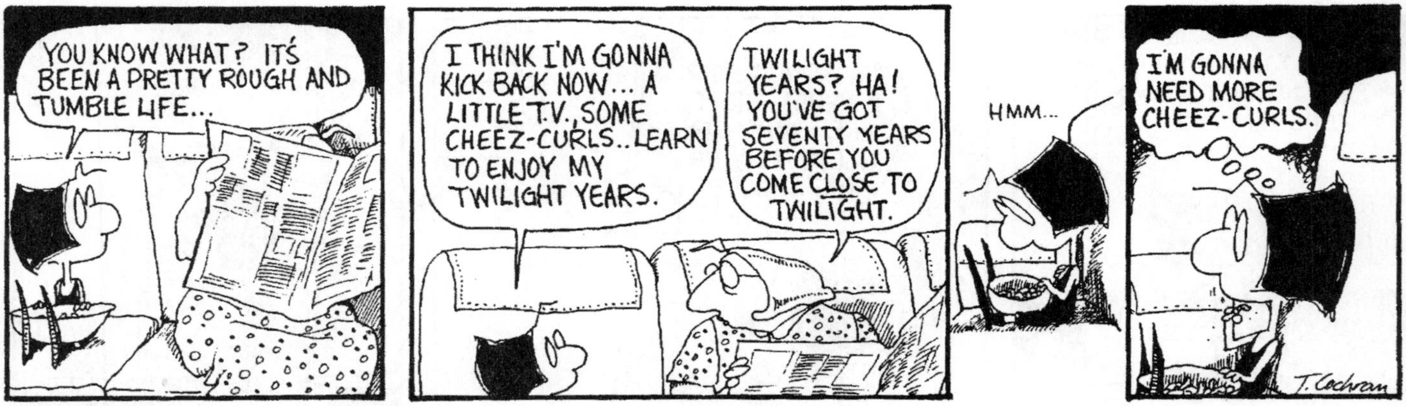
YOU KNOW WHAT? IT'S BEEN A PRETTY ROUGH AND TUMBLE LIFE...
I THINK I'M GONNA KICK BACK NOW... A LITTLE T.V., SOME CHEEZ-CURLS.. LEARN TO ENJOY MY TWILIGHT YEARS.
TWILIGHT YEARS? HA! YOU'VE GOT SEVENTY YEARS BEFORE YOU COME CLOSE TO TWILIGHT.
HMM...
I'M GONNA NEED MORE CHEEZ-CURLS.
T. Cochran

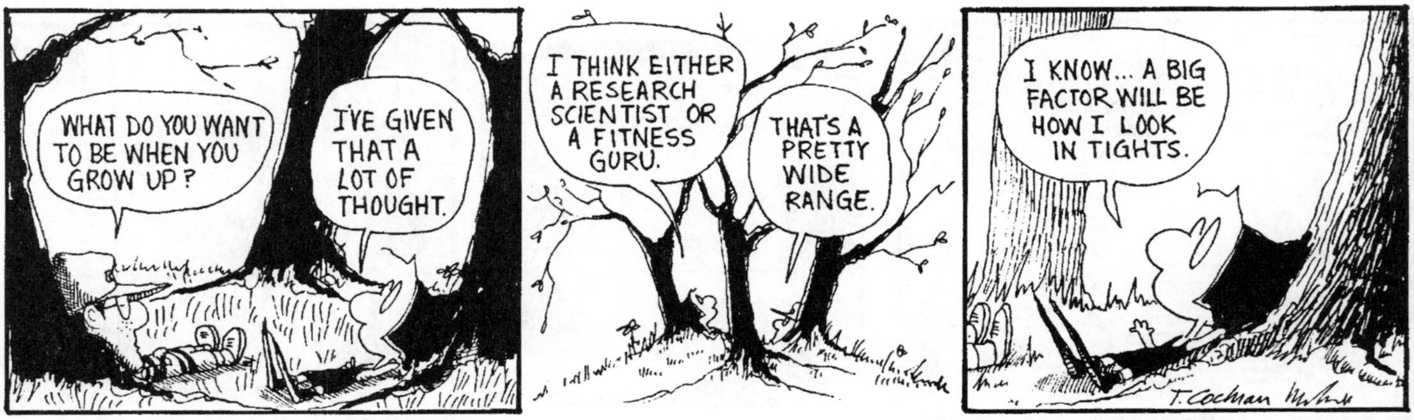
WHAT DO YOU WANT TO BE WHEN YOU GROW UP?
I'VE GIVEN THAT A LOT OF THOUGHT.
I THINK EITHER A RESEARCH SCIENTIST OR A FITNESS GURU.
THAT'S A PRETTY WIDE RANGE.
I KNOW... A BIG FACTOR WILL BE HOW I LOOK IN TIGHTS.
T. Cochran

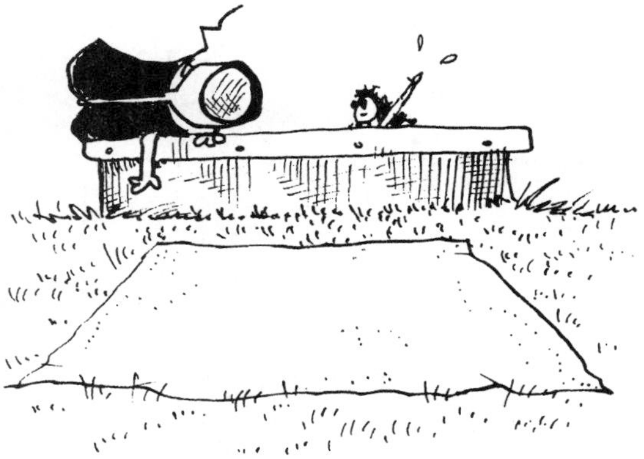

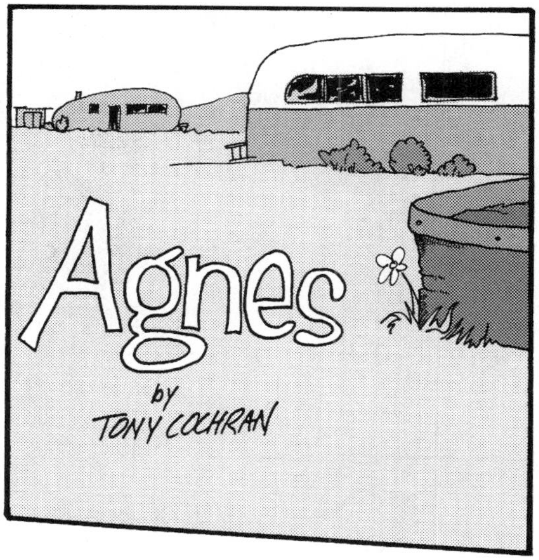
Agnes
by
TONY COCHRAN

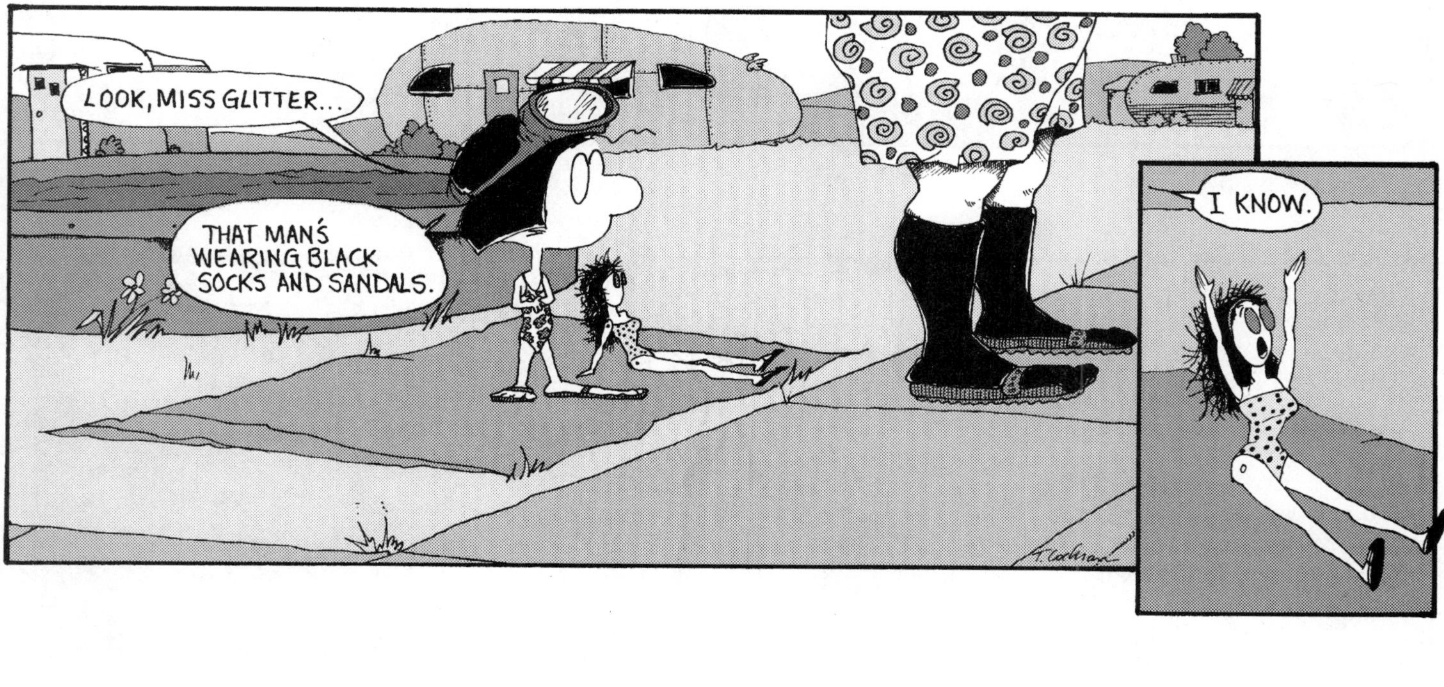
LOOK, MISS GLITTER...
THAT MAN'S WEARING BLACK SOCKS AND SANDALS.
I KNOW.

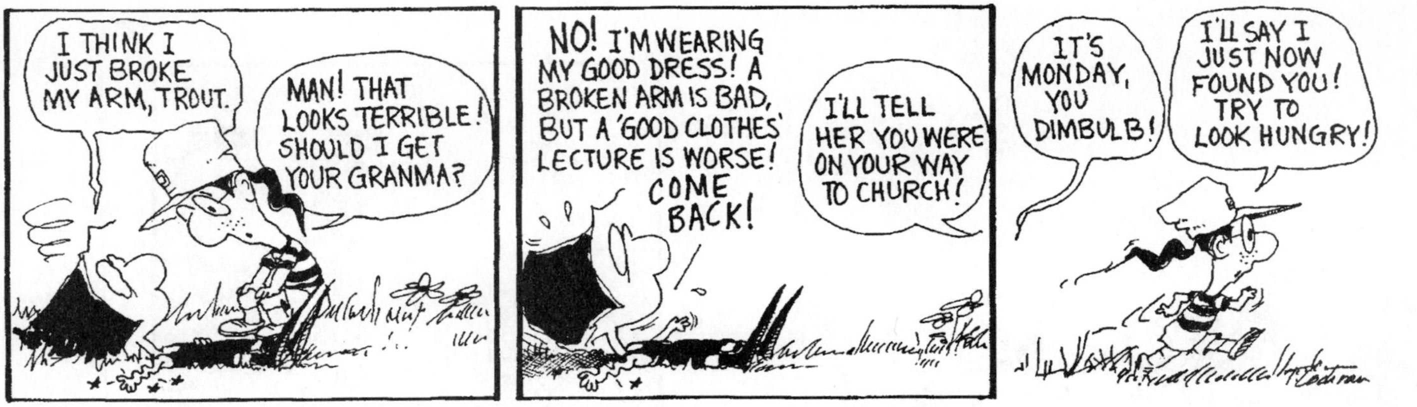
I THINK I JUST BROKE MY ARM, TROUT.
MAN! THAT LOOKS TERRIBLE! SHOULD I GET YOUR GRANMA?
NO! I'M WEARING MY GOOD DRESS! A BROKEN ARM IS BAD, BUT A 'GOOD CLOTHES' LECTURE IS WORSE!
COME BACK!
I'LL TELL HER YOU WERE ON YOUR WAY TO CHURCH!
IT'S MONDAY, YOU DIMBULB!
I'LL SAY I JUST NOW FOUND YOU! TRY TO LOOK HUNGRY!

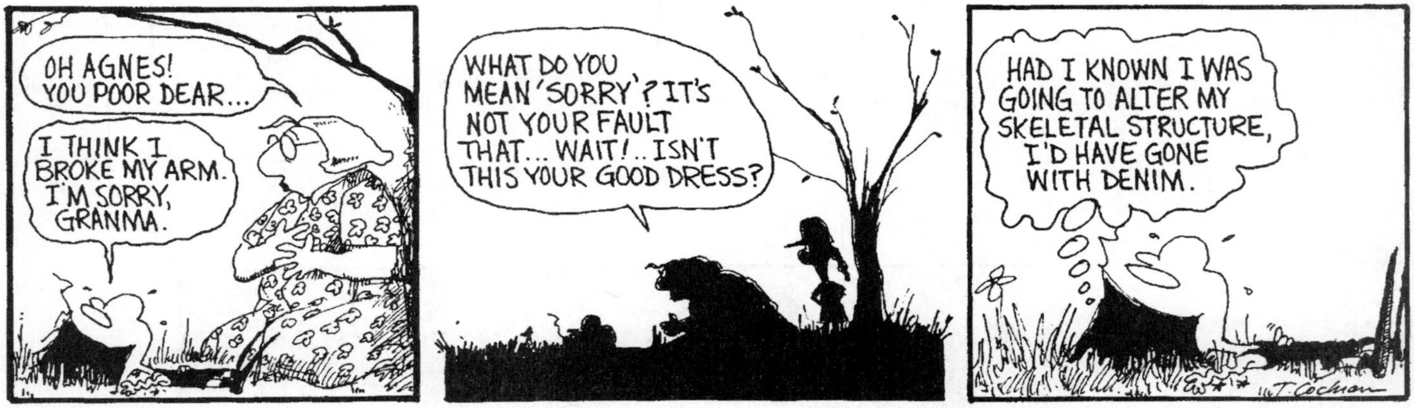
OH AGNES! YOU POOR DEAR...
I THINK I BROKE MY ARM. I'M SORRY, GRANMA.
WHAT DO YOU MEAN 'SORRY'? IT'S NOT YOUR FAULT THAT... WAIT!.. ISN'T THIS YOUR GOOD DRESS?
HAD I KNOWN I WAS GOING TO ALTER MY SKELETAL STRUCTURE, I'D HAVE GONE WITH DENIM.

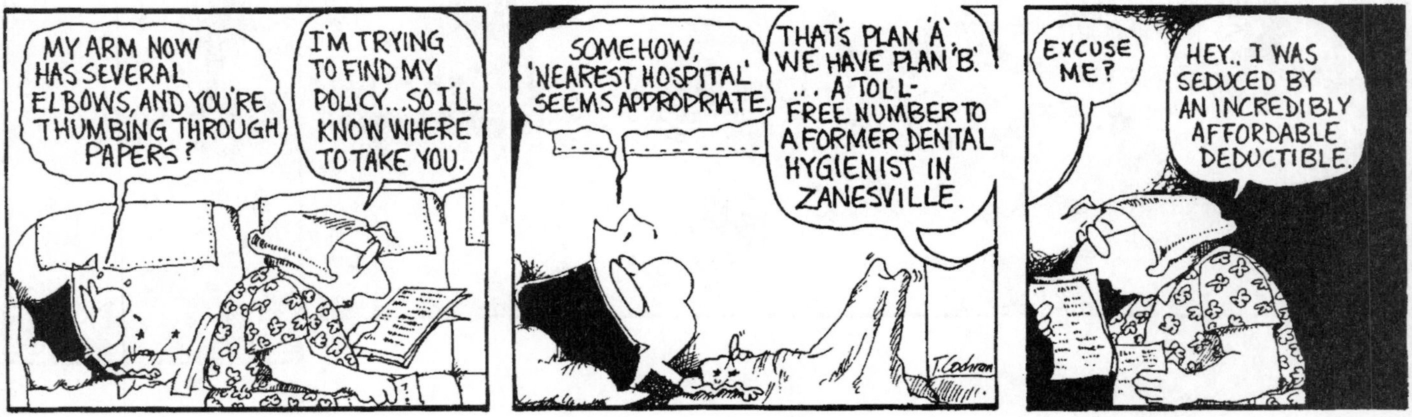
MY ARM NOW HAS SEVERAL ELBOWS, AND YOU'RE THUMBING THROUGH PAPERS?
I'M TRYING TO FIND MY POLICY... SO I'LL KNOW WHERE TO TAKE YOU.
SOMEHOW, 'NEAREST HOSPITAL' SEEMS APPROPRIATE.
THAT'S PLAN 'A'. WE HAVE PLAN 'B'. ... A TOLL-FREE NUMBER TO A FORMER DENTAL HYGIENIST IN ZANESVILLE.
EXCUSE ME?
HEY.. I WAS SEDUCED BY AN INCREDIBLY AFFORDABLE DEDUCTIBLE.

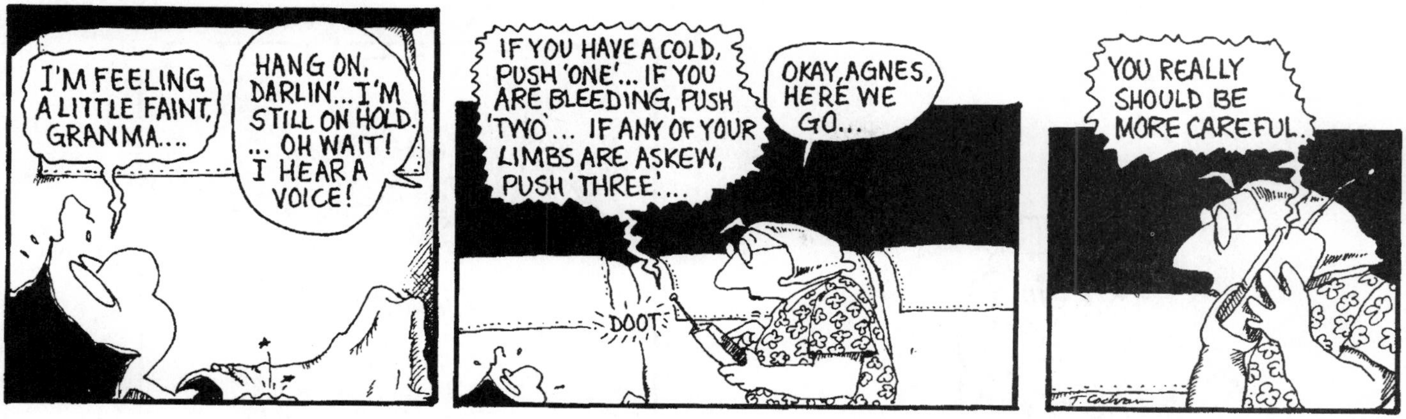
I'M FEELING A LITTLE FAINT, GRANMA....
HANG ON, DARLIN'... I'M STILL ON HOLD. ... OH WAIT! I HEAR A VOICE!
IF YOU HAVE A COLD, PUSH 'ONE'... IF YOU ARE BLEEDING, PUSH 'TWO'... IF ANY OF YOUR LIMBS ARE ASKEW, PUSH 'THREE'...
OKAY, AGNES, HERE WE GO...
DOOT
YOU REALLY SHOULD BE MORE CAREFUL.

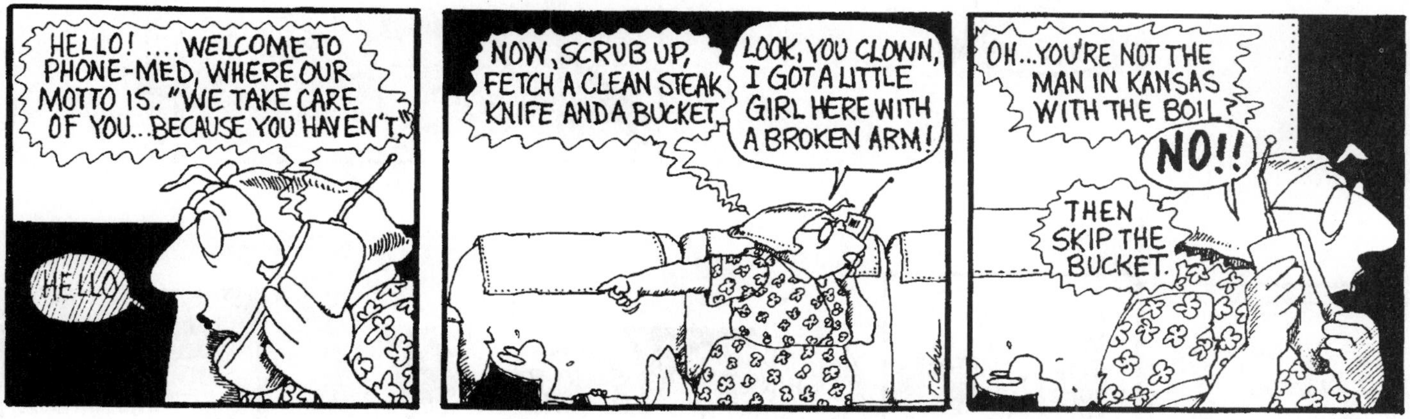
HELLO! .... WELCOME TO PHONE-MED, WHERE OUR MOTTO IS, "WE TAKE CARE OF YOU.. BECAUSE YOU HAVEN'T."
HELLO
NOW, SCRUB UP, FETCH A CLEAN STEAK KNIFE AND A BUCKET.
LOOK, YOU CLOWN, I GOT A LITTLE GIRL HERE WITH A BROKEN ARM!
OH... YOU'RE NOT THE MAN IN KANSAS WITH THE BOIL?
NO!!
THEN SKIP THE BUCKET.

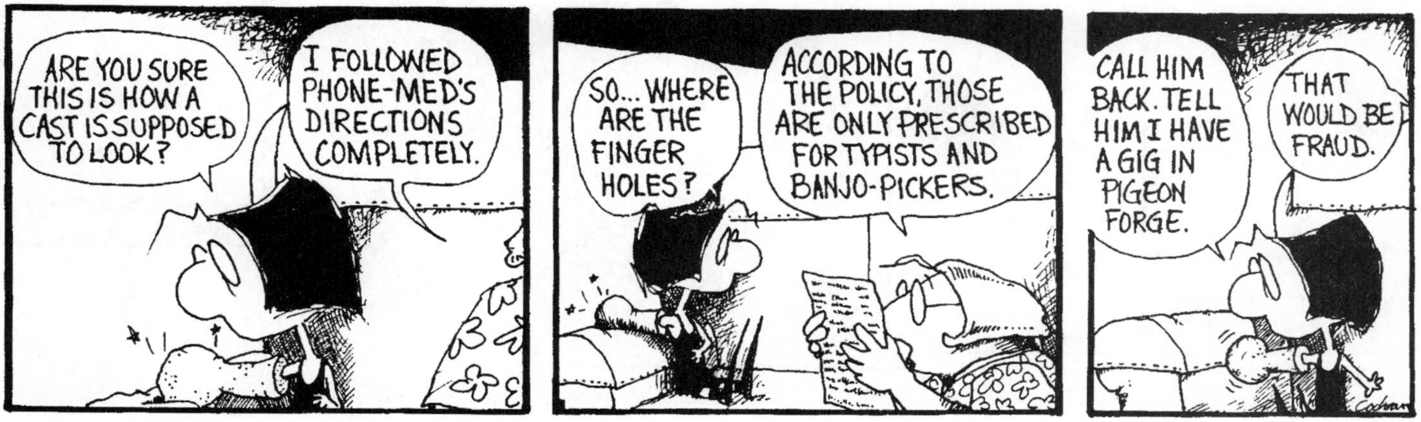
ARE YOU SURE THIS IS HOW A CAST IS SUPPOSED TO LOOK?
I FOLLOWED PHONE-MED'S DIRECTIONS COMPLETELY.
SO... WHERE ARE THE FINGER HOLES?
ACCORDING TO THE POLICY, THOSE ARE ONLY PRESCRIBED FOR TYPISTS AND BANJO-PICKERS.
CALL HIM BACK. TELL HIM I HAVE A GIG IN PIGEON FORGE.
THAT WOULD BE FRAUD.

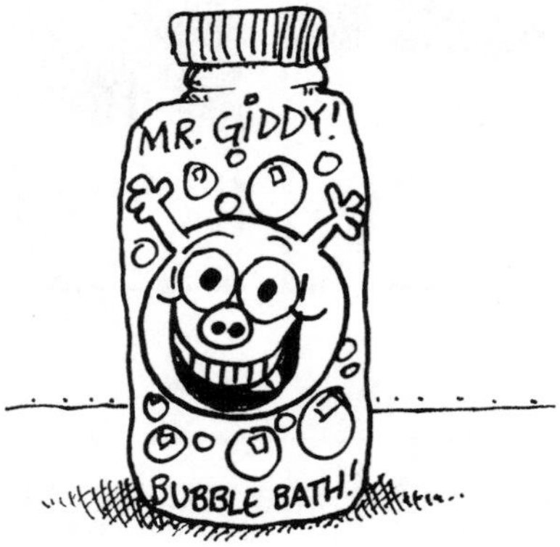
MR. GIDDY!
BUBBLE BATH!

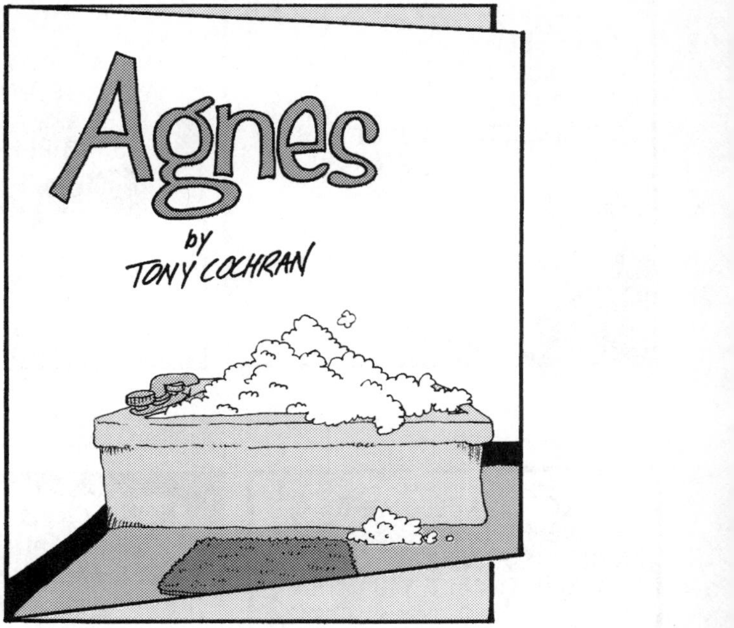
Agnes
by
TONY COCHRAN

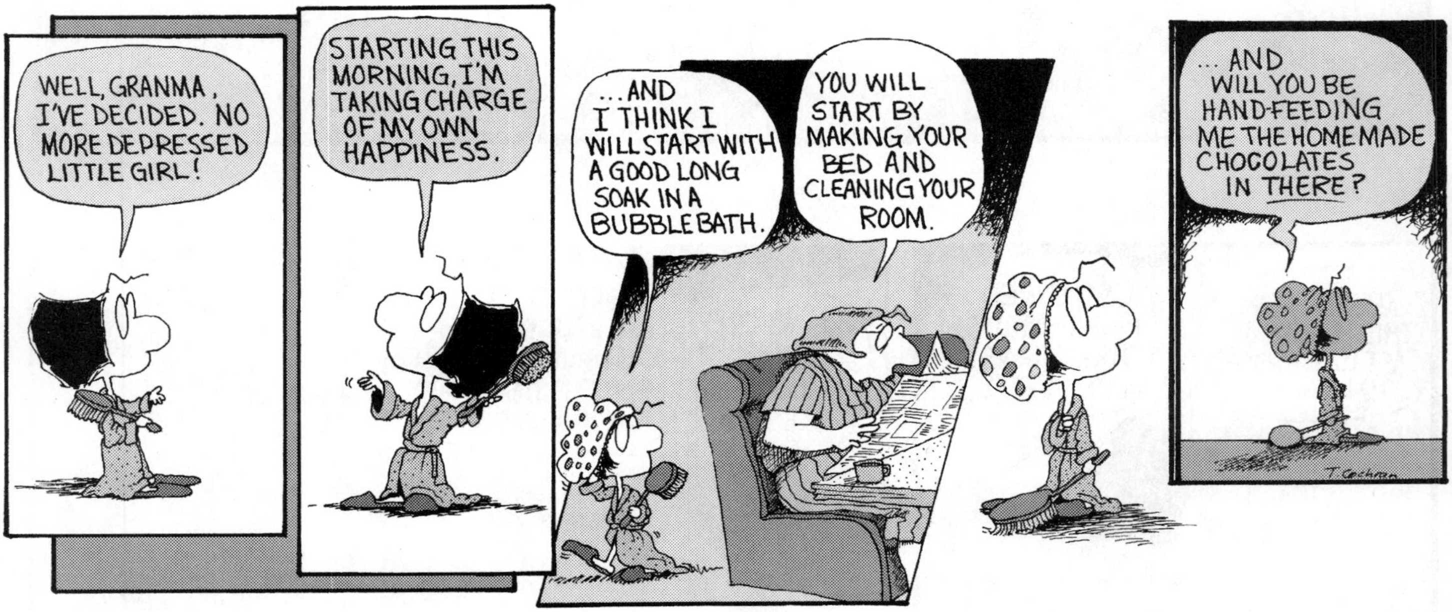
WELL, GRANMA, I'VE DECIDED. NO MORE DEPRESSED LITTLE GIRL!
STARTING THIS MORNING, I'M TAKING CHARGE OF MY OWN HAPPINESS.
...AND I THINK I WILL START WITH A GOOD LONG SOAK IN A BUBBLE BATH.
YOU WILL START BY MAKING YOUR BED AND CLEANING YOUR ROOM.
...AND WILL YOU BE HAND-FEEDING ME THE HOMEMADE CHOCOLATES IN THERE?
T. Cochran

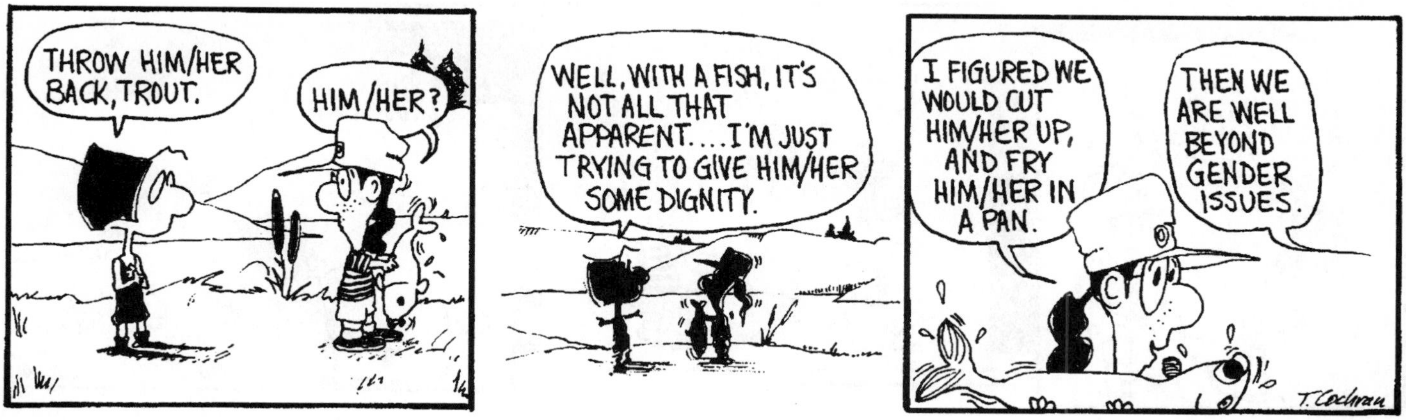
THROW HIM/HER BACK, TROUT.
HIM/HER?
WELL, WITH A FISH, IT'S NOT ALL THAT APPARENT.... I'M JUST TRYING TO GIVE HIM/HER SOME DIGNITY.
I FIGURED WE WOULD CUT HIM/HER UP, AND FRY HIM/HER IN A PAN.
THEN WE ARE WELL BEYOND GENDER ISSUES.
T. Cochran

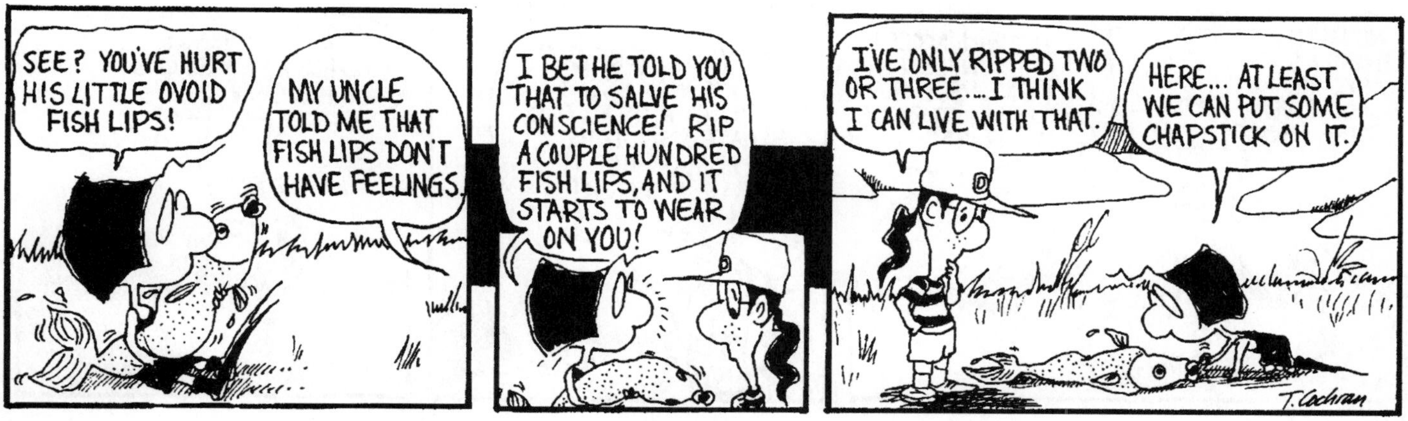
SEE? YOU'VE HURT HIS LITTLE OVOID FISH LIPS!
MY UNCLE TOLD ME THAT FISH LIPS DON'T HAVE FEELINGS.
I BET HE TOLD YOU THAT TO SALVE HIS CONSCIENCE! RIP A COUPLE HUNDRED FISH LIPS, AND IT STARTS TO WEAR ON YOU!
I'VE ONLY RIPPED TWO OR THREE... I THINK I CAN LIVE WITH THAT.
HERE... AT LEAST WE CAN PUT SOME CHAPSTICK ON IT.
T. Cochran

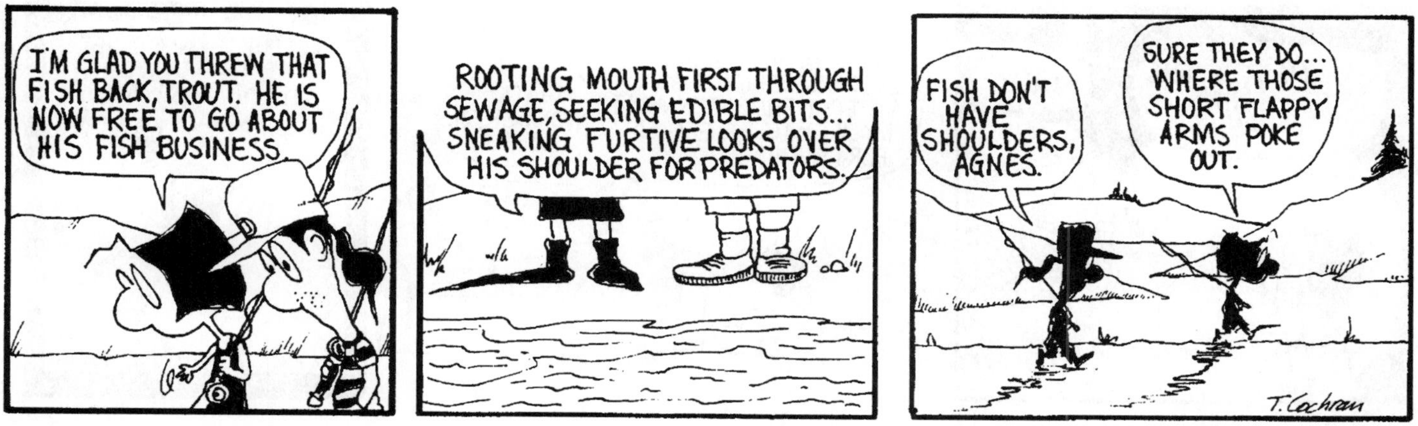
I'M GLAD YOU THREW THAT FISH BACK, TROUT. HE IS NOW FREE TO GO ABOUT HIS FISH BUSINESS.
ROOTING MOUTH FIRST THROUGH SEWAGE, SEEKING EDIBLE BITS... SNEAKING FURTIVE LOOKS OVER HIS SHOULDER FOR PREDATORS.
FISH DON'T HAVE SHOULDERS, AGNES.
SURE THEY DO... WHERE THOSE SHORT FLAPPY ARMS POKE OUT.
T. Cochran

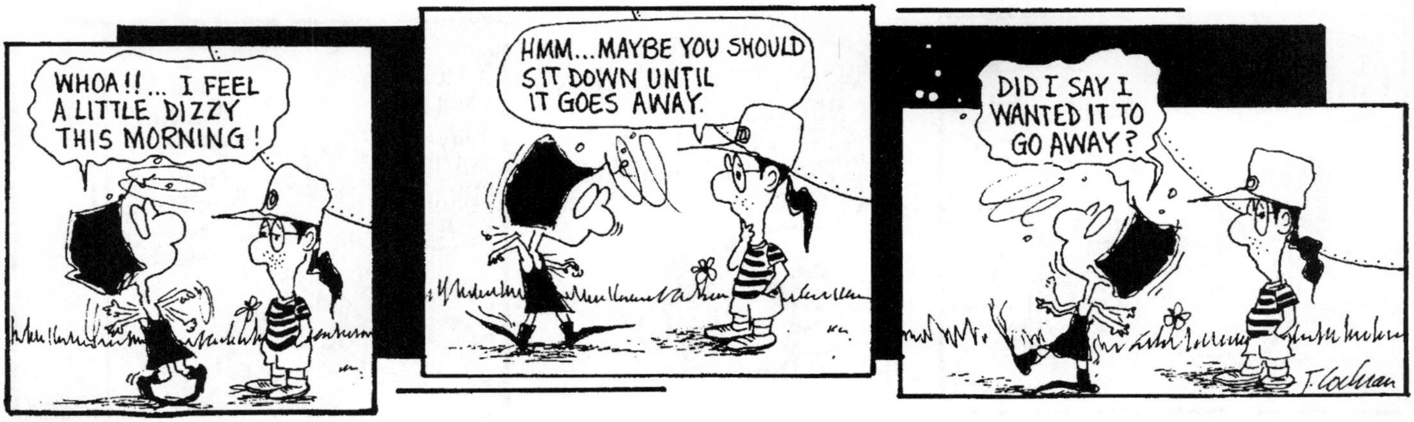
WHOA!!... I FEEL A LITTLE DIZZY THIS MORNING!
HMM... MAYBE YOU SHOULD SIT DOWN UNTIL IT GOES AWAY.
DID I SAY I WANTED IT TO GO AWAY?
T. Cochran

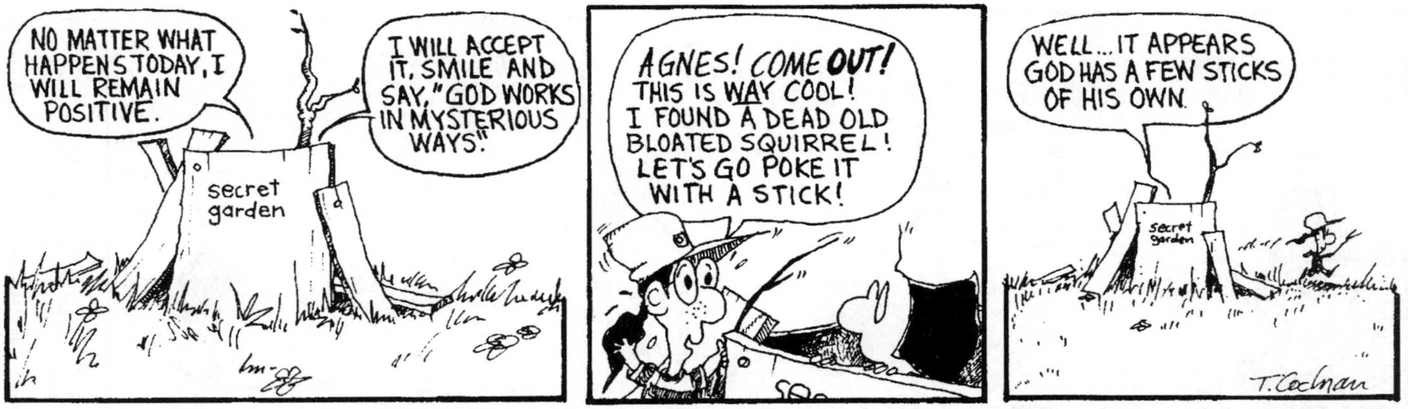
NO MATTER WHAT HAPPENS TODAY, I WILL REMAIN POSITIVE.
I WILL ACCEPT IT, SMILE AND SAY, "GOD WORKS IN MYSTERIOUS WAYS."
secret garden
AGNES! COME OUT! THIS IS WAY COOL! I FOUND A DEAD OLD BLOATED SQUIRREL! LET'S GO POKE IT WITH A STICK!
WELL... IT APPEARS GOD HAS A FEW STICKS OF HIS OWN.
secret garden
T. Cochran

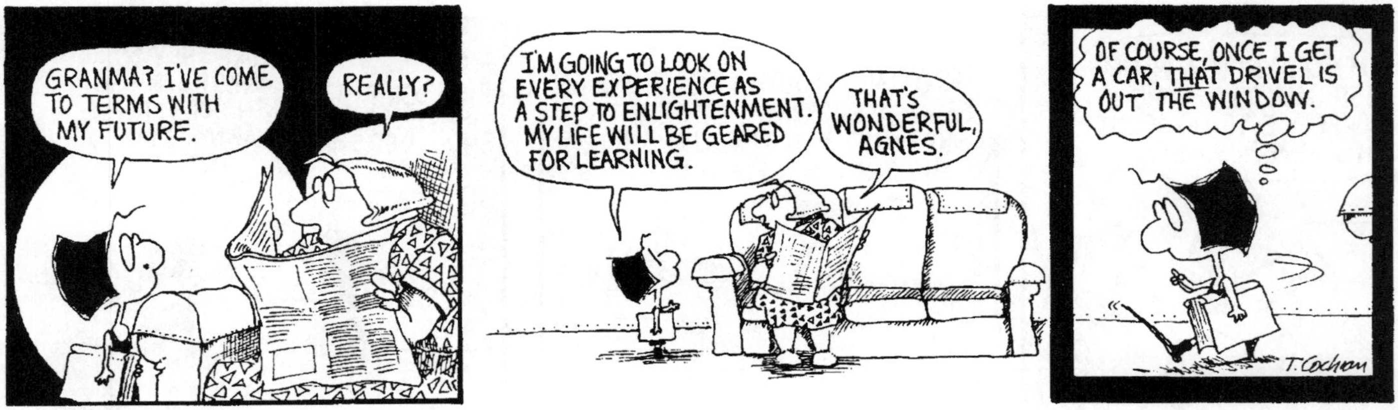
GRANMA? I'VE COME TO TERMS WITH MY FUTURE.
REALLY?
I'M GOING TO LOOK ON EVERY EXPERIENCE AS A STEP TO ENLIGHTENMENT. MY LIFE WILL BE GEARED FOR LEARNING.
THAT'S WONDERFUL, AGNES.
OF COURSE, ONCE I GET A CAR, THAT DRIVEL IS OUT THE WINDOW.
T. Cochran

Agnes

by TONY COCHRAN

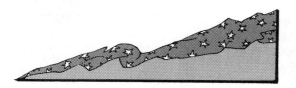

BEHOLD! I AM 'QUEEN LIBERTY', AND I HAVE COME TO BID MY LOWLY SUBJECTS A HALE AND HEARTY FOURTH. GIFTS AND FINE CANDIES CAN BE LEFT ON THE PORCH.

THE FOURTH OF JULY REPRESENTS THE INDEPENDENCE FROM A MONARCHY. THERE IS NO 'QUEEN LIBERTY.'

THAT'S <u>IT</u>? A HOT DOG AND A SPARKLER?

IT'S NOT A RELIGIOUS HOLIDAY.

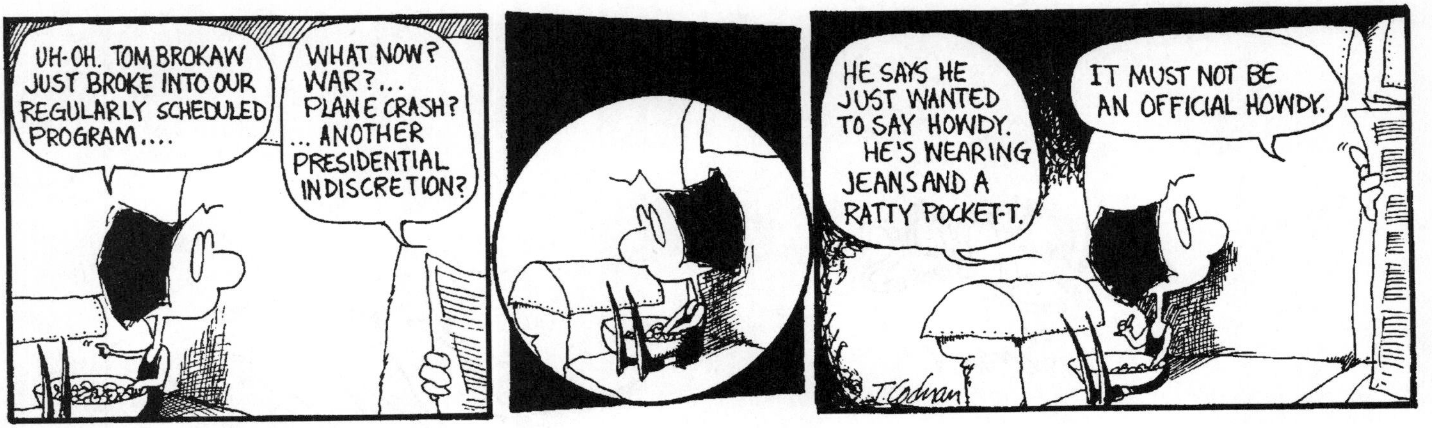
UH-OH. TOM BROKAW JUST BROKE INTO OUR REGULARLY SCHEDULED PROGRAM....
WHAT NOW? WAR?... PLANE CRASH? ...ANOTHER PRESIDENTIAL INDISCRETION?
HE SAYS HE JUST WANTED TO SAY HOWDY. HE'S WEARING JEANS AND A RATTY POCKET-T.
IT MUST NOT BE AN OFFICIAL HOWDY.

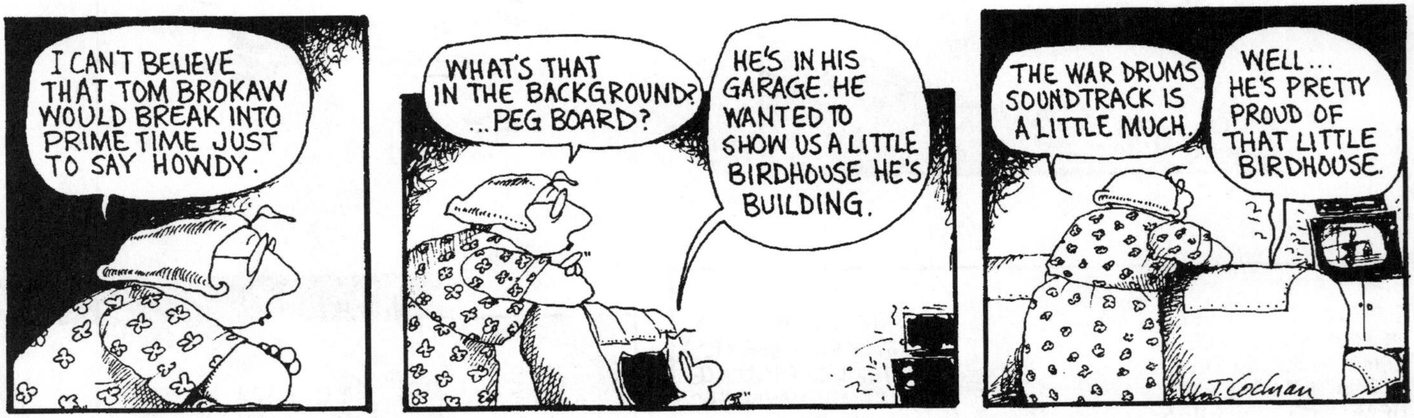
I CAN'T BELIEVE THAT TOM BROKAW WOULD BREAK INTO PRIME TIME JUST TO SAY HOWDY.
WHAT'S THAT IN THE BACKGROUND? ...PEG BOARD?
HE'S IN HIS GARAGE. HE WANTED TO SHOW US A LITTLE BIRDHOUSE HE'S BUILDING.
THE WAR DRUMS SOUNDTRACK IS A LITTLE MUCH.
WELL... HE'S PRETTY PROUD OF THAT LITTLE BIRDHOUSE.

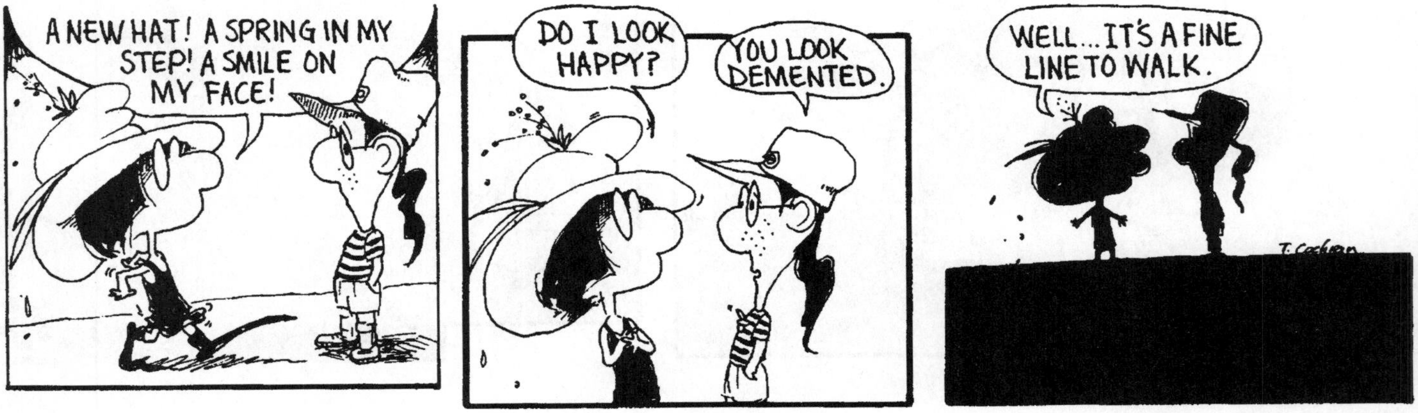
A NEW HAT! A SPRING IN MY STEP! A SMILE ON MY FACE!
DO I LOOK HAPPY?
YOU LOOK DEMENTED.
WELL...IT'S A FINE LINE TO WALK.

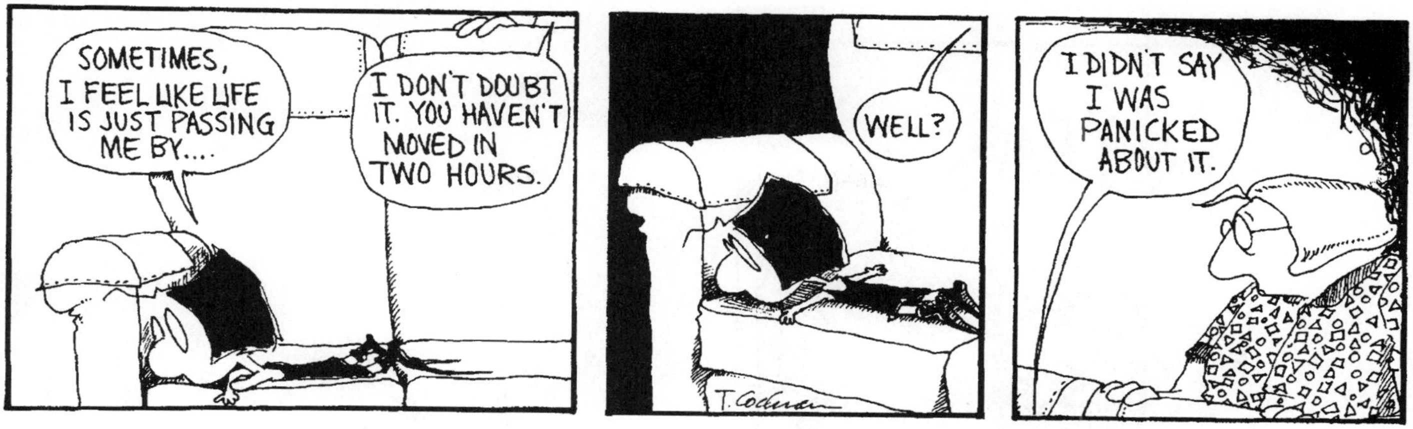
SOMETIMES, I FEEL LIKE LIFE IS JUST PASSING ME BY....
I DON'T DOUBT IT. YOU HAVEN'T MOVED IN TWO HOURS.
WELL?
I DIDN'T SAY I WAS PANICKED ABOUT IT.
T. Cochran

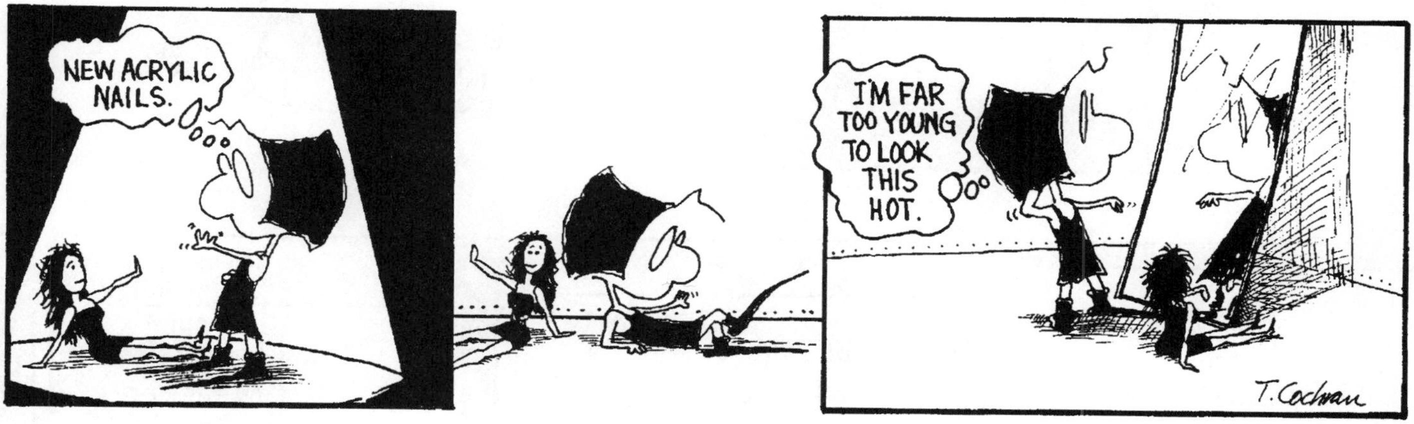
NEW ACRYLIC NAILS.
I'M FAR TOO YOUNG TO LOOK THIS HOT.
T. Cochran

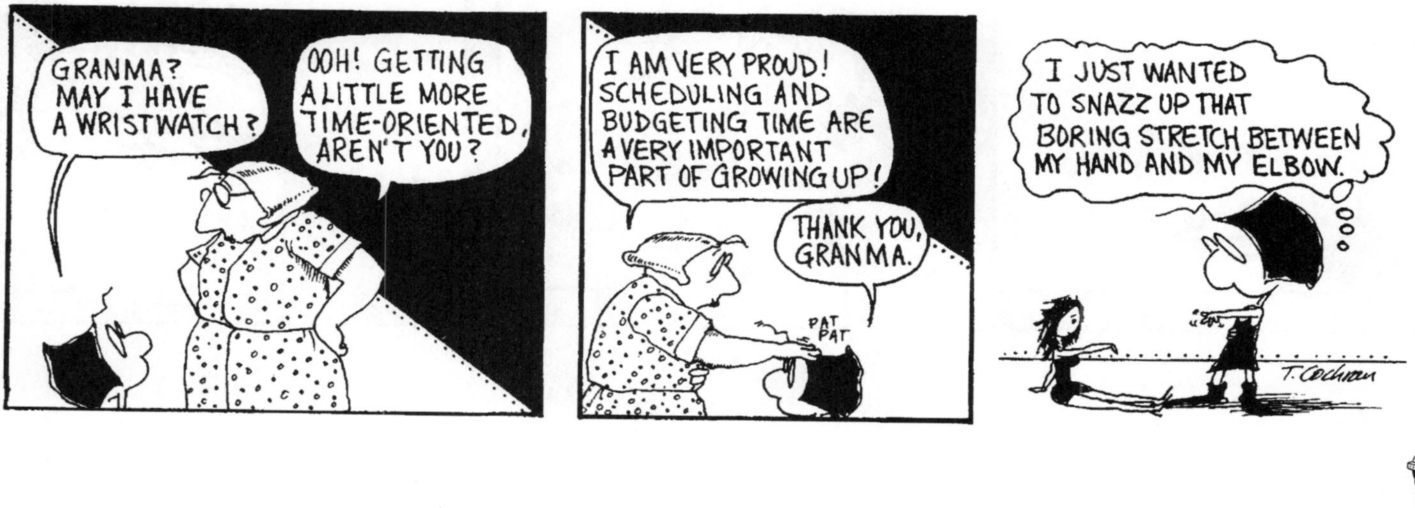
GRANMA? MAY I HAVE A WRISTWATCH?
OOH! GETTING A LITTLE MORE TIME-ORIENTED, AREN'T YOU?
I AM VERY PROUD! SCHEDULING AND BUDGETING TIME ARE A VERY IMPORTANT PART OF GROWING UP!
PAT PAT
THANK YOU, GRANMA.
I JUST WANTED TO SNAZZ UP THAT BORING STRETCH BETWEEN MY HAND AND MY ELBOW.
T. Cochran

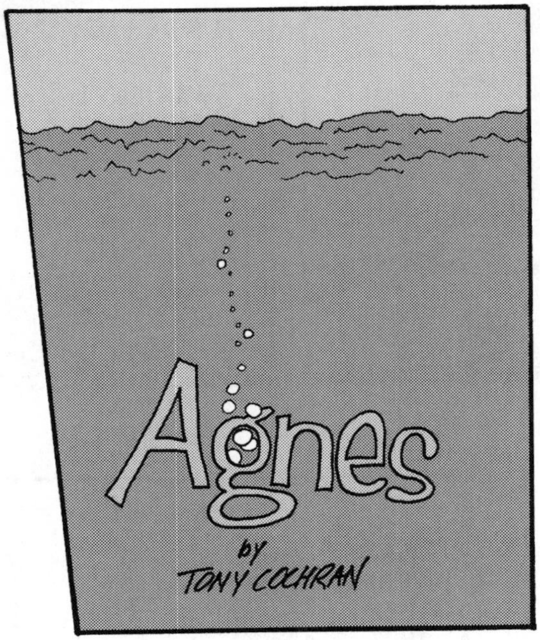
Agnes
by
TONY COCHRAN

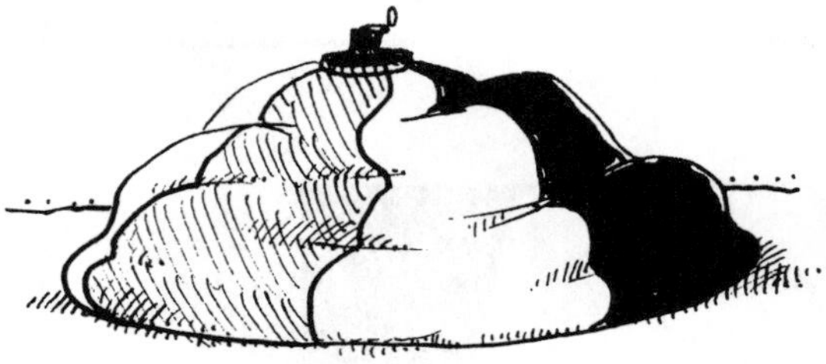

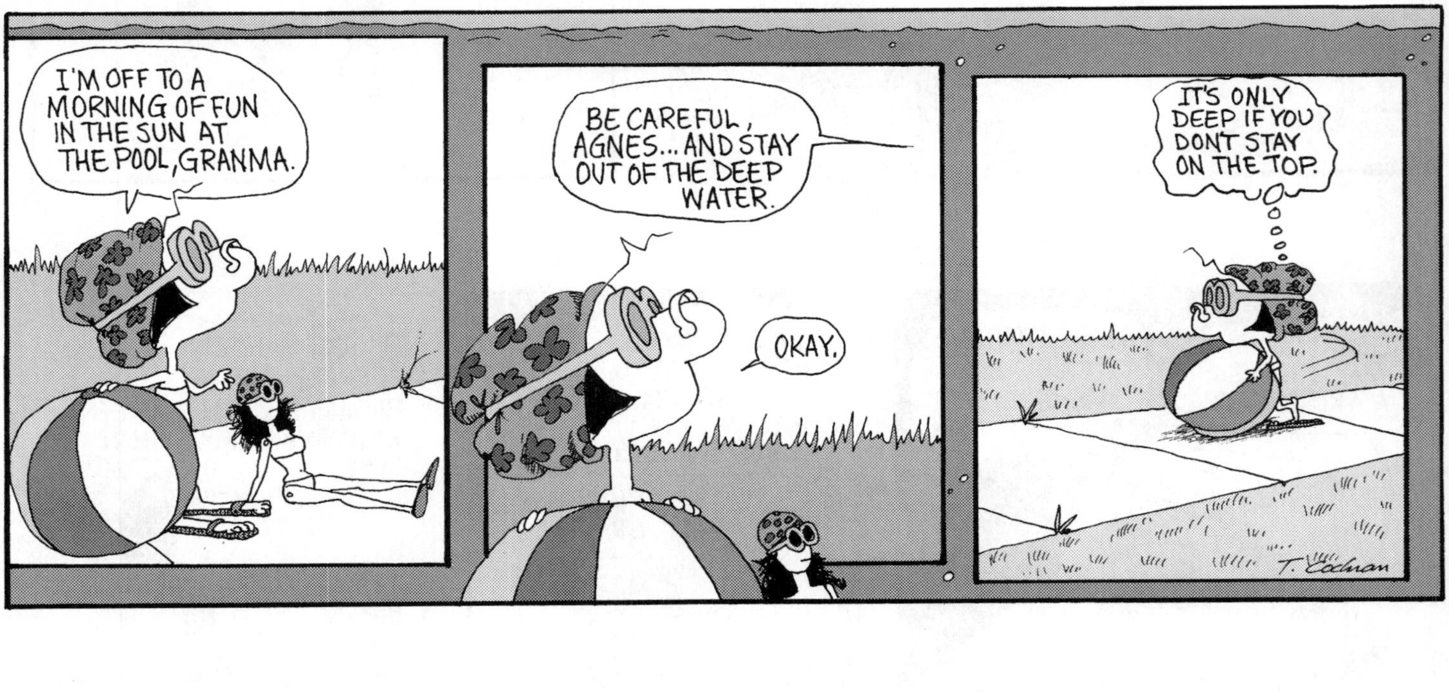
I'M OFF TO A MORNING OF FUN IN THE SUN AT THE POOL, GRANMA.
BE CAREFUL, AGNES... AND STAY OUT OF THE DEEP WATER.
OKAY.
IT'S ONLY DEEP IF YOU DON'T STAY ON THE TOP.
T. Cochran

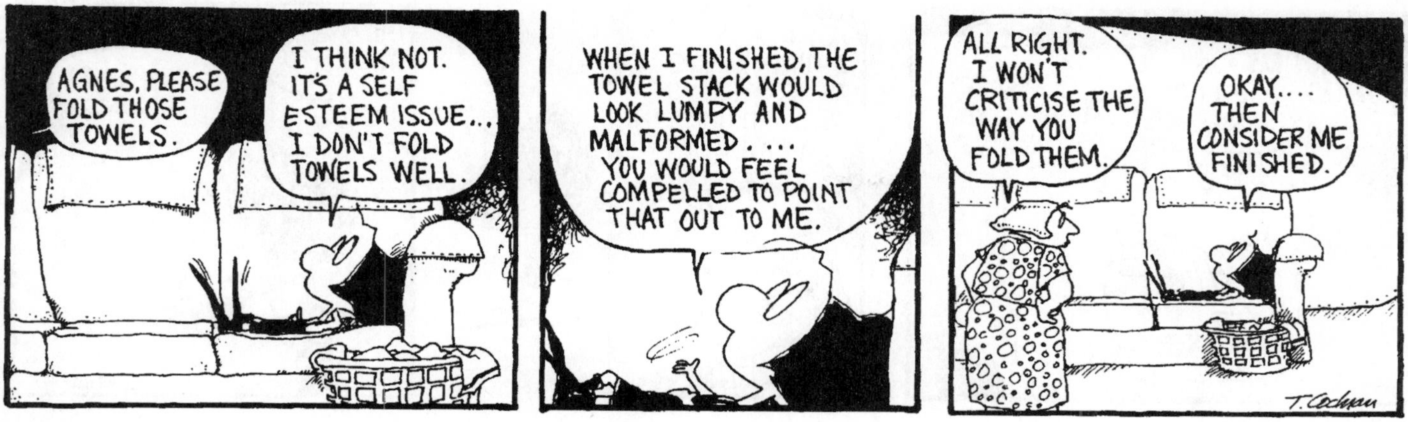
AGNES, PLEASE FOLD THOSE TOWELS.
I THINK NOT. IT'S A SELF ESTEEM ISSUE... I DON'T FOLD TOWELS WELL.
WHEN I FINISHED, THE TOWEL STACK WOULD LOOK LUMPY AND MALFORMED. ... YOU WOULD FEEL COMPELLED TO POINT THAT OUT TO ME.
ALL RIGHT. I WON'T CRITICISE THE WAY YOU FOLD THEM.
OKAY.... THEN CONSIDER ME FINISHED.
T. Cochran

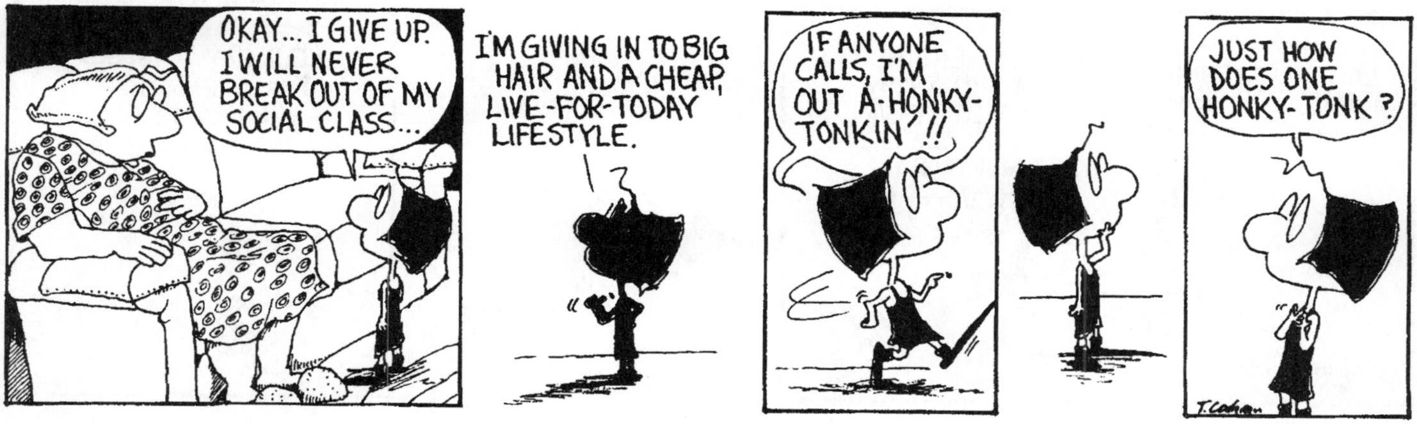
OKAY... I GIVE UP. I WILL NEVER BREAK OUT OF MY SOCIAL CLASS...
I'M GIVING IN TO BIG HAIR AND A CHEAP, LIVE-FOR-TODAY LIFESTYLE.
IF ANYONE CALLS, I'M OUT A-HONKY-TONKIN'!!
JUST HOW DOES ONE HONKY-TONK?
T. Cochran

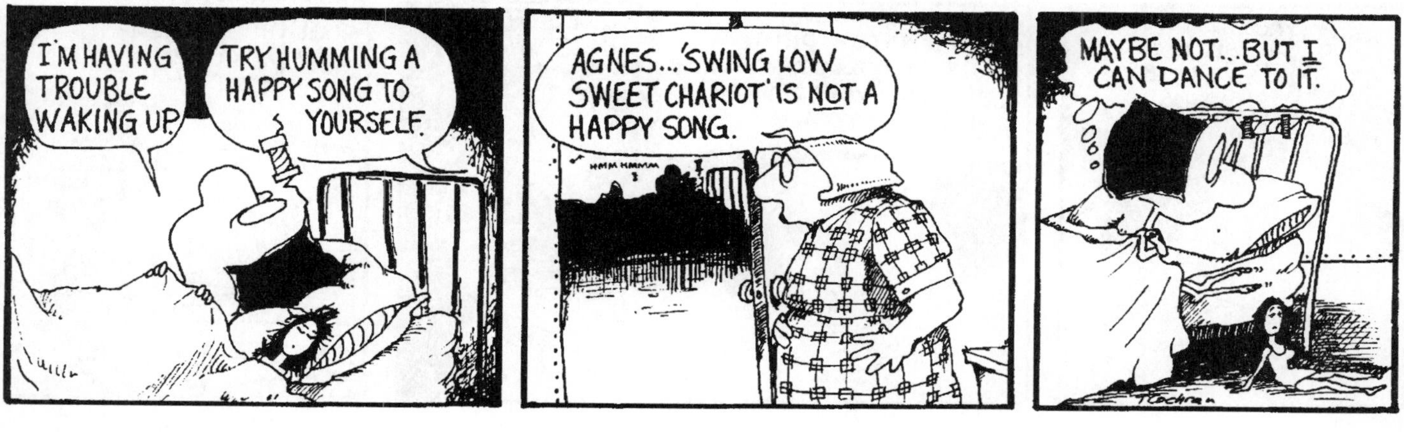
I'M HAVING TROUBLE WAKING UP.
TRY HUMMING A HAPPY SONG TO YOURSELF.
AGNES...'SWING LOW SWEET CHARIOT' IS NOT A HAPPY SONG.
HMM HMMM
MAYBE NOT...BUT I CAN DANCE TO IT.
T. Cochran

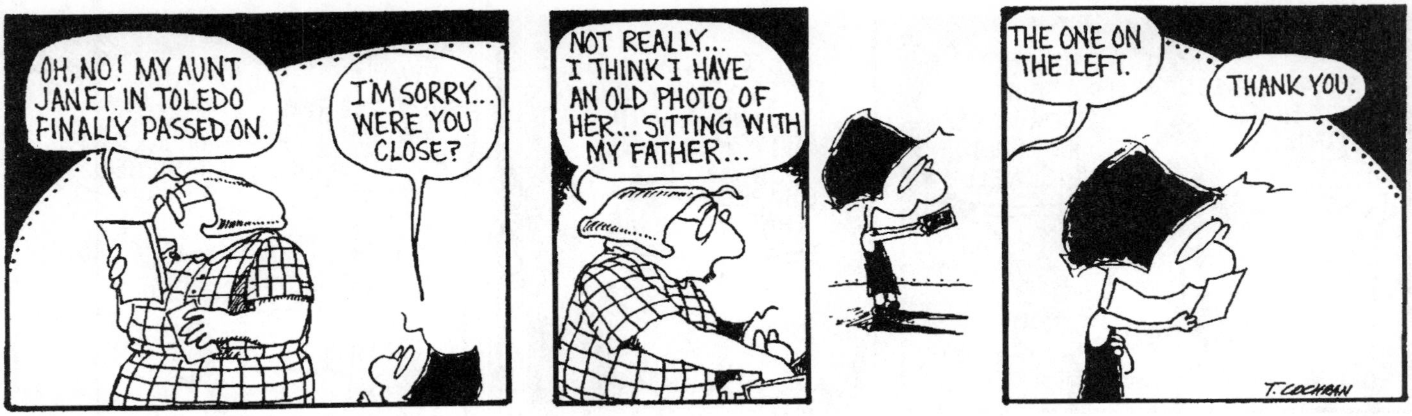
OH, NO! MY AUNT JANET IN TOLEDO FINALLY PASSED ON.
I'M SORRY... WERE YOU CLOSE?
NOT REALLY... I THINK I HAVE AN OLD PHOTO OF HER... SITTING WITH MY FATHER...
THE ONE ON THE LEFT.
THANK YOU.
T. COCHRAN

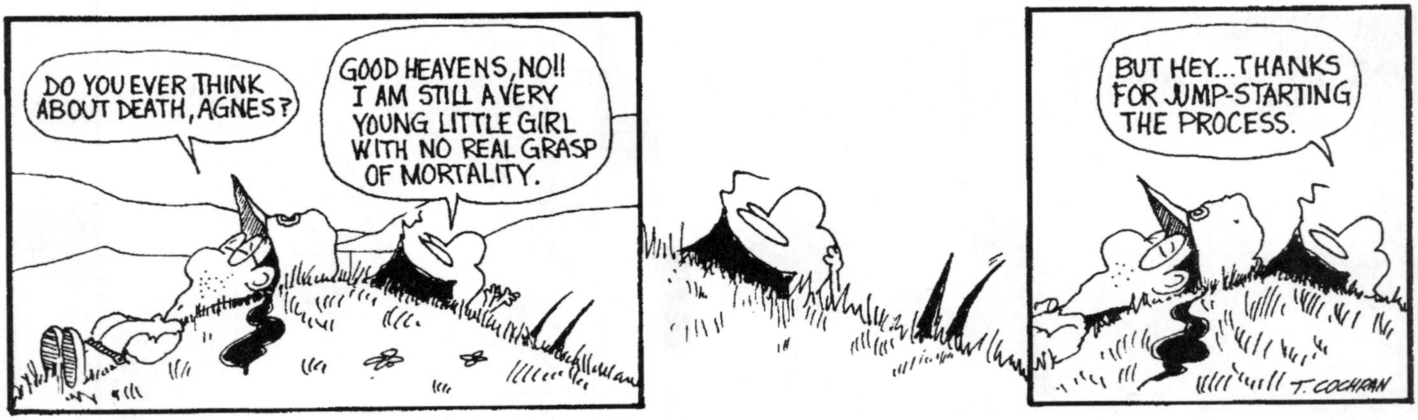
DO YOU EVER THINK ABOUT DEATH, AGNES?
GOOD HEAVENS, NO!! I AM STILL A VERY YOUNG LITTLE GIRL WITH NO REAL GRASP OF MORTALITY.
BUT HEY...THANKS FOR JUMP-STARTING THE PROCESS.
T. COCHRAN

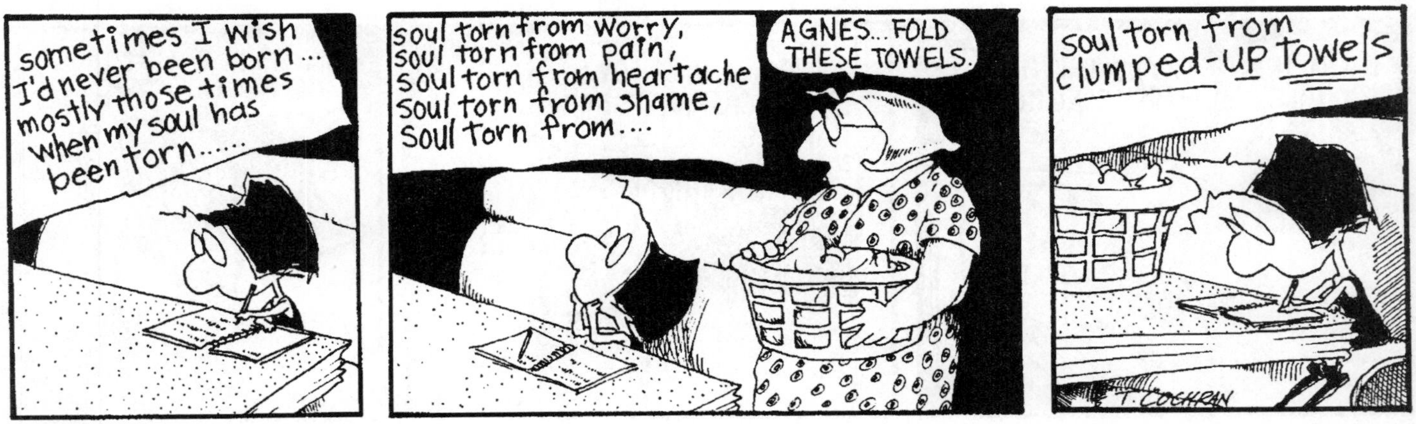
sometimes I wish I'd never been born... mostly those times when my soul has been torn......
soul torn from worry, soul torn from pain, soul torn from heartache soul torn from shame, soul torn from....
AGNES... FOLD THESE TOWELS.
soul torn from clumped-up towels
T. COCHRAN

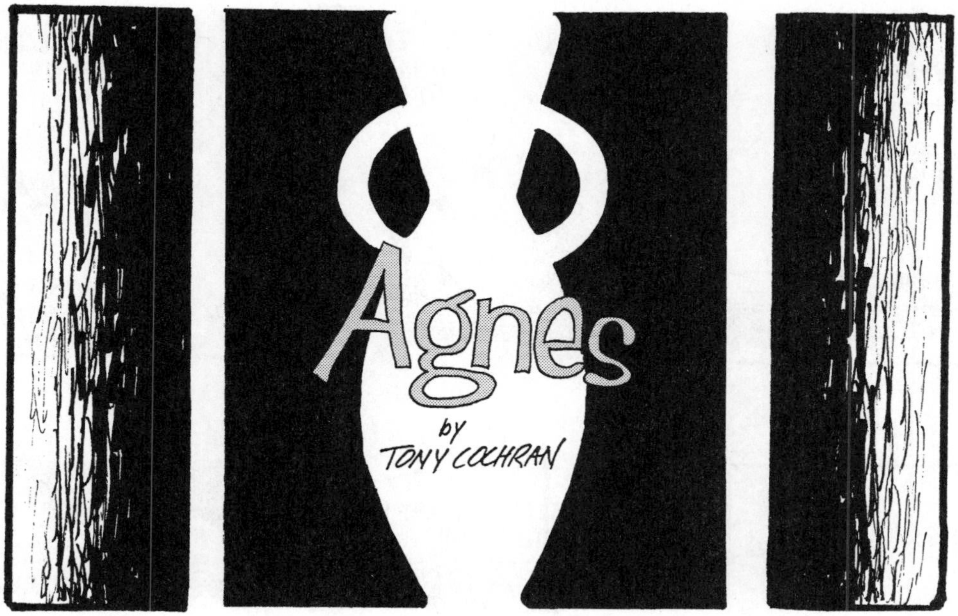
Agnes
by
TONY COCHRAN

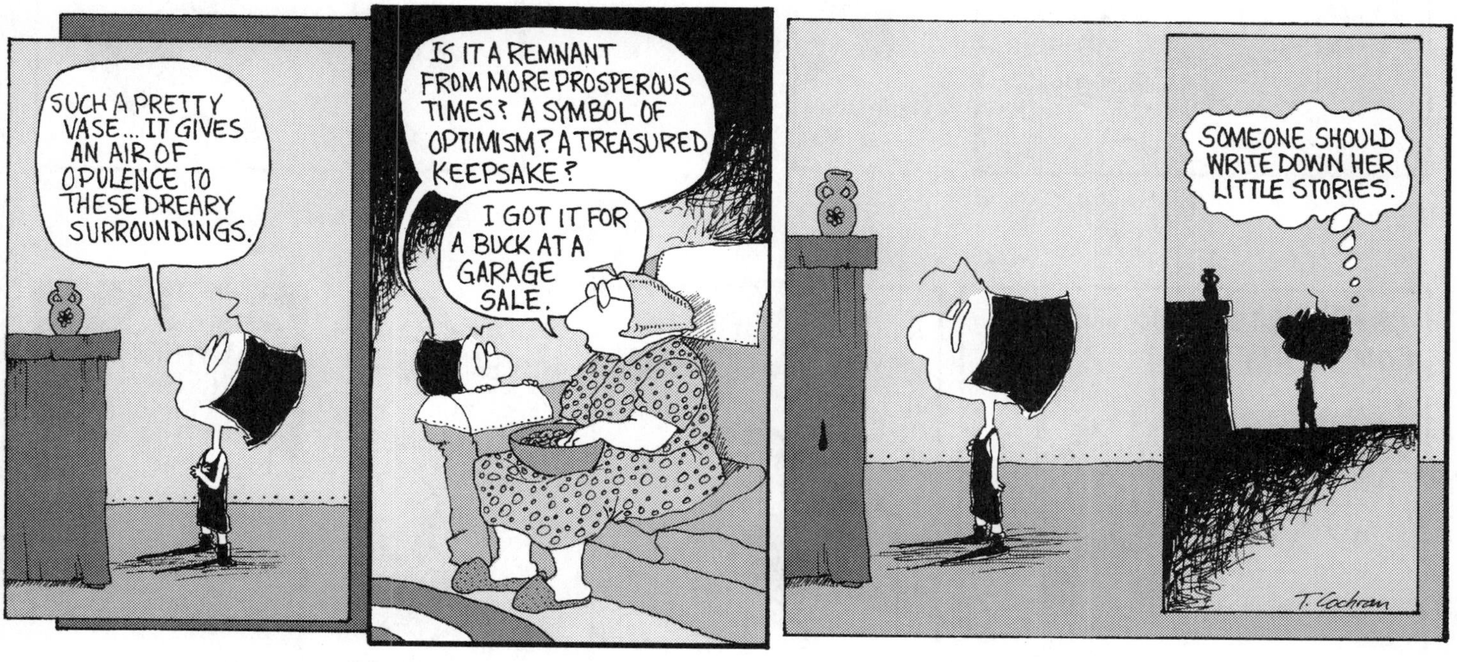
SUCH A PRETTY VASE... IT GIVES AN AIR OF OPULENCE TO THESE DREARY SURROUNDINGS.
IS IT A REMNANT FROM MORE PROSPEROUS TIMES? A SYMBOL OF OPTIMISM? A TREASURED KEEPSAKE?
I GOT IT FOR A BUCK AT A GARAGE SALE.
SOMEONE SHOULD WRITE DOWN HER LITTLE STORIES.
T. Cochran

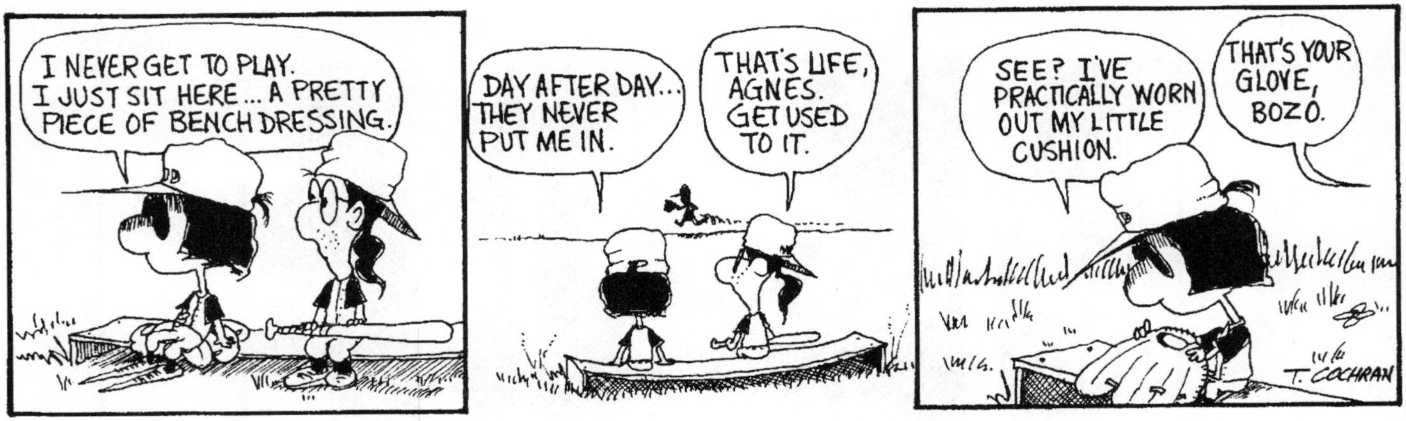
I NEVER GET TO PLAY. I JUST SIT HERE... A PRETTY PIECE OF BENCH DRESSING.
DAY AFTER DAY... THEY NEVER PUT ME IN.
THAT'S LIFE, AGNES. GET USED TO IT.
SEE? I'VE PRACTICALLY WORN OUT MY LITTLE CUSHION.
THAT'S YOUR GLOVE, BOZO.
T. COCHRAN

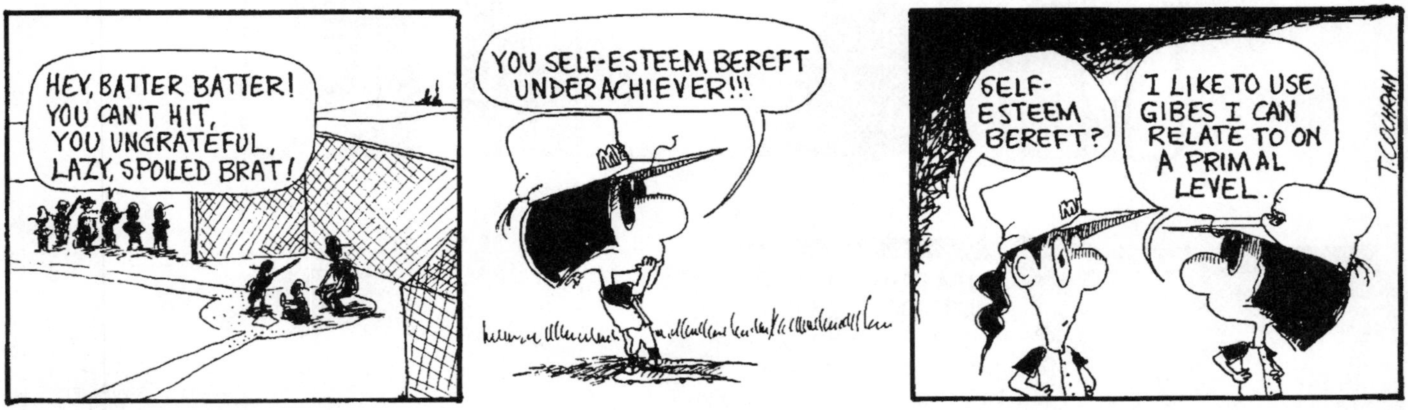
HEY, BATTER BATTER! YOU CAN'T HIT, YOU UNGRATEFUL, LAZY, SPOILED BRAT!
YOU SELF-ESTEEM BEREFT UNDERACHIEVER!!!
SELF-ESTEEM BEREFT?
I LIKE TO USE GIBES I CAN RELATE TO ON A PRIMAL LEVEL.
T. COCHRAN

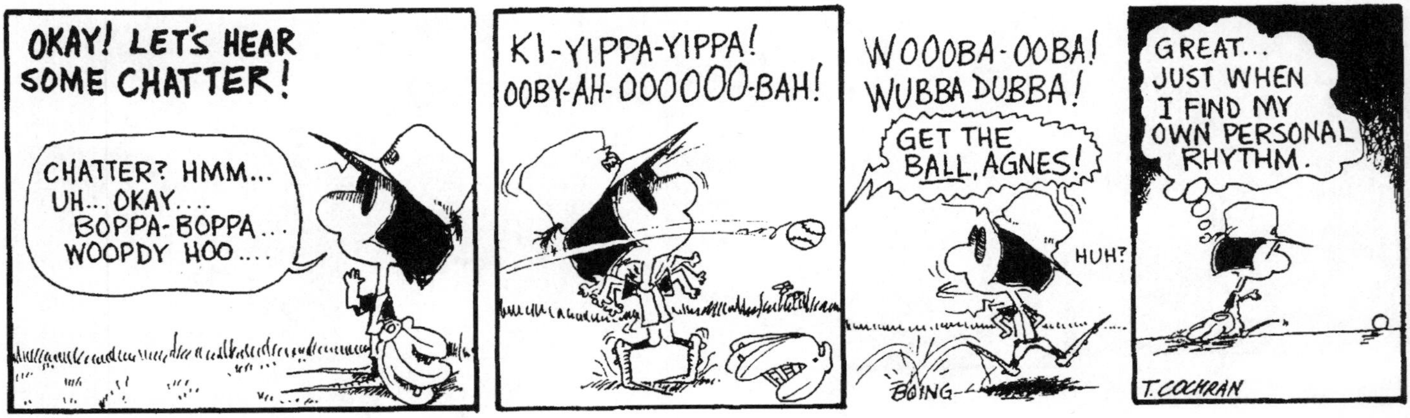
OKAY! LET'S HEAR SOME CHATTER!
CHATTER? HMM... UH... OKAY.... BOPPA-BOPPA... WOOPDY HOO....
KI-YIPPA-YIPPA! OOBY-AH-OOOOOO-BAH!
WOOOBA-OOBA! WUBBA DUBBA!
GET THE BALL, AGNES!
HUH?
BOING
GREAT... JUST WHEN I FIND MY OWN PERSONAL RHYTHM.
T. COCHRAN

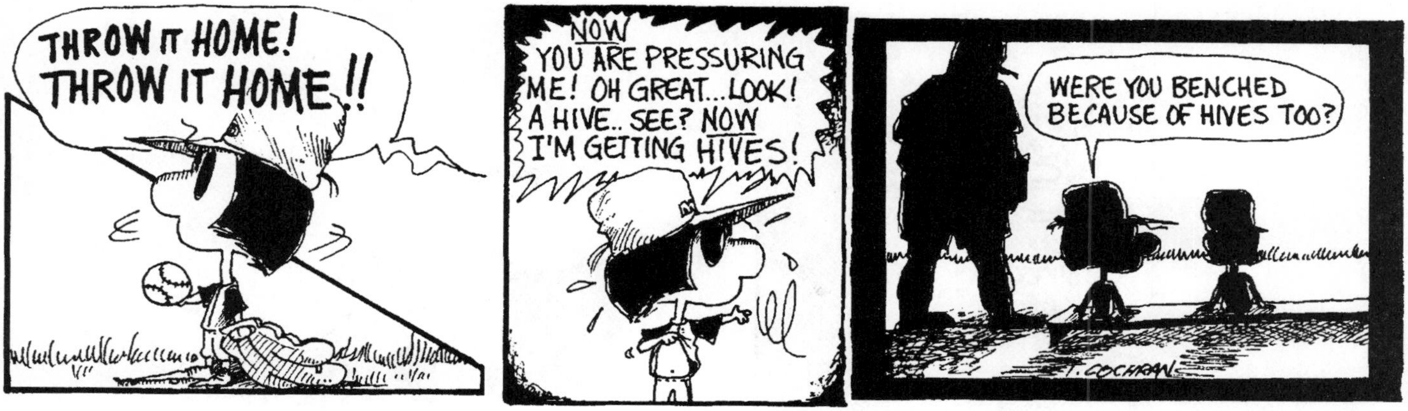
THROW IT HOME! THROW IT HOME!!
NOW YOU ARE PRESSURING ME! OH GREAT...LOOK! A HIVE.. SEE? NOW I'M GETTING HIVES!
WERE YOU BENCHED BECAUSE OF HIVES TOO?
T. COCHRAN

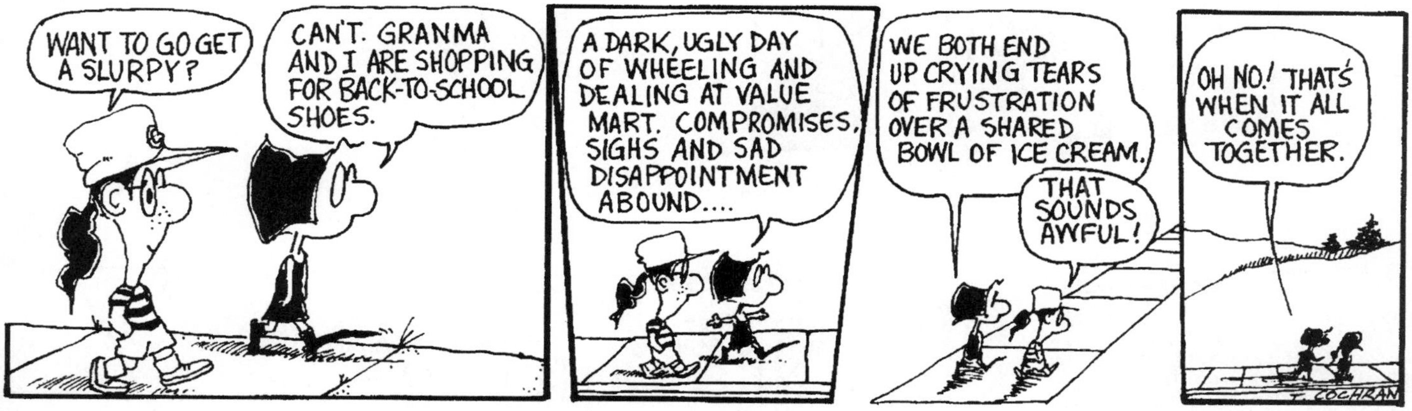
WANT TO GO GET A SLURPY?
CAN'T. GRANMA AND I ARE SHOPPING FOR BACK-TO-SCHOOL SHOES.
A DARK, UGLY DAY OF WHEELING AND DEALING AT VALUE MART. COMPROMISES, SIGHS AND SAD DISAPPOINTMENT ABOUND....
WE BOTH END UP CRYING TEARS OF FRUSTRATION OVER A SHARED BOWL OF ICE CREAM.
THAT SOUNDS AWFUL!
OH NO! THAT'S WHEN IT ALL COMES TOGETHER.
T. COCHRAN

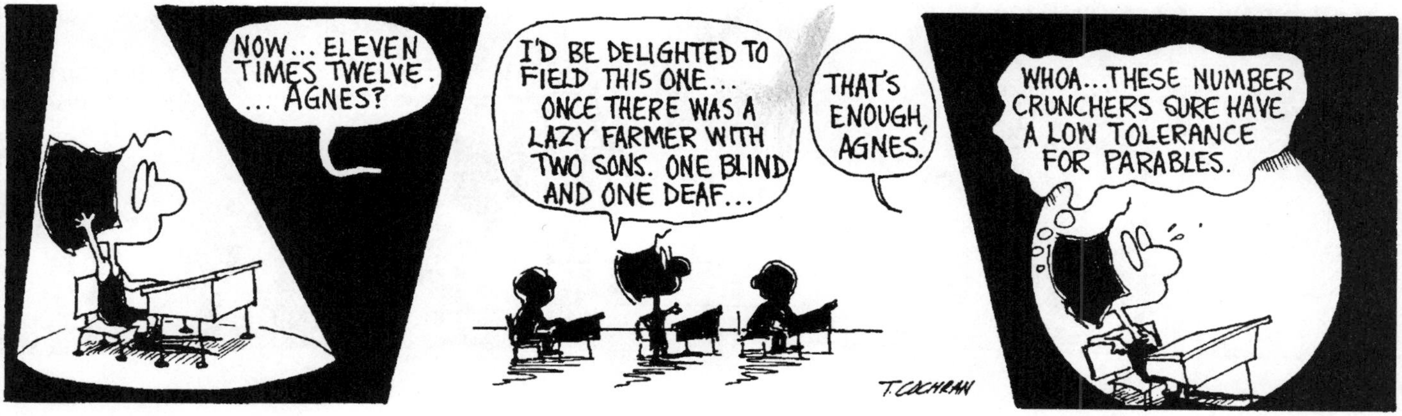
NOW... ELEVEN TIMES TWELVE. ... AGNES?
I'D BE DELIGHTED TO FIELD THIS ONE... ONCE THERE WAS A LAZY FARMER WITH TWO SONS. ONE BLIND AND ONE DEAF...
THAT'S ENOUGH, AGNES.
T. COCHRAN
WHOA...THESE NUMBER CRUNCHERS SURE HAVE A LOW TOLERANCE FOR PARABLES.

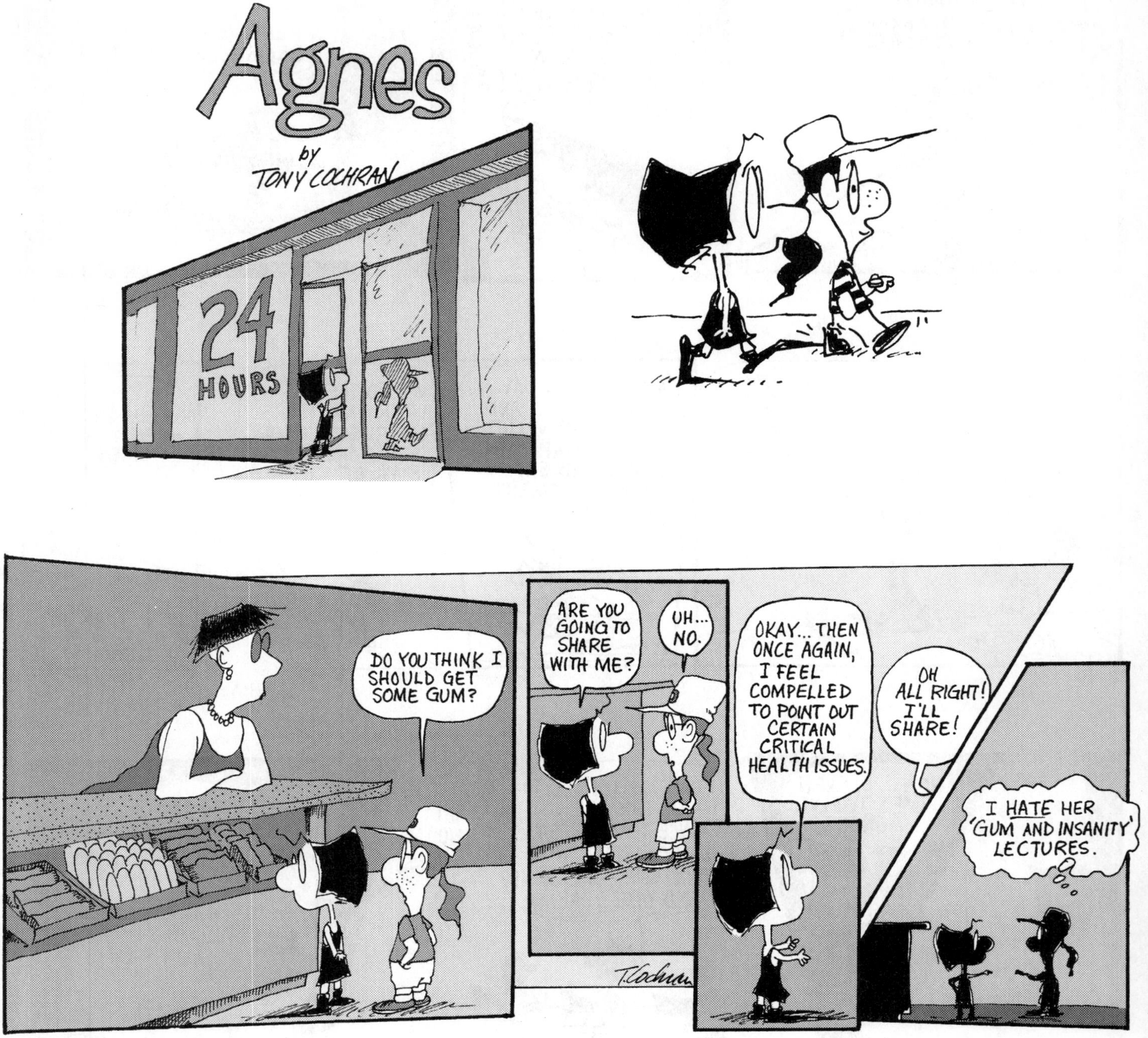

Agnes
by TONY COCHRAN
24 HOURS
DO YOU THINK I SHOULD GET SOME GUM?
ARE YOU GOING TO SHARE WITH ME?
UH... NO.
OKAY... THEN ONCE AGAIN, I FEEL COMPELLED TO POINT OUT CERTAIN CRITICAL HEALTH ISSUES.
OH ALL RIGHT! I'LL SHARE!
I HATE HER 'GUM AND INSANITY' LECTURES.
T. Cochran

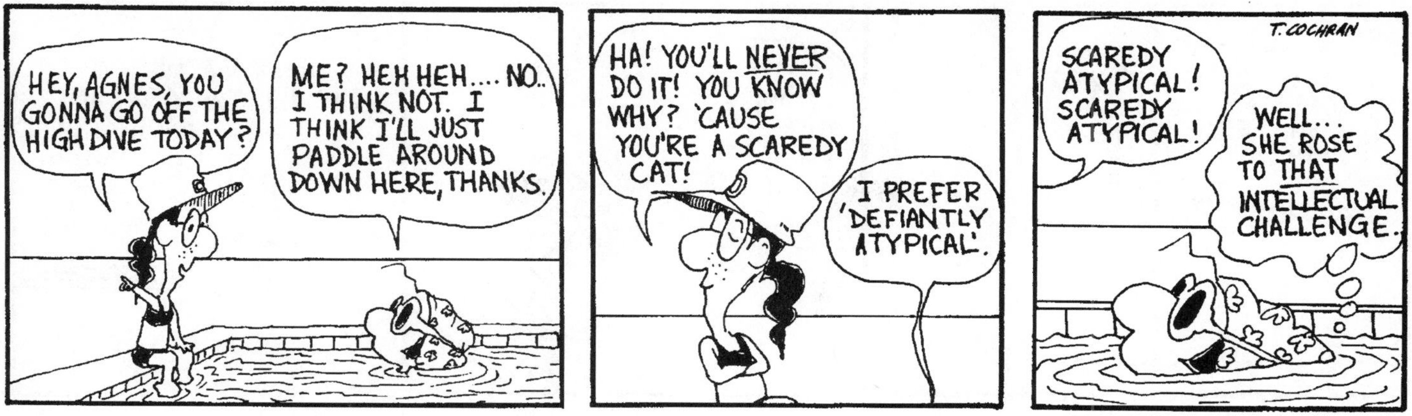
T. COCHRAN
HEY, AGNES, YOU GONNA GO OFF THE HIGH DIVE TODAY?
ME? HEH HEH.... NO.. I THINK NOT. I THINK I'LL JUST PADDLE AROUND DOWN HERE, THANKS.
HA! YOU'LL NEVER DO IT! YOU KNOW WHY? 'CAUSE YOU'RE A SCAREDY CAT!
I PREFER 'DEFIANTLY ATYPICAL'.
SCAREDY ATYPICAL! SCAREDY ATYPICAL!
WELL... SHE ROSE TO THAT INTELLECTUAL CHALLENGE..

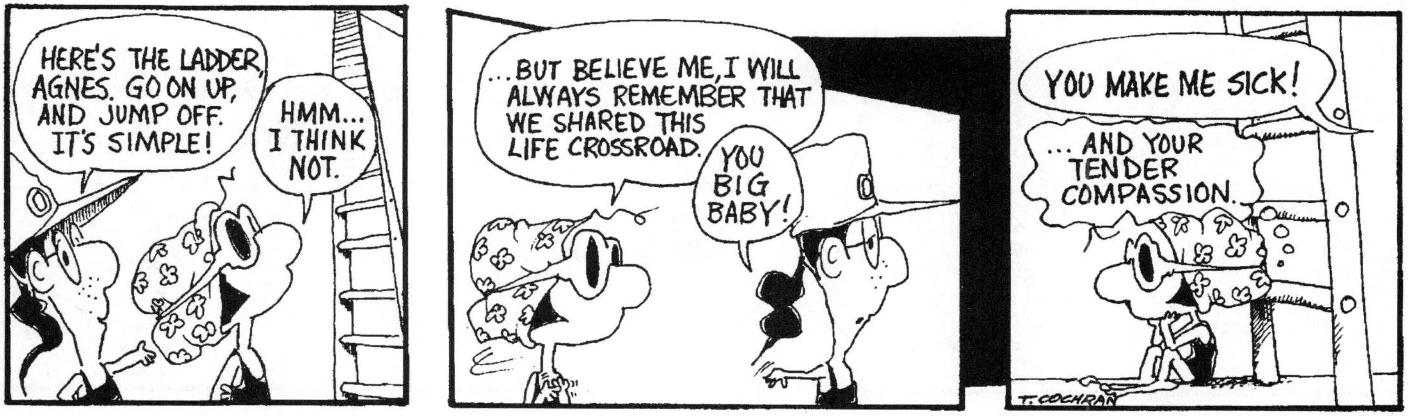
HERE'S THE LADDER, AGNES. GO ON UP, AND JUMP OFF. IT'S SIMPLE!
HMM... I THINK NOT.
...BUT BELIEVE ME, I WILL ALWAYS REMEMBER THAT WE SHARED THIS LIFE CROSSROAD.
YOU BIG BABY!
YOU MAKE ME SICK!
... AND YOUR TENDER COMPASSION.
T. COCHRAN

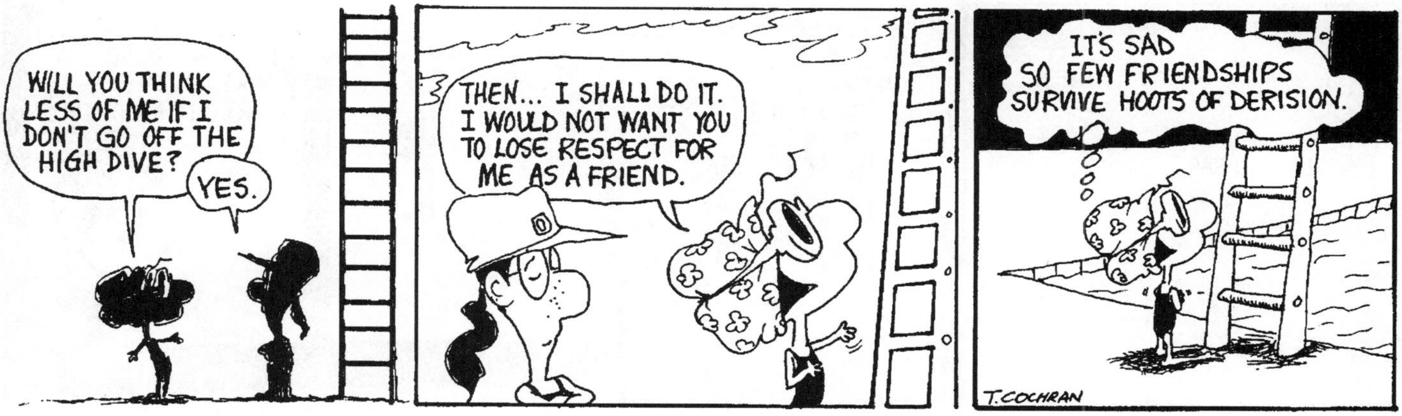
WILL YOU THINK LESS OF ME IF I DON'T GO OFF THE HIGH DIVE?
YES.
THEN... I SHALL DO IT. I WOULD NOT WANT YOU TO LOSE RESPECT FOR ME AS A FRIEND.
IT'S SAD SO FEW FRIENDSHIPS SURVIVE HOOTS OF DERISION.
T. COCHRAN

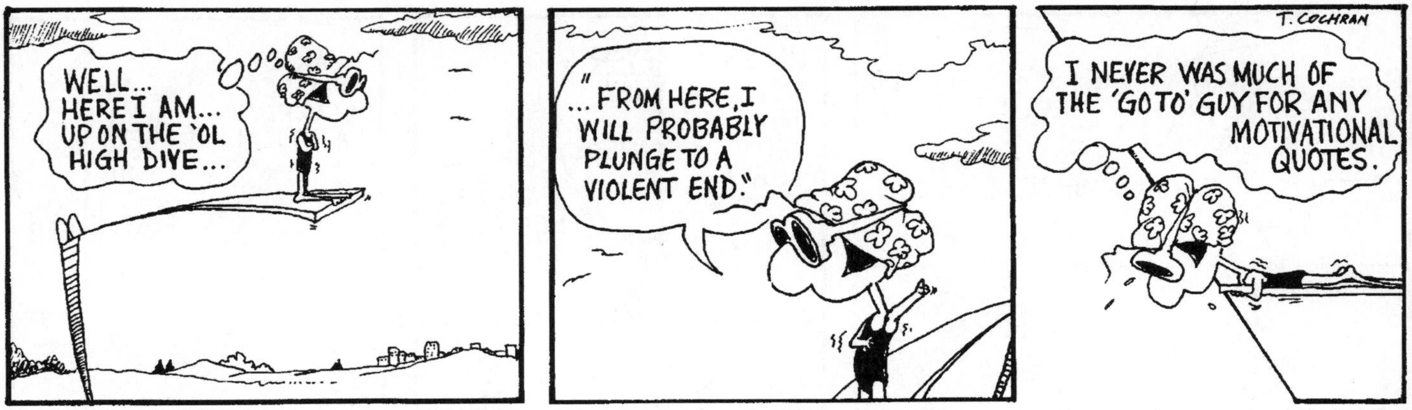
WELL... HERE I AM... UP ON THE 'OL HIGH DIVE...
"... FROM HERE, I WILL PROBABLY PLUNGE TO A VIOLENT END."
T. COCHRAN
I NEVER WAS MUCH OF THE 'GO TO' GUY FOR ANY MOTIVATIONAL QUOTES.

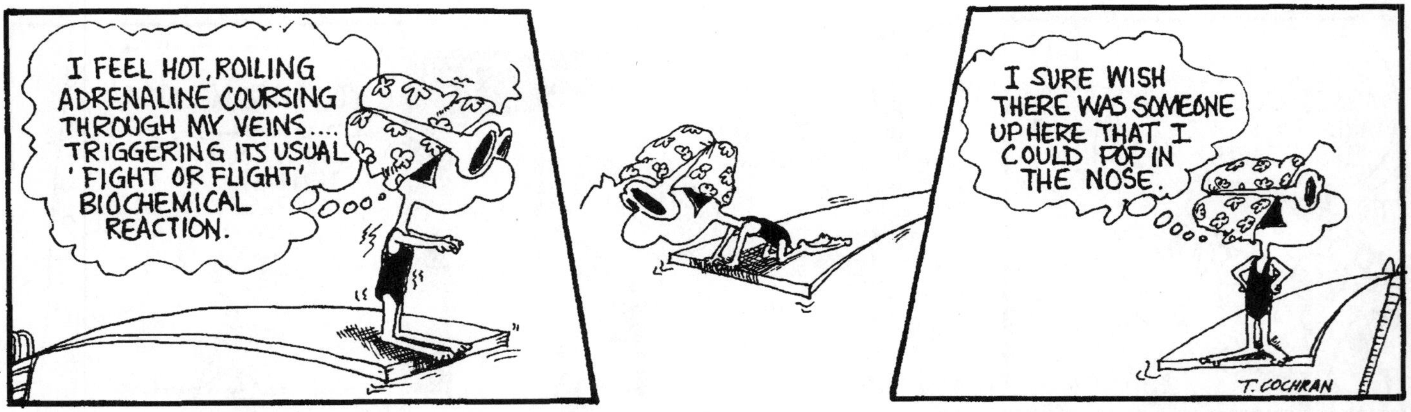
I FEEL HOT, ROILING ADRENALINE COURSING THROUGH MY VEINS.... TRIGGERING ITS USUAL 'FIGHT OR FLIGHT' BIOCHEMICAL REACTION.
I SURE WISH THERE WAS SOMEONE UP HERE THAT I COULD POP IN THE NOSE.
T. COCHRAN

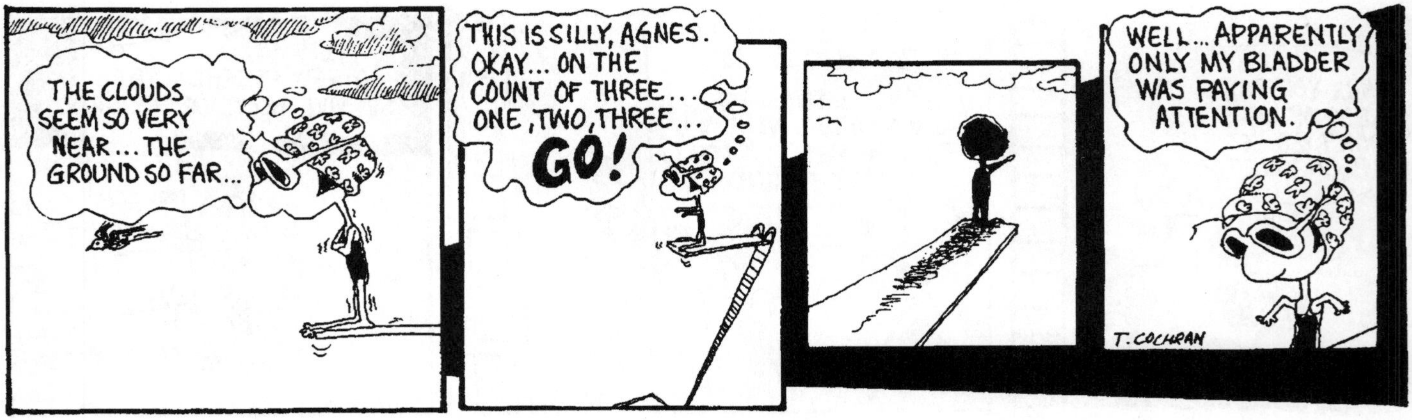
THE CLOUDS SEEM SO VERY NEAR... THE GROUND SO FAR...
THIS IS SILLY, AGNES. OKAY... ON THE COUNT OF THREE... ONE, TWO, THREE...
GO!
WELL... APPARENTLY ONLY MY BLADDER WAS PAYING ATTENTION.
T. COCHRAN

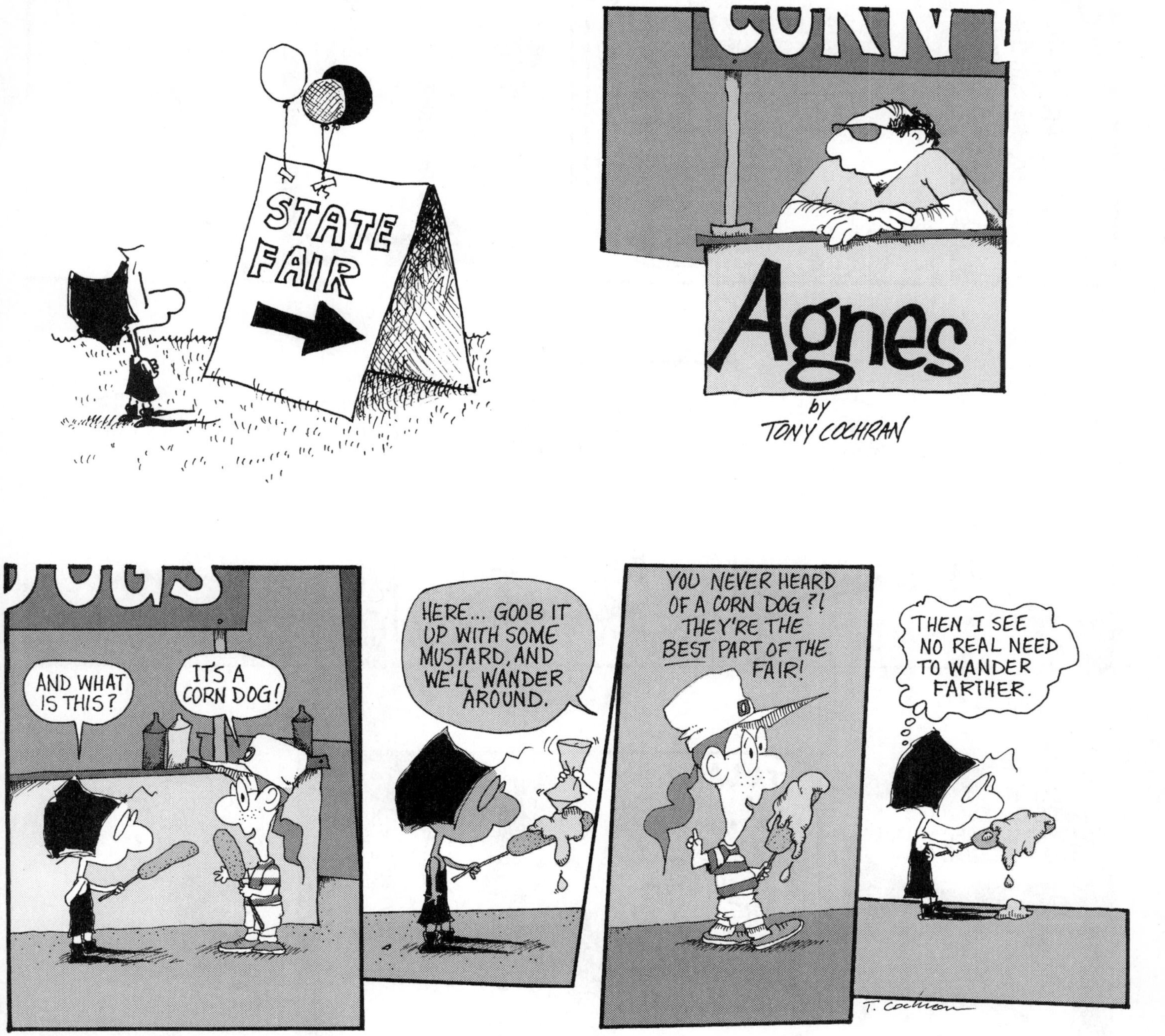
STATE FAIR
CORN DOGS
Agnes
by TONY COCHRAN
AND WHAT IS THIS?
IT'S A CORN DOG!
HERE... GOOB IT UP WITH SOME MUSTARD, AND WE'LL WANDER AROUND.
YOU NEVER HEARD OF A CORN DOG ?! THEY'RE THE BEST PART OF THE FAIR!
THEN I SEE NO REAL NEED TO WANDER FARTHER.
T. Cochran

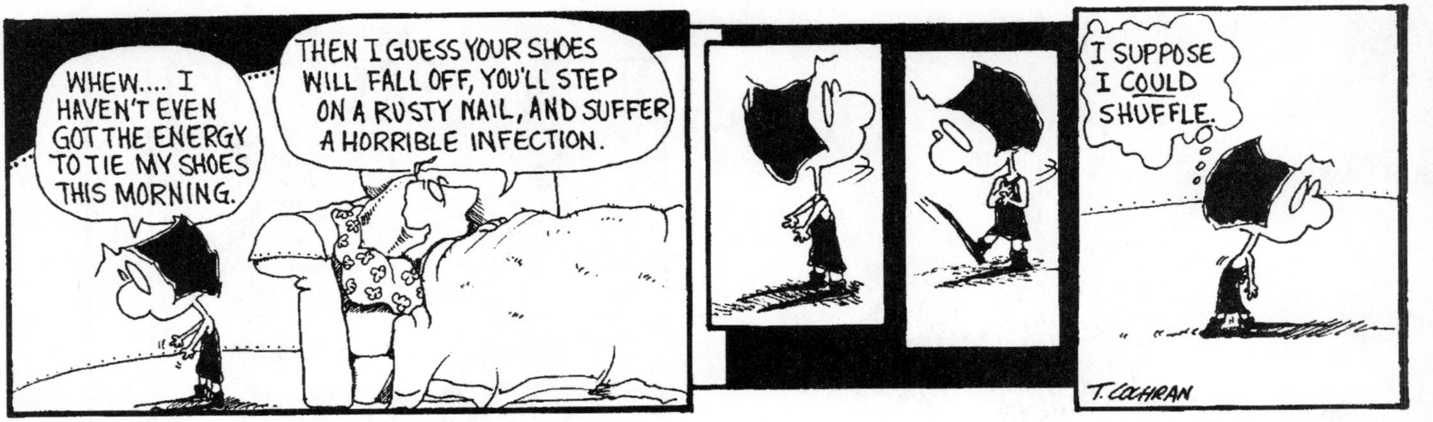
WHEW.... I HAVEN'T EVEN GOT THE ENERGY TO TIE MY SHOES THIS MORNING.
THEN I GUESS YOUR SHOES WILL FALL OFF, YOU'LL STEP ON A RUSTY NAIL, AND SUFFER A HORRIBLE INFECTION.
I SUPPOSE I COULD SHUFFLE.
T. COCHRAN

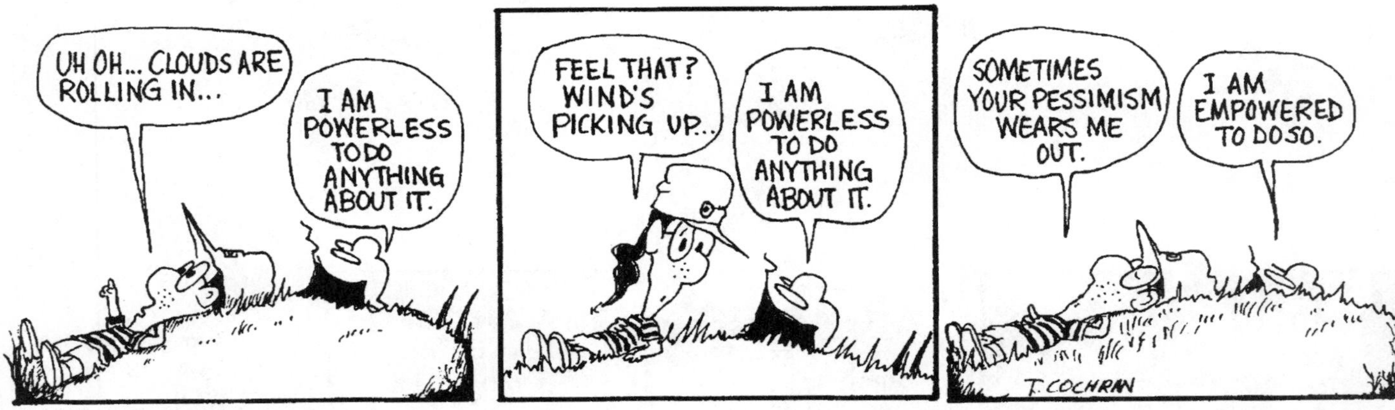
UH OH... CLOUDS ARE ROLLING IN...
I AM POWERLESS TO DO ANYTHING ABOUT IT.
FEEL THAT? WIND'S PICKING UP...
I AM POWERLESS TO DO ANYTHING ABOUT IT.
SOMETIMES YOUR PESSIMISM WEARS ME OUT.
I AM EMPOWERED TO DO SO.
T. COCHRAN

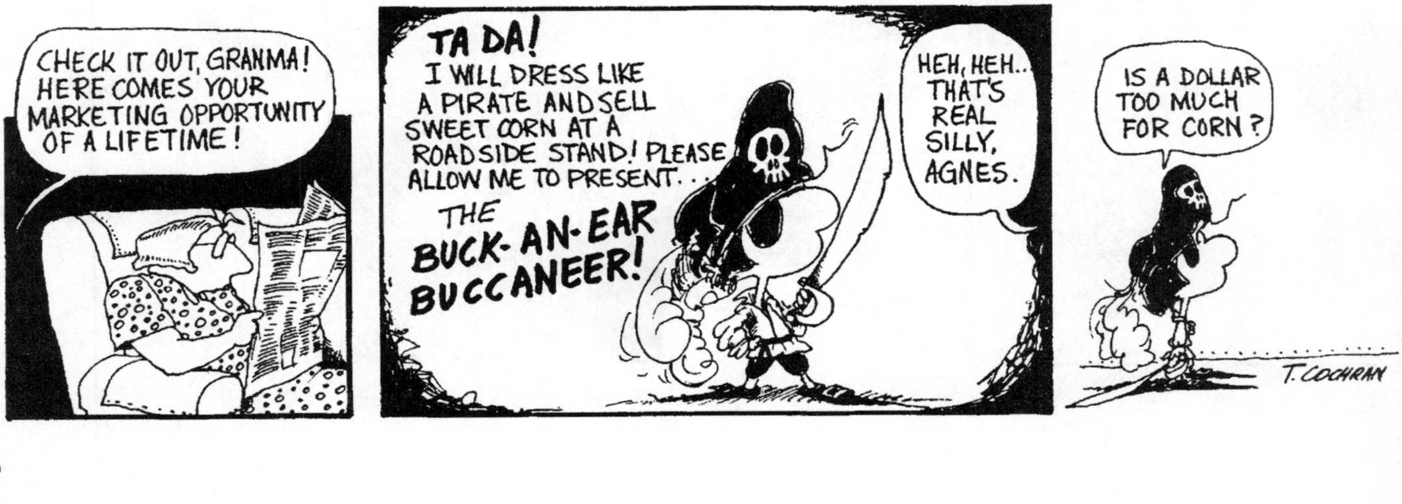
CHECK IT OUT, GRANMA! HERE COMES YOUR MARKETING OPPORTUNITY OF A LIFETIME!
TA DA! I WILL DRESS LIKE A PIRATE AND SELL SWEET CORN AT A ROADSIDE STAND! PLEASE ALLOW ME TO PRESENT. . .
THE BUCK-AN-EAR BUCCANEER!
HEH, HEH.. THAT'S REAL SILLY, AGNES.
IS A DOLLAR TOO MUCH FOR CORN?
T. COCHRAN

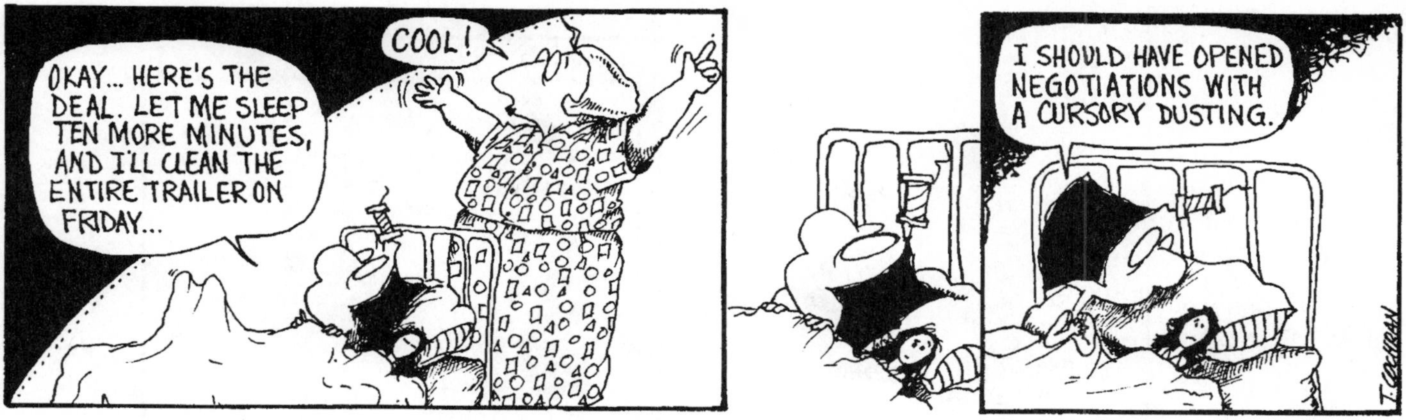
OKAY... HERE'S THE DEAL. LET ME SLEEP TEN MORE MINUTES, AND I'LL CLEAN THE ENTIRE TRAILER ON FRIDAY...
COOL!
I SHOULD HAVE OPENED NEGOTIATIONS WITH A CURSORY DUSTING.
T. COCHRAN

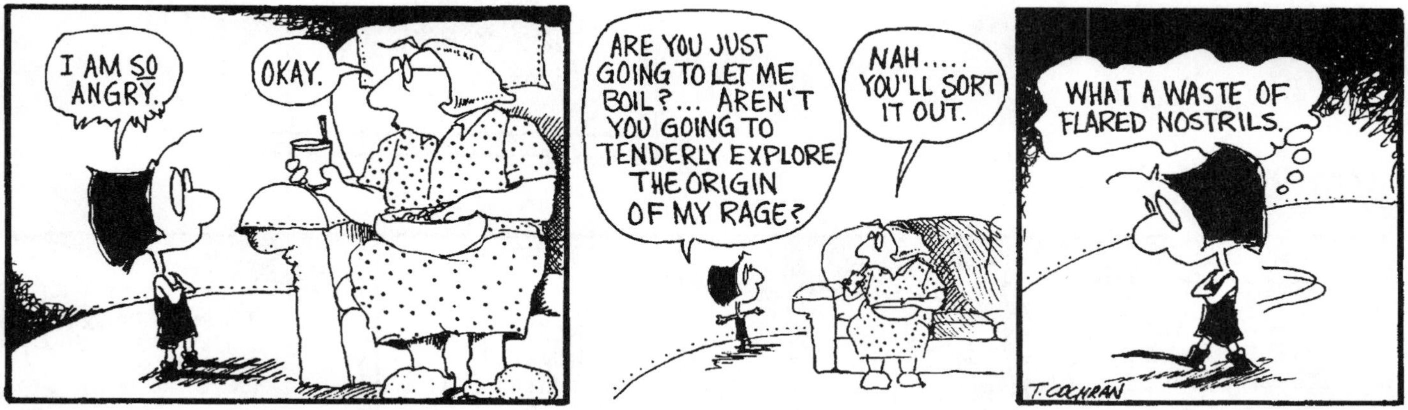
I AM SO ANGRY.
OKAY.
ARE YOU JUST GOING TO LET ME BOIL?... AREN'T YOU GOING TO TENDERLY EXPLORE THE ORIGIN OF MY RAGE?
NAH..... YOU'LL SORT IT OUT.
WHAT A WASTE OF FLARED NOSTRILS.
T. COCHRAN

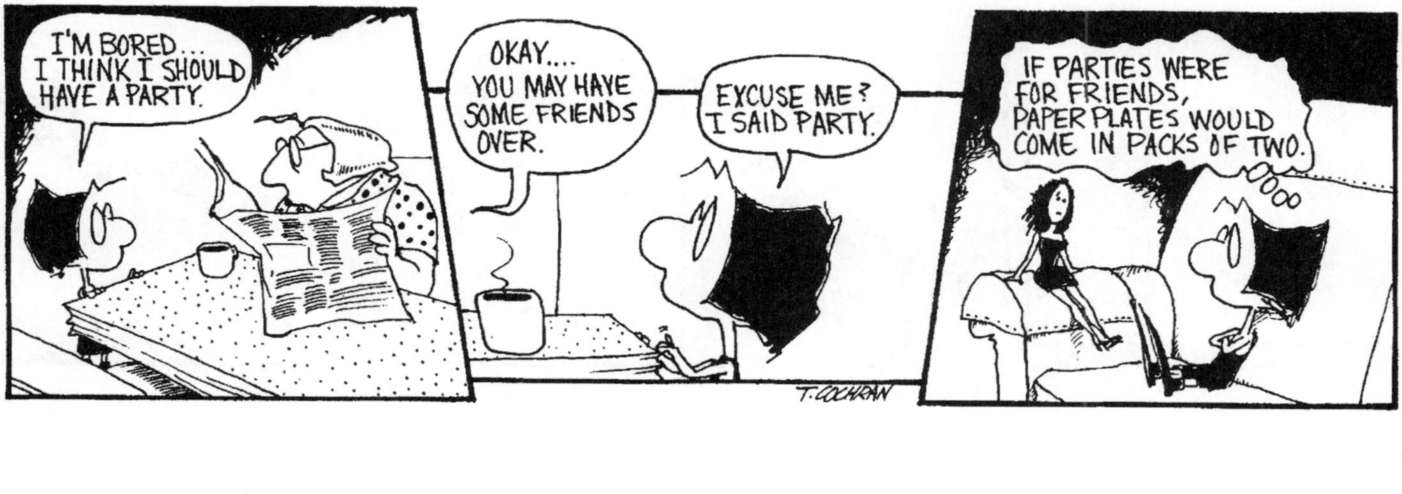
I'M BORED... I THINK I SHOULD HAVE A PARTY.
OKAY.... YOU MAY HAVE SOME FRIENDS OVER.
EXCUSE ME? I SAID PARTY.
IF PARTIES WERE FOR FRIENDS, PAPER PLATES WOULD COME IN PACKS OF TWO.
T. COCHRAN

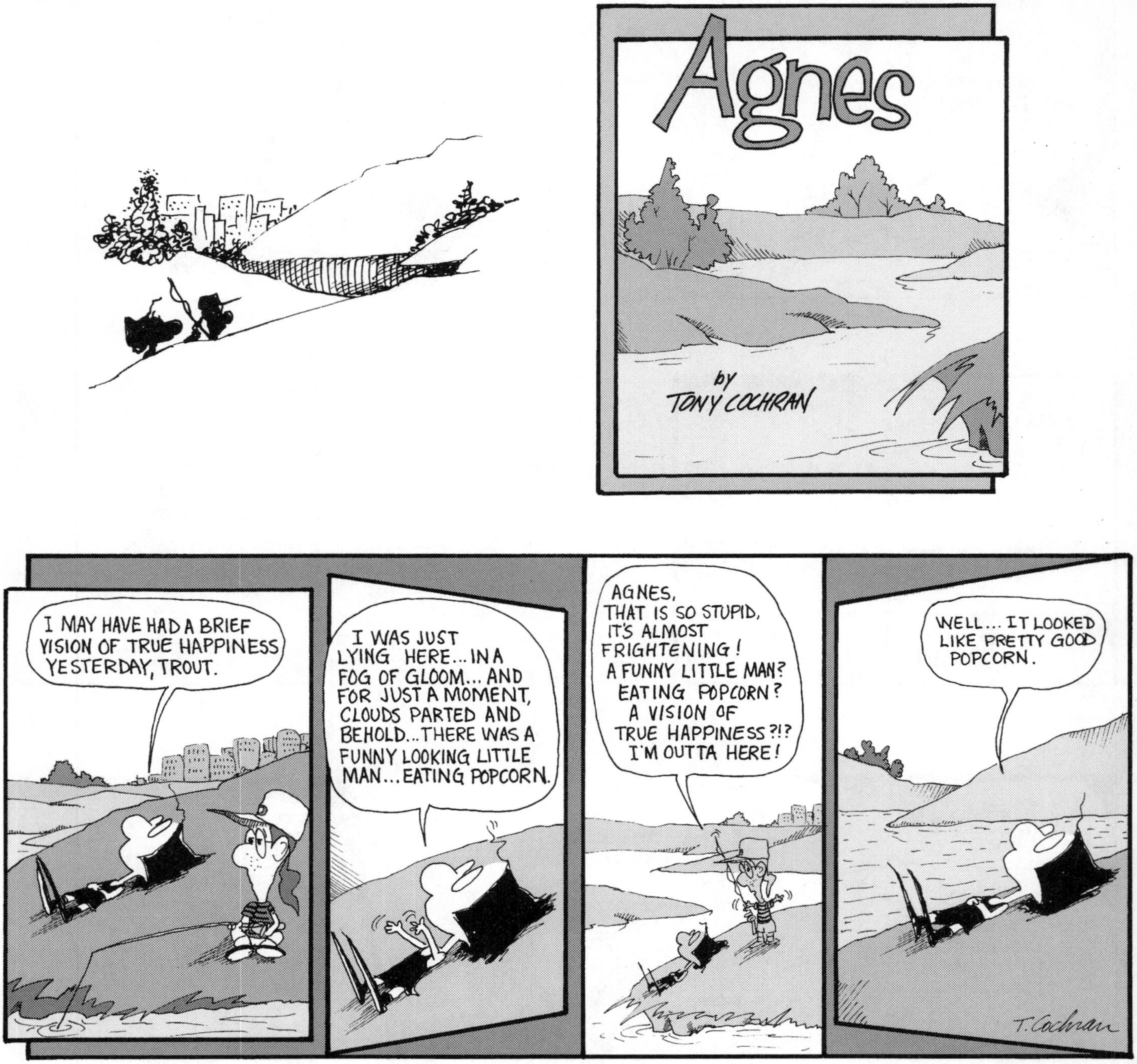
Agnes
by
TONY COCHRAN
I MAY HAVE HAD A BRIEF VISION OF TRUE HAPPINESS YESTERDAY, TROUT.
I WAS JUST LYING HERE... IN A FOG OF GLOOM... AND FOR JUST A MOMENT, CLOUDS PARTED AND BEHOLD... THERE WAS A FUNNY LOOKING LITTLE MAN... EATING POPCORN.
AGNES, THAT IS SO STUPID, IT'S ALMOST FRIGHTENING! A FUNNY LITTLE MAN? EATING POPCORN? A VISION OF TRUE HAPPINESS?!? I'M OUTTA HERE!
WELL... IT LOOKED LIKE PRETTY GOOD POPCORN.
T. Cochran

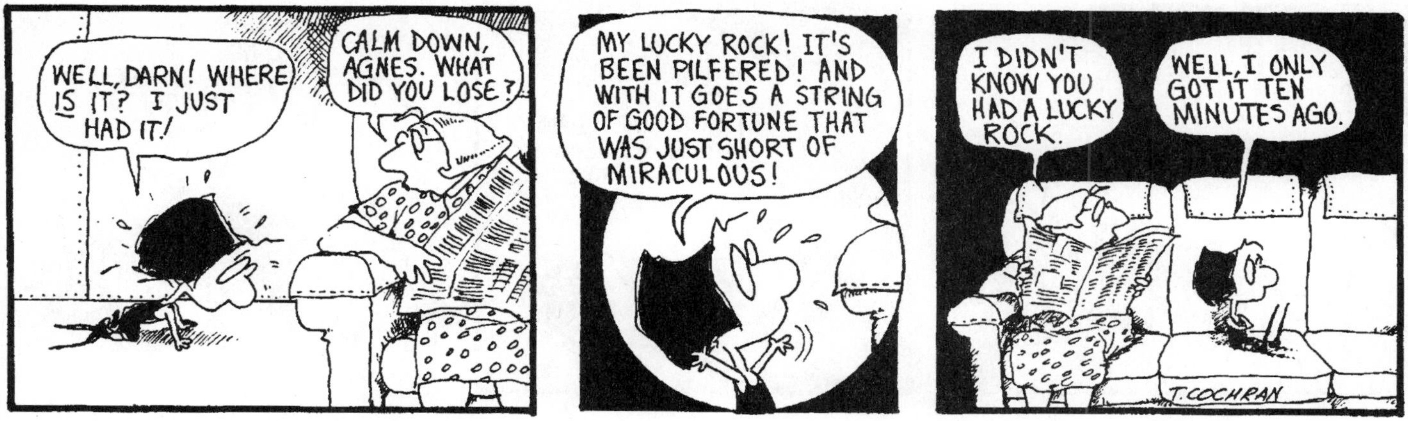
WELL, DARN! WHERE IS IT? I JUST HAD IT!
CALM DOWN, AGNES. WHAT DID YOU LOSE?
MY LUCKY ROCK! IT'S BEEN PILFERED! AND WITH IT GOES A STRING OF GOOD FORTUNE THAT WAS JUST SHORT OF MIRACULOUS!
I DIDN'T KNOW YOU HAD A LUCKY ROCK.
WELL, I ONLY GOT IT TEN MINUTES AGO.
T. COCHRAN

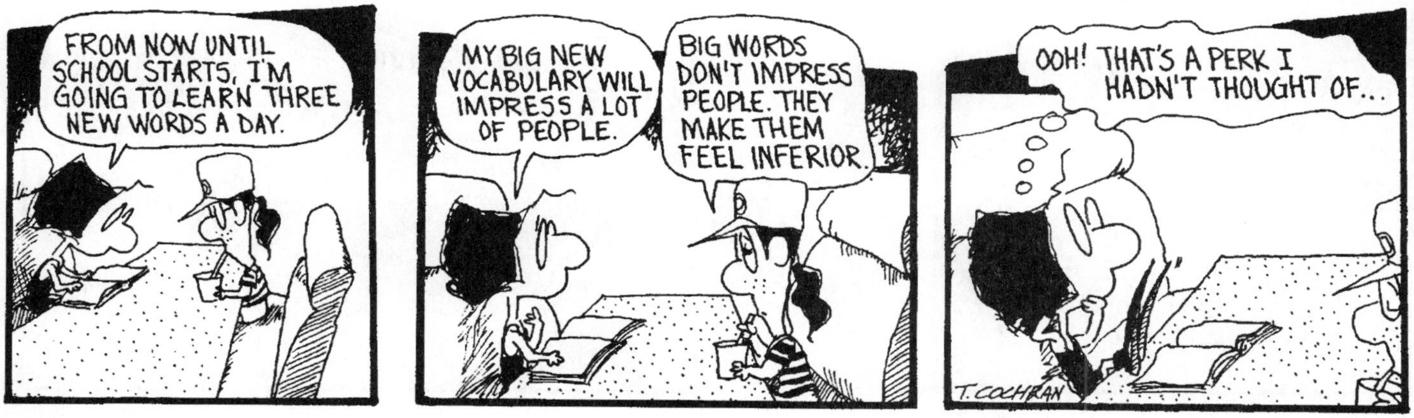
FROM NOW UNTIL SCHOOL STARTS, I'M GOING TO LEARN THREE NEW WORDS A DAY.
MY BIG NEW VOCABULARY WILL IMPRESS A LOT OF PEOPLE.
BIG WORDS DON'T IMPRESS PEOPLE. THEY MAKE THEM FEEL INFERIOR.
OOH! THAT'S A PERK I HADN'T THOUGHT OF...
T. COCHRAN

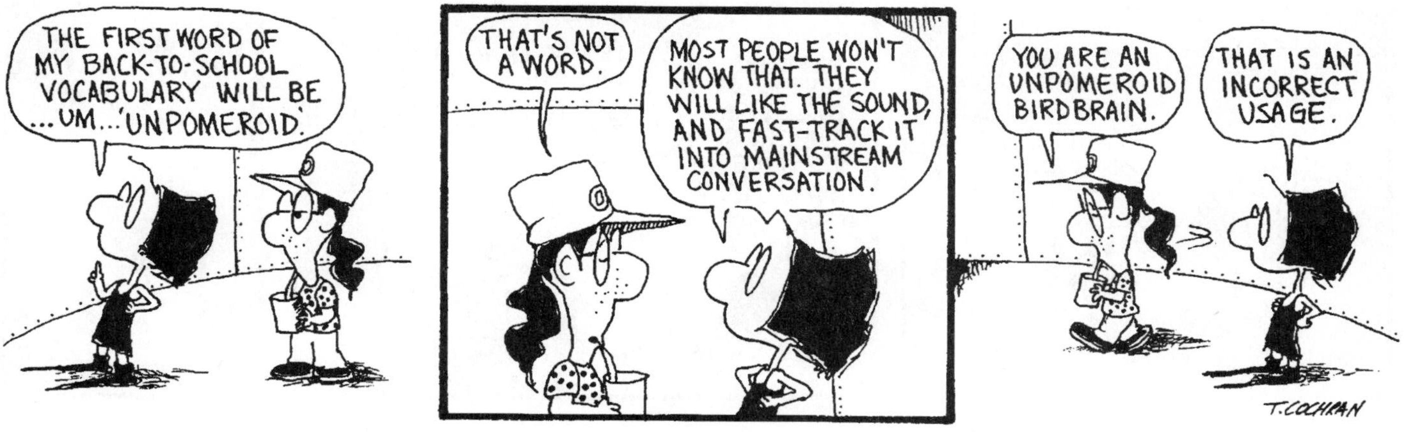
THE FIRST WORD OF MY BACK-TO-SCHOOL VOCABULARY WILL BE ...UM...'UNPOMEROID.'
THAT'S NOT A WORD.
MOST PEOPLE WON'T KNOW THAT. THEY WILL LIKE THE SOUND, AND FAST-TRACK IT INTO MAINSTREAM CONVERSATION.
YOU ARE AN UNPOMEROID BIRDBRAIN.
THAT IS AN INCORRECT USAGE.
T. COCHRAN

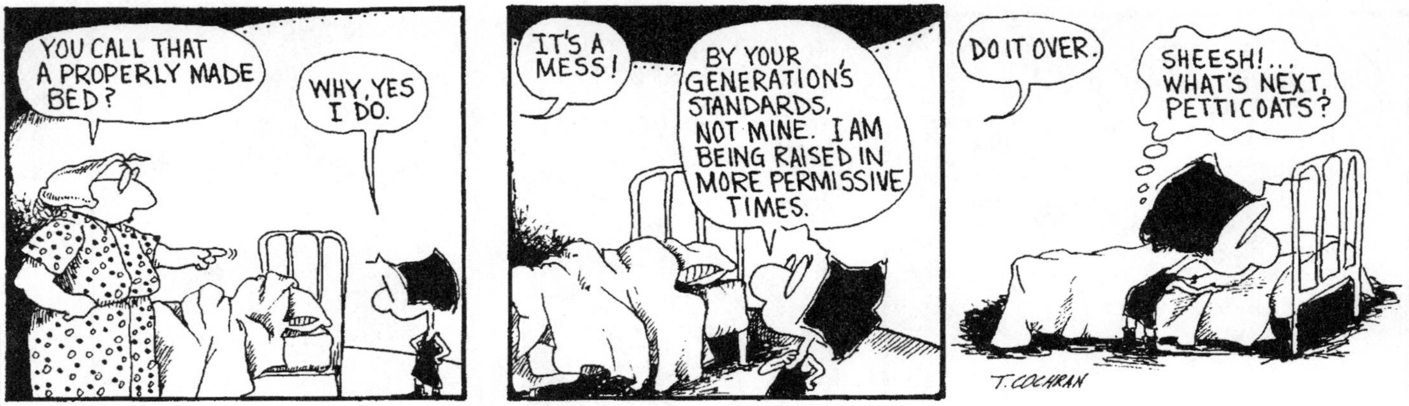
YOU CALL THAT A PROPERLY MADE BED?
WHY, YES I DO.
IT'S A MESS!
BY YOUR GENERATION'S STANDARDS, NOT MINE. I AM BEING RAISED IN MORE PERMISSIVE TIMES.
DO IT OVER.
SHEESH!... WHAT'S NEXT, PETTICOATS?
T. COCHRAN

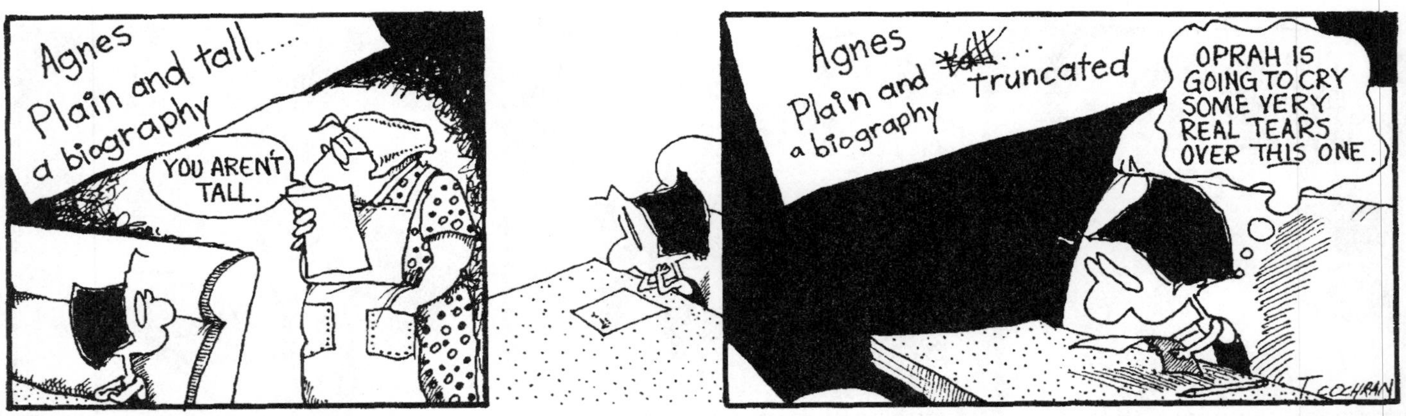
Agnes
Plain and tall.....
a biography
YOU AREN'T TALL.
Agnes
Plain and ~~tall~~.... truncated
a biography
OPRAH IS GOING TO CRY SOME VERY REAL TEARS OVER THIS ONE.
T. COCHRAN

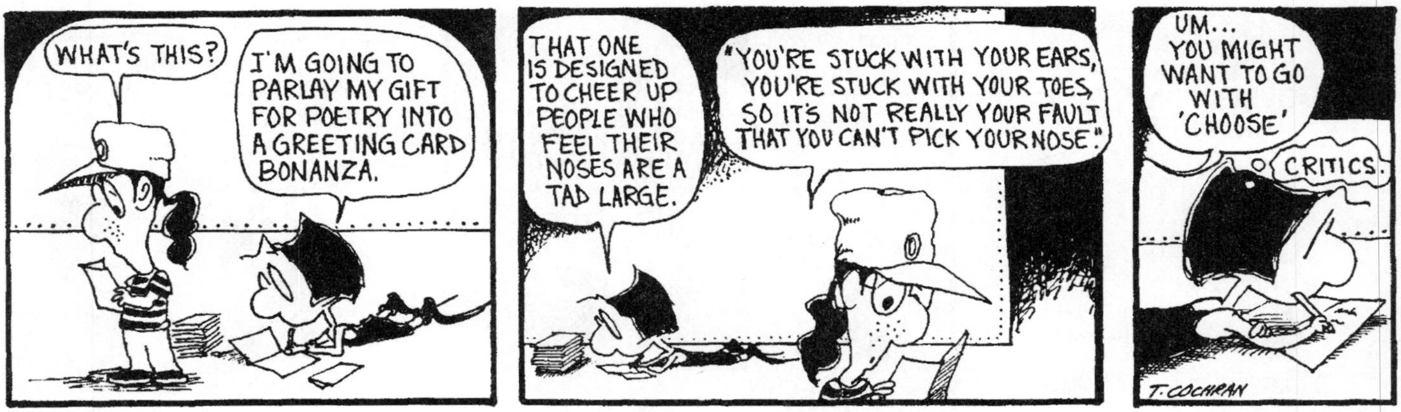
WHAT'S THIS?
I'M GOING TO PARLAY MY GIFT FOR POETRY INTO A GREETING CARD BONANZA.
THAT ONE IS DESIGNED TO CHEER UP PEOPLE WHO FEEL THEIR NOSES ARE A TAD LARGE.
"YOU'RE STUCK WITH YOUR EARS, YOU'RE STUCK WITH YOUR TOES, SO IT'S NOT REALLY YOUR FAULT THAT YOU CAN'T PICK YOUR NOSE."
UM... YOU MIGHT WANT TO GO WITH 'CHOOSE'
CRITICS.
T. COCHRAN

Agnes
by Tony Cochran

AGNES!

YIKES

AGNES, DID YOU LEAVE THIS BIG GLOB OF TOOTHPASTE IN THE SINK?

PERHAPS.

I SURELY WOULDN'T CALL THAT A BIG GLOB, THOUGH. THIS IS MORE OF A SPECK... MAYBE A DAB.

A BIG GLOB WOULD HAVE A ROUNDER, FULLER LOOK.

DON'T CRITIQUE IT. JUST CLEAN IT UP.

SEE?.... I DON'T EVEN NEED THE TONGS THIS TIME.

T. Cochran

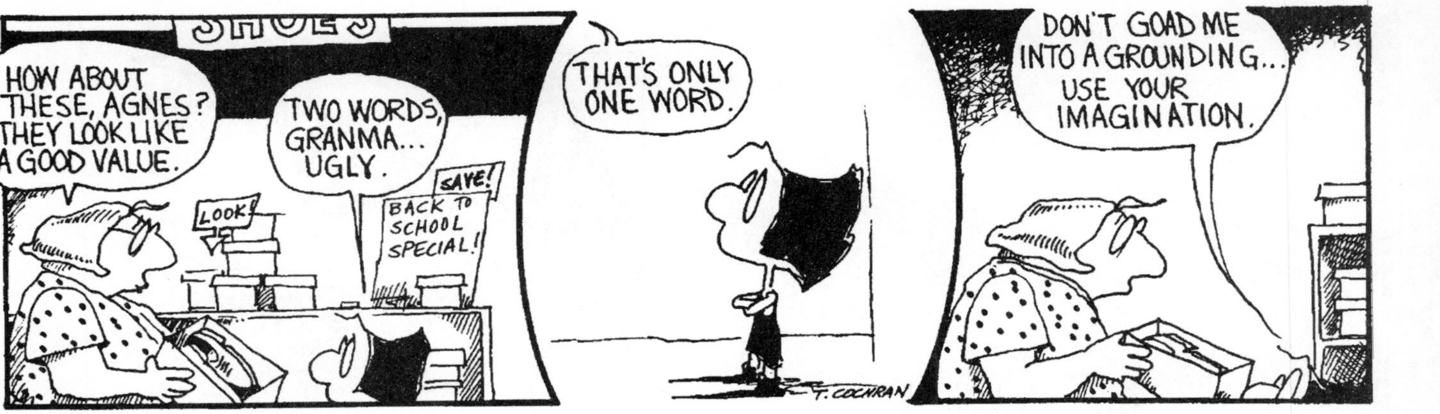
HOW ABOUT THESE, AGNES? THEY LOOK LIKE A GOOD VALUE.
TWO WORDS, GRANMA... UGLY.
LOOK!
SAVE!
BACK TO SCHOOL SPECIAL!
THAT'S ONLY ONE WORD.
T. COCHRAN
DON'T GOAD ME INTO A GROUNDING... USE YOUR IMAGINATION.

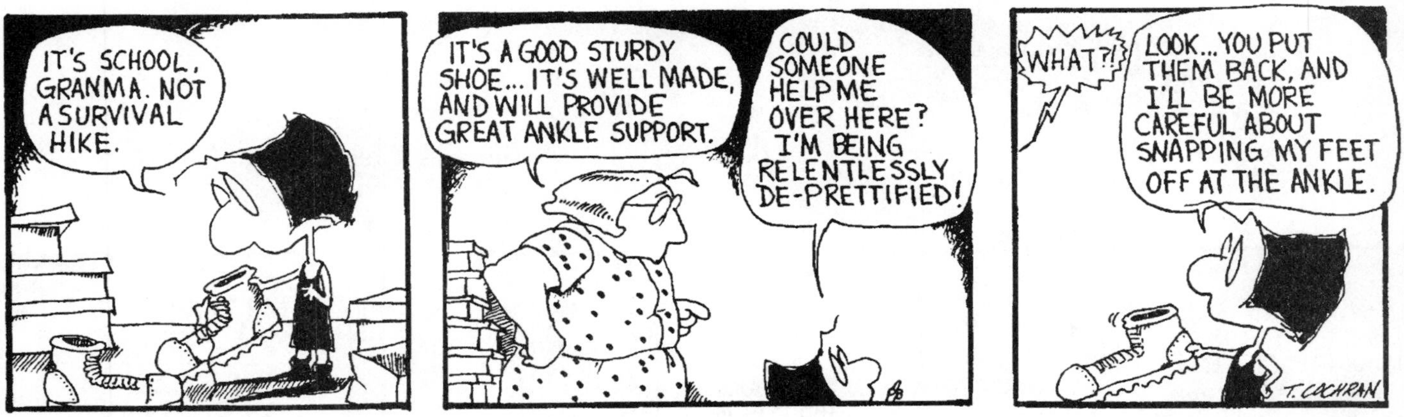
IT'S SCHOOL, GRANMA. NOT A SURVIVAL HIKE.
IT'S A GOOD STURDY SHOE... IT'S WELL MADE, AND WILL PROVIDE GREAT ANKLE SUPPORT.
COULD SOMEONE HELP ME OVER HERE? I'M BEING RELENTLESSLY DE-PRETTIFIED!
WHAT?!
LOOK... YOU PUT THEM BACK, AND I'LL BE MORE CAREFUL ABOUT SNAPPING MY FEET OFF AT THE ANKLE.
T. COCHRAN

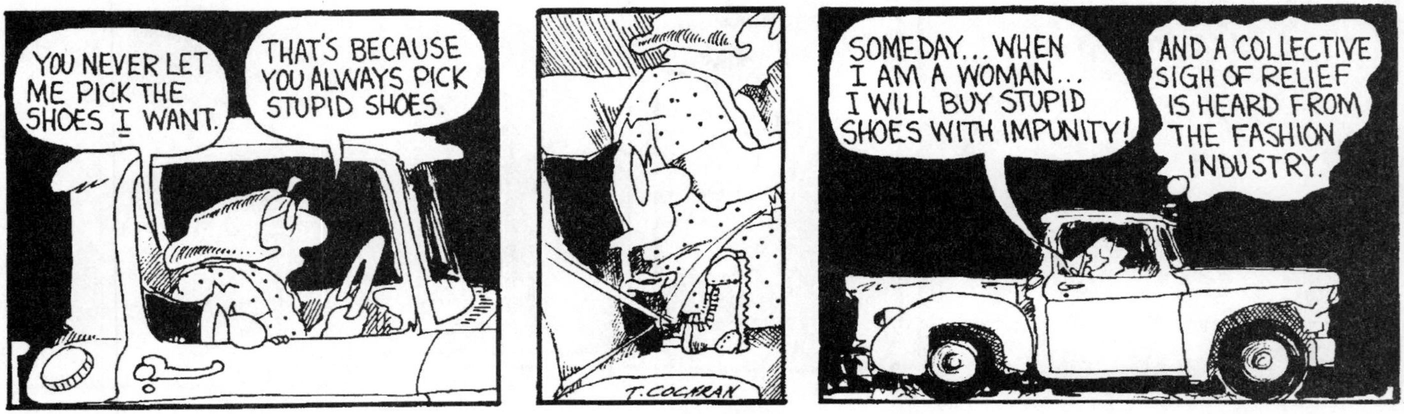
YOU NEVER LET ME PICK THE SHOES I WANT.
THAT'S BECAUSE YOU ALWAYS PICK STUPID SHOES.
T. COCHRAN
SOMEDAY... WHEN I AM A WOMAN... I WILL BUY STUPID SHOES WITH IMPUNITY!
AND A COLLECTIVE SIGH OF RELIEF IS HEARD FROM THE FASHION INDUSTRY.

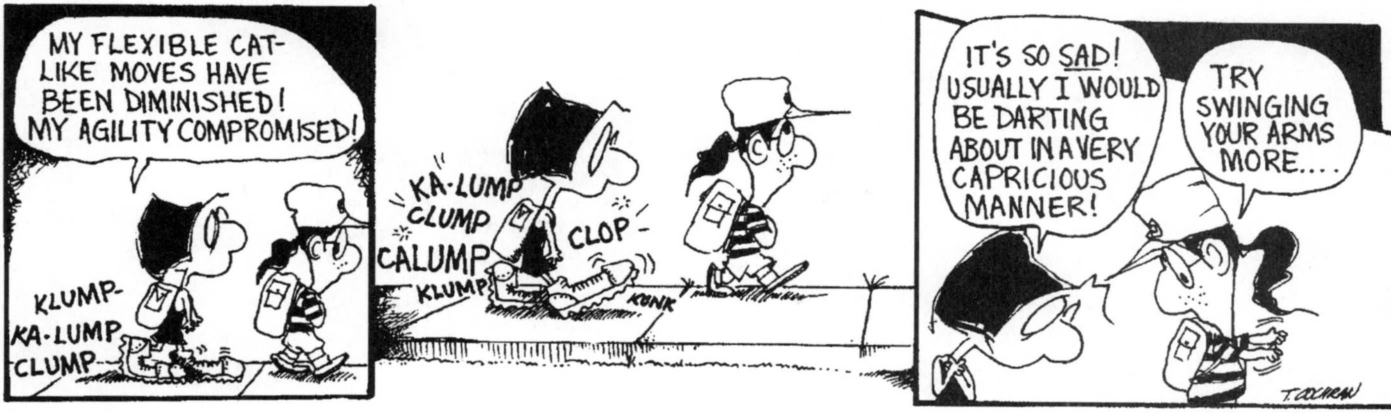
MY FLEXIBLE CAT-LIKE MOVES HAVE BEEN DIMINISHED! MY AGILITY COMPROMISED!
KLUMP-
KA-LUMP
CLUMP
KA-LUMP
CLUMP
CALUMP
KLUMP
CLOP
KUNK
IT'S SO SAD! USUALLY I WOULD BE DARTING ABOUT IN A VERY CAPRICIOUS MANNER!
TRY SWINGING YOUR ARMS MORE....
T. COCHRAN

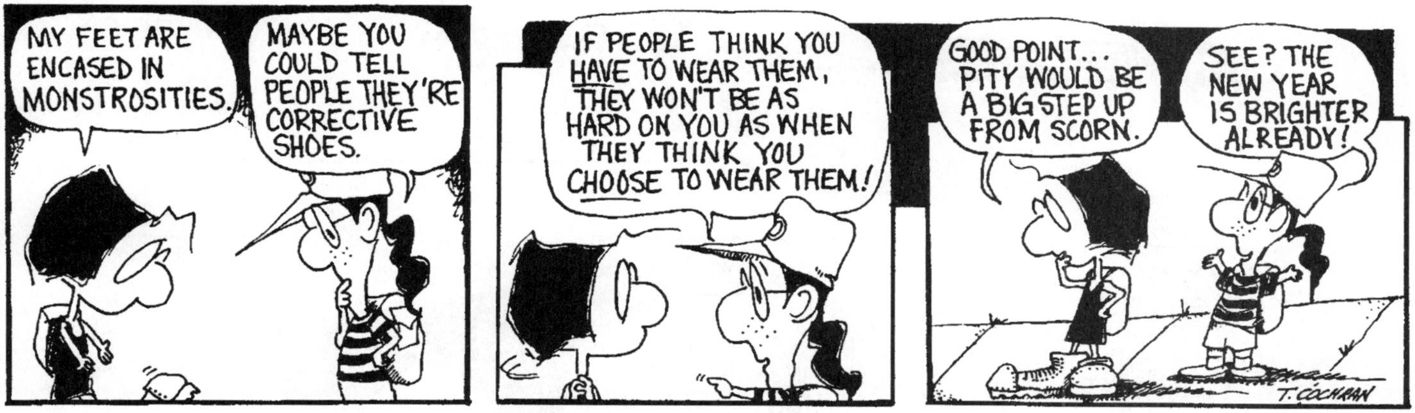
MY FEET ARE ENCASED IN MONSTROSITIES.
MAYBE YOU COULD TELL PEOPLE THEY'RE CORRECTIVE SHOES.
IF PEOPLE THINK YOU HAVE TO WEAR THEM, THEY WON'T BE AS HARD ON YOU AS WHEN THEY THINK YOU CHOOSE TO WEAR THEM!
GOOD POINT... PITY WOULD BE A BIG STEP UP FROM SCORN.
SEE? THE NEW YEAR IS BRIGHTER ALREADY!
T. COCHRAN

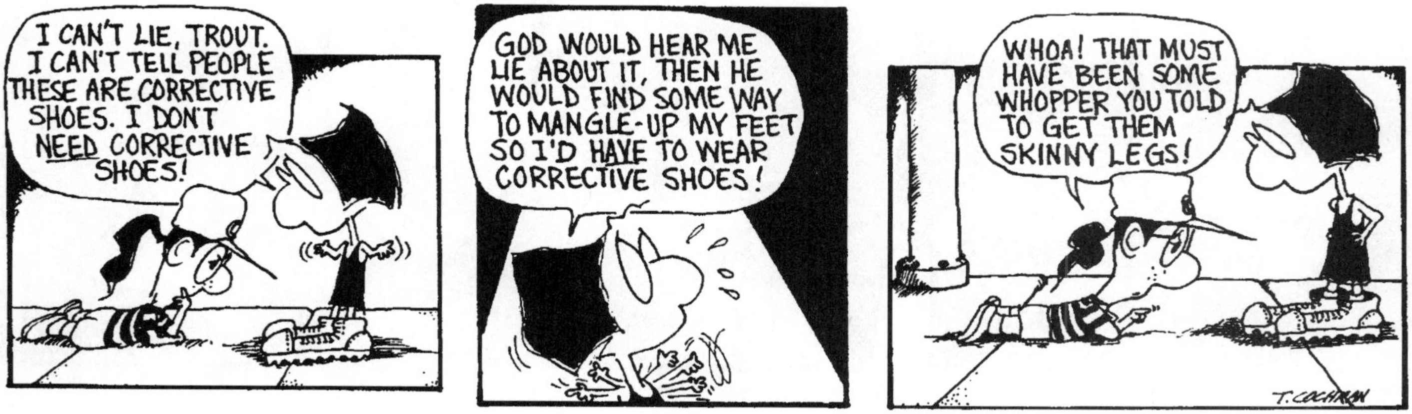
I CAN'T LIE, TROUT. I CAN'T TELL PEOPLE THESE ARE CORRECTIVE SHOES. I DON'T NEED CORRECTIVE SHOES!
GOD WOULD HEAR ME LIE ABOUT IT, THEN HE WOULD FIND SOME WAY TO MANGLE-UP MY FEET SO I'D HAVE TO WEAR CORRECTIVE SHOES!
WHOA! THAT MUST HAVE BEEN SOME WHOPPER YOU TOLD TO GET THEM SKINNY LEGS!
T. COCHRAN

Agnes
by TONY COCHRAN
TRUTH
Bill's Goldfish
BILL'S GOLDFISH BILL GOT A GOLDFISH. TWO MONTHS LATER, HIS FISH WENT BELLY UP AND DIED. BILL WAS DEVASTATED. THE END
MAYBE YOU COULD PUT IN SOME THINGS TO LIGHTEN THIS UP. ...... SOME MEMORIES OF THE GOOD TIMES, PERHAPS.
~~The End~~
Suddenly, Bill remembered eating some real good ice cream a week prior to the fish's death.
T. COCHRAN

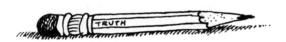

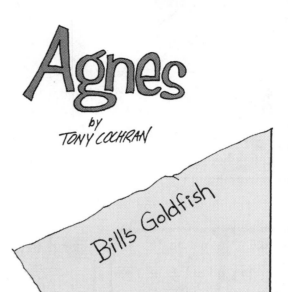

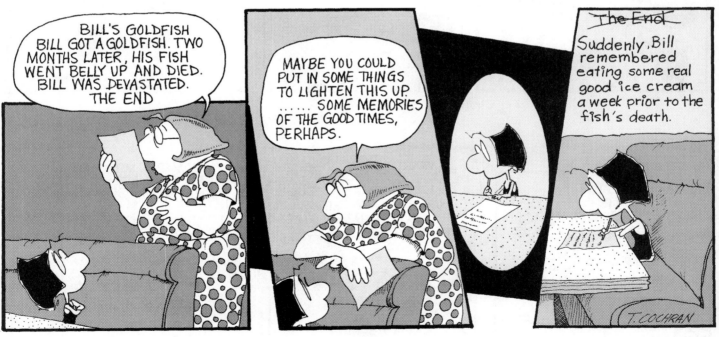

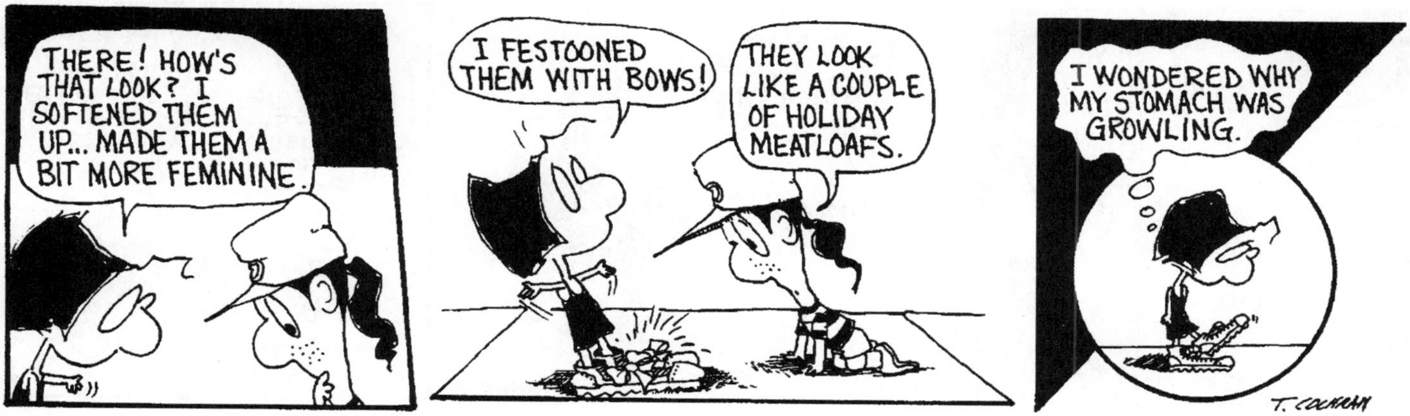
THERE! HOW'S THAT LOOK? I SOFTENED THEM UP... MADE THEM A BIT MORE FEMININE.
I FESTOONED THEM WITH BOWS!
THEY LOOK LIKE A COUPLE OF HOLIDAY MEATLOAFS.
I WONDERED WHY MY STOMACH WAS GROWLING.
T. COCHRAN

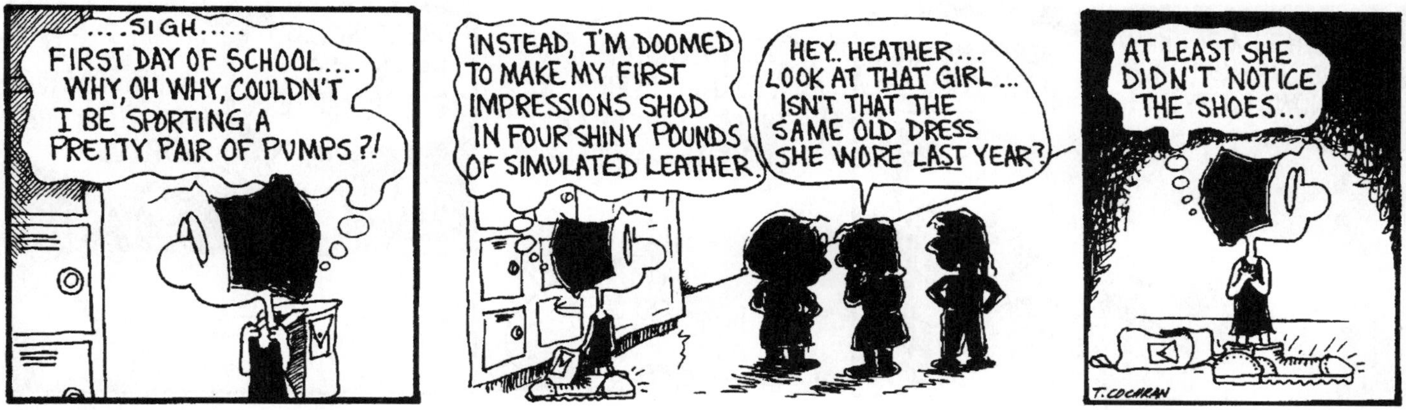
....SIGH.....
FIRST DAY OF SCHOOL.... WHY, OH WHY, COULDN'T I BE SPORTING A PRETTY PAIR OF PUMPS?!
INSTEAD, I'M DOOMED TO MAKE MY FIRST IMPRESSIONS SHOD IN FOUR SHINY POUNDS OF SIMULATED LEATHER.
HEY.. HEATHER... LOOK AT THAT GIRL... ISN'T THAT THE SAME OLD DRESS SHE WORE LAST YEAR?
AT LEAST SHE DIDN'T NOTICE THE SHOES...
T. COCHRAN

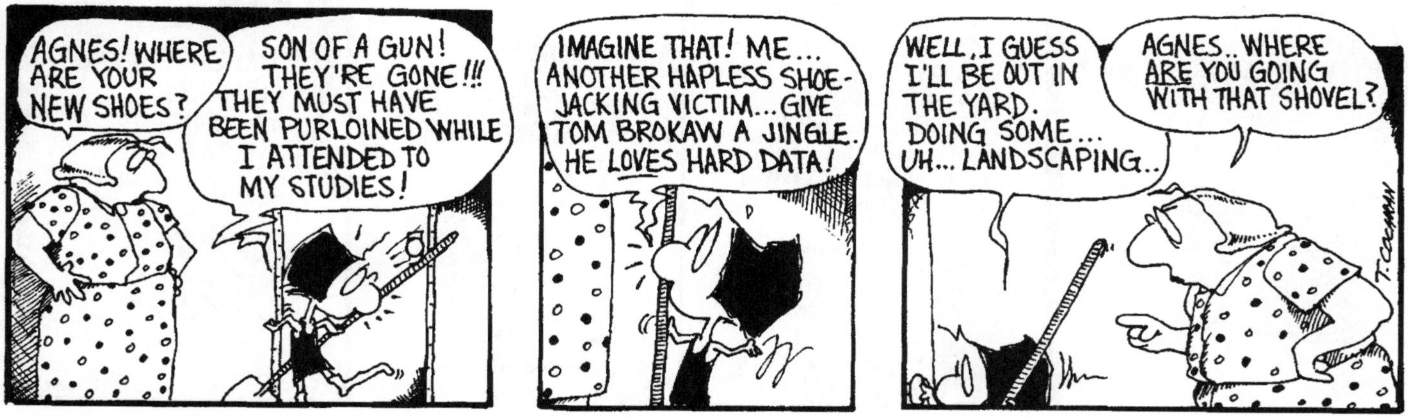
AGNES! WHERE ARE YOUR NEW SHOES?
SON OF A GUN! THEY'RE GONE!!! THEY MUST HAVE BEEN PURLOINED WHILE I ATTENDED TO MY STUDIES!
IMAGINE THAT! ME... ANOTHER HAPLESS SHOE-JACKING VICTIM... GIVE TOM BROKAW A JINGLE. HE LOVES HARD DATA!
WELL, I GUESS I'LL BE OUT IN THE YARD. DOING SOME... UH... LANDSCAPING..
AGNES.. WHERE ARE YOU GOING WITH THAT SHOVEL?
T. COCHRAN

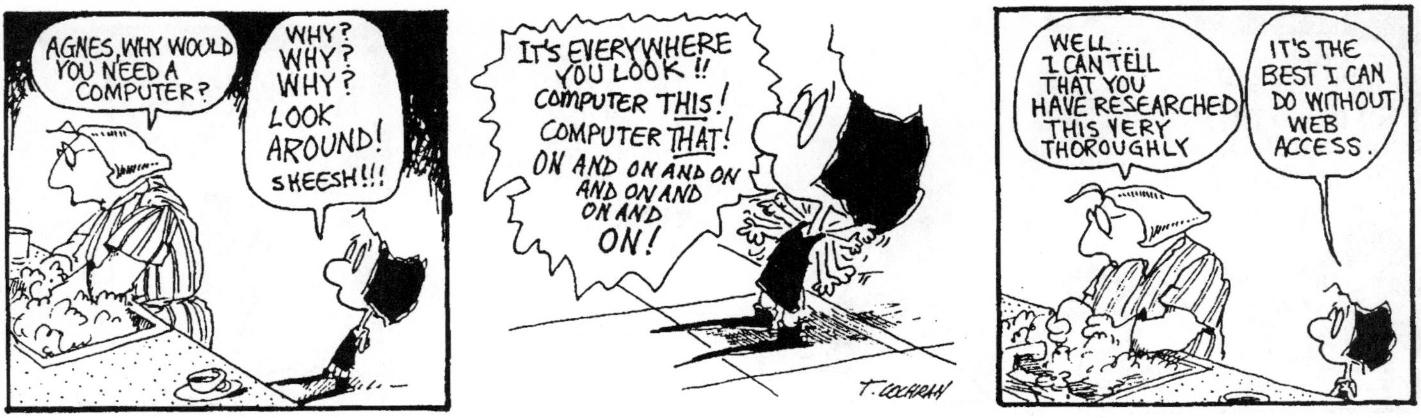
AGNES, WHY WOULD YOU NEED A COMPUTER?
WHY? WHY? WHY? LOOK AROUND! SHEESH!!!
IT'S EVERYWHERE YOU LOOK!! COMPUTER THIS! COMPUTER THAT! ON AND ON AND ON AND ON AND ON AND ON!
T. COCHRAN
WELL... I CAN TELL THAT YOU HAVE RESEARCHED THIS VERY THOROUGHLY
IT'S THE BEST I CAN DO WITHOUT WEB ACCESS.

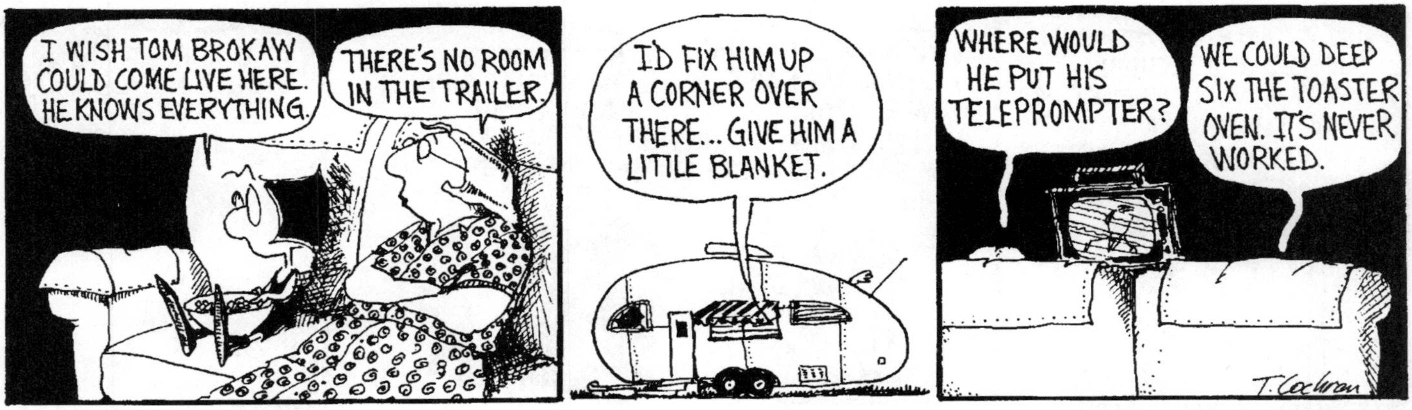
I WISH TOM BROKAW COULD COME LIVE HERE. HE KNOWS EVERYTHING.
THERE'S NO ROOM IN THE TRAILER.
I'D FIX HIM UP A CORNER OVER THERE... GIVE HIM A LITTLE BLANKET.
WHERE WOULD HE PUT HIS TELEPROMPTER?
WE COULD DEEP SIX THE TOASTER OVEN. IT'S NEVER WORKED.
T. Cochran

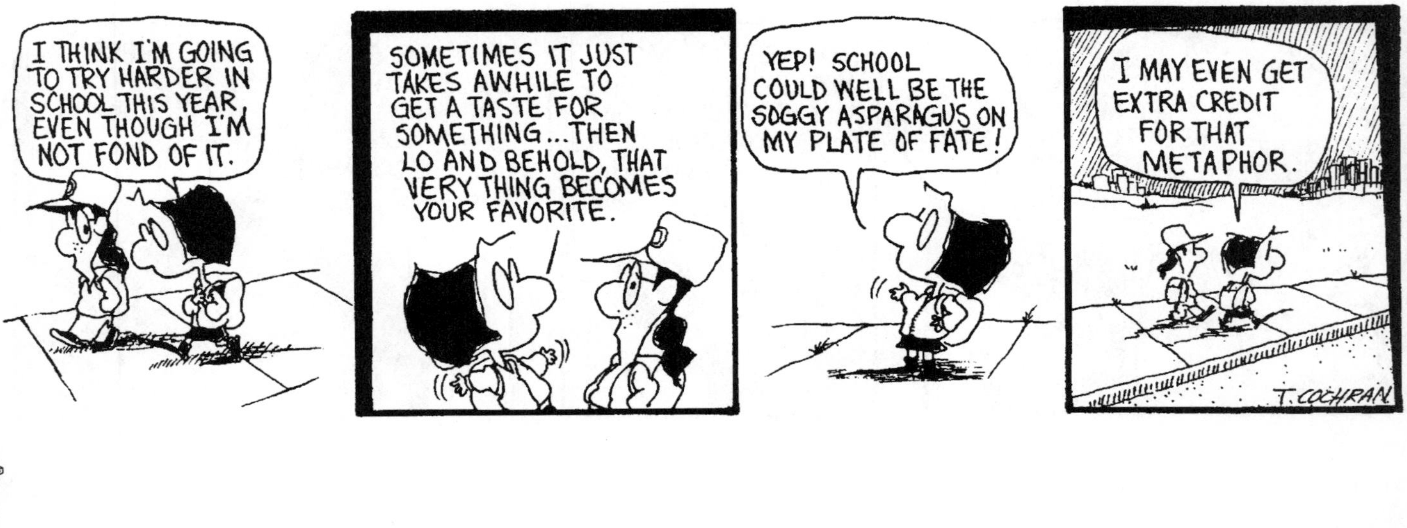
I THINK I'M GOING TO TRY HARDER IN SCHOOL THIS YEAR, EVEN THOUGH I'M NOT FOND OF IT.
SOMETIMES IT JUST TAKES AWHILE TO GET A TASTE FOR SOMETHING... THEN LO AND BEHOLD, THAT VERY THING BECOMES YOUR FAVORITE.
YEP! SCHOOL COULD WELL BE THE SOGGY ASPARAGUS ON MY PLATE OF FATE!
I MAY EVEN GET EXTRA CREDIT FOR THAT METAPHOR.
T. COCHRAN

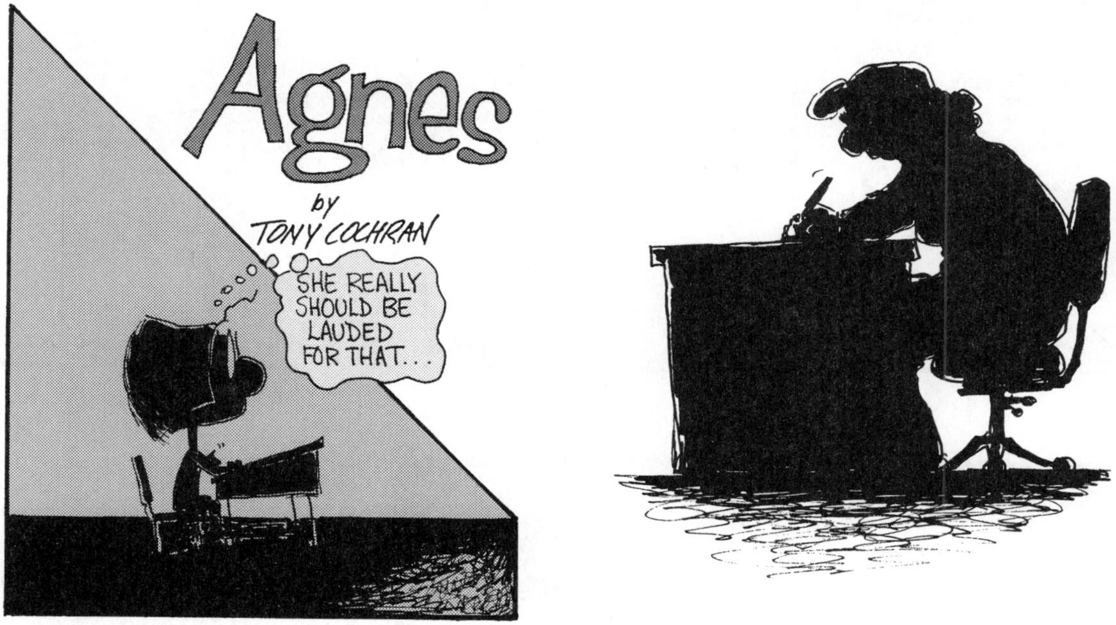
Agnes
by TONY COCHRAN
SHE REALLY SHOULD BE LAUDED FOR THAT...

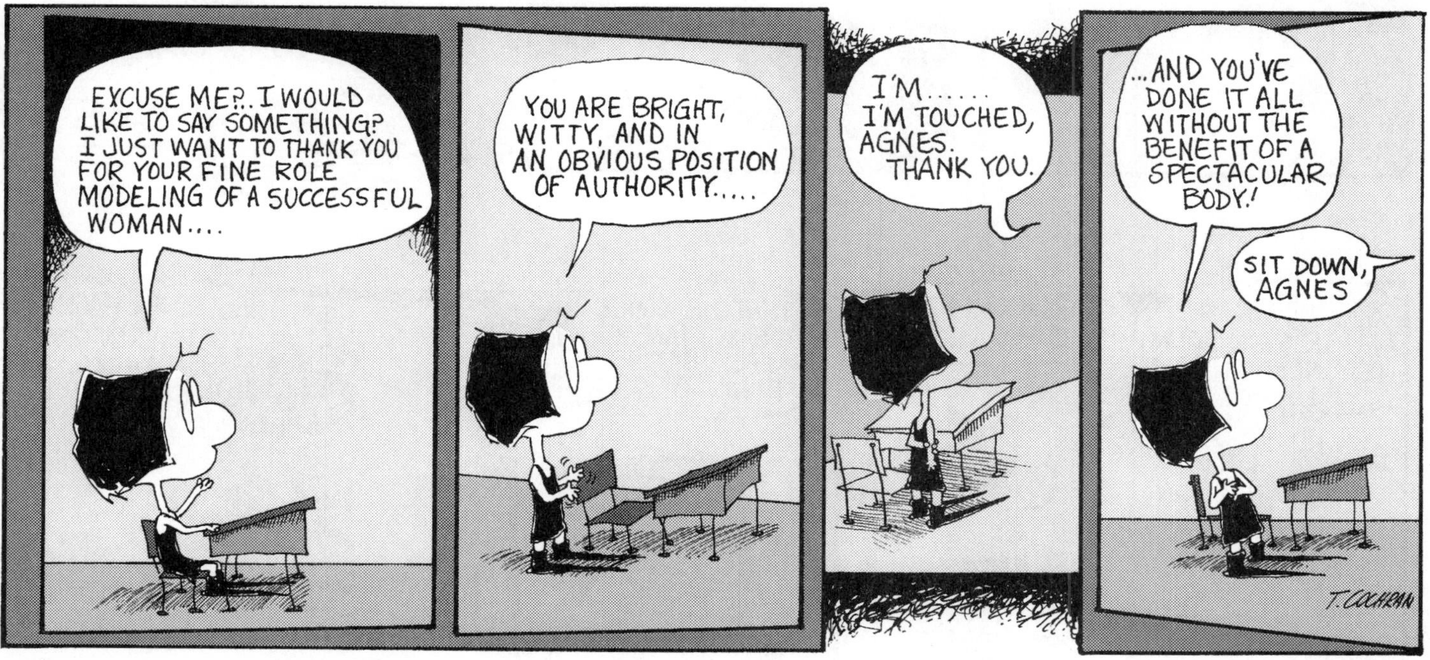
EXCUSE ME?.. I WOULD LIKE TO SAY SOMETHING? I JUST WANT TO THANK YOU FOR YOUR FINE ROLE MODELING OF A SUCCESSFUL WOMAN....
YOU ARE BRIGHT, WITTY, AND IN AN OBVIOUS POSITION OF AUTHORITY.....
I'M...... I'M TOUCHED, AGNES. THANK YOU.
...AND YOU'VE DONE IT ALL WITHOUT THE BENEFIT OF A SPECTACULAR BODY!
SIT DOWN, AGNES
T. COCHRAN

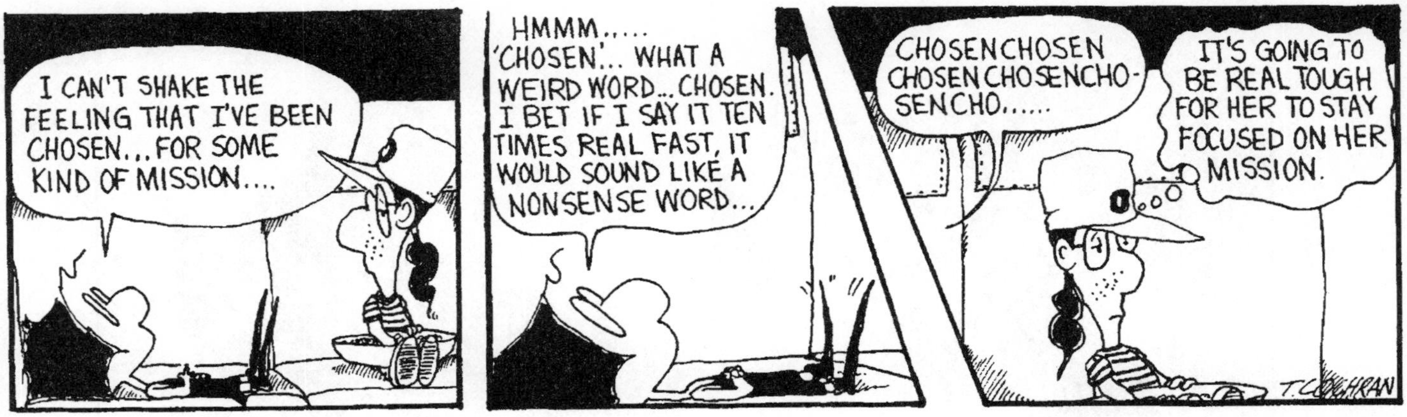
I CAN'T SHAKE THE FEELING THAT I'VE BEEN CHOSEN... FOR SOME KIND OF MISSION....
HMMM..... 'CHOSEN'... WHAT A WEIRD WORD... CHOSEN. I BET IF I SAY IT TEN TIMES REAL FAST, IT WOULD SOUND LIKE A NONSENSE WORD...
CHOSENCHOSEN CHOSENCHOSENCHO-SENCHO......
IT'S GOING TO BE REAL TOUGH FOR HER TO STAY FOCUSED ON HER MISSION.
T. COCHRAN

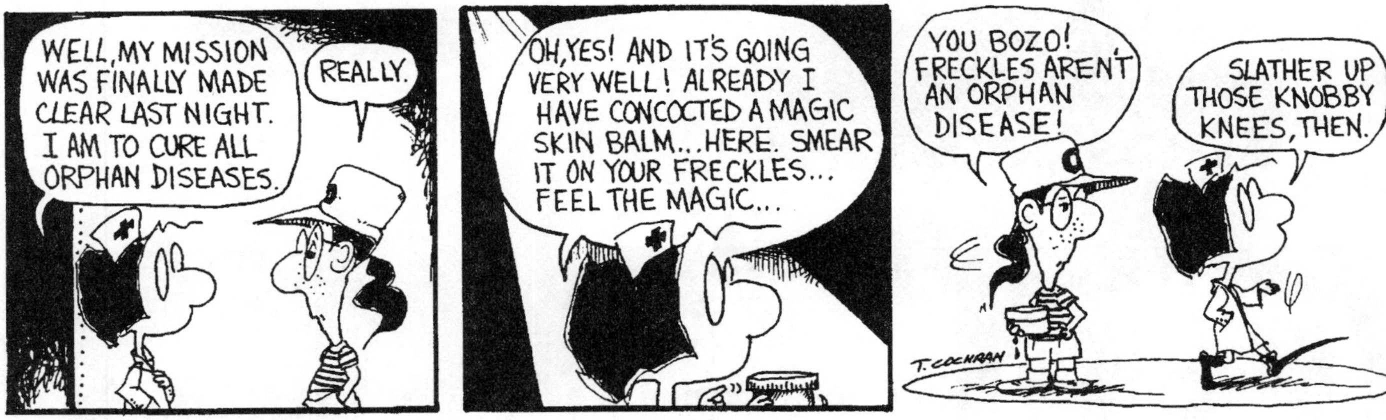
WELL, MY MISSION WAS FINALLY MADE CLEAR LAST NIGHT. I AM TO CURE ALL ORPHAN DISEASES.
REALLY.
OH, YES! AND IT'S GOING VERY WELL! ALREADY I HAVE CONCOCTED A MAGIC SKIN BALM... HERE. SMEAR IT ON YOUR FRECKLES... FEEL THE MAGIC...
YOU BOZO! FRECKLES AREN'T AN ORPHAN DISEASE!
SLATHER UP THOSE KNOBBY KNEES, THEN.
T. COCHRAN

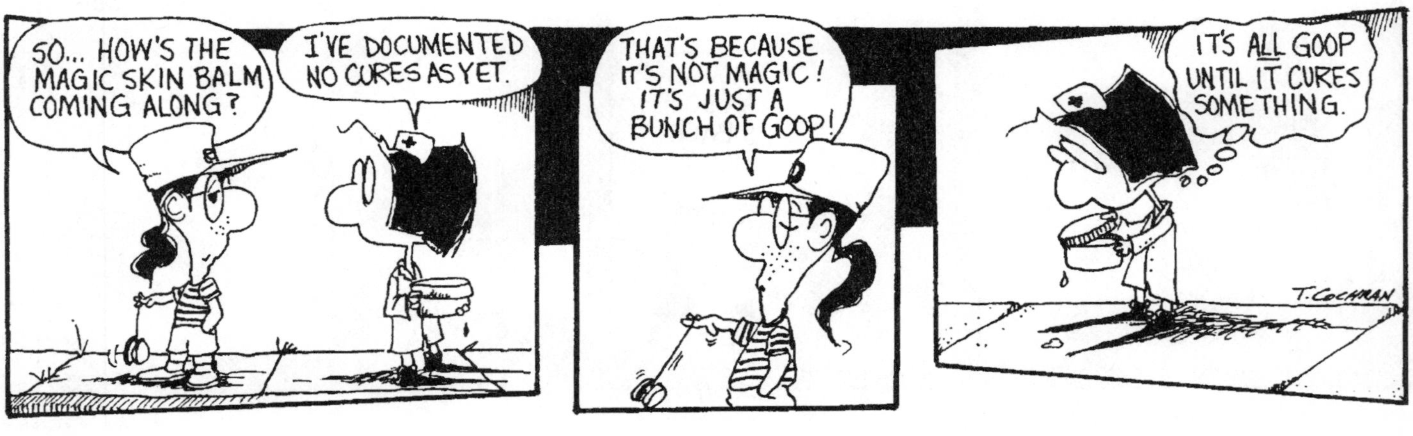
SO... HOW'S THE MAGIC SKIN BALM COMING ALONG?
I'VE DOCUMENTED NO CURES AS YET.
THAT'S BECAUSE IT'S NOT MAGIC! IT'S JUST A BUNCH OF GOOP!
IT'S ALL GOOP UNTIL IT CURES SOMETHING.
T. COCHRAN

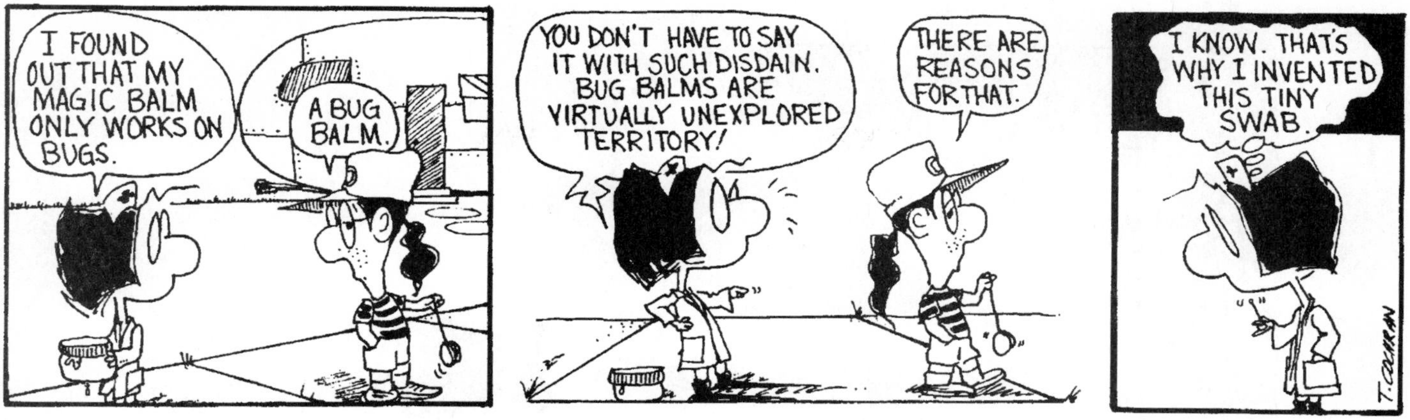
I FOUND OUT THAT MY MAGIC BALM ONLY WORKS ON BUGS.
A BUG BALM.
YOU DON'T HAVE TO SAY IT WITH SUCH DISDAIN. BUG BALMS ARE VIRTUALLY UNEXPLORED TERRITORY!
THERE ARE REASONS FOR THAT.
I KNOW. THAT'S WHY I INVENTED THIS TINY SWAB.
T. COCHRAN

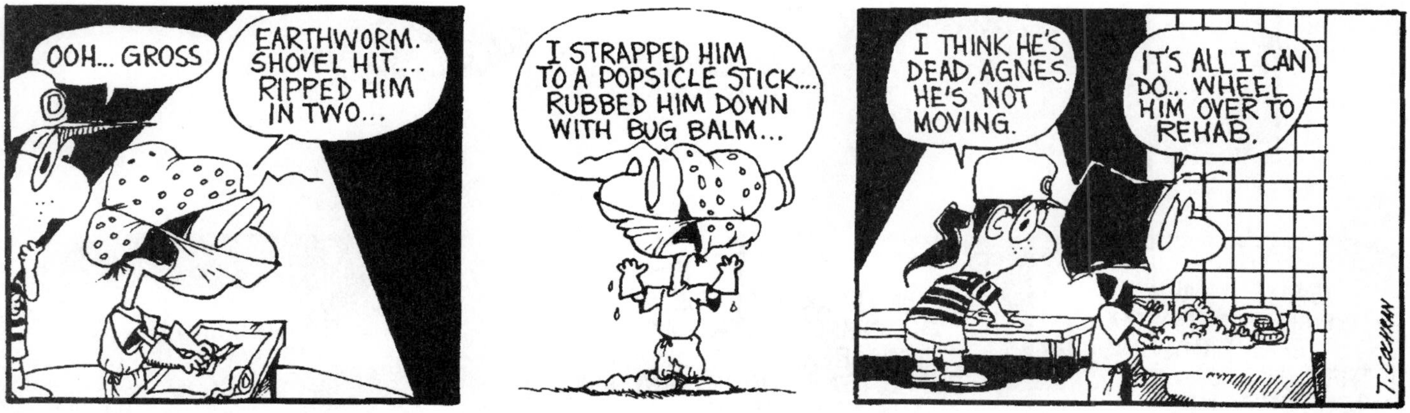
OOH... GROSS
EARTHWORM. SHOVEL HIT.... RIPPED HIM IN TWO...
I STRAPPED HIM TO A POPSICLE STICK... RUBBED HIM DOWN WITH BUG BALM...
I THINK HE'S DEAD, AGNES. HE'S NOT MOVING.
IT'S ALL I CAN DO... WHEEL HIM OVER TO REHAB.
T. COCHRAN

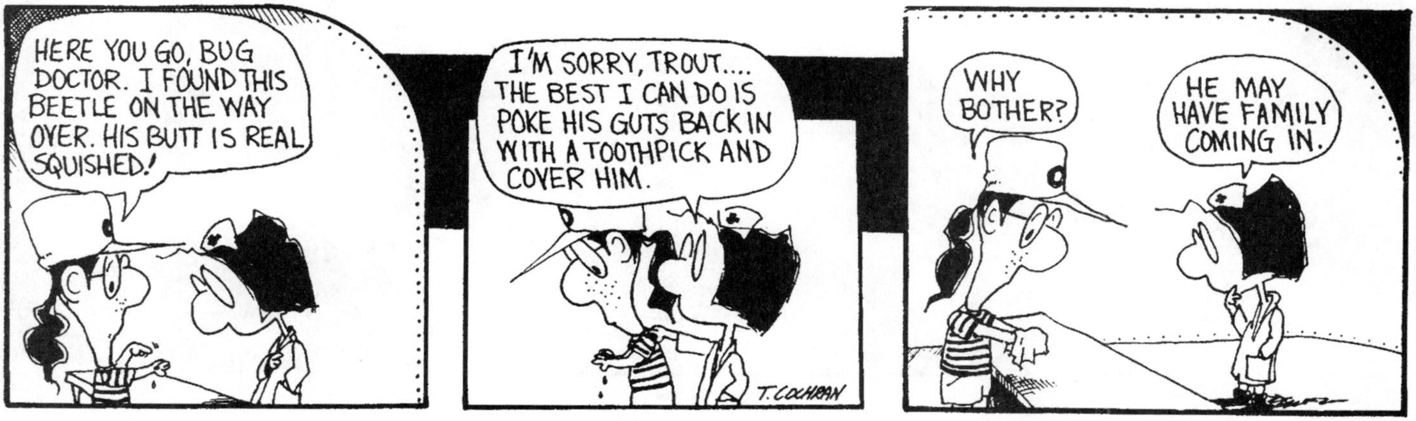
HERE YOU GO, BUG DOCTOR. I FOUND THIS BEETLE ON THE WAY OVER. HIS BUTT IS REAL SQUISHED!
I'M SORRY, TROUT.... THE BEST I CAN DO IS POKE HIS GUTS BACK IN WITH A TOOTHPICK AND COVER HIM.
T. COCHRAN
WHY BOTHER?
HE MAY HAVE FAMILY COMING IN.

Agnes

by TONY COCHRAN

HEAR YE, HEAR YE! WE ARE BUT TINY DUCKS, ... MERELY BOBBING ON THE ...UM.. SURFACE TENSION OF LIFE......

UH.. WE THANK THEE FOR THE CHANCE TO POKE OUR LITTLE BEAKS THROUGH THE FLOTSAM AND JETSAM OF THIS STINKY RIVER .... SEEKING SUSTENANCE, ... AMEN.

THAT WAS SAYING GRACE?

GOOD ENOUGH FOR BOILED HOT DOGS.

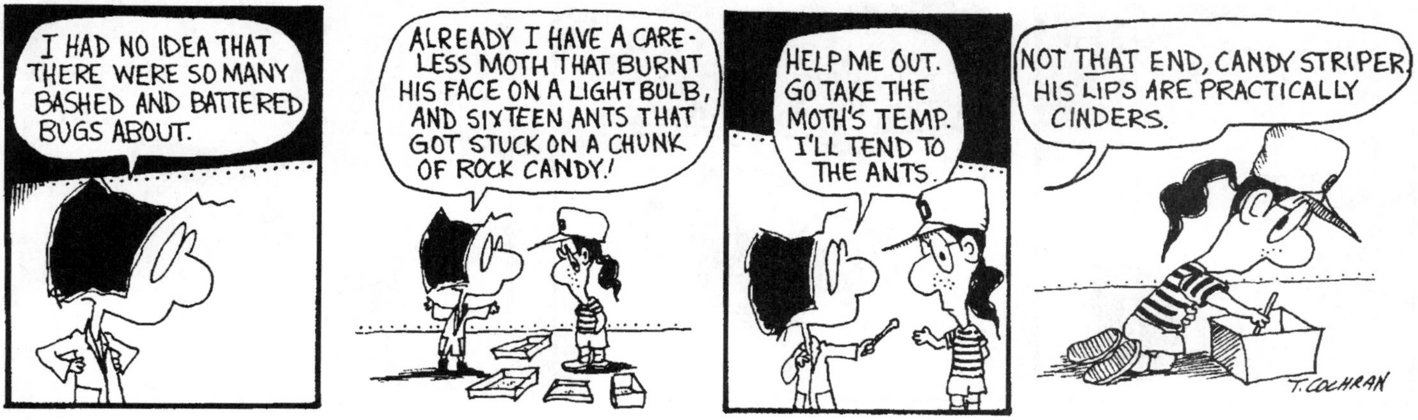
I HAD NO IDEA THAT THERE WERE SO MANY BASHED AND BATTERED BUGS ABOUT.
ALREADY I HAVE A CARELESS MOTH THAT BURNT HIS FACE ON A LIGHT BULB, AND SIXTEEN ANTS THAT GOT STUCK ON A CHUNK OF ROCK CANDY!
HELP ME OUT. GO TAKE THE MOTH'S TEMP. I'LL TEND TO THE ANTS.
NOT THAT END, CANDY STRIPER. HIS LIPS ARE PRACTICALLY CINDERS.
T. COCHRAN

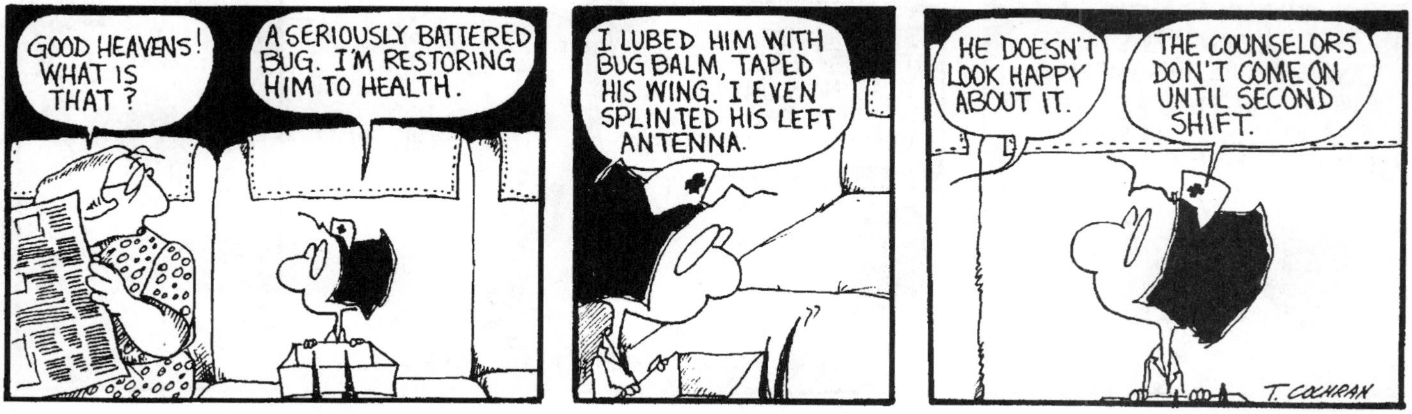
GOOD HEAVENS! WHAT IS THAT?
A SERIOUSLY BATTERED BUG. I'M RESTORING HIM TO HEALTH.
I LUBED HIM WITH BUG BALM, TAPED HIS WING. I EVEN SPLINTED HIS LEFT ANTENNA.
HE DOESN'T LOOK HAPPY ABOUT IT.
THE COUNSELORS DON'T COME ON UNTIL SECOND SHIFT.
T. COCHRAN

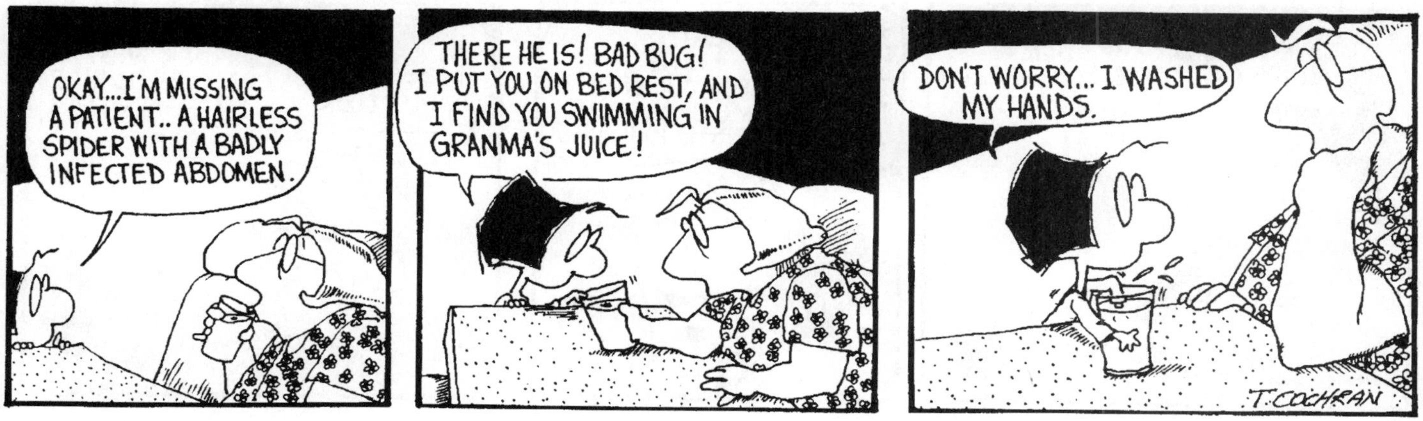
OKAY...I'M MISSING A PATIENT.. A HAIRLESS SPIDER WITH A BADLY INFECTED ABDOMEN.
THERE HE IS! BAD BUG! I PUT YOU ON BED REST, AND I FIND YOU SWIMMING IN GRANMA'S JUICE!
DON'T WORRY... I WASHED MY HANDS.
T. COCHRAN

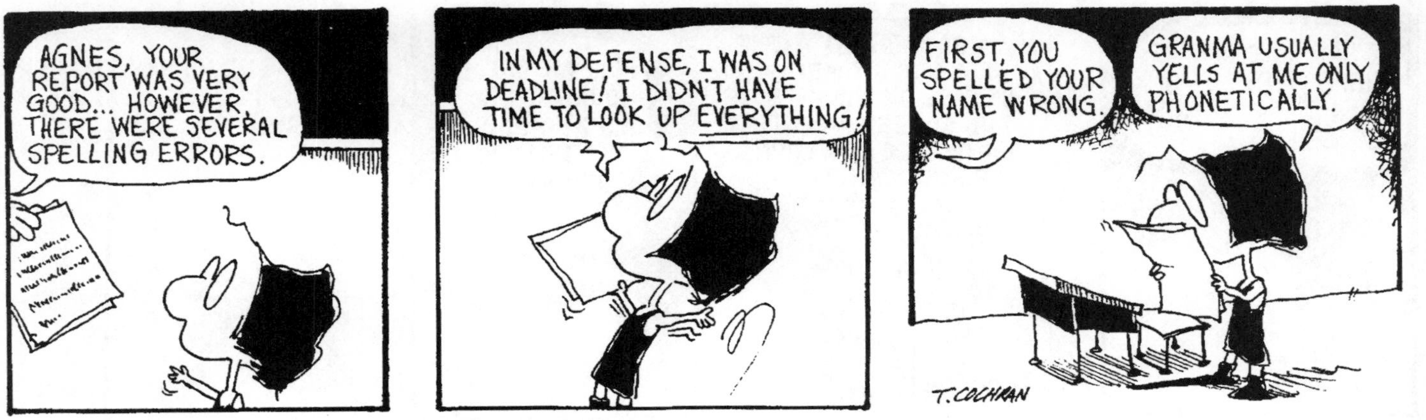
AGNES, YOUR REPORT WAS VERY GOOD... HOWEVER, THERE WERE SEVERAL SPELLING ERRORS.
IN MY DEFENSE, I WAS ON DEADLINE! I DIDN'T HAVE TIME TO LOOK UP EVERYTHING!
FIRST, YOU SPELLED YOUR NAME WRONG.
GRANMA USUALLY YELLS AT ME ONLY PHONETICALLY.
T. COCHRAN

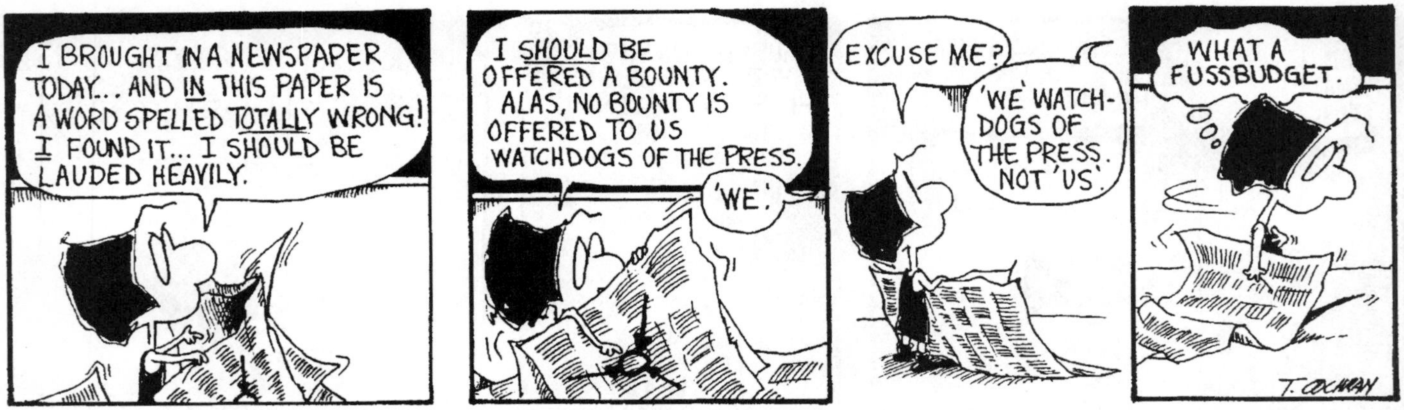
I BROUGHT IN A NEWSPAPER TODAY... AND IN THIS PAPER IS A WORD SPELLED TOTALLY WRONG! I FOUND IT... I SHOULD BE LAUDED HEAVILY.
I SHOULD BE OFFERED A BOUNTY. ALAS, NO BOUNTY IS OFFERED TO US WATCHDOGS OF THE PRESS.
'WE'.
EXCUSE ME?
'WE' WATCHDOGS OF THE PRESS. NOT 'US'.
WHAT A FUSSBUDGET.
T. COCHRAN

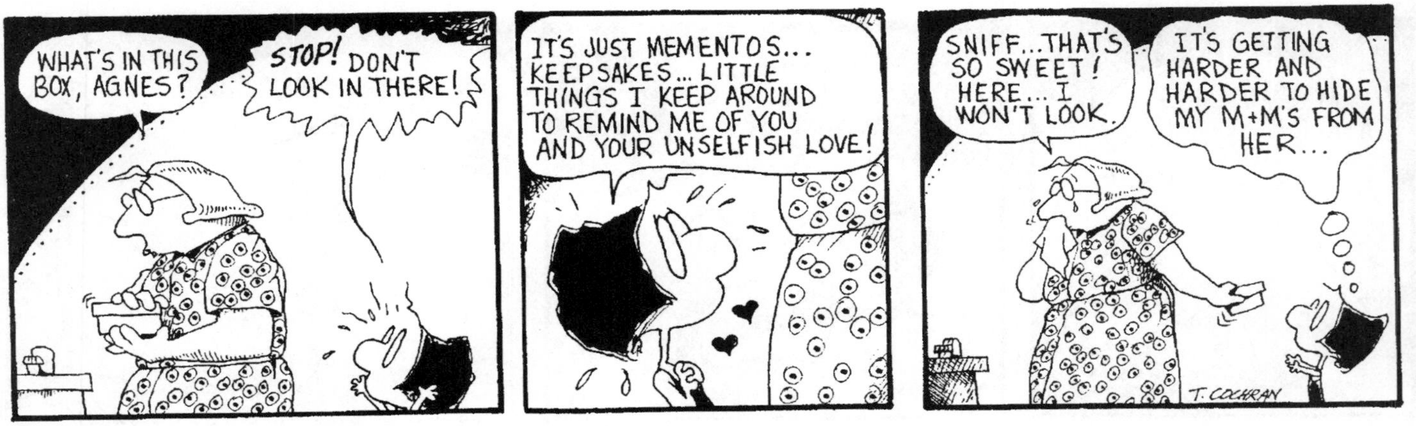
WHAT'S IN THIS BOX, AGNES?
STOP! DON'T LOOK IN THERE!
IT'S JUST MEMENTOS... KEEPSAKES... LITTLE THINGS I KEEP AROUND TO REMIND ME OF YOU AND YOUR UNSELFISH LOVE!
SNIFF...THAT'S SO SWEET! HERE... I WON'T LOOK.
IT'S GETTING HARDER AND HARDER TO HIDE MY M+M'S FROM HER...
T. COCHRAN

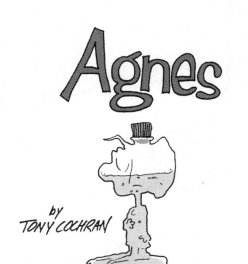

Agnes

by
TONY COCHRAN

SPLAPPITA! SPLIPPITA!

SPLAP!

SPLIP!

GRANMA, YOU ARE THE FIRST TO SNIFF A WHIFF OF MY NEW SIGNATURE COLOGNE.

TENTATIVELY LABELED 'AGNES PETALS', IT IS A DELIGHTFUL ELIXIR OF BLENDED FLORALS AND ORIENTAL SPICES... ENJOY...

SNIFF... YOU SMELL LIKE SPAGHETTI-O'S.

OKAY... YOU WERE RIGHT. OREGANO IS NOT ORIENTAL.

T. COCHRAN

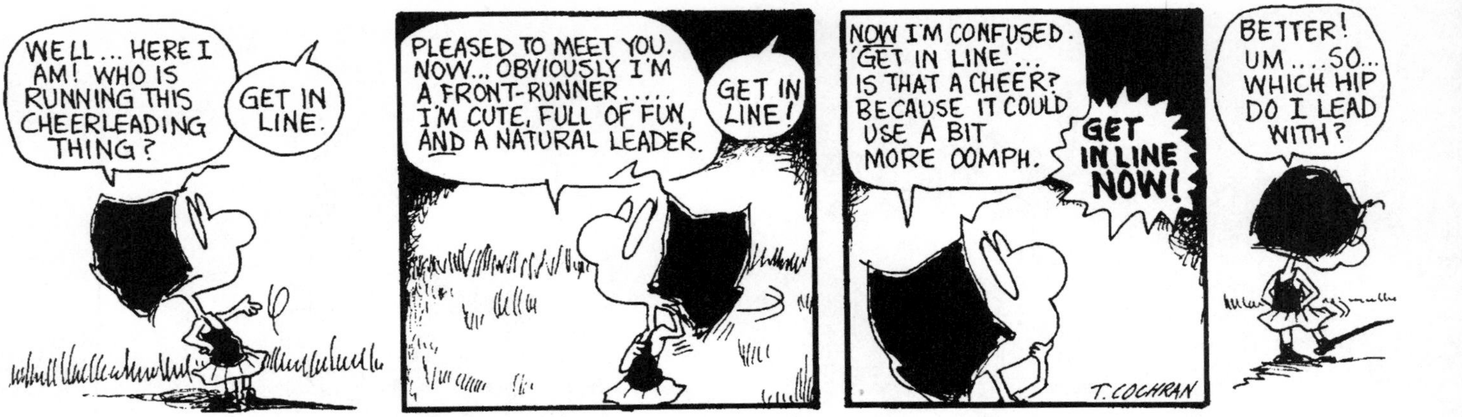
WELL... HERE I AM! WHO IS RUNNING THIS CHEERLEADING THING?
GET IN LINE.
PLEASED TO MEET YOU. NOW... OBVIOUSLY I'M A FRONT-RUNNER..... I'M CUTE, FULL OF FUN, AND A NATURAL LEADER.
GET IN LINE!
NOW I'M CONFUSED. 'GET IN LINE'... IS THAT A CHEER? BECAUSE IT COULD USE A BIT MORE OOMPH.
GET IN LINE NOW!
BETTER! UM....SO... WHICH HIP DO I LEAD WITH?
T. COCHRAN

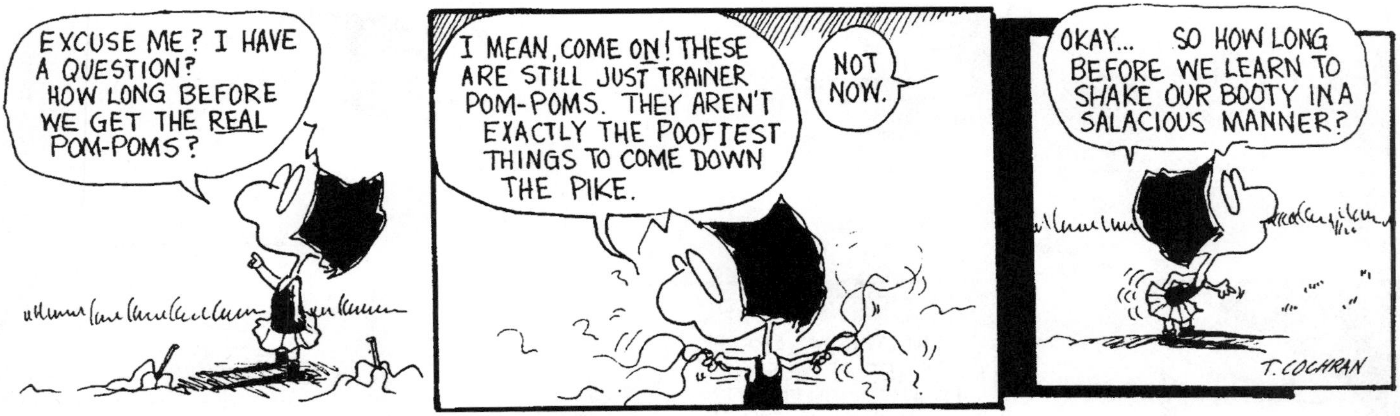
EXCUSE ME? I HAVE A QUESTION? HOW LONG BEFORE WE GET THE REAL POM-POMS?
I MEAN, COME ON! THESE ARE STILL JUST TRAINER POM-POMS. THEY AREN'T EXACTLY THE POOFIEST THINGS TO COME DOWN THE PIKE.
NOT NOW.
OKAY... SO HOW LONG BEFORE WE LEARN TO SHAKE OUR BOOTY IN A SALACIOUS MANNER?
T. COCHRAN

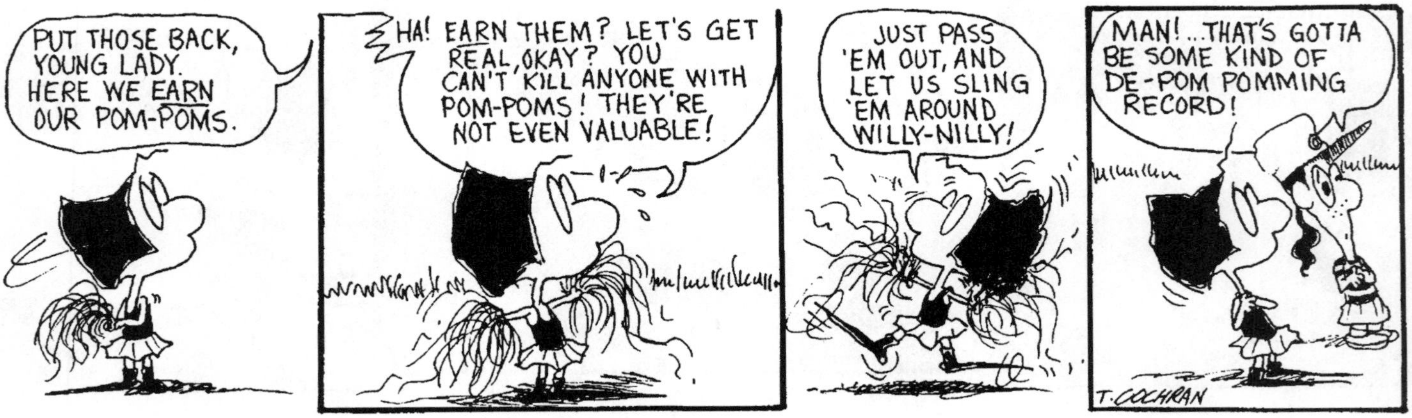
PUT THOSE BACK, YOUNG LADY. HERE WE EARN OUR POM-POMS.
HA! EARN THEM? LET'S GET REAL, OKAY? YOU CAN'T KILL ANYONE WITH POM-POMS! THEY'RE NOT EVEN VALUABLE!
JUST PASS 'EM OUT, AND LET US SLING 'EM AROUND WILLY-NILLY!
MAN! ...THAT'S GOTTA BE SOME KIND OF DE-POM POMMING RECORD!
T. COCHRAN

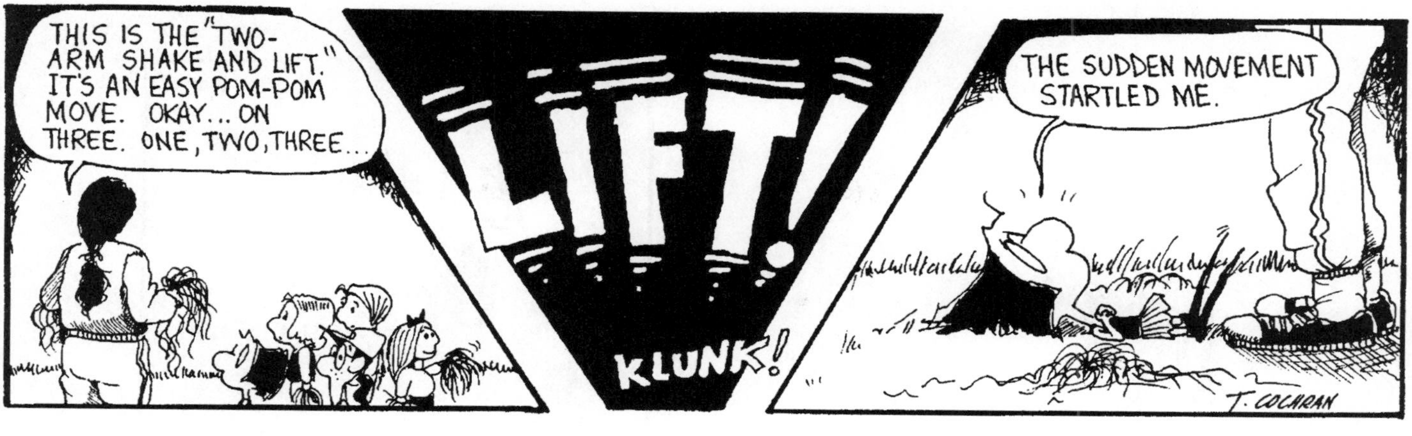
THIS IS THE "TWO-ARM SHAKE AND LIFT." IT'S AN EASY POM-POM MOVE. OKAY... ON THREE. ONE, TWO, THREE...
LIFT!
KLUNK!
THE SUDDEN MOVEMENT STARTLED ME.
T. COCHRAN

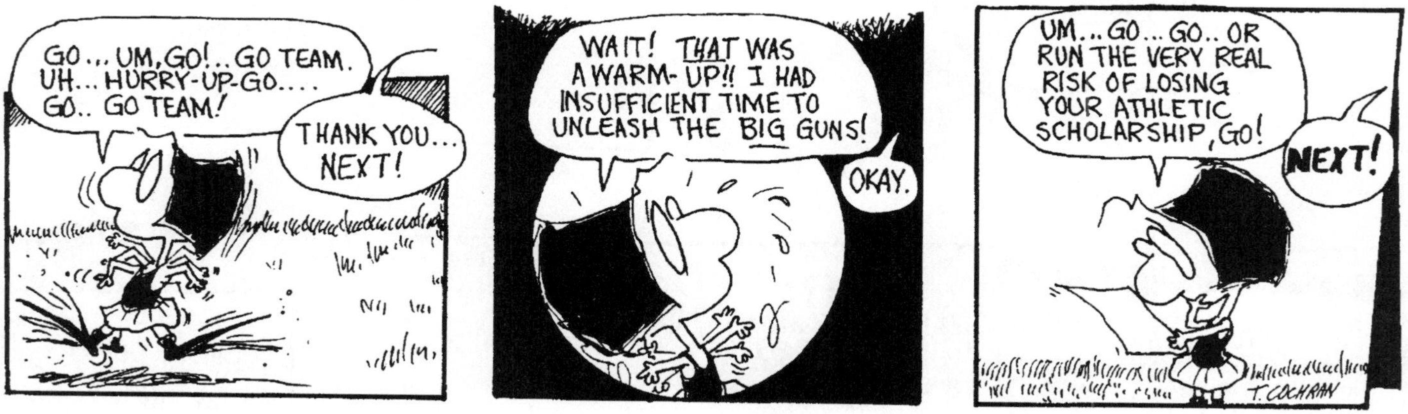
GO... UM, GO!... GO TEAM. UH... HURRY-UP-GO.... GO.. GO TEAM!
THANK YOU... NEXT!
WAIT! THAT WAS A WARM-UP!! I HAD INSUFFICIENT TIME TO UNLEASH THE BIG GUNS!
OKAY.
UM... GO... GO.. OR RUN THE VERY REAL RISK OF LOSING YOUR ATHLETIC SCHOLARSHIP, GO!
NEXT!
T. COCHRAN

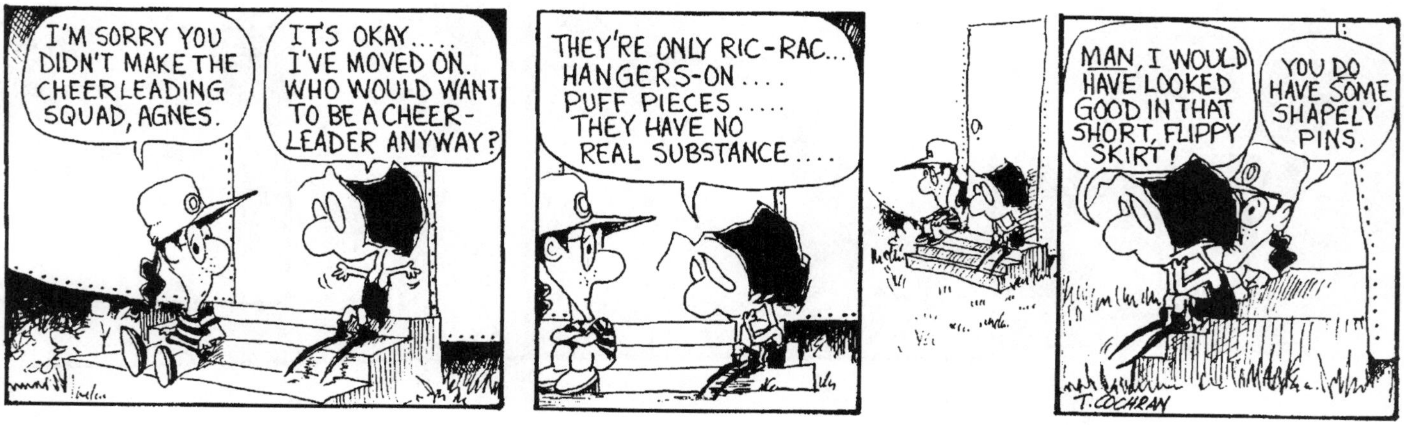
I'M SORRY YOU DIDN'T MAKE THE CHEERLEADING SQUAD, AGNES.
IT'S OKAY..... I'VE MOVED ON. WHO WOULD WANT TO BE A CHEER-LEADER ANYWAY?
THEY'RE ONLY RIC-RAC... HANGERS-ON.... PUFF PIECES..... THEY HAVE NO REAL SUBSTANCE....
MAN, I WOULD HAVE LOOKED GOOD IN THAT SHORT, FLIPPY SKIRT!
YOU DO HAVE SOME SHAPELY PINS.
T. COCHRAN

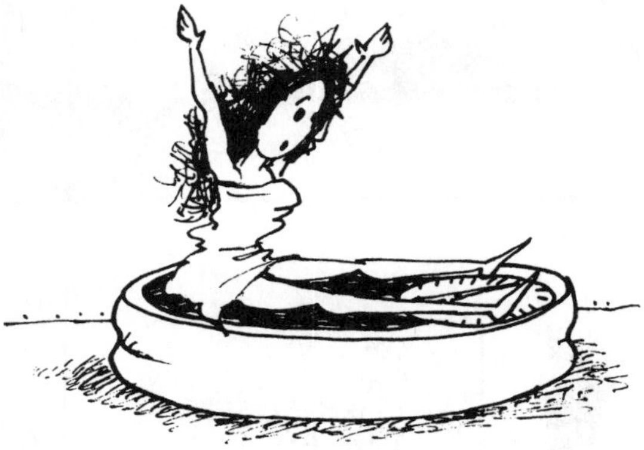

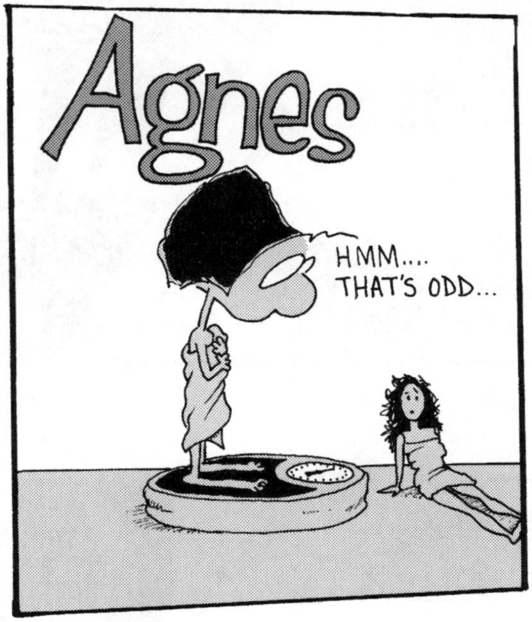
Agnes
HMM....
THAT'S ODD...

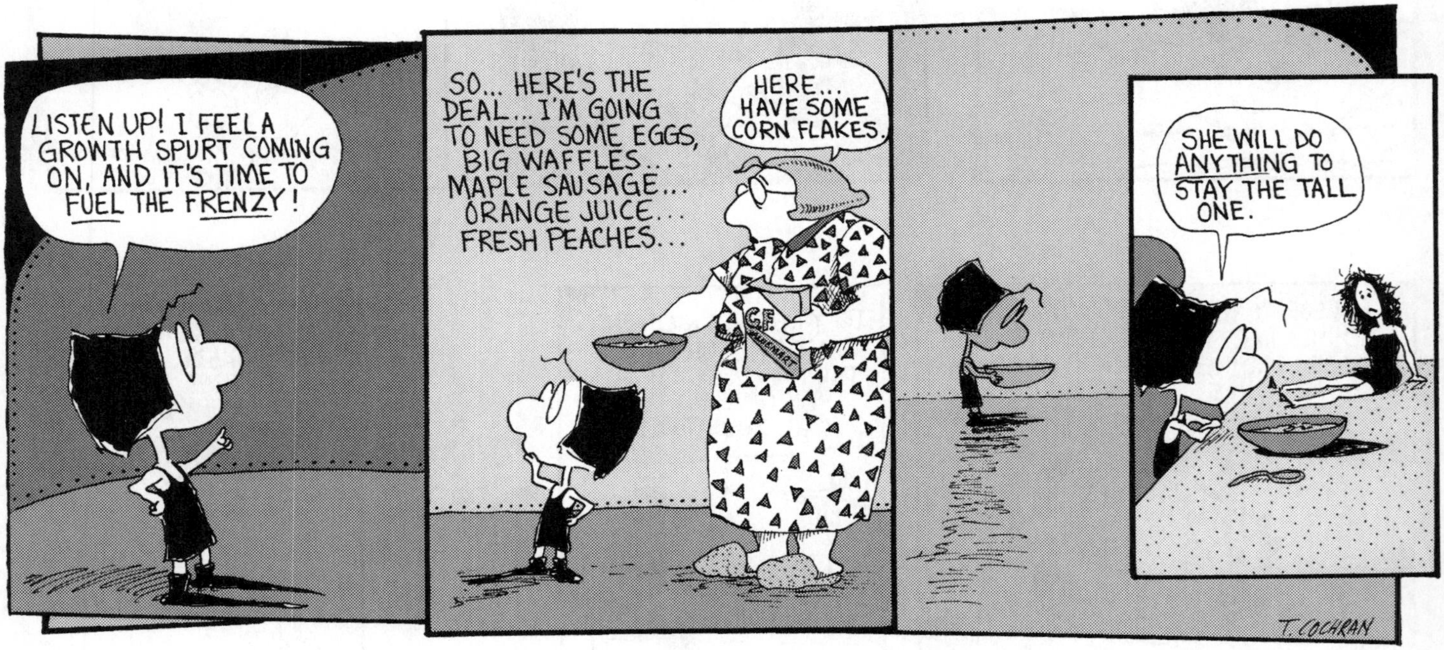
LISTEN UP! I FEEL A GROWTH SPURT COMING ON, AND IT'S TIME TO FUEL THE FRENZY!
SO... HERE'S THE DEAL... I'M GOING TO NEED SOME EGGS, BIG WAFFLES... MAPLE SAUSAGE... ORANGE JUICE... FRESH PEACHES...
HERE... HAVE SOME CORN FLAKES.
C.F.
SHE WILL DO ANYTHING TO STAY THE TALL ONE.
T. COCHRAN

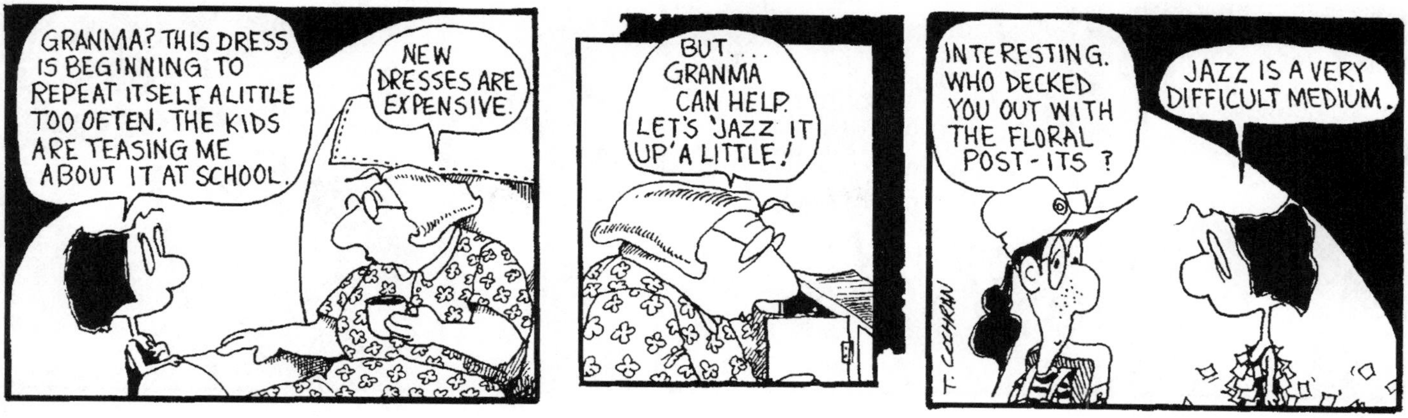
GRANMA? THIS DRESS IS BEGINNING TO REPEAT ITSELF A LITTLE TOO OFTEN. THE KIDS ARE TEASING ME ABOUT IT AT SCHOOL.
NEW DRESSES ARE EXPENSIVE.
BUT.... GRANMA CAN HELP. LET'S 'JAZZ' IT UP' A LITTLE!
INTERESTING. WHO DECKED YOU OUT WITH THE FLORAL POST-ITS ?
JAZZ IS A VERY DIFFICULT MEDIUM.
T. COCHRAN

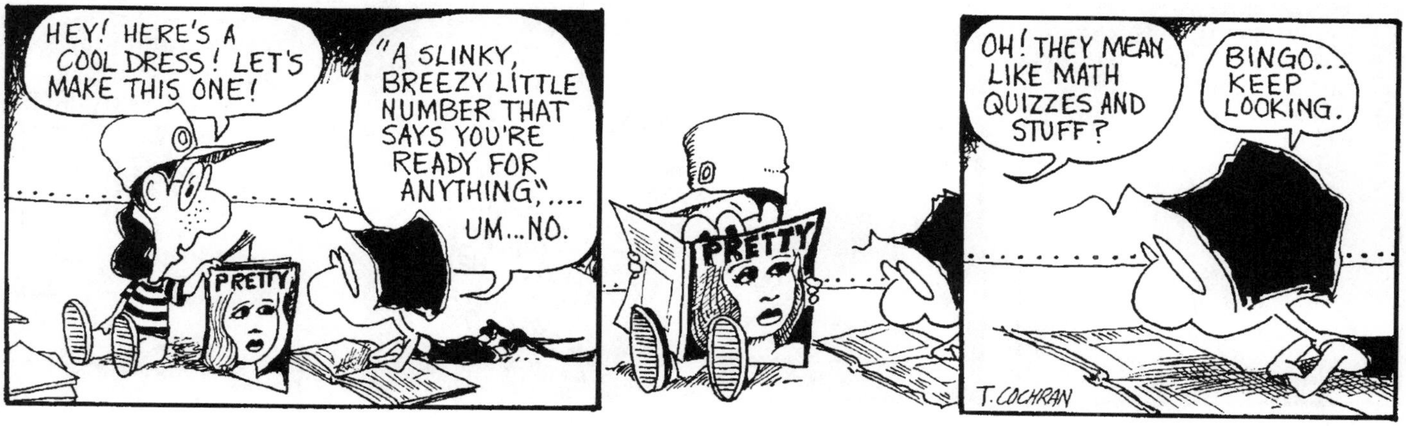
HEY! HERE'S A COOL DRESS! LET'S MAKE THIS ONE!
"A SLINKY, BREEZY LITTLE NUMBER THAT SAYS YOU'RE READY FOR ANYTHING,".... UM...NO.
PRETTY
PRETTY
OH! THEY MEAN LIKE MATH QUIZZES AND STUFF?
BINGO... KEEP LOOKING.
T. COCHRAN

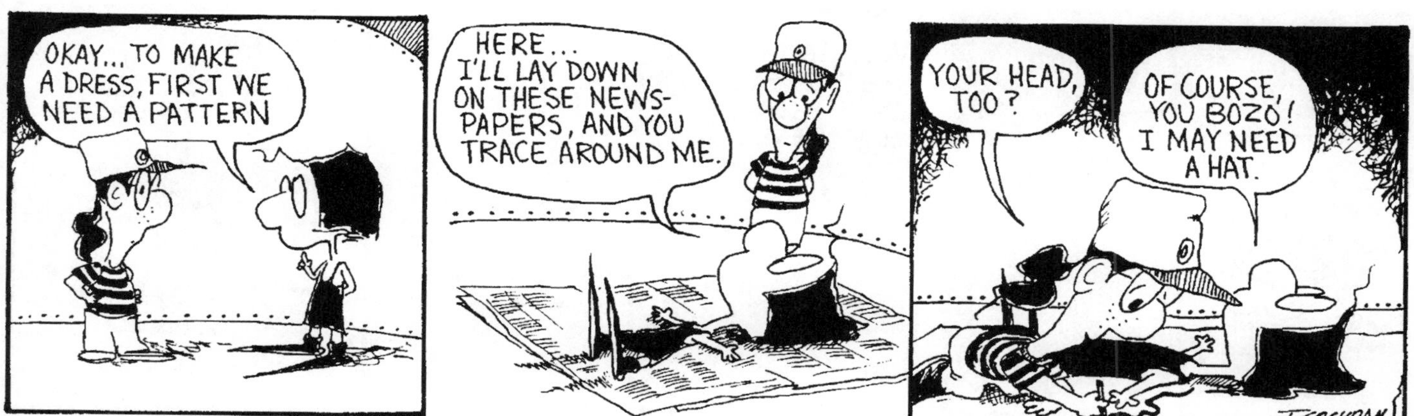
OKAY... TO MAKE A DRESS, FIRST WE NEED A PATTERN
HERE... I'LL LAY DOWN ON THESE NEWS-PAPERS, AND YOU TRACE AROUND ME.
YOUR HEAD, TOO?
OF COURSE, YOU BOZO! I MAY NEED A HAT.
T. COCHRAN

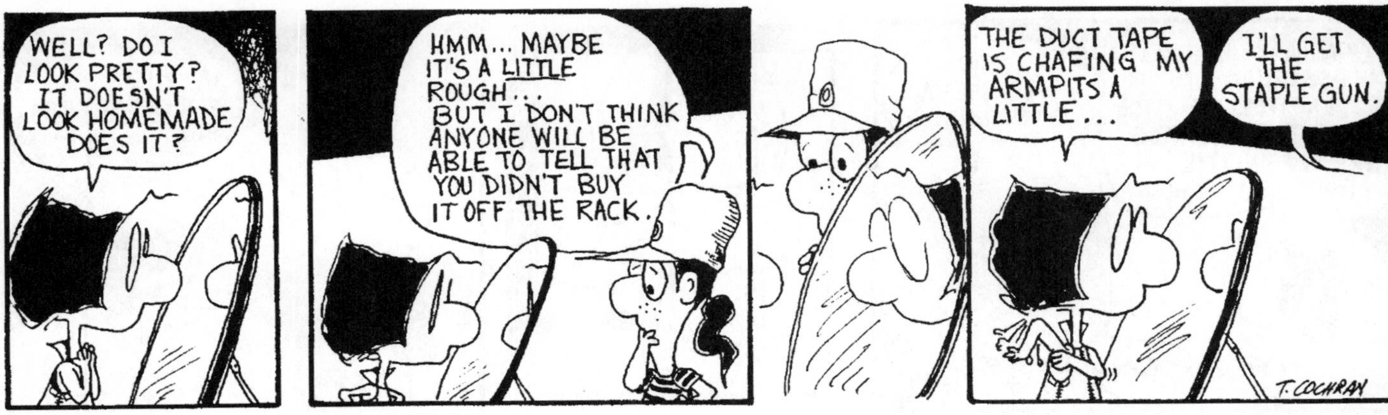
WELL? DO I LOOK PRETTY? IT DOESN'T LOOK HOMEMADE DOES IT?
HMM... MAYBE IT'S A LITTLE ROUGH... BUT I DON'T THINK ANYONE WILL BE ABLE TO TELL THAT YOU DIDN'T BUY IT OFF THE RACK.
THE DUCT TAPE IS CHAFING MY ARMPITS A LITTLE...
I'LL GET THE STAPLE GUN.
T. COCHRAN

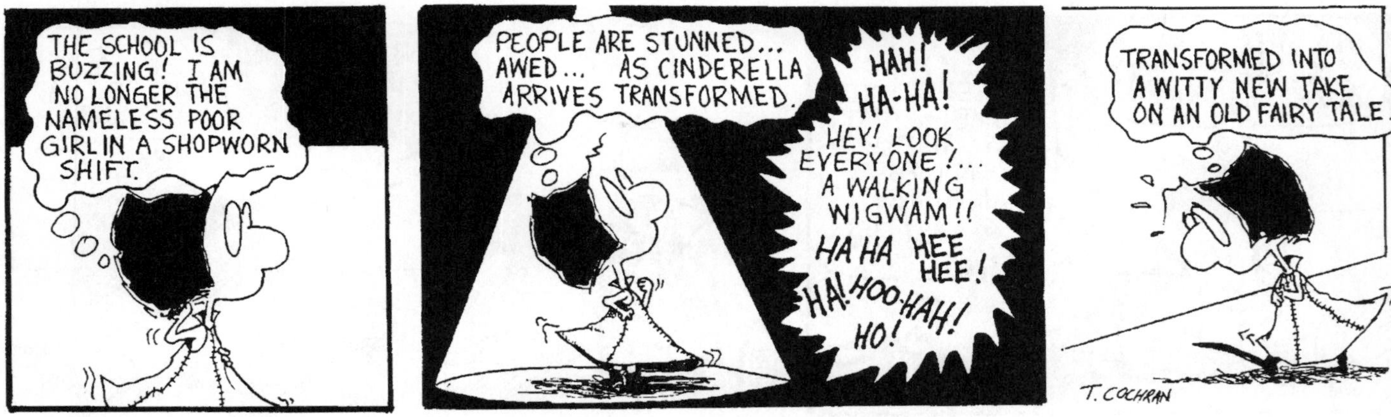
THE SCHOOL IS BUZZING! I AM NO LONGER THE NAMELESS POOR GIRL IN A SHOPWORN SHIFT.
PEOPLE ARE STUNNED... AWED... AS CINDERELLA ARRIVES TRANSFORMED.
HAH! HA-HA! HEY! LOOK EVERYONE!... A WALKING WIGWAM!! HA HA HEE HEE! HA! HOO-HAH! HO!
TRANSFORMED INTO A WITTY NEW TAKE ON AN OLD FAIRY TALE.
T. COCHRAN

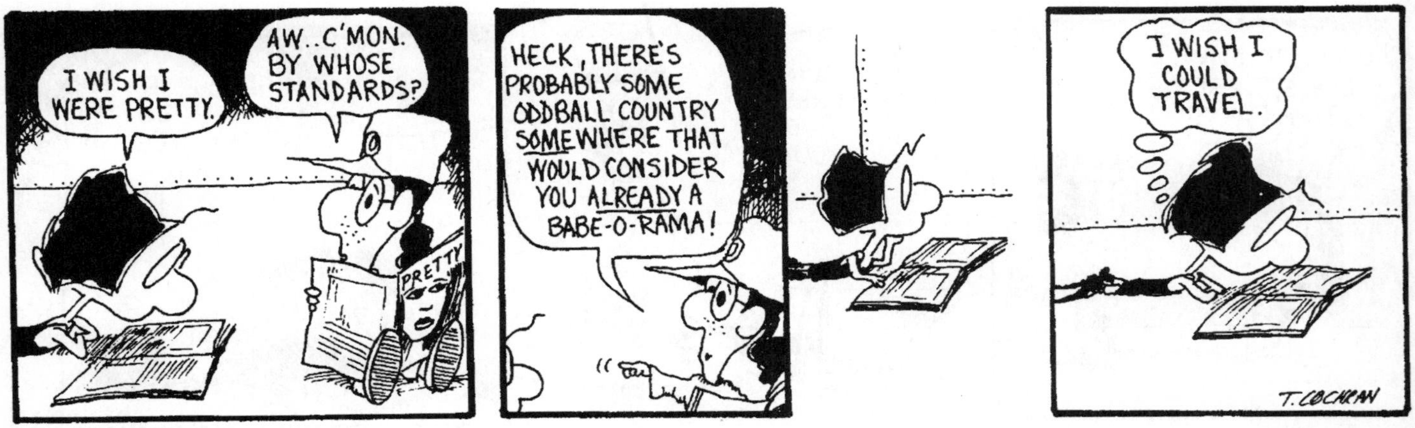
I WISH I WERE PRETTY.
AW.. C'MON. BY WHOSE STANDARDS?
PRETTY
HECK, THERE'S PROBABLY SOME ODDBALL COUNTRY SOMEWHERE THAT WOULD CONSIDER YOU ALREADY A BABE-O-RAMA!
I WISH I COULD TRAVEL.
T. COCHRAN

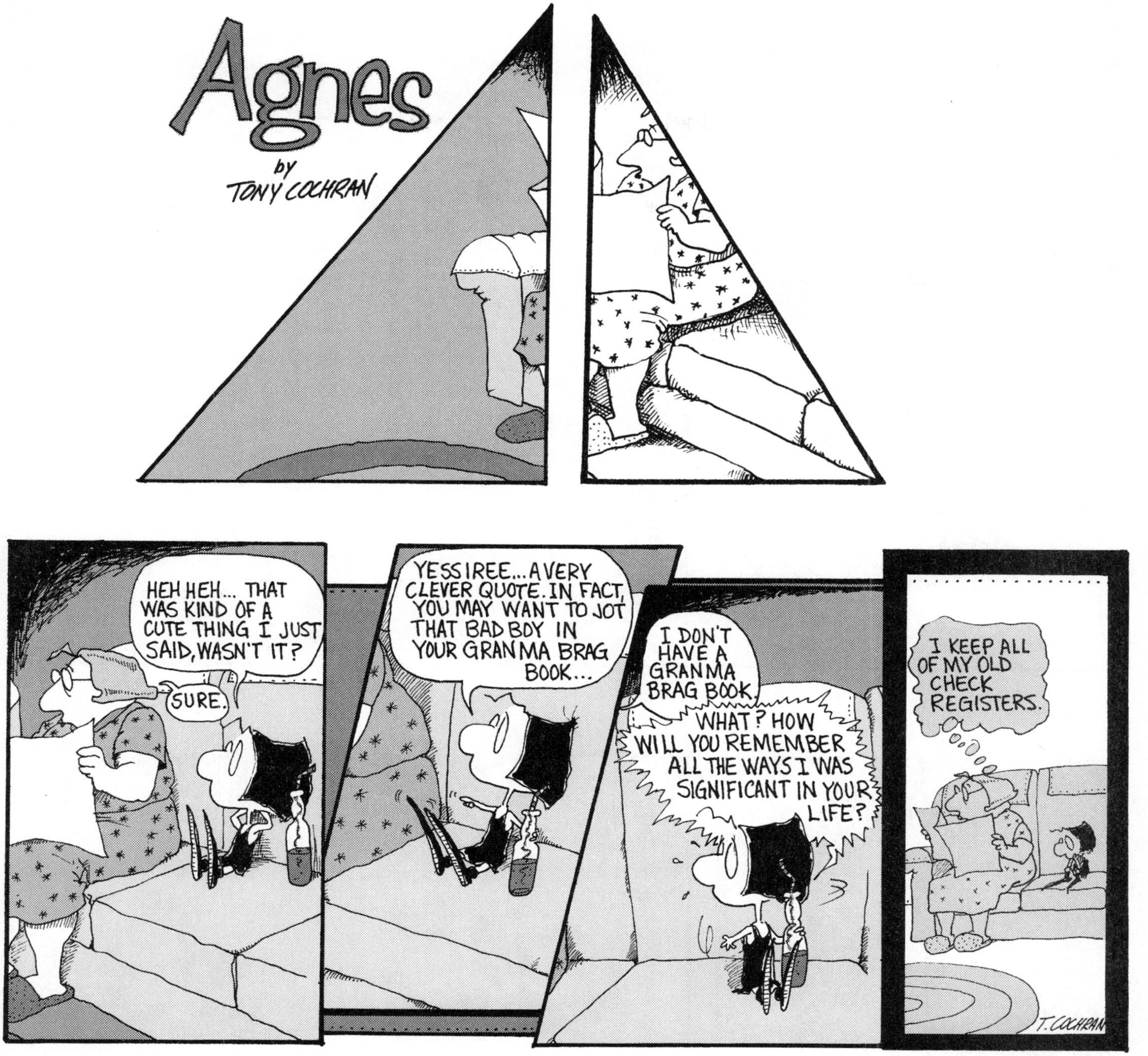
Agnes
by TONY COCHRAN
HEH HEH... THAT WAS KIND OF A CUTE THING I JUST SAID, WASN'T IT?
SURE.
YESSIREE... A VERY CLEVER QUOTE. IN FACT, YOU MAY WANT TO JOT THAT BAD BOY IN YOUR GRANMA BRAG BOOK...
I DON'T HAVE A GRANMA BRAG BOOK.
WHAT? HOW WILL YOU REMEMBER ALL THE WAYS I WAS SIGNIFICANT IN YOUR LIFE?
I KEEP ALL OF MY OLD CHECK REGISTERS.
T. COCHRAN

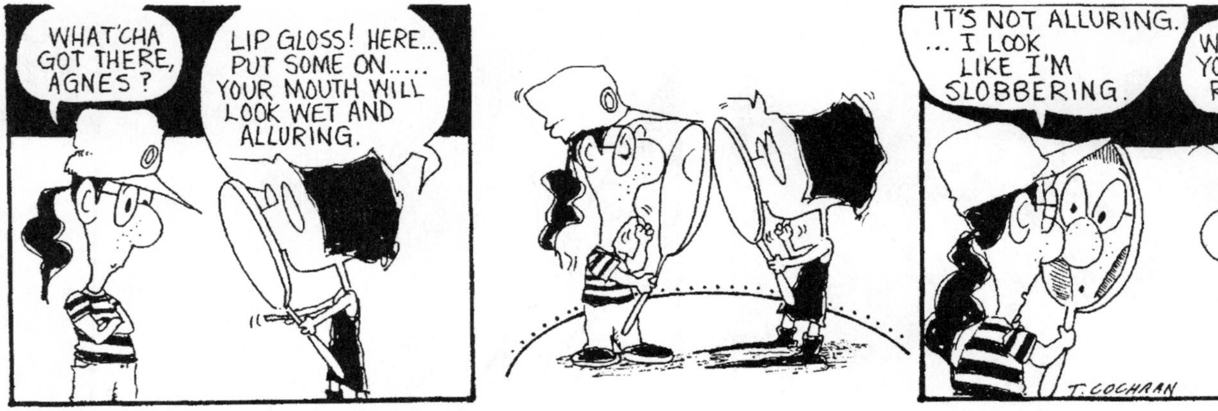
WHAT'CHA GOT THERE, AGNES?
LIP GLOSS! HERE.. PUT SOME ON..... YOUR MOUTH WILL LOOK WET AND ALLURING.
IT'S NOT ALLURING. ... I LOOK LIKE I'M SLOBBERING.
WIPE IT OFF YOUR CHIN, ROOKIE.
T. COCHRAN

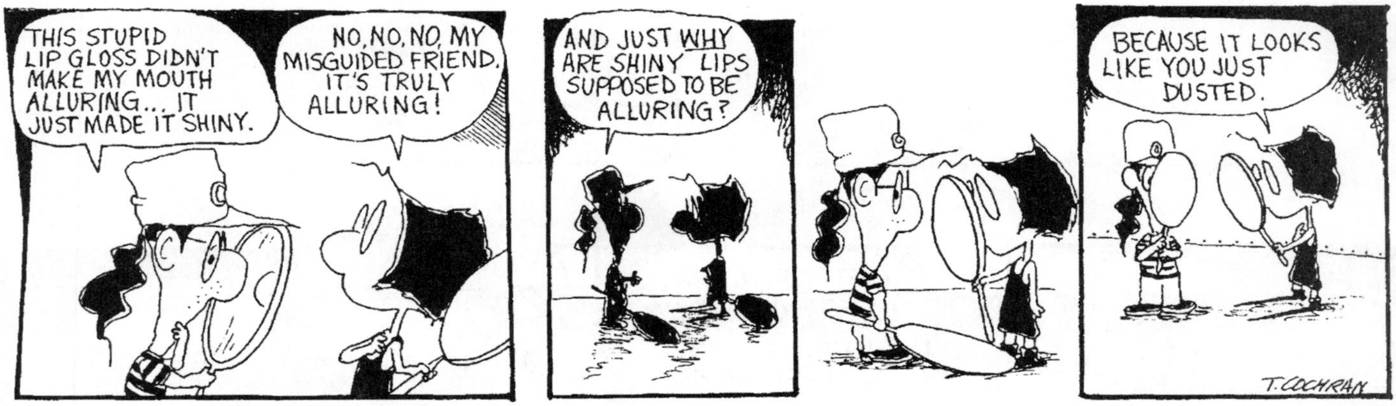
THIS STUPID LIP GLOSS DIDN'T MAKE MY MOUTH ALLURING... IT JUST MADE IT SHINY.
NO, NO, NO, MY MISGUIDED FRIEND. IT'S TRULY ALLURING!
AND JUST WHY ARE SHINY LIPS SUPPOSED TO BE ALLURING?
BECAUSE IT LOOKS LIKE YOU JUST DUSTED.
T. COCHRAN

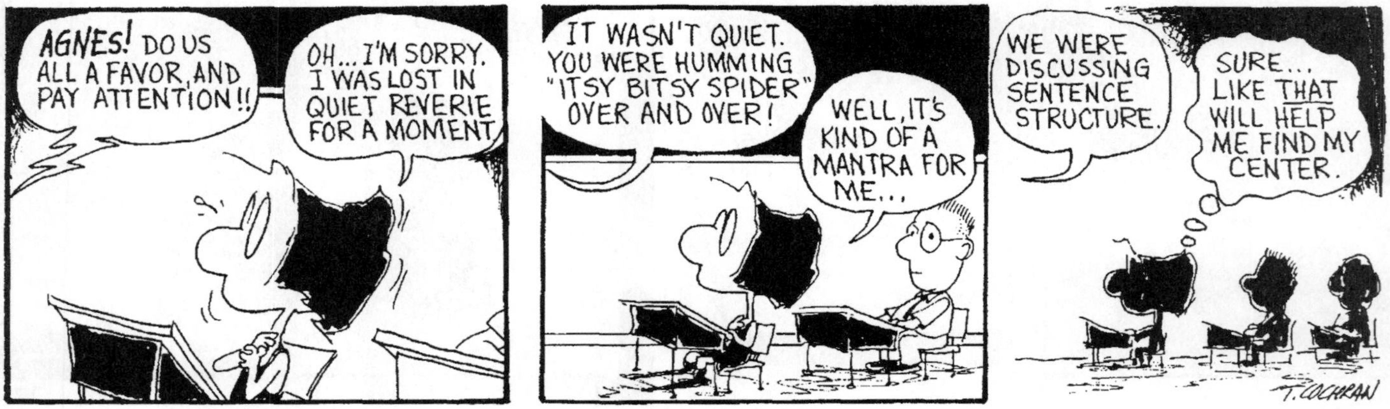
AGNES! DO US ALL A FAVOR, AND PAY ATTENTION!!
OH... I'M SORRY. I WAS LOST IN QUIET REVERIE FOR A MOMENT.
IT WASN'T QUIET. YOU WERE HUMMING "ITSY BITSY SPIDER" OVER AND OVER!
WELL, IT'S KIND OF A MANTRA FOR ME...
WE WERE DISCUSSING SENTENCE STRUCTURE.
SURE... LIKE THAT WILL HELP ME FIND MY CENTER.
T. COCHRAN

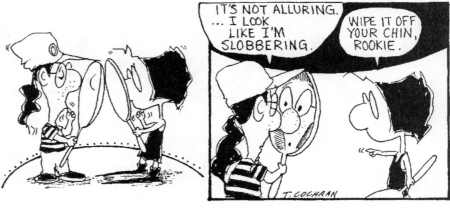

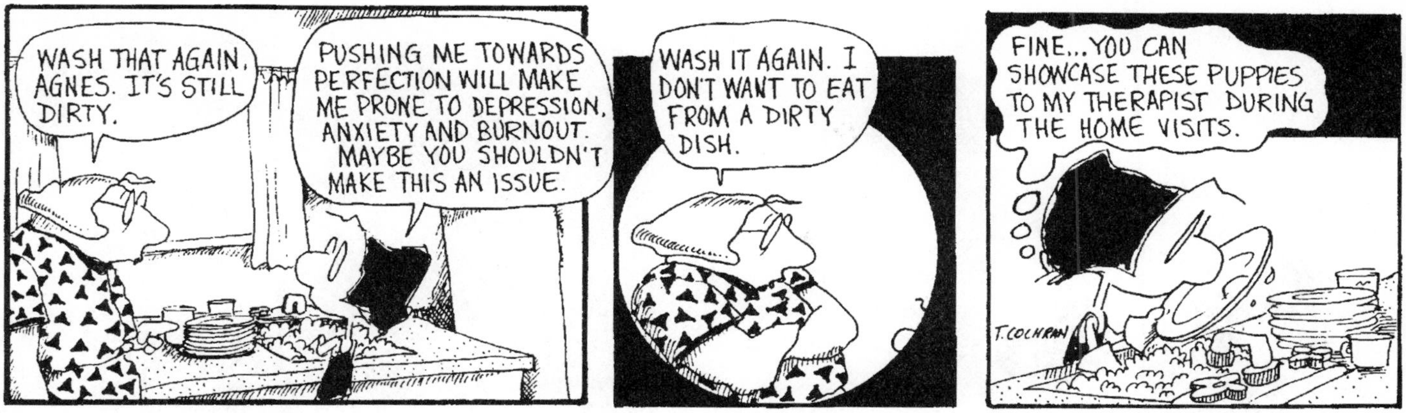
WASH THAT AGAIN, AGNES. IT'S STILL DIRTY.
PUSHING ME TOWARDS PERFECTION WILL MAKE ME PRONE TO DEPRESSION, ANXIETY AND BURNOUT. MAYBE YOU SHOULDN'T MAKE THIS AN ISSUE.
WASH IT AGAIN. I DON'T WANT TO EAT FROM A DIRTY DISH.
FINE... YOU CAN SHOWCASE THESE PUPPIES TO MY THERAPIST DURING THE HOME VISITS.
T. COCHRAN

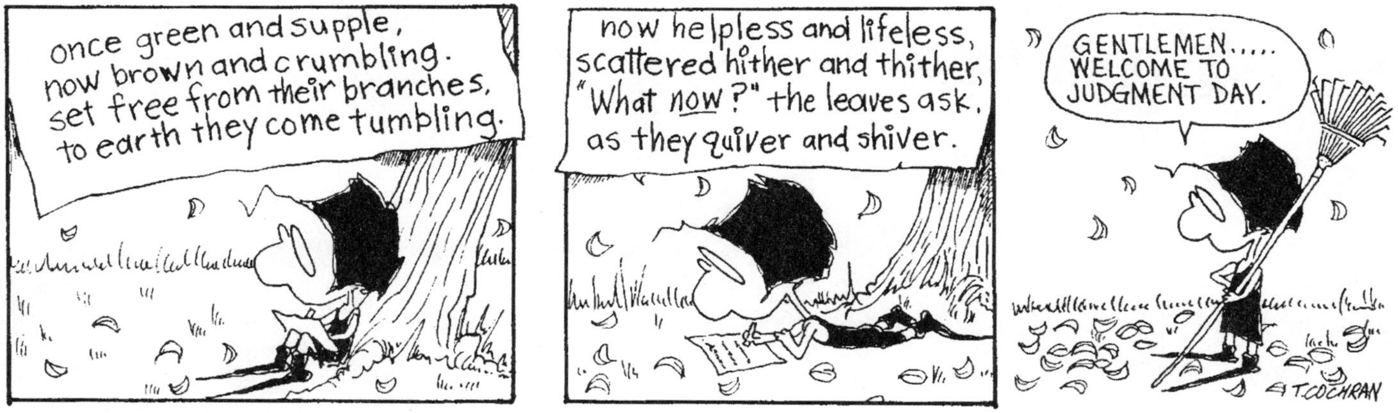
once green and supple, now brown and crumbling. set free from their branches, to earth they come tumbling.
now helpless and lifeless, scattered hither and thither, "What now?" the leaves ask, as they quiver and shiver.
GENTLEMEN..... WELCOME TO JUDGMENT DAY.
T. COCHRAN

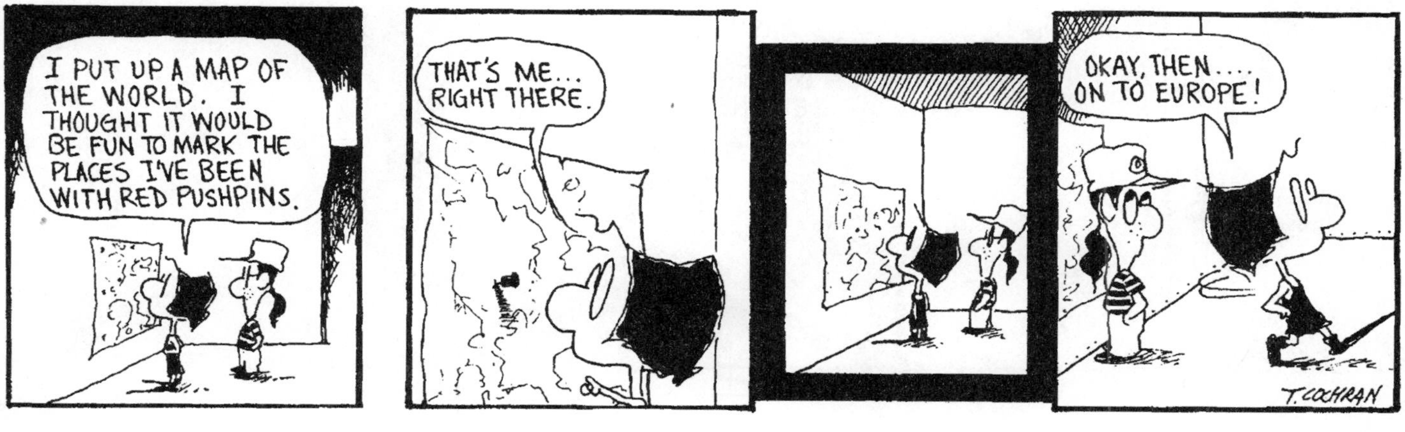
I PUT UP A MAP OF THE WORLD. I THOUGHT IT WOULD BE FUN TO MARK THE PLACES I'VE BEEN WITH RED PUSHPINS.
THAT'S ME... RIGHT THERE.
OKAY, THEN.... ON TO EUROPE!
T. COCHRAN

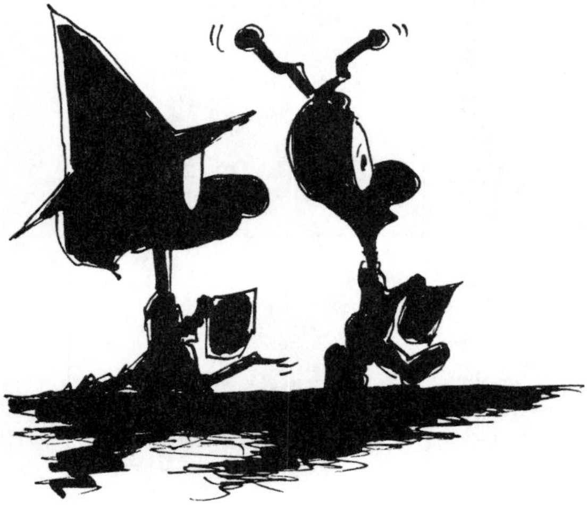

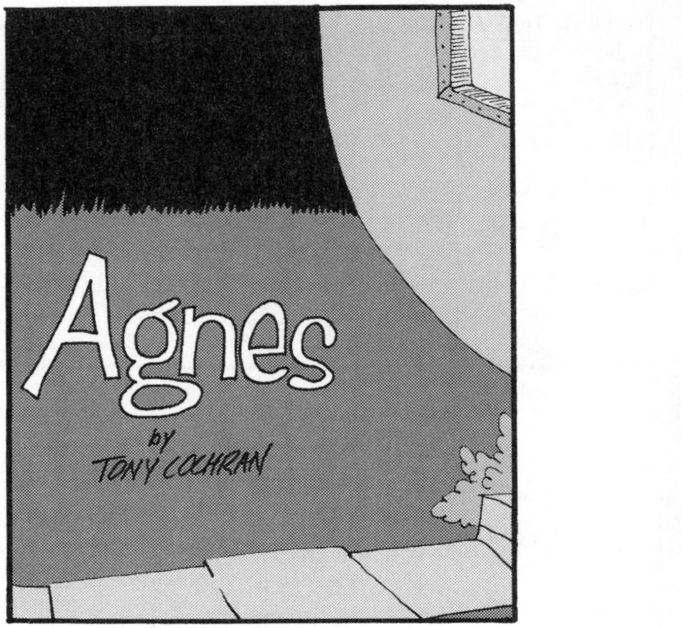
Agnes
by
TONY COCHRAN

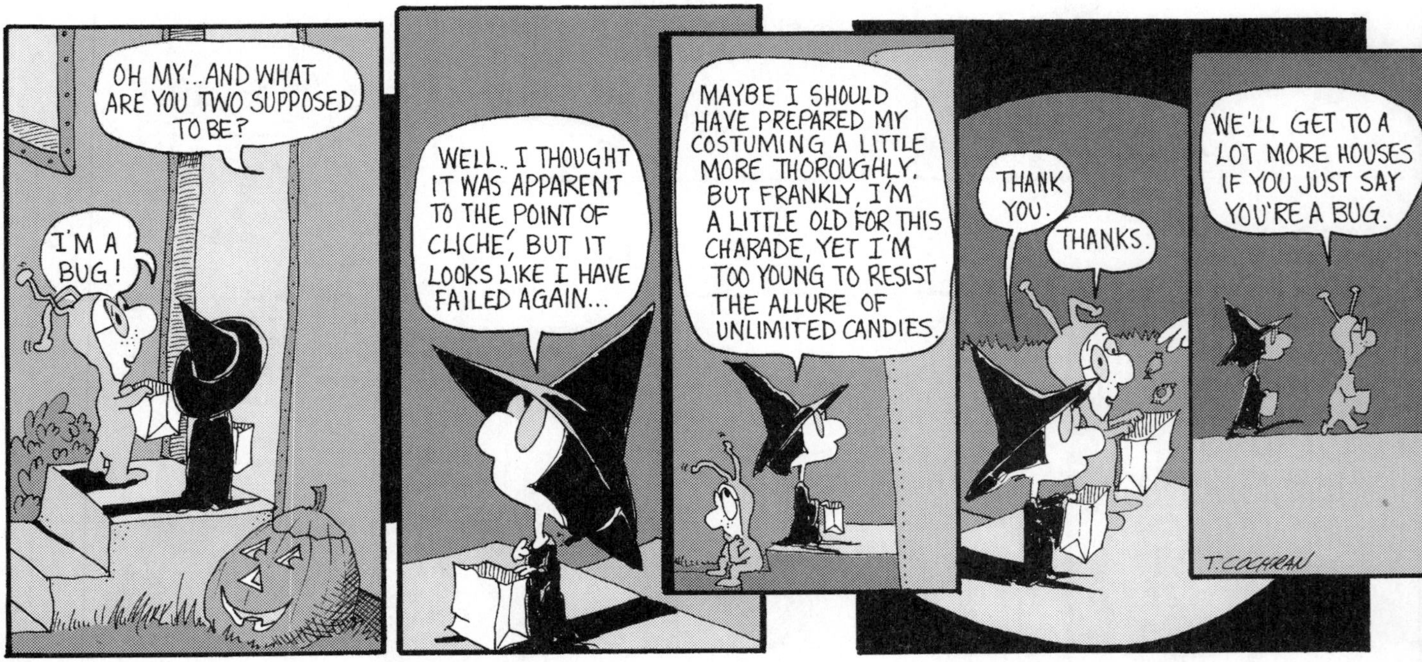
OH MY!..AND WHAT ARE YOU TWO SUPPOSED TO BE?
I'M A BUG!
WELL.. I THOUGHT IT WAS APPARENT TO THE POINT OF CLICHE', BUT IT LOOKS LIKE I HAVE FAILED AGAIN...
MAYBE I SHOULD HAVE PREPARED MY COSTUMING A LITTLE MORE THOROUGHLY. BUT FRANKLY, I'M A LITTLE OLD FOR THIS CHARADE, YET I'M TOO YOUNG TO RESIST THE ALLURE OF UNLIMITED CANDIES.
THANK YOU.
THANKS.
WE'LL GET TO A LOT MORE HOUSES IF YOU JUST SAY YOU'RE A BUG.
T. COCHRAN

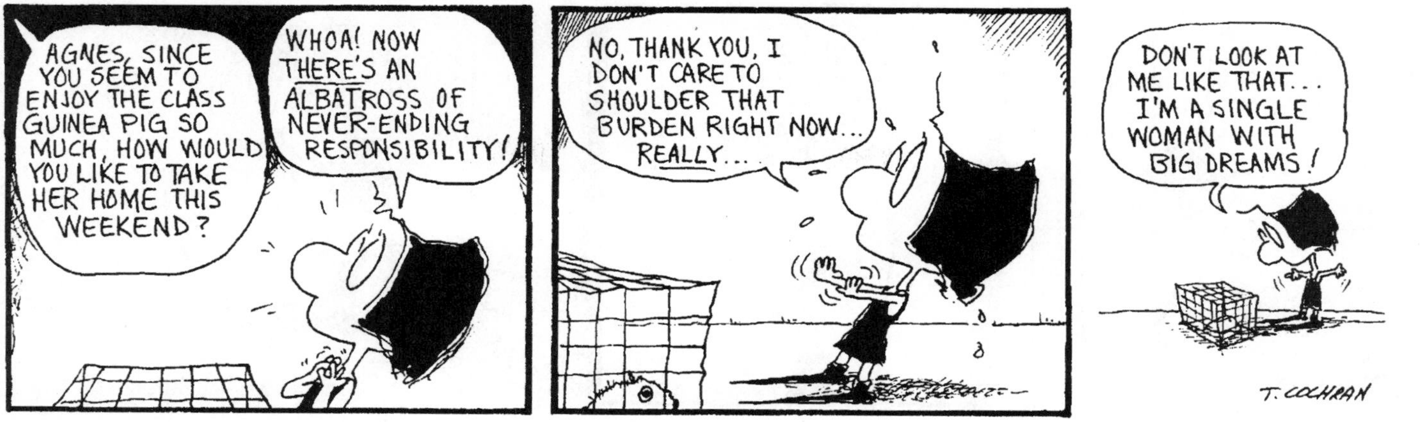
AGNES, SINCE YOU SEEM TO ENJOY THE CLASS GUINEA PIG SO MUCH, HOW WOULD YOU LIKE TO TAKE HER HOME THIS WEEKEND?
WHOA! NOW THERE'S AN ALBATROSS OF NEVER-ENDING RESPONSIBILITY!
NO, THANK YOU, I DON'T CARE TO SHOULDER THAT BURDEN RIGHT NOW... REALLY...
DON'T LOOK AT ME LIKE THAT... I'M A SINGLE WOMAN WITH BIG DREAMS!
T. COCHRAN

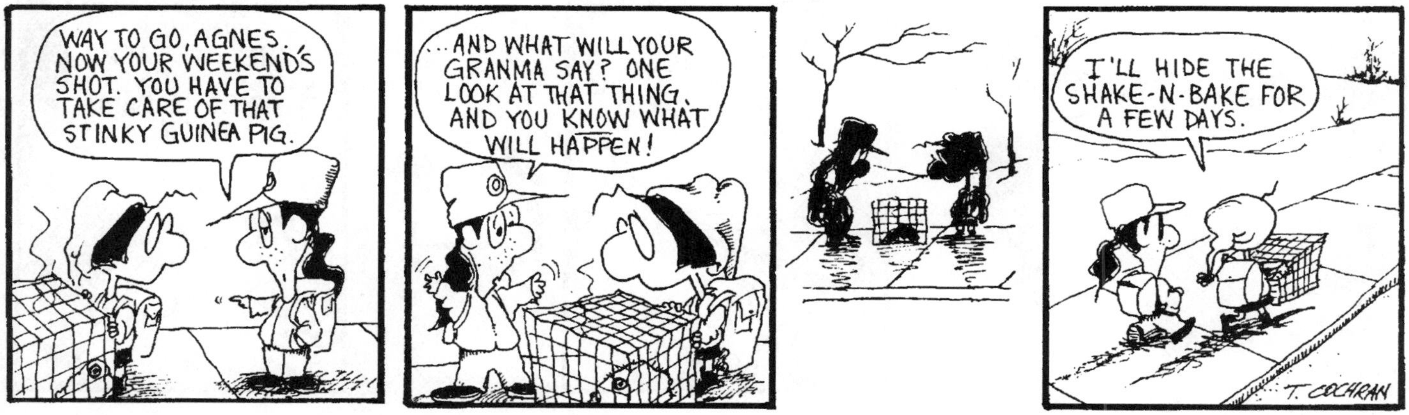
WAY TO GO, AGNES. NOW YOUR WEEKEND'S SHOT. YOU HAVE TO TAKE CARE OF THAT STINKY GUINEA PIG.
...AND WHAT WILL YOUR GRANMA SAY? ONE LOOK AT THAT THING, AND YOU KNOW WHAT WILL HAPPEN!
I'LL HIDE THE SHAKE-N-BAKE FOR A FEW DAYS.
T. COCHRAN

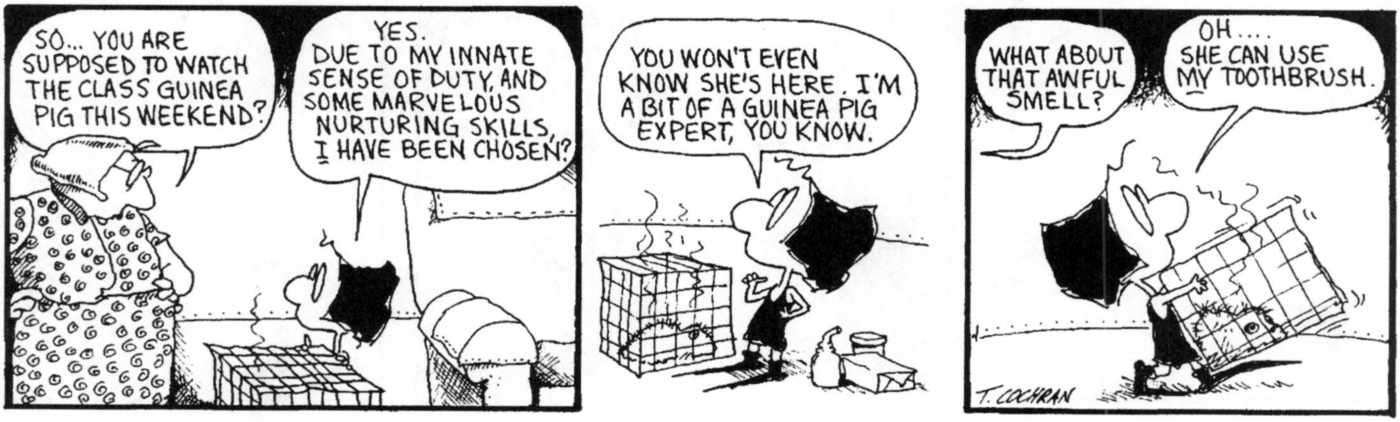
SO... YOU ARE SUPPOSED TO WATCH THE CLASS GUINEA PIG THIS WEEKEND?
YES. DUE TO MY INNATE SENSE OF DUTY, AND SOME MARVELOUS NURTURING SKILLS, I HAVE BEEN CHOSEN!
YOU WON'T EVEN KNOW SHE'S HERE. I'M A BIT OF A GUINEA PIG EXPERT, YOU KNOW.
WHAT ABOUT THAT AWFUL SMELL?
OH.... SHE CAN USE MY TOOTHBRUSH.
T. COCHRAN

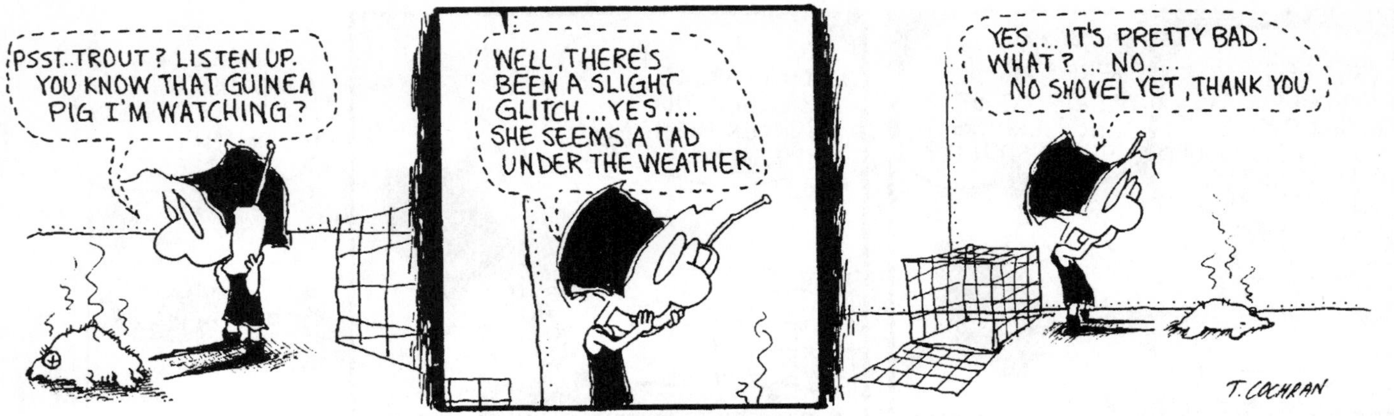
PSST..TROUT? LISTEN UP. YOU KNOW THAT GUINEA PIG I'M WATCHING?
WELL, THERE'S BEEN A SLIGHT GLITCH...YES.... SHE SEEMS A TAD UNDER THE WEATHER.
YES.... IT'S PRETTY BAD. WHAT?... NO.... NO SHOVEL YET, THANK YOU.
T. COCHRAN

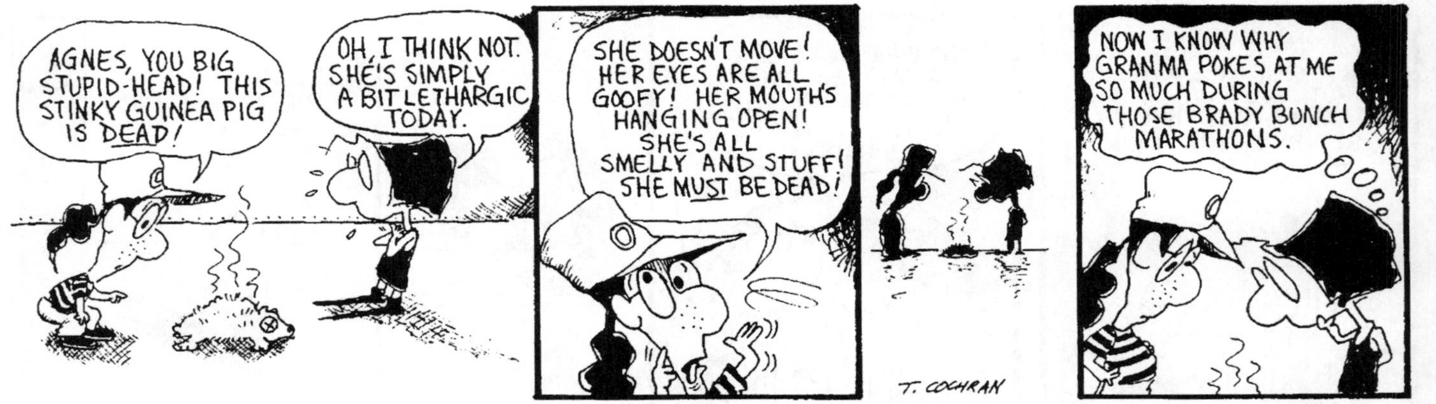
AGNES, YOU BIG STUPID-HEAD! THIS STINKY GUINEA PIG IS DEAD!
OH, I THINK NOT. SHE'S SIMPLY A BIT LETHARGIC TODAY.
SHE DOESN'T MOVE! HER EYES ARE ALL GOOFY! HER MOUTH'S HANGING OPEN! SHE'S ALL SMELLY AND STUFF! SHE MUST BE DEAD!
T. COCHRAN
NOW I KNOW WHY GRANMA POKES AT ME SO MUCH DURING THOSE BRADY BUNCH MARATHONS.

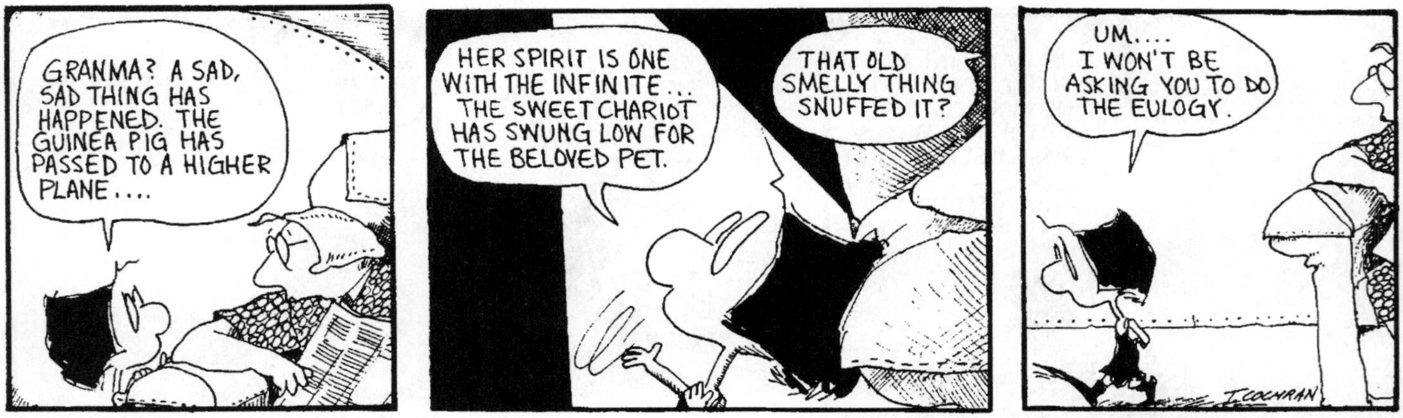
GRANMA? A SAD, SAD THING HAS HAPPENED. THE GUINEA PIG HAS PASSED TO A HIGHER PLANE....
HER SPIRIT IS ONE WITH THE INFINITE... THE SWEET CHARIOT HAS SWUNG LOW FOR THE BELOVED PET.
THAT OLD SMELLY THING SNUFFED IT?
UM.... I WON'T BE ASKING YOU TO DO THE EULOGY.
T. COCHRAN

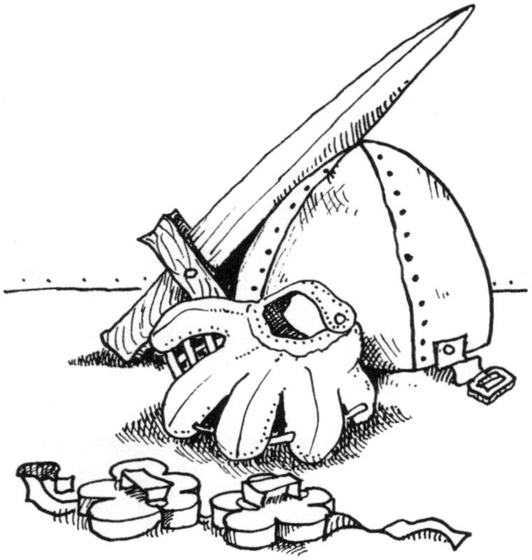

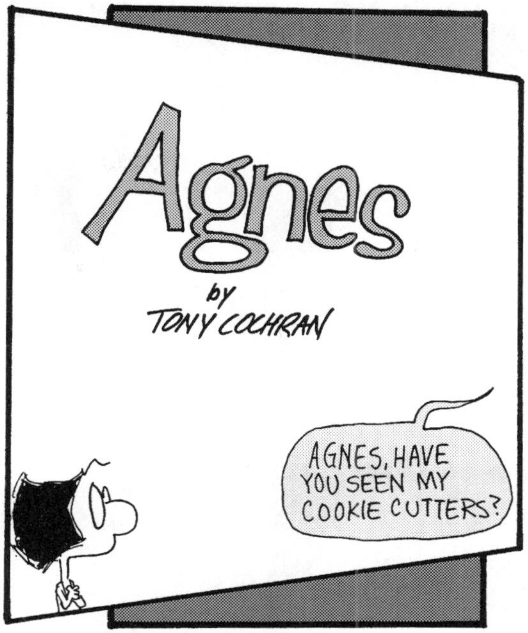
Agnes
by TONY COCHRAN
AGNES, HAVE YOU SEEN MY COOKIE CUTTERS?

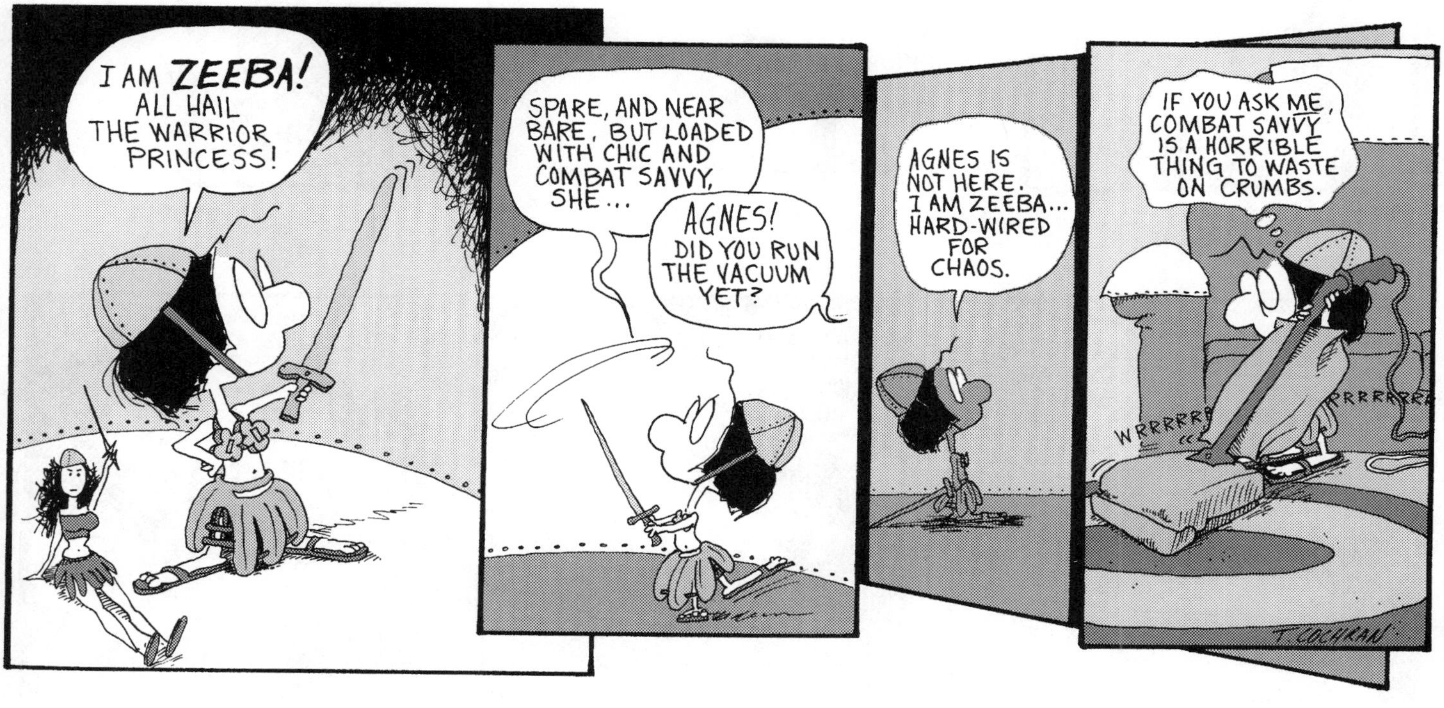
I AM ZEEBA! ALL HAIL THE WARRIOR PRINCESS!
SPARE, AND NEAR BARE, BUT LOADED WITH CHIC AND COMBAT SAVVY, SHE...
AGNES! DID YOU RUN THE VACUUM YET?
AGNES IS NOT HERE. I AM ZEEBA... HARD-WIRED FOR CHAOS.
IF YOU ASK ME, COMBAT SAVVY IS A HORRIBLE THING TO WASTE ON CRUMBS.
T. COCHRAN

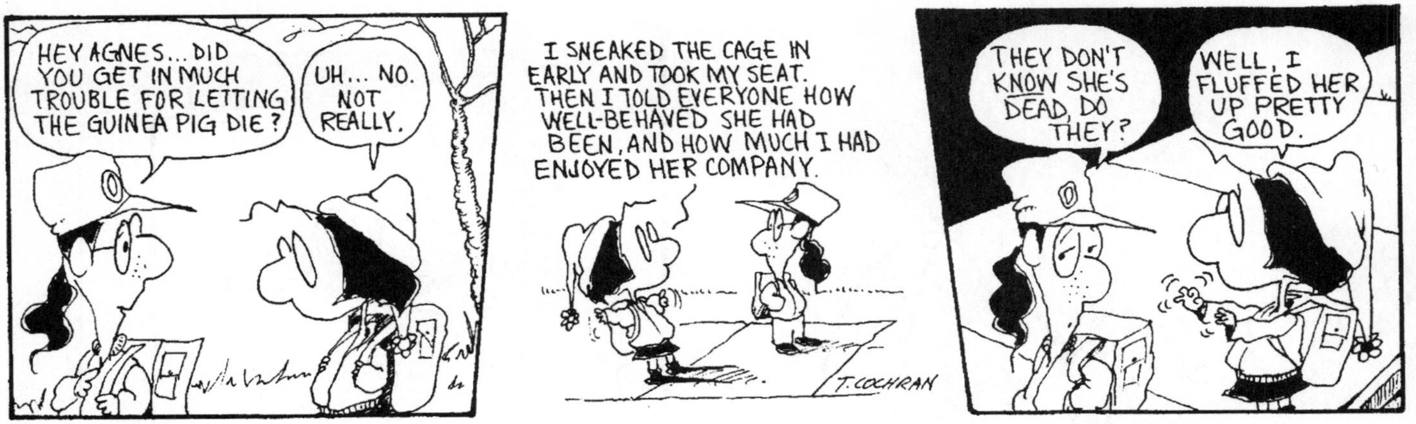
HEY AGNES... DID YOU GET IN MUCH TROUBLE FOR LETTING THE GUINEA PIG DIE?
UH... NO. NOT REALLY.
I SNEAKED THE CAGE IN EARLY AND TOOK MY SEAT. THEN I TOLD EVERYONE HOW WELL-BEHAVED SHE HAD BEEN, AND HOW MUCH I HAD ENJOYED HER COMPANY.
T. COCHRAN
THEY DON'T KNOW SHE'S DEAD, DO THEY?
WELL, I FLUFFED HER UP PRETTY GOOD.

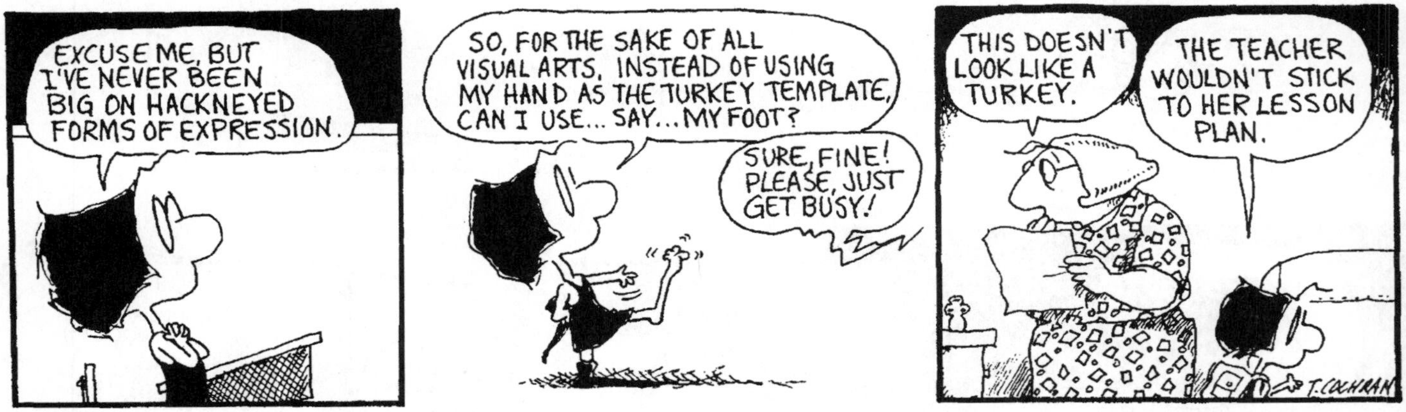
EXCUSE ME, BUT I'VE NEVER BEEN BIG ON HACKNEYED FORMS OF EXPRESSION.
SO, FOR THE SAKE OF ALL VISUAL ARTS, INSTEAD OF USING MY HAND AS THE TURKEY TEMPLATE, CAN I USE... SAY... MY FOOT?
SURE, FINE! PLEASE, JUST GET BUSY!
THIS DOESN'T LOOK LIKE A TURKEY.
THE TEACHER WOULDN'T STICK TO HER LESSON PLAN.
T. COCHRAN

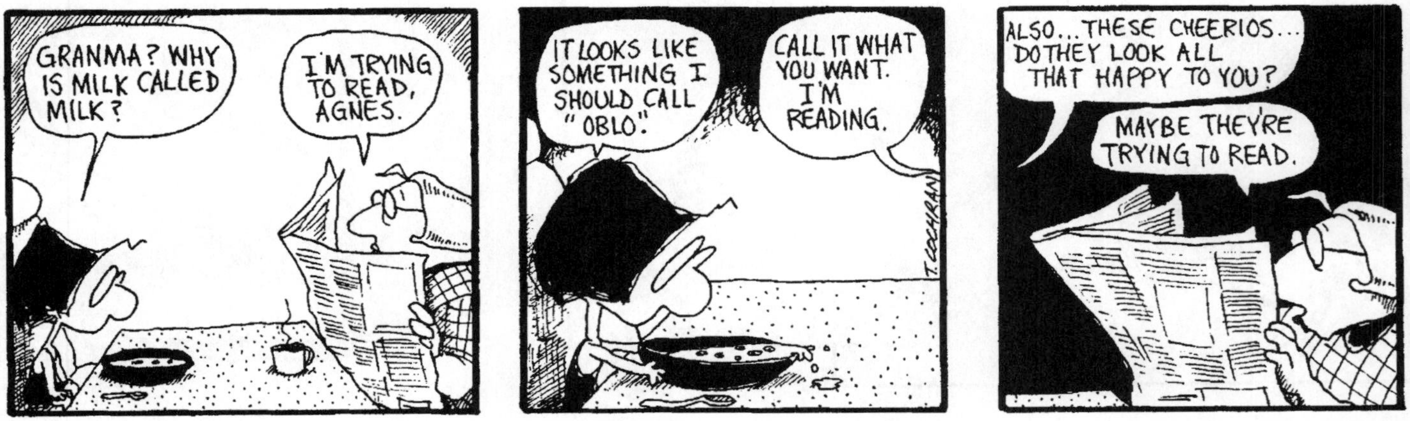
GRANMA? WHY IS MILK CALLED MILK?
I'M TRYING TO READ, AGNES.
IT LOOKS LIKE SOMETHING I SHOULD CALL "OBLO."
CALL IT WHAT YOU WANT. I'M READING.
T. COCHRAN
ALSO... THESE CHEERIOS... DO THEY LOOK ALL THAT HAPPY TO YOU?
MAYBE THEY'RE TRYING TO READ.

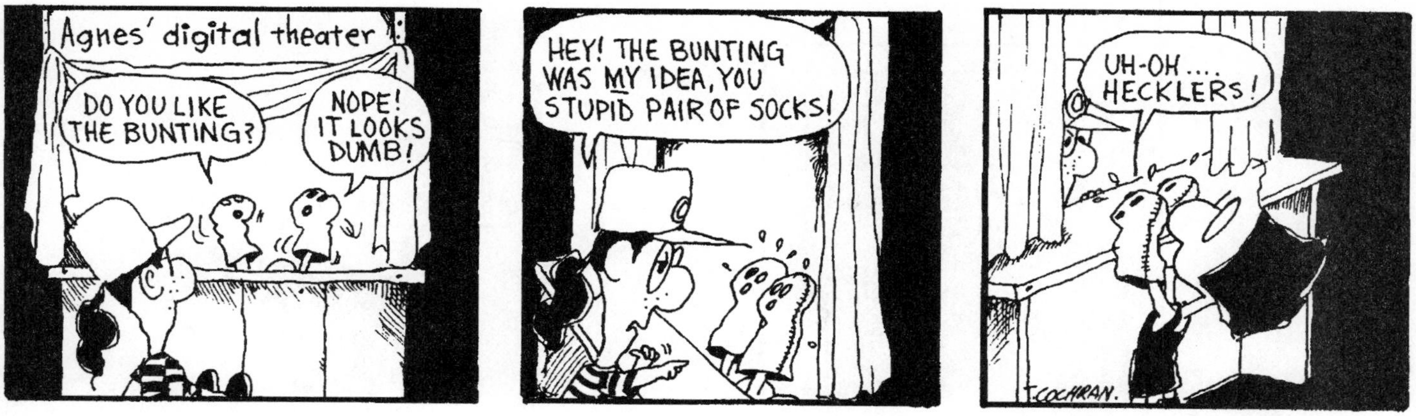
Agnes' digital theater
DO YOU LIKE THE BUNTING?
NOPE! IT LOOKS DUMB!
HEY! THE BUNTING WAS MY IDEA, YOU STUPID PAIR OF SOCKS!
UH-OH.... HECKLERS!
T. COCHRAN.

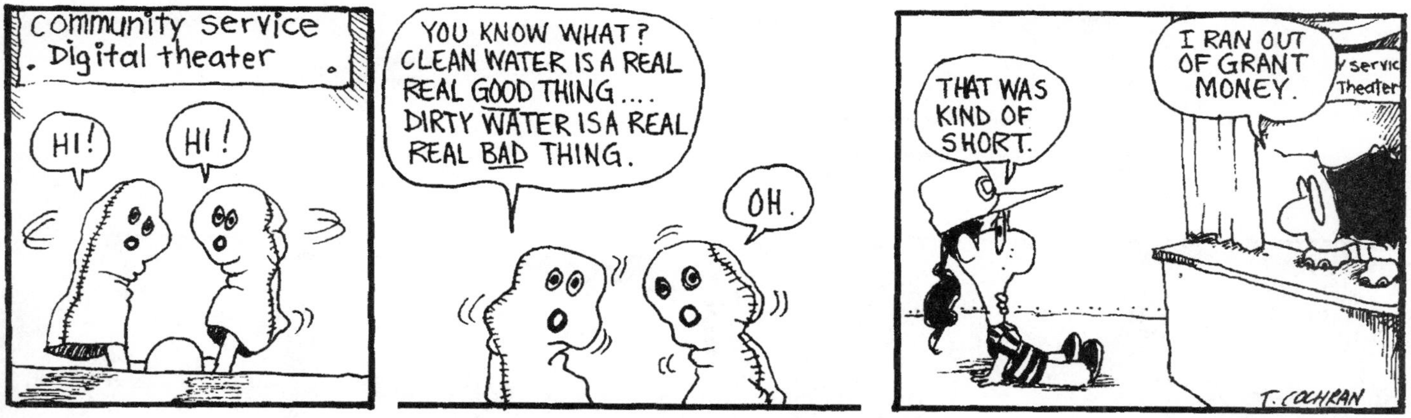
community service Digital theater
HI!
HI!
YOU KNOW WHAT? CLEAN WATER IS A REAL REAL GOOD THING.... DIRTY WATER IS A REAL REAL BAD THING.
OH.
THAT WAS KIND OF SHORT.
I RAN OUT OF GRANT MONEY.
T. COCHRAN

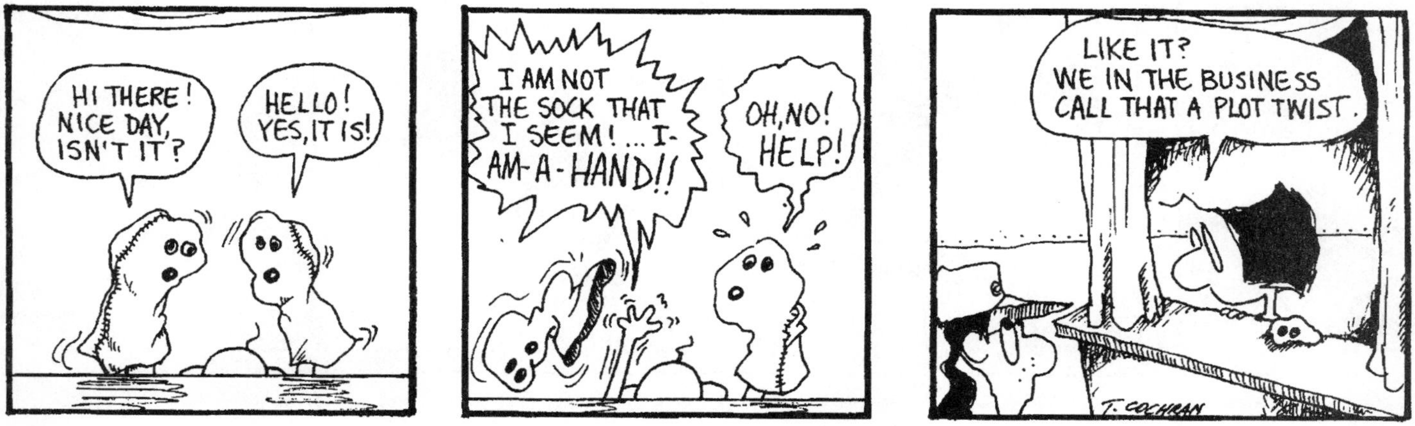
HI THERE! NICE DAY, ISN'T IT?
HELLO! YES, IT IS!
I AM NOT THE SOCK THAT I SEEM!... I-AM-A-HAND!!
OH, NO! HELP!
LIKE IT? WE IN THE BUSINESS CALL THAT A PLOT TWIST.
T. COCHRAN

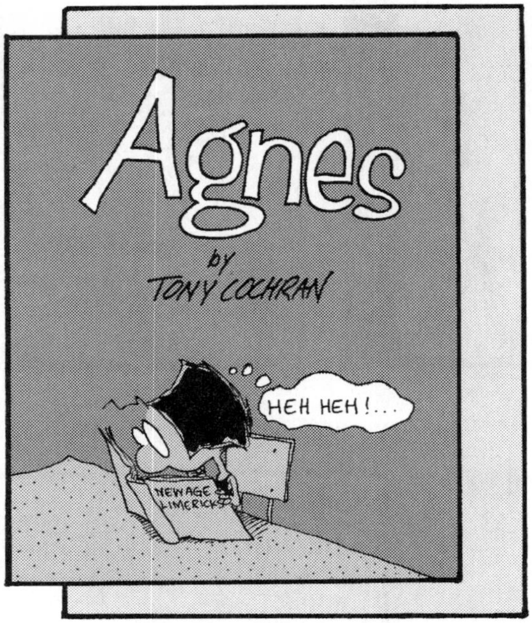
Agnes
by
TONY COCHRAN
HEH HEH!...
NEWAGE LIMERICKS

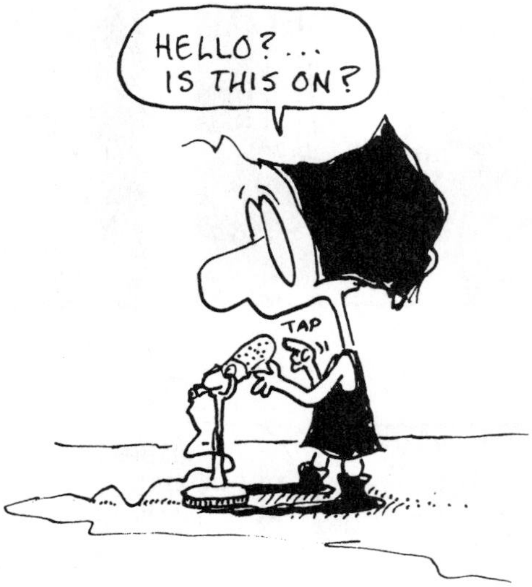
HELLO?... IS THIS ON?
TAP

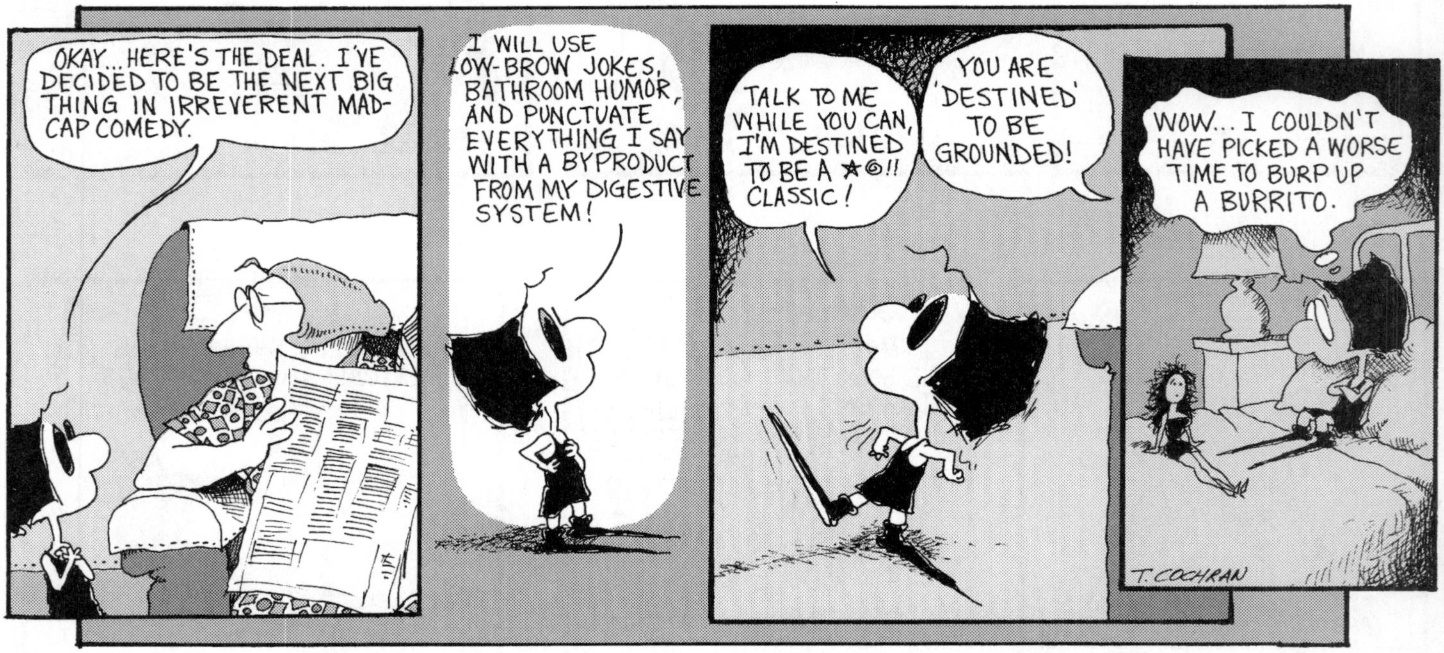
OKAY... HERE'S THE DEAL. I'VE DECIDED TO BE THE NEXT BIG THING IN IRREVERENT MAD-CAP COMEDY.
I WILL USE LOW-BROW JOKES, BATHROOM HUMOR, AND PUNCTUATE EVERYTHING I SAY WITH A BYPRODUCT FROM MY DIGESTIVE SYSTEM!
TALK TO ME WHILE YOU CAN, I'M DESTINED TO BE A ★◎!! CLASSIC!
YOU ARE 'DESTINED' TO BE GROUNDED!
WOW... I COULDN'T HAVE PICKED A WORSE TIME TO BURP UP A BURRITO.
T. COCHRAN

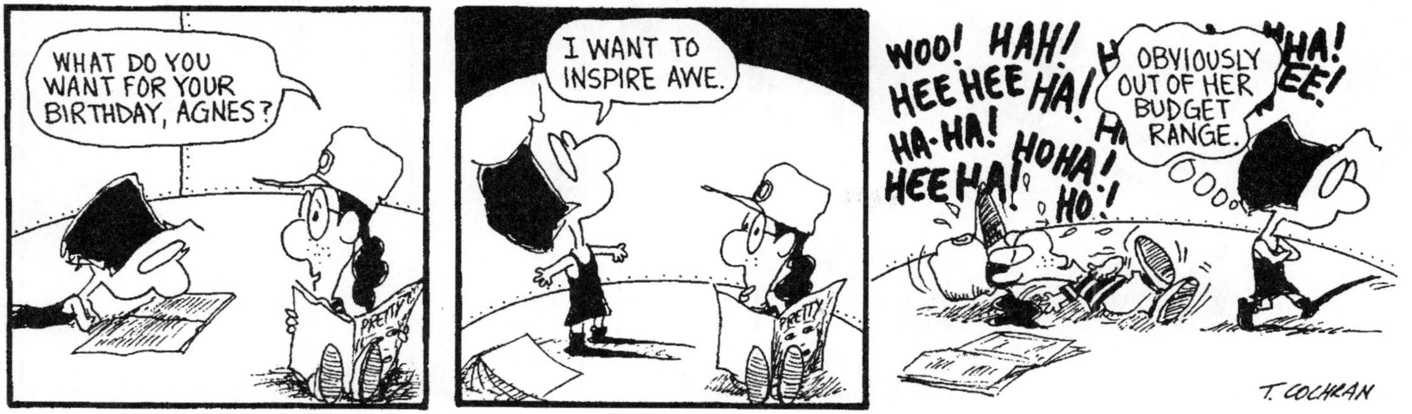
WHAT DO YOU WANT FOR YOUR BIRTHDAY, AGNES?
PRETTY
I WANT TO INSPIRE AWE.
PRETTY
WOO! HAH!
HEE HEE HA!
HA-HA! HOHA!
HEE HA! HO!
HA!
EE!
OBVIOUSLY OUT OF HER BUDGET RANGE.
T. COCHRAN

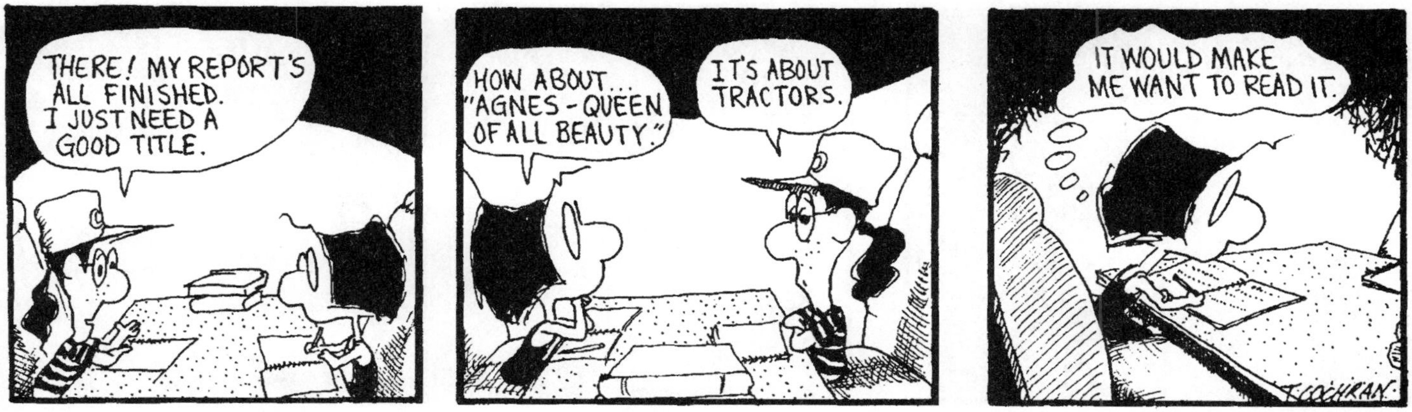
THERE! MY REPORT'S ALL FINISHED. I JUST NEED A GOOD TITLE.
HOW ABOUT... "AGNES - QUEEN OF ALL BEAUTY."
IT'S ABOUT TRACTORS.
IT WOULD MAKE ME WANT TO READ IT.
T. COCHRAN

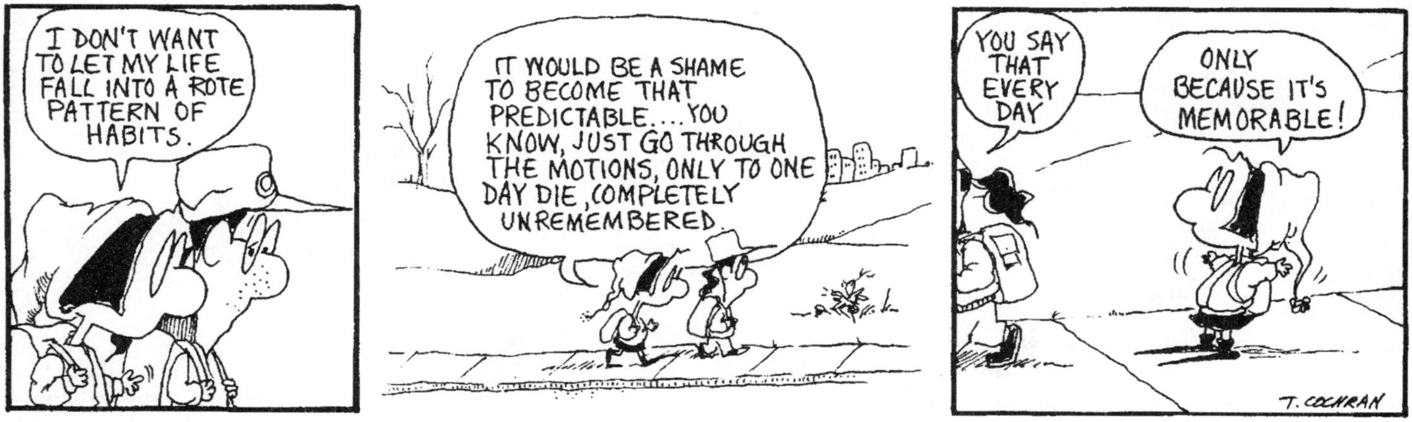
I DON'T WANT TO LET MY LIFE FALL INTO A ROTE PATTERN OF HABITS.
IT WOULD BE A SHAME TO BECOME THAT PREDICTABLE.... YOU KNOW, JUST GO THROUGH THE MOTIONS, ONLY TO ONE DAY DIE, COMPLETELY UNREMEMBERED.
YOU SAY THAT EVERY DAY
ONLY BECAUSE IT'S MEMORABLE!
T. COCHRAN

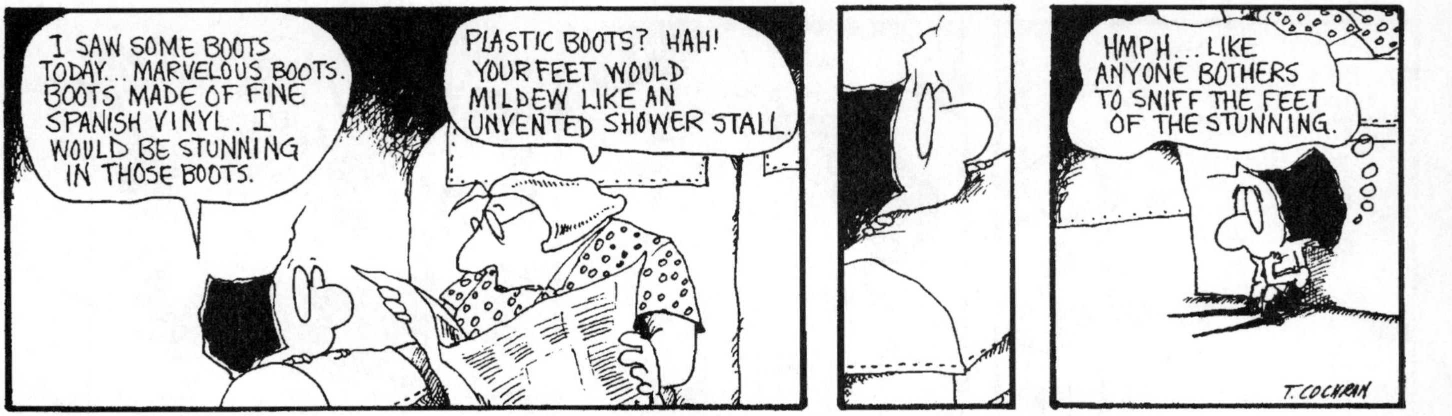
I SAW SOME BOOTS TODAY... MARVELOUS BOOTS. BOOTS MADE OF FINE SPANISH VINYL. I WOULD BE STUNNING IN THOSE BOOTS.
PLASTIC BOOTS? HAH! YOUR FEET WOULD MILDEW LIKE AN UNVENTED SHOWER STALL.
HMPH... LIKE ANYONE BOTHERS TO SNIFF THE FEET OF THE STUNNING.
T. COCHRAN

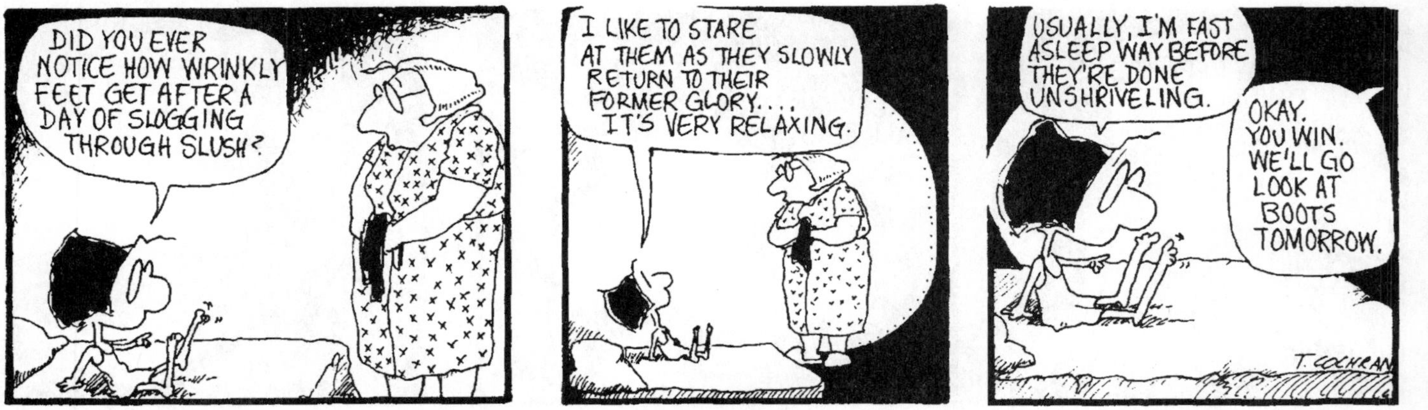
DID YOU EVER NOTICE HOW WRINKLY FEET GET AFTER A DAY OF SLOGGING THROUGH SLUSH?
I LIKE TO STARE AT THEM AS THEY SLOWLY RETURN TO THEIR FORMER GLORY.... IT'S VERY RELAXING.
USUALLY, I'M FAST ASLEEP WAY BEFORE THEY'RE DONE UNSHRIVELING.
OKAY. YOU WIN. WE'LL GO LOOK AT BOOTS TOMORROW.
T. COCHRAN

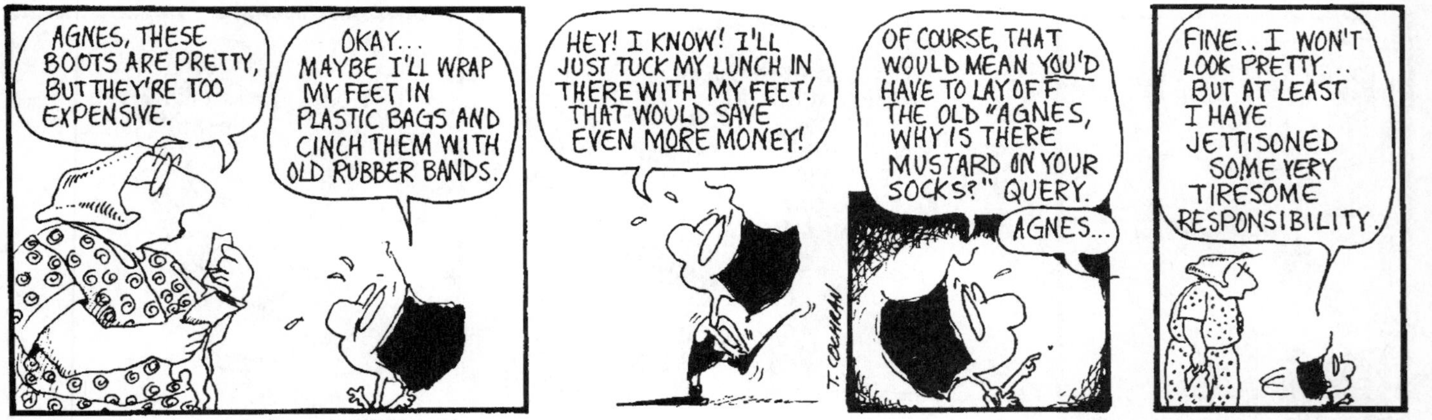
AGNES, THESE BOOTS ARE PRETTY, BUT THEY'RE TOO EXPENSIVE.
OKAY... MAYBE I'LL WRAP MY FEET IN PLASTIC BAGS AND CINCH THEM WITH OLD RUBBER BANDS.
HEY! I KNOW! I'LL JUST TUCK MY LUNCH IN THERE WITH MY FEET! THAT WOULD SAVE EVEN MORE MONEY!
T. COCHRAN
OF COURSE, THAT WOULD MEAN YOU'D HAVE TO LAY OFF THE OLD "AGNES, WHY IS THERE MUSTARD ON YOUR SOCKS?" QUERY.
AGNES...
FINE.. I WON'T LOOK PRETTY... BUT AT LEAST I HAVE JETTISONED SOME VERY TIRESOME RESPONSIBILITY.

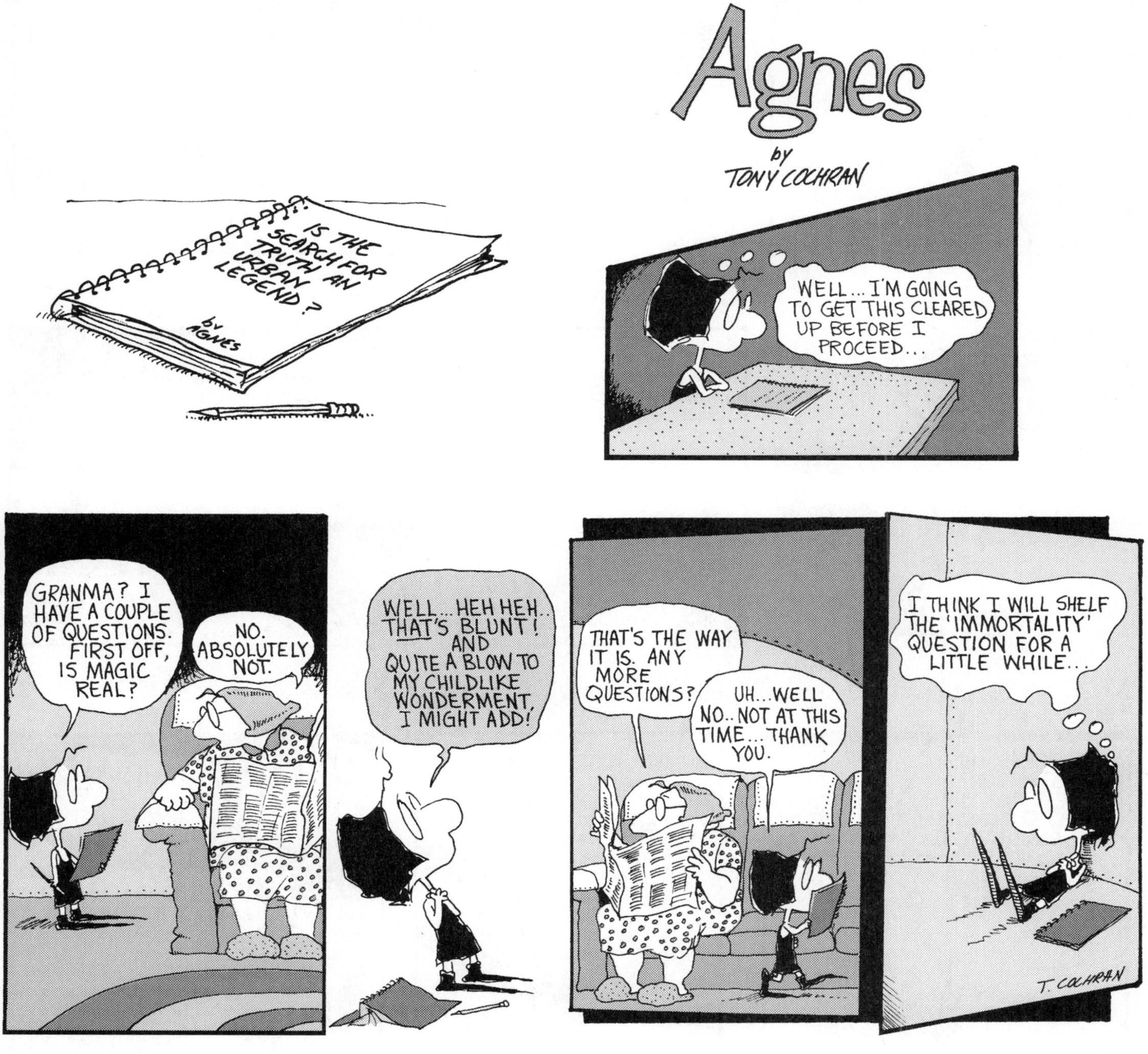
Agnes
by TONY COCHRAN
IS THE SEARCH FOR TRUTH AN URBAN LEGEND?
by AGNES
WELL... I'M GOING TO GET THIS CLEARED UP BEFORE I PROCEED...
GRANMA? I HAVE A COUPLE OF QUESTIONS. FIRST OFF, IS MAGIC REAL?
NO. ABSOLUTELY NOT.
WELL... HEH HEH... THAT'S BLUNT! AND QUITE A BLOW TO MY CHILDLIKE WONDERMENT, I MIGHT ADD!
THAT'S THE WAY IT IS. ANY MORE QUESTIONS?
UH... WELL NO.. NOT AT THIS TIME... THANK YOU.
I THINK I WILL SHELF THE 'IMMORTALITY' QUESTION FOR A LITTLE WHILE...
T. COCHRAN

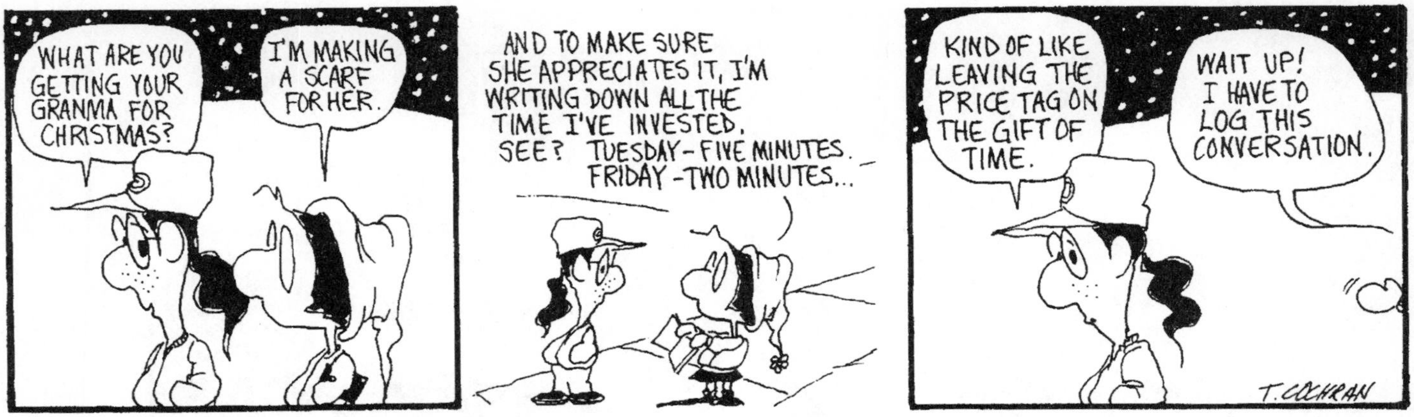
WHAT ARE YOU GETTING YOUR GRANMA FOR CHRISTMAS?
I'M MAKING A SCARF FOR HER.
AND TO MAKE SURE SHE APPRECIATES IT, I'M WRITING DOWN ALL THE TIME I'VE INVESTED. SEE? TUESDAY - FIVE MINUTES. FRIDAY - TWO MINUTES...
KIND OF LIKE LEAVING THE PRICE TAG ON THE GIFT OF TIME.
WAIT UP! I HAVE TO LOG THIS CONVERSATION.
T. COCHRAN

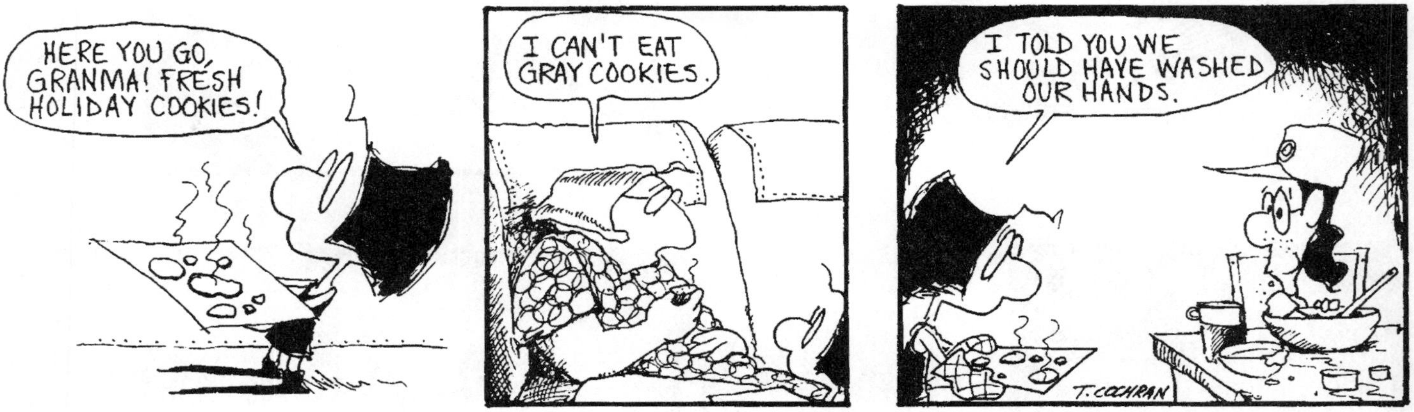
HERE YOU GO, GRANMA! FRESH HOLIDAY COOKIES!
I CAN'T EAT GRAY COOKIES.
I TOLD YOU WE SHOULD HAVE WASHED OUR HANDS.
T. COCHRAN

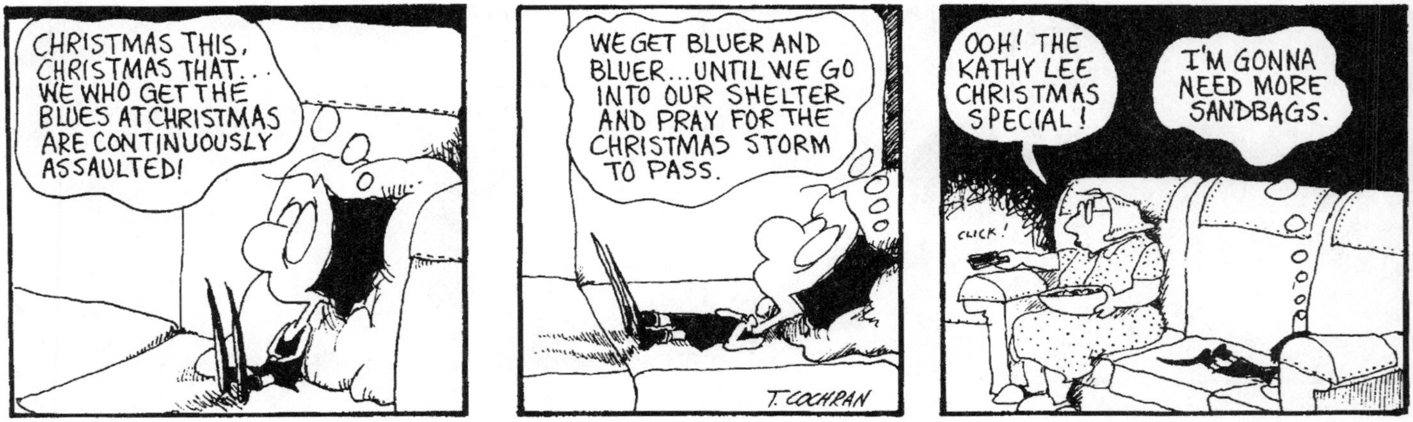
CHRISTMAS THIS, CHRISTMAS THAT... WE WHO GET THE BLUES AT CHRISTMAS ARE CONTINUOUSLY ASSAULTED!
WE GET BLUER AND BLUER... UNTIL WE GO INTO OUR SHELTER AND PRAY FOR THE CHRISTMAS STORM TO PASS.
T. COCHRAN
CLICK!
OOH! THE KATHY LEE CHRISTMAS SPECIAL!
I'M GONNA NEED MORE SANDBAGS.

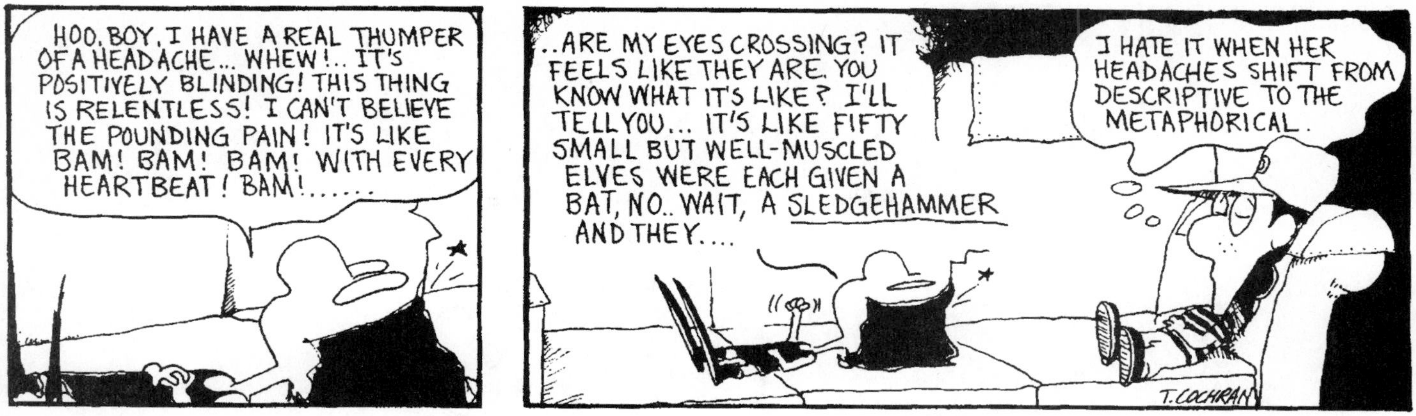
HOO, BOY, I HAVE A REAL THUMPER OF A HEADACHE... WHEW!.. IT'S POSITIVELY BLINDING! THIS THING IS RELENTLESS! I CAN'T BELIEVE THE POUNDING PAIN! IT'S LIKE BAM! BAM! BAM! WITH EVERY HEARTBEAT! BAM!......
..ARE MY EYES CROSSING? IT FEELS LIKE THEY ARE. YOU KNOW WHAT IT'S LIKE? I'LL TELL YOU... IT'S LIKE FIFTY SMALL BUT WELL-MUSCLED ELVES WERE EACH GIVEN A BAT, NO.. WAIT, A SLEDGEHAMMER AND THEY....
I HATE IT WHEN HER HEADACHES SHIFT FROM DESCRIPTIVE TO THE METAPHORICAL.
T. COCHRAN

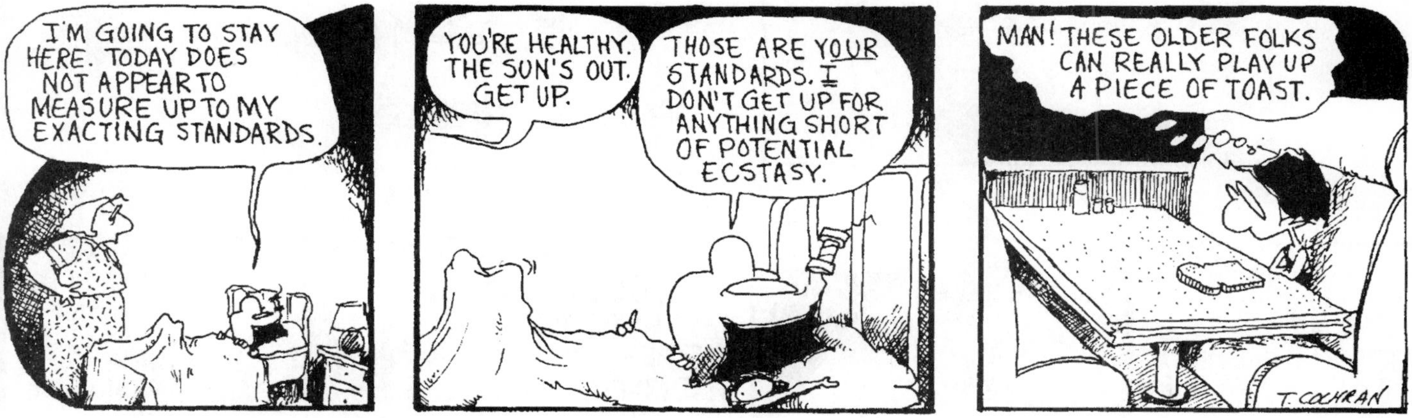
I'M GOING TO STAY HERE. TODAY DOES NOT APPEAR TO MEASURE UP TO MY EXACTING STANDARDS.
YOU'RE HEALTHY. THE SUN'S OUT. GET UP.
THOSE ARE YOUR STANDARDS. I DON'T GET UP FOR ANYTHING SHORT OF POTENTIAL ECSTASY.
MAN! THESE OLDER FOLKS CAN REALLY PLAY UP A PIECE OF TOAST.
T. COCHRAN

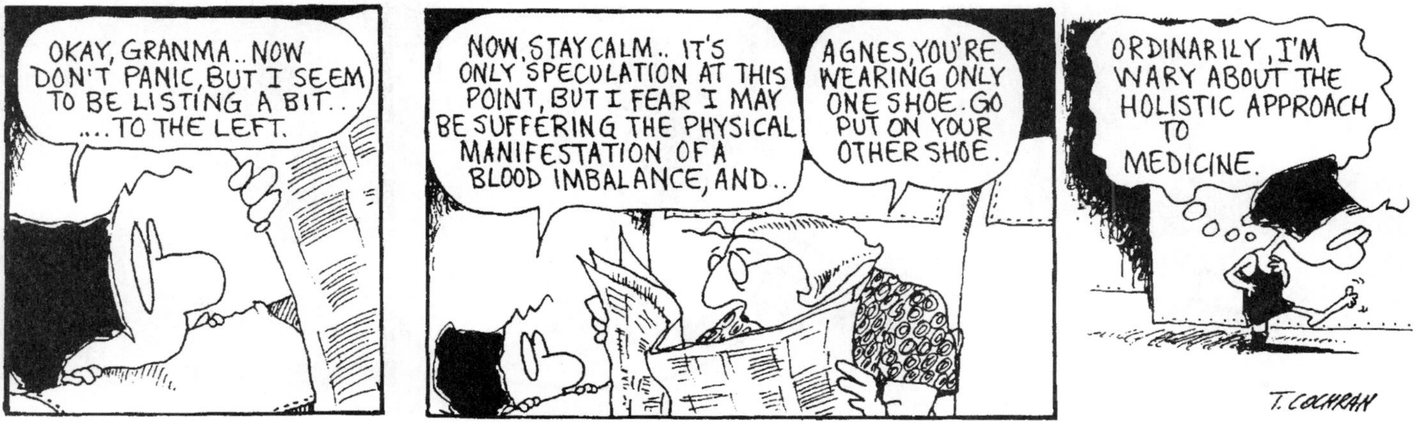
OKAY, GRANMA.. NOW DON'T PANIC, BUT I SEEM TO BE LISTING A BIT.. ....TO THE LEFT.
NOW, STAY CALM.. IT'S ONLY SPECULATION AT THIS POINT, BUT I FEAR I MAY BE SUFFERING THE PHYSICAL MANIFESTATION OF A BLOOD IMBALANCE, AND..
AGNES, YOU'RE WEARING ONLY ONE SHOE. GO PUT ON YOUR OTHER SHOE.
ORDINARILY, I'M WARY ABOUT THE HOLISTIC APPROACH TO MEDICINE.
T. COCHRAN

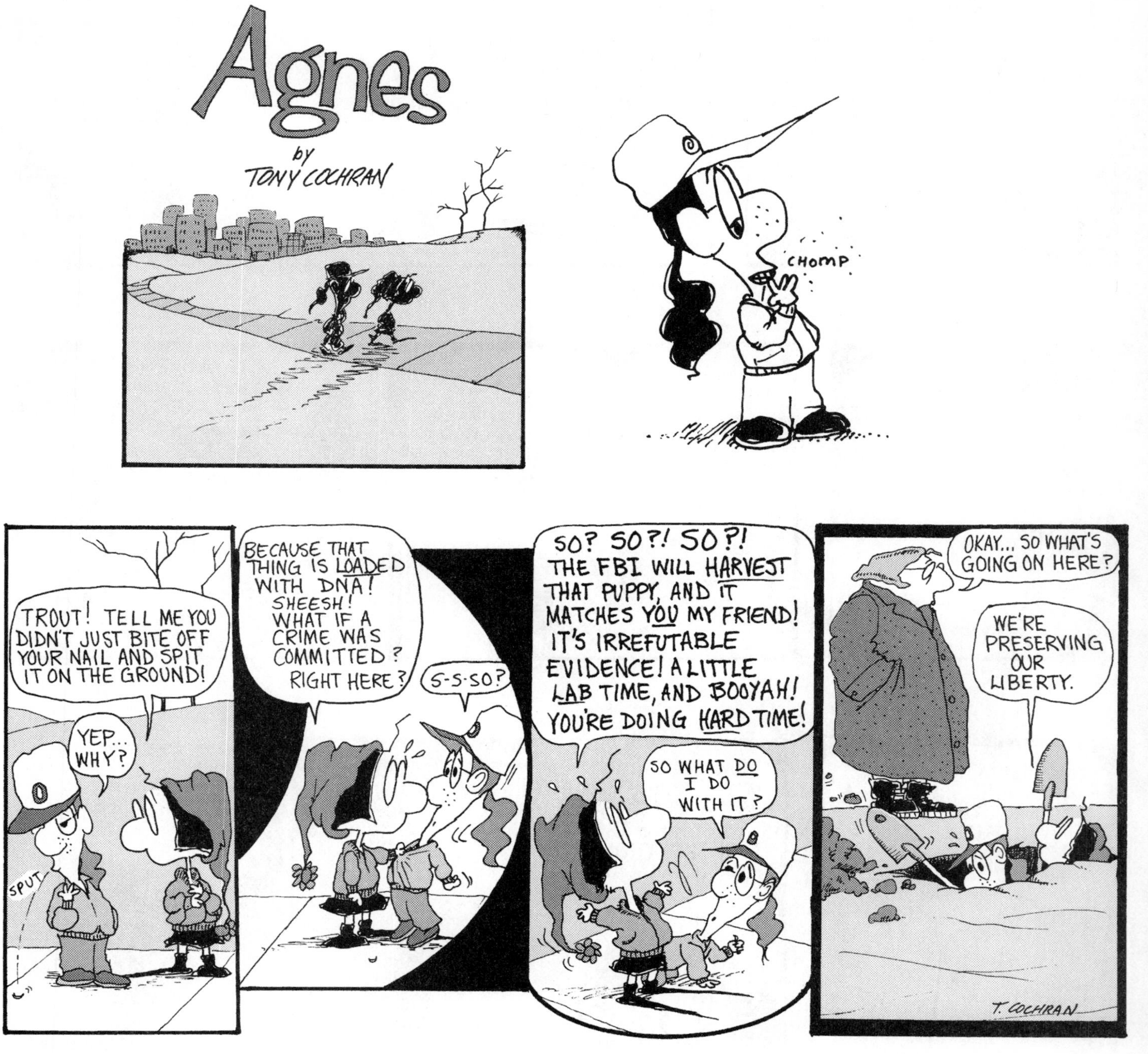
Agnes
by
TONY COCHRAN
CHOMP
TROUT! TELL ME YOU DIDN'T JUST BITE OFF YOUR NAIL AND SPIT IT ON THE GROUND!
YEP... WHY?
SPUT
BECAUSE THAT THING IS LOADED WITH DNA! SHEESH! WHAT IF A CRIME WAS COMMITTED? RIGHT HERE?
S-S-SO?
SO? SO?! SO?! THE FBI WILL HARVEST THAT PUPPY, AND IT MATCHES YOU MY FRIEND! IT'S IRREFUTABLE EVIDENCE! A LITTLE LAB TIME, AND BOOYAH! YOU'RE DOING HARD TIME!
SO WHAT DO I DO WITH IT?
OKAY... SO WHAT'S GOING ON HERE?
WE'RE PRESERVING OUR LIBERTY.
T. COCHRAN

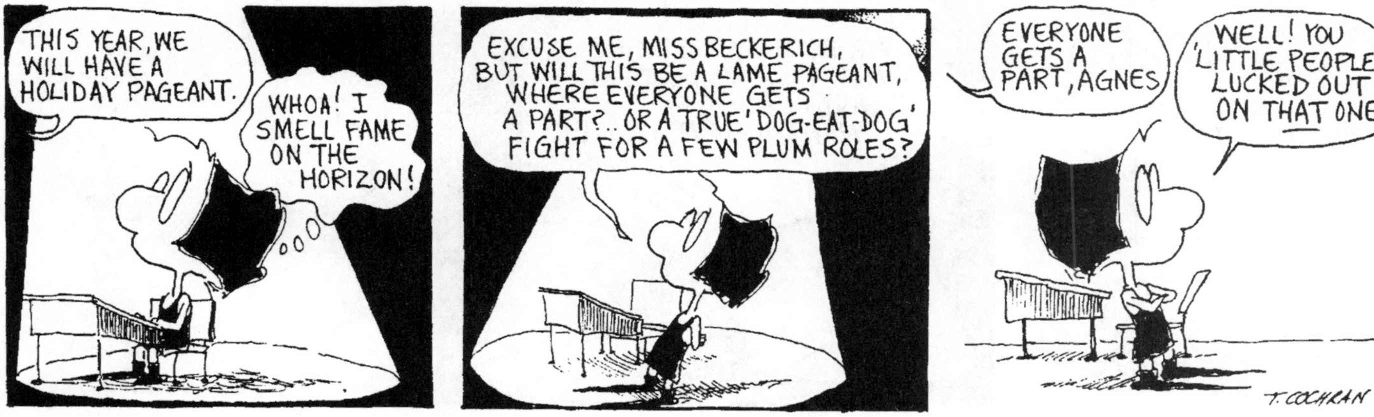
THIS YEAR, WE WILL HAVE A HOLIDAY PAGEANT.
WHOA! I SMELL FAME ON THE HORIZON!
EXCUSE ME, MISS BECKERICH, BUT WILL THIS BE A LAME PAGEANT, WHERE EVERYONE GETS A PART?.. OR A TRUE 'DOG-EAT-DOG' FIGHT FOR A FEW PLUM ROLES?
EVERYONE GETS A PART, AGNES
WELL! YOU 'LITTLE PEOPLE' LUCKED OUT ON THAT ONE!
T. COCHRAN

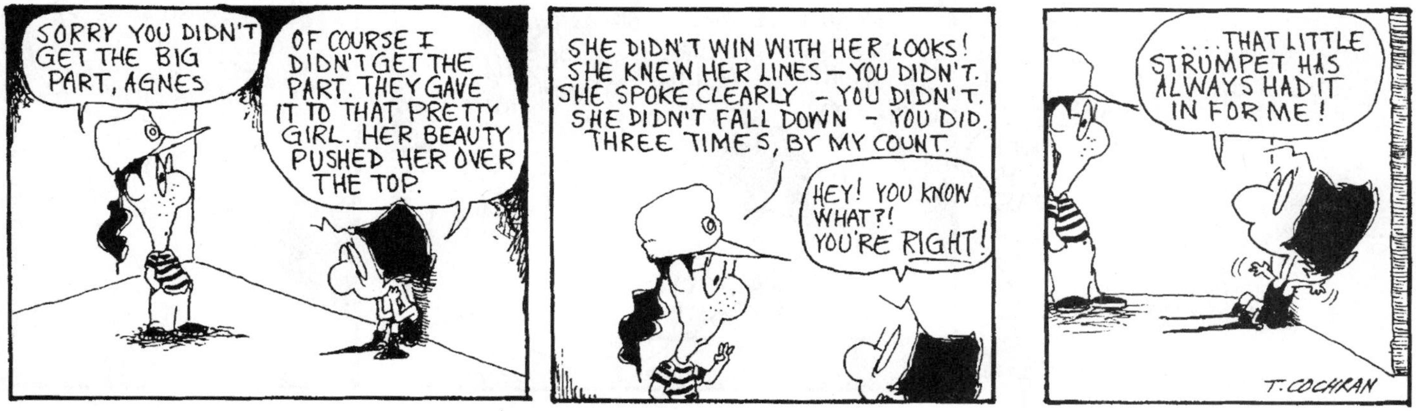
SORRY YOU DIDN'T GET THE BIG PART, AGNES
OF COURSE I DIDN'T GET THE PART. THEY GAVE IT TO THAT PRETTY GIRL. HER BEAUTY PUSHED HER OVER THE TOP.
SHE DIDN'T WIN WITH HER LOOKS! SHE KNEW HER LINES — YOU DIDN'T. SHE SPOKE CLEARLY - YOU DIDN'T. SHE DIDN'T FALL DOWN - YOU DID. THREE TIMES, BY MY COUNT.
HEY! YOU KNOW WHAT?! YOU'RE RIGHT!
....THAT LITTLE STRUMPET HAS ALWAYS HAD IT IN FOR ME!
T. COCHRAN

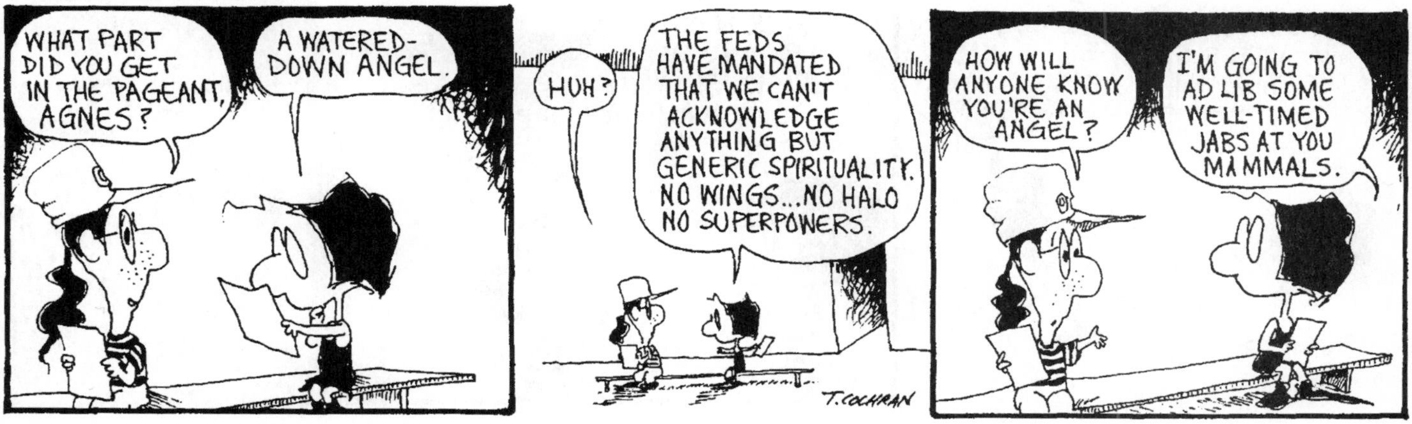
WHAT PART DID YOU GET IN THE PAGEANT, AGNES?
A WATERED-DOWN ANGEL.
HUH?
THE FEDS HAVE MANDATED THAT WE CAN'T ACKNOWLEDGE ANYTHING BUT GENERIC SPIRITUALITY. NO WINGS...NO HALO NO SUPERPOWERS.
T. COCHRAN
HOW WILL ANYONE KNOW YOU'RE AN ANGEL?
I'M GOING TO AD LIB SOME WELL-TIMED JABS AT YOU MAMMALS.

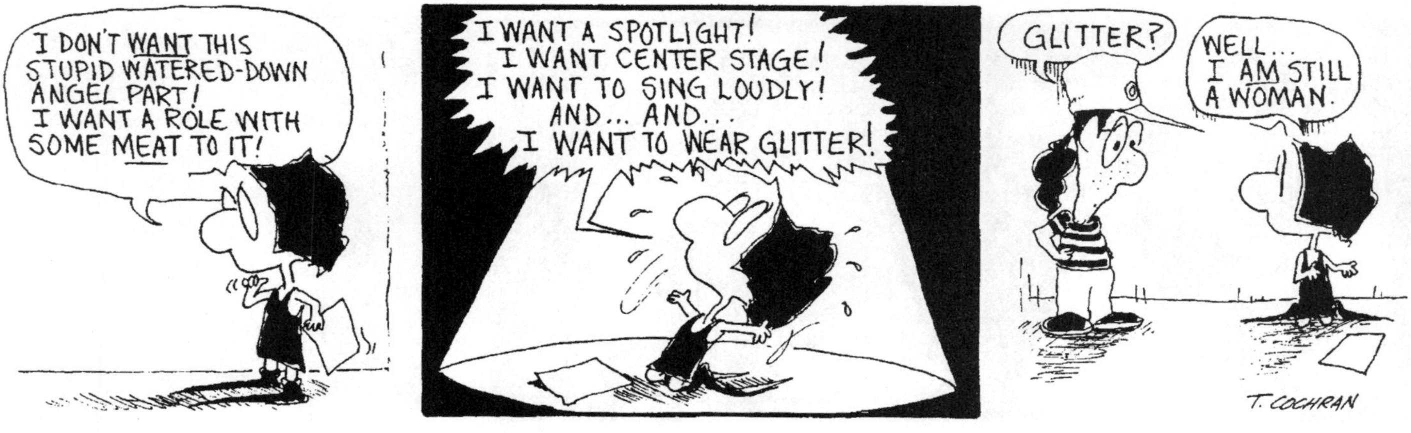
I DON'T WANT THIS STUPID WATERED-DOWN ANGEL PART! I WANT A ROLE WITH SOME MEAT TO IT!
I WANT A SPOTLIGHT! I WANT CENTER STAGE! I WANT TO SING LOUDLY! AND... AND... I WANT TO WEAR GLITTER!
GLITTER?
WELL... I AM STILL A WOMAN.
T. COCHRAN

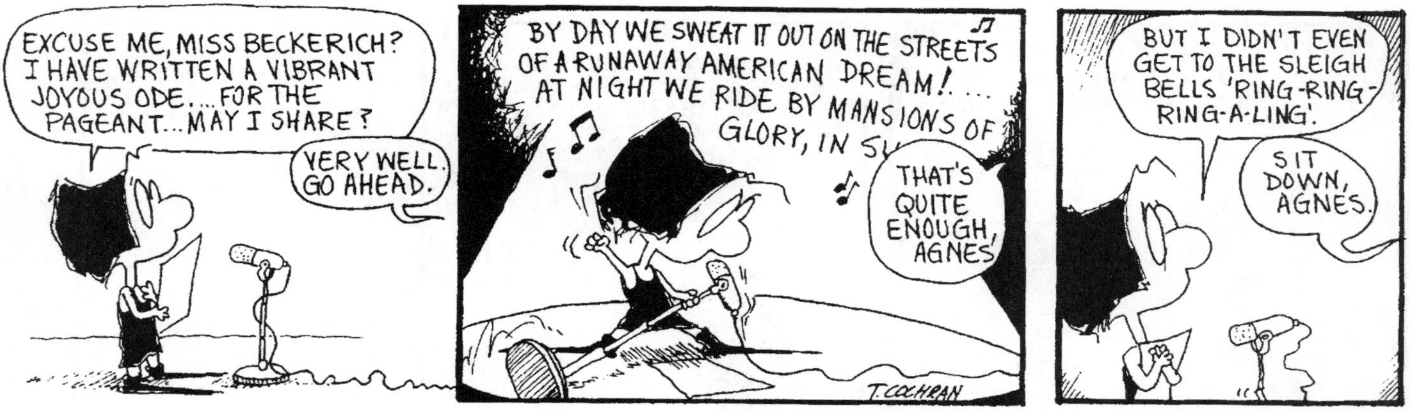
EXCUSE ME, MISS BECKERICH? I HAVE WRITTEN A VIBRANT JOYOUS ODE.... FOR THE PAGEANT... MAY I SHARE?
VERY WELL. GO AHEAD.
BY DAY WE SWEAT IT OUT ON THE STREETS OF A RUNAWAY AMERICAN DREAM!... AT NIGHT WE RIDE BY MANSIONS OF GLORY, IN SU
THAT'S QUITE ENOUGH, AGNES!
T. COCHRAN
BUT I DIDN'T EVEN GET TO THE SLEIGH BELLS 'RING-RING-RING-A-LING'.
SIT DOWN, AGNES.

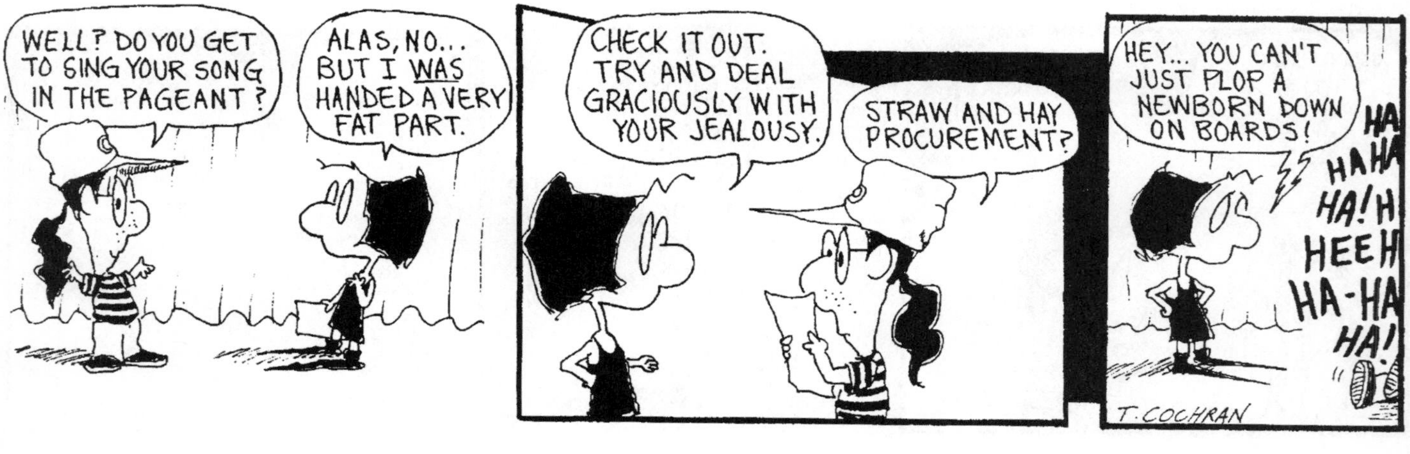
WELL? DO YOU GET TO SING YOUR SONG IN THE PAGEANT?
ALAS, NO... BUT I WAS HANDED A VERY FAT PART.
CHECK IT OUT. TRY AND DEAL GRACIOUSLY WITH YOUR JEALOUSY.
STRAW AND HAY PROCUREMENT?
HEY... YOU CAN'T JUST PLOP A NEWBORN DOWN ON BOARDS!
HA
HAHA
HA! H
HEEH
HA-HA
HA!
T. COCHRAN

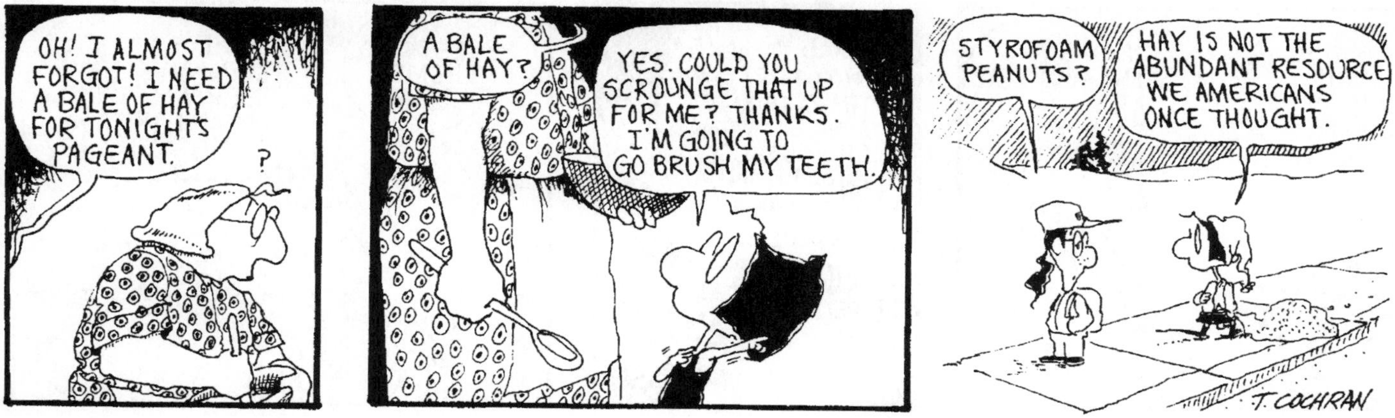
OH! I ALMOST FORGOT! I NEED A BALE OF HAY FOR TONIGHT'S PAGEANT.
?
A BALE OF HAY?
YES. COULD YOU SCROUNGE THAT UP FOR ME? THANKS. I'M GOING TO GO BRUSH MY TEETH.
STYROFOAM PEANUTS?
HAY IS NOT THE ABUNDANT RESOURCE WE AMERICANS ONCE THOUGHT.
T. COCHRAN

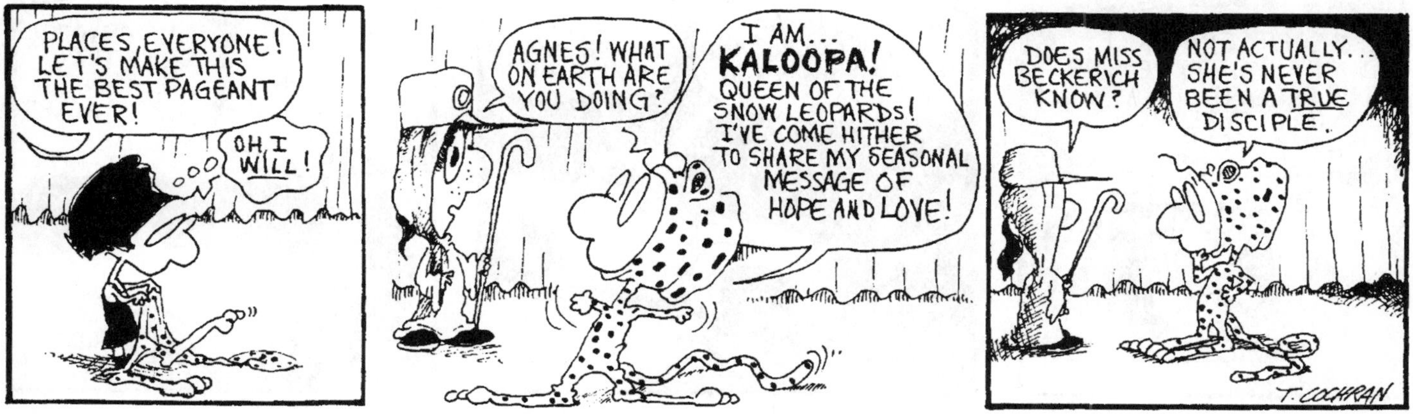
PLACES, EVERYONE! LET'S MAKE THIS THE BEST PAGEANT EVER!
OH, I WILL!
AGNES! WHAT ON EARTH ARE YOU DOING?
I AM... KALOOPA! QUEEN OF THE SNOW LEOPARDS! I'VE COME HITHER TO SHARE MY SEASONAL MESSAGE OF HOPE AND LOVE!
DOES MISS BECKERICH KNOW?
NOT ACTUALLY... SHE'S NEVER BEEN A TRUE DISCIPLE.
T. COCHRAN

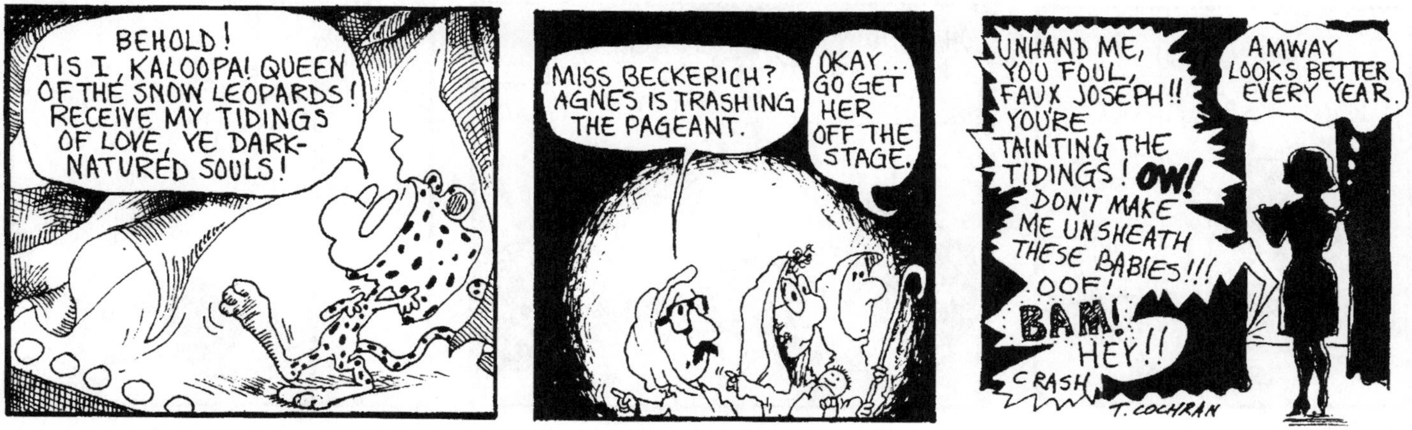
BEHOLD! 'TIS I, KALOOPA! QUEEN OF THE SNOW LEOPARDS! RECEIVE MY TIDINGS OF LOVE, YE DARK-NATURED SOULS!
MISS BECKERICH? AGNES IS TRASHING THE PAGEANT.
OKAY... GO GET HER OFF THE STAGE.
UNHAND ME, YOU FOUL, FAUX JOSEPH!! YOU'RE TAINTING THE TIDINGS! OW! DON'T MAKE ME UNSHEATH THESE BABIES!!! OOF! BAM! HEY!!
CRASH
AMWAY LOOKS BETTER EVERY YEAR.
T. COCHRAN

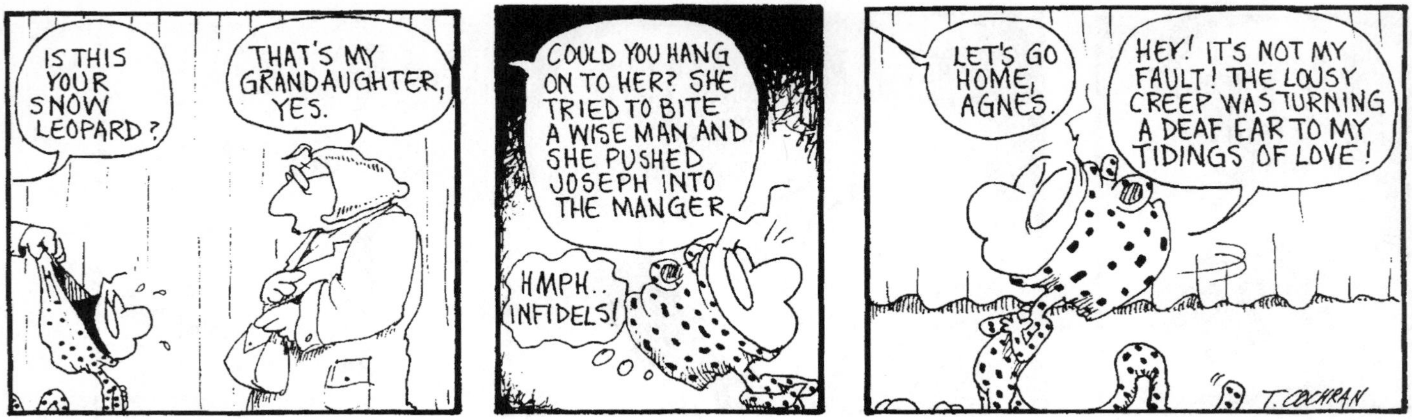
IS THIS YOUR SNOW LEOPARD?
THAT'S MY GRANDAUGHTER, YES.
COULD YOU HANG ON TO HER? SHE TRIED TO BITE A WISE MAN AND SHE PUSHED JOSEPH INTO THE MANGER.
HMPH.. INFIDELS!
LET'S GO HOME, AGNES.
HEY! IT'S NOT MY FAULT! THE LOUSY CREEP WAS TURNING A DEAF EAR TO MY TIDINGS OF LOVE!
T. COCHRAN

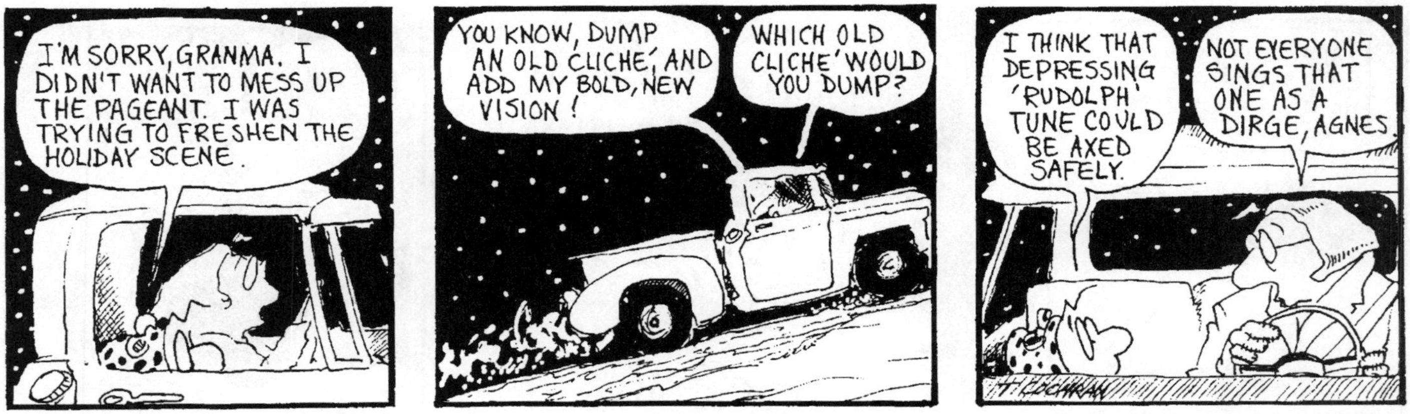
I'M SORRY, GRANMA. I DIDN'T WANT TO MESS UP THE PAGEANT. I WAS TRYING TO FRESHEN THE HOLIDAY SCENE.
YOU KNOW, DUMP AN OLD CLICHE', AND ADD MY BOLD, NEW VISION!
WHICH OLD CLICHE' WOULD YOU DUMP?
I THINK THAT DEPRESSING 'RUDOLPH' TUNE COULD BE AXED SAFELY.
NOT EVERYONE SINGS THAT ONE AS A DIRGE, AGNES.

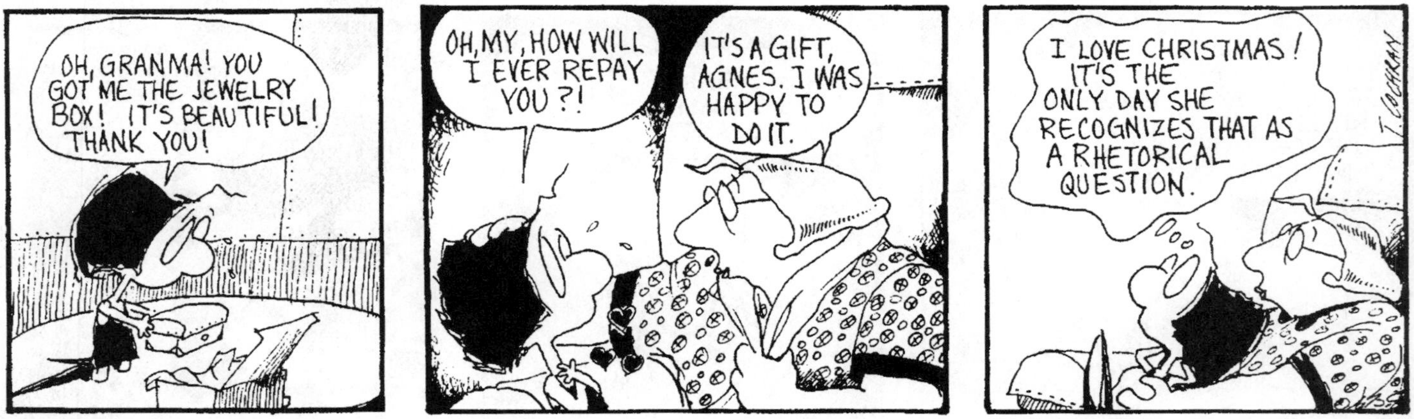
OH, GRANMA! YOU GOT ME THE JEWELRY BOX! IT'S BEAUTIFUL! THANK YOU!
OH, MY, HOW WILL I EVER REPAY YOU?!
IT'S A GIFT, AGNES. I WAS HAPPY TO DO IT.
I LOVE CHRISTMAS! IT'S THE ONLY DAY SHE RECOGNIZES THAT AS A RHETORICAL QUESTION.
T. COCHRAN

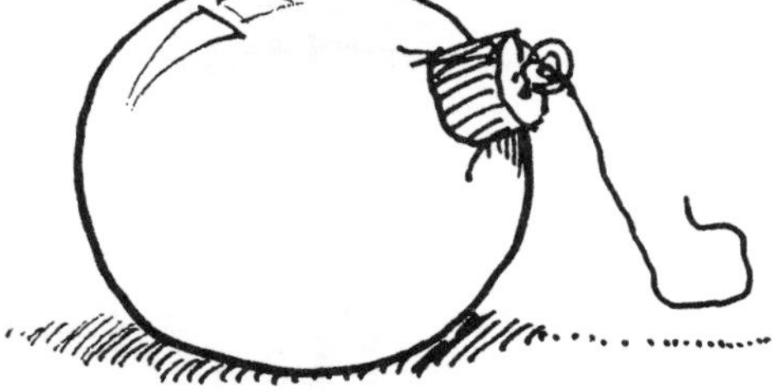

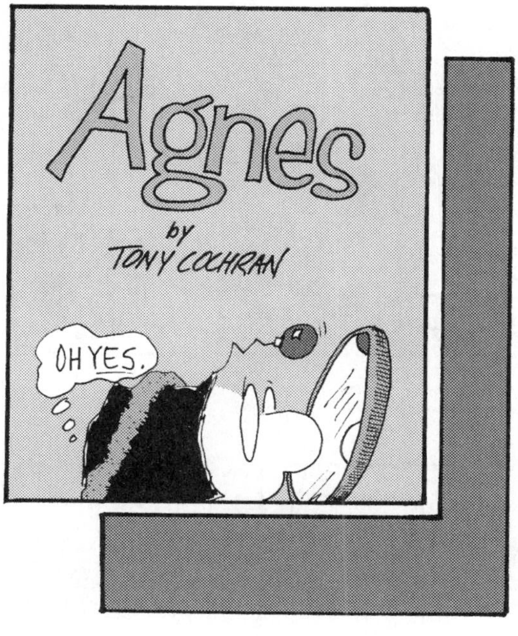
Agnes
by
TONY COCHRAN
OH YES.

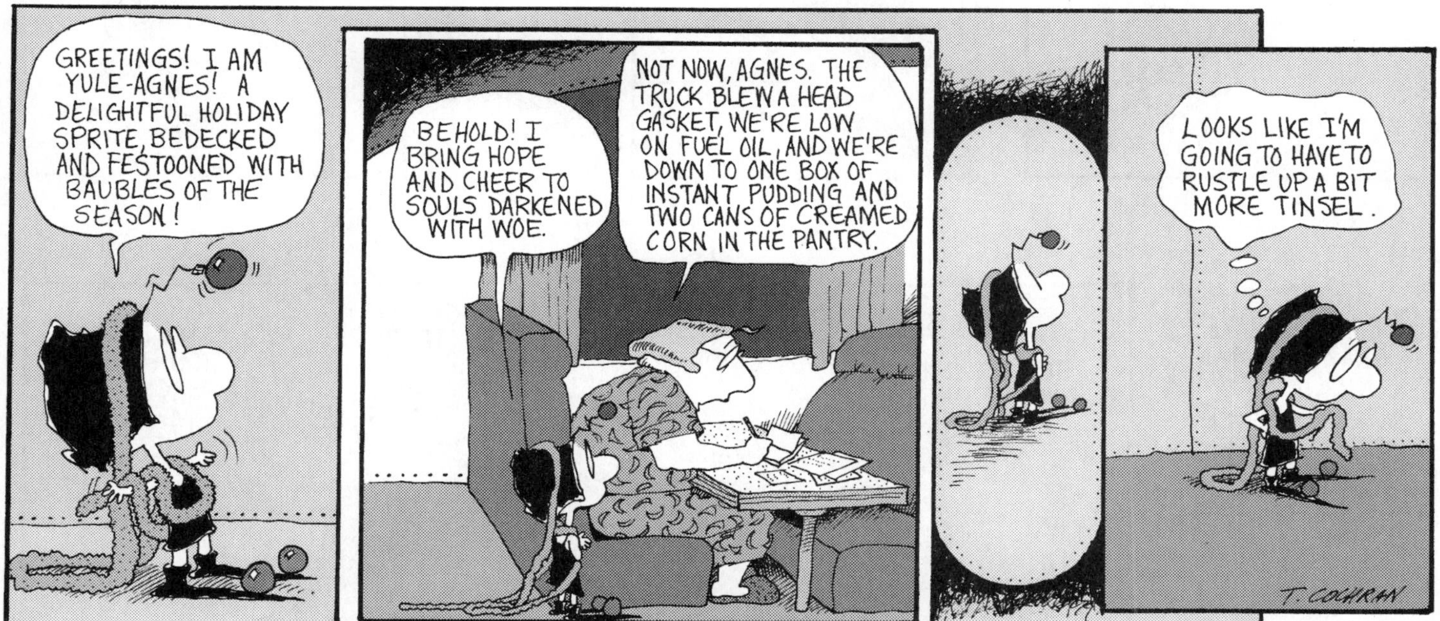
GREETINGS! I AM YULE-AGNES! A DELIGHTFUL HOLIDAY SPRITE, BEDECKED AND FESTOONED WITH BAUBLES OF THE SEASON!
BEHOLD! I BRING HOPE AND CHEER TO SOULS DARKENED WITH WOE.
NOT NOW, AGNES. THE TRUCK BLEW A HEAD GASKET, WE'RE LOW ON FUEL OIL, AND WE'RE DOWN TO ONE BOX OF INSTANT PUDDING AND TWO CANS OF CREAMED CORN IN THE PANTRY.
LOOKS LIKE I'M GOING TO HAVE TO RUSTLE UP A BIT MORE TINSEL.
T. COCHRAN

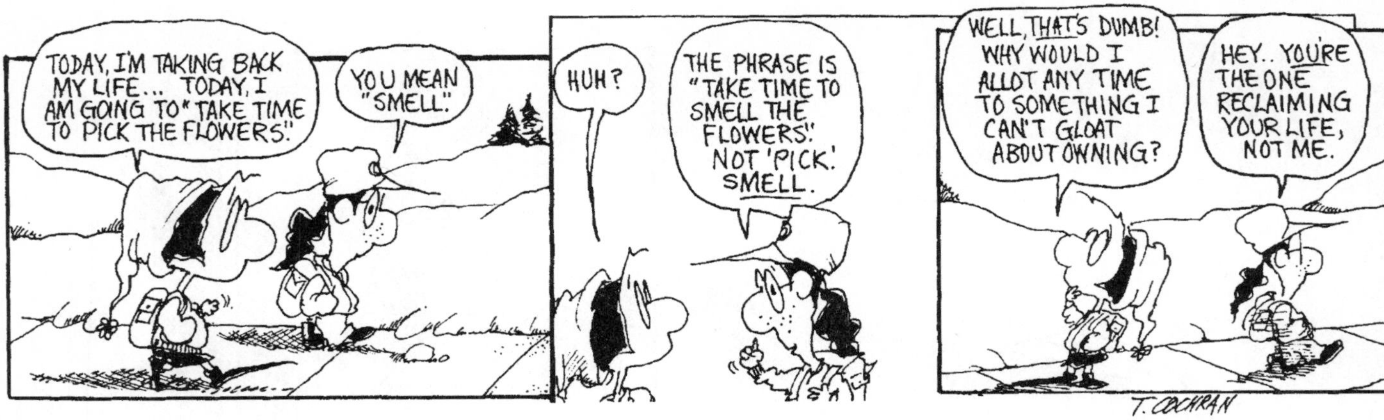
TODAY, I'M TAKING BACK MY LIFE... TODAY, I AM GOING TO "TAKE TIME TO PICK THE FLOWERS."
YOU MEAN "SMELL."
HUH?
THE PHRASE IS "TAKE TIME TO SMELL THE FLOWERS." NOT 'PICK.' SMELL.
WELL, THAT'S DUMB! WHY WOULD I ALLOT ANY TIME TO SOMETHING I CAN'T GLOAT ABOUT OWNING?
HEY.. YOU'RE THE ONE RECLAIMING YOUR LIFE, NOT ME.
T. COCHRAN

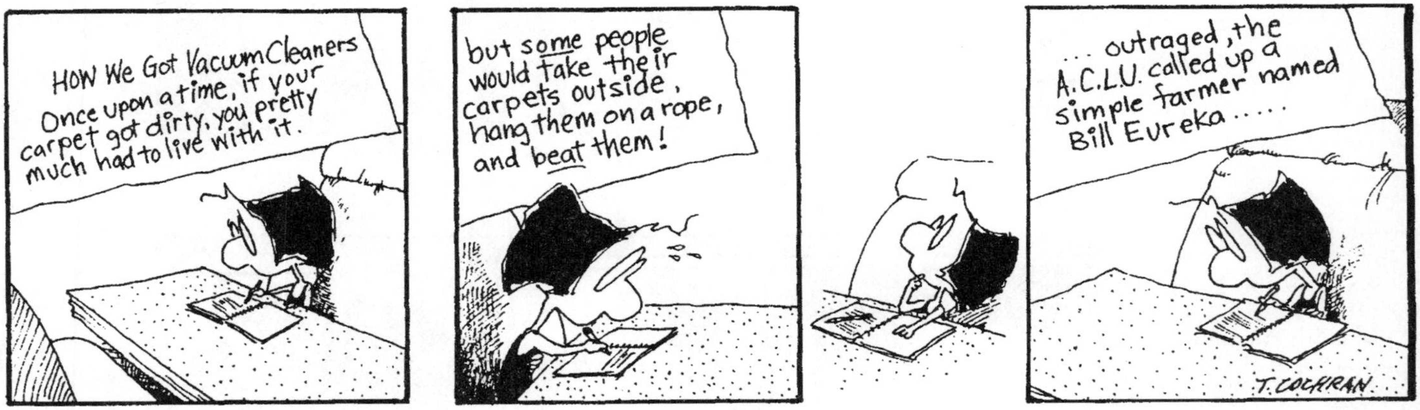
HOW We Got Vacuum Cleaners
Once upon a time, if your carpet got dirty, you pretty much had to live with it.
but some people would take their carpets outside, hang them on a rope, and beat them!
... outraged, the A.C.L.U. called up a simple farmer named Bill Eureka.....
T. COCHRAN

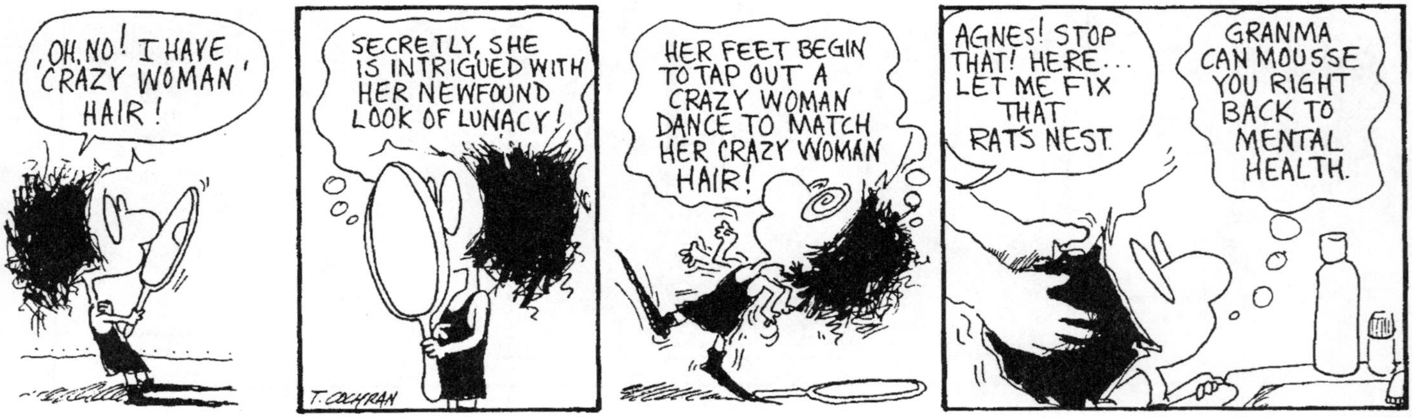
OH, NO! I HAVE 'CRAZY WOMAN' HAIR!
SECRETLY, SHE IS INTRIGUED WITH HER NEWFOUND LOOK OF LUNACY!
T. COCHRAN
HER FEET BEGIN TO TAP OUT A CRAZY WOMAN DANCE TO MATCH HER CRAZY WOMAN HAIR!
AGNES! STOP THAT! HERE... LET ME FIX THAT RAT'S NEST.
GRANMA CAN MOUSSE YOU RIGHT BACK TO MENTAL HEALTH.

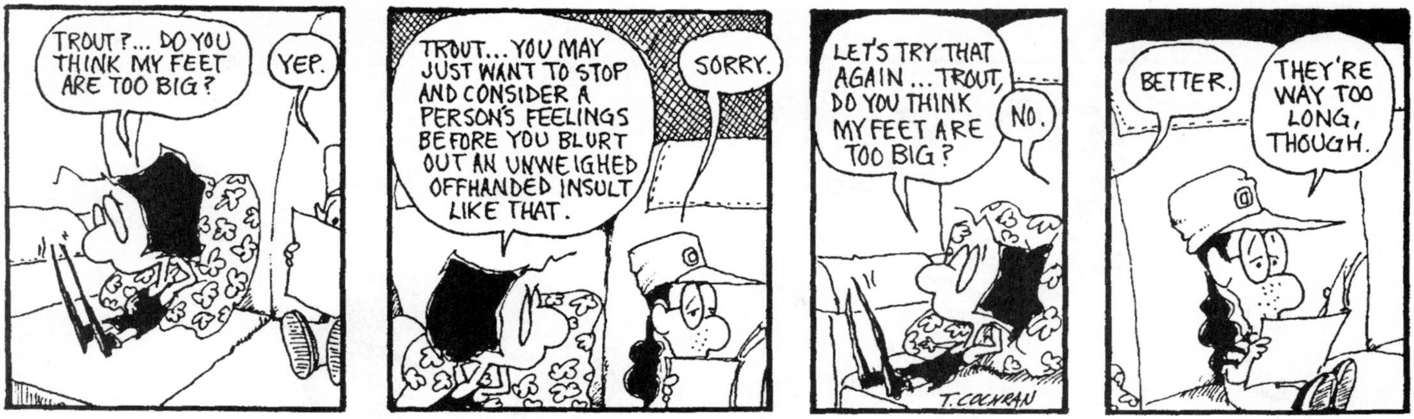
TROUT?... DO YOU THINK MY FEET ARE TOO BIG?
YEP.
TROUT... YOU MAY JUST WANT TO STOP AND CONSIDER A PERSON'S FEELINGS BEFORE YOU BLURT OUT AN UNWEIGHED OFFHANDED INSULT LIKE THAT.
SORRY.
LET'S TRY THAT AGAIN... TROUT, DO YOU THINK MY FEET ARE TOO BIG?
NO.
BETTER.
THEY'RE WAY TOO LONG, THOUGH.
T. COCHRAN

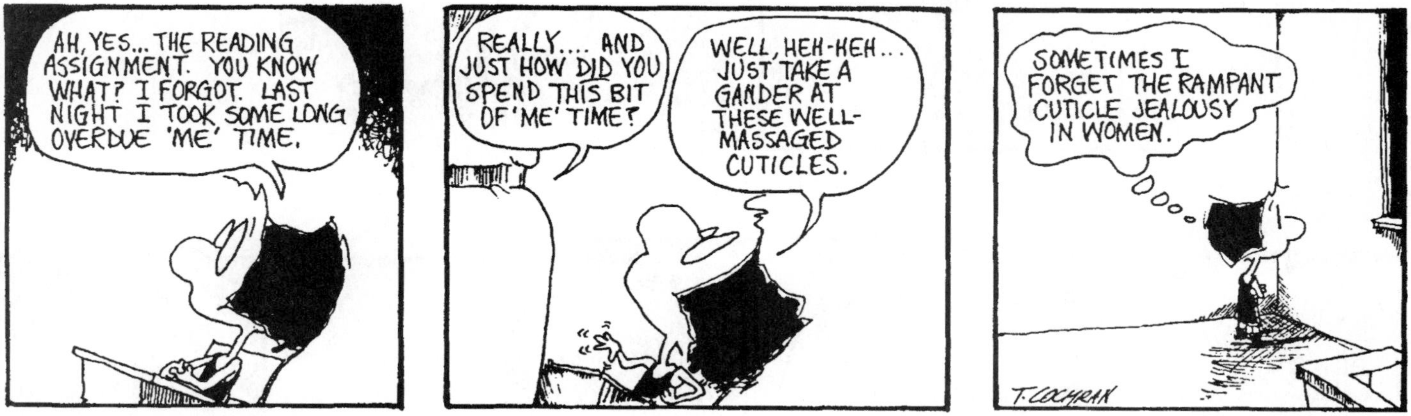
AH, YES... THE READING ASSIGNMENT. YOU KNOW WHAT? I FORGOT. LAST NIGHT I TOOK SOME LONG OVERDUE 'ME' TIME.
REALLY.... AND JUST HOW DID YOU SPEND THIS BIT OF 'ME' TIME?
WELL, HEH-HEH... JUST TAKE A GANDER AT THESE WELL-MASSAGED CUTICLES.
SOMETIMES I FORGET THE RAMPANT CUTICLE JEALOUSY IN WOMEN.
T. COCHRAN

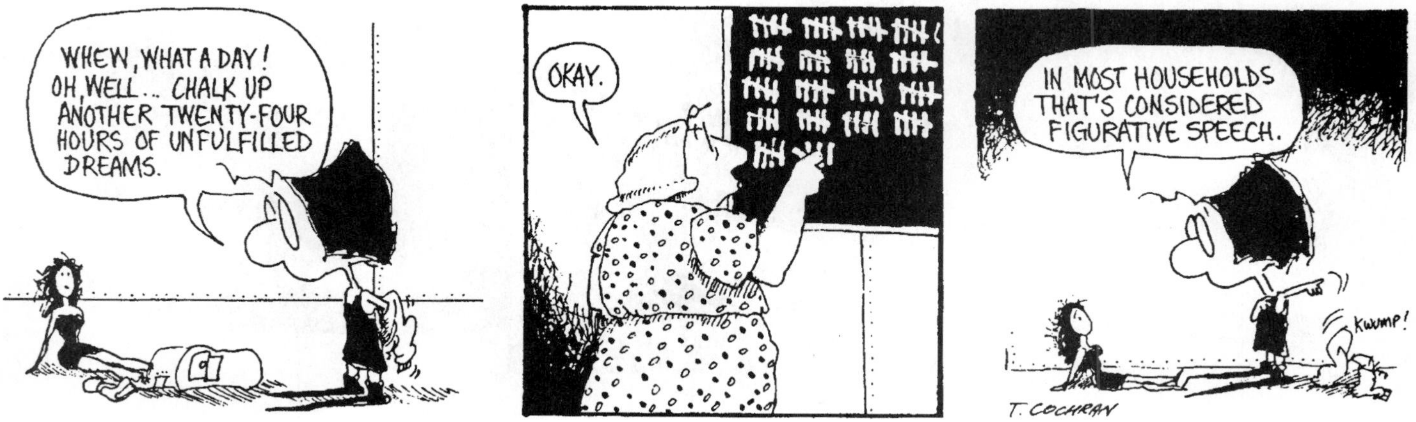
WHEW, WHAT A DAY! OH, WELL... CHALK UP ANOTHER TWENTY-FOUR HOURS OF UNFULFILLED DREAMS.
OKAY.
IN MOST HOUSEHOLDS THAT'S CONSIDERED FIGURATIVE SPEECH.
KWUMP!
T. COCHRAN

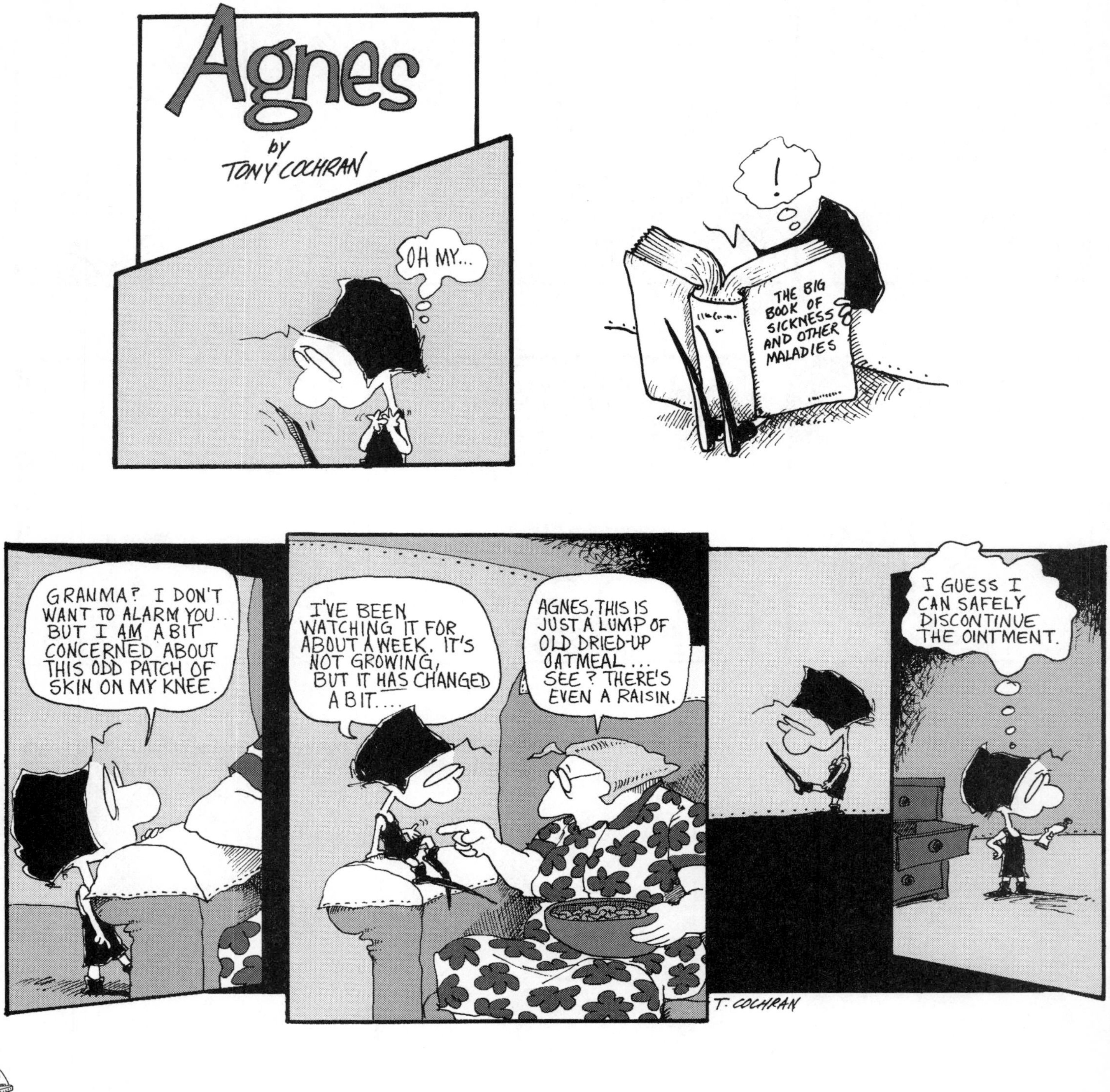
Agnes
by
TONY COCHRAN
OH MY...
!
THE BIG BOOK OF SICKNESS AND OTHER MALADIES
GRANMA? I DON'T WANT TO ALARM YOU... BUT I AM A BIT CONCERNED ABOUT THIS ODD PATCH OF SKIN ON MY KNEE.
I'VE BEEN WATCHING IT FOR ABOUT A WEEK. IT'S NOT GROWING, BUT IT HAS CHANGED A BIT....
AGNES, THIS IS JUST A LUMP OF OLD DRIED-UP OATMEAL... SEE? THERE'S EVEN A RAISIN.
I GUESS I CAN SAFELY DISCONTINUE THE OINTMENT.
T. COCHRAN

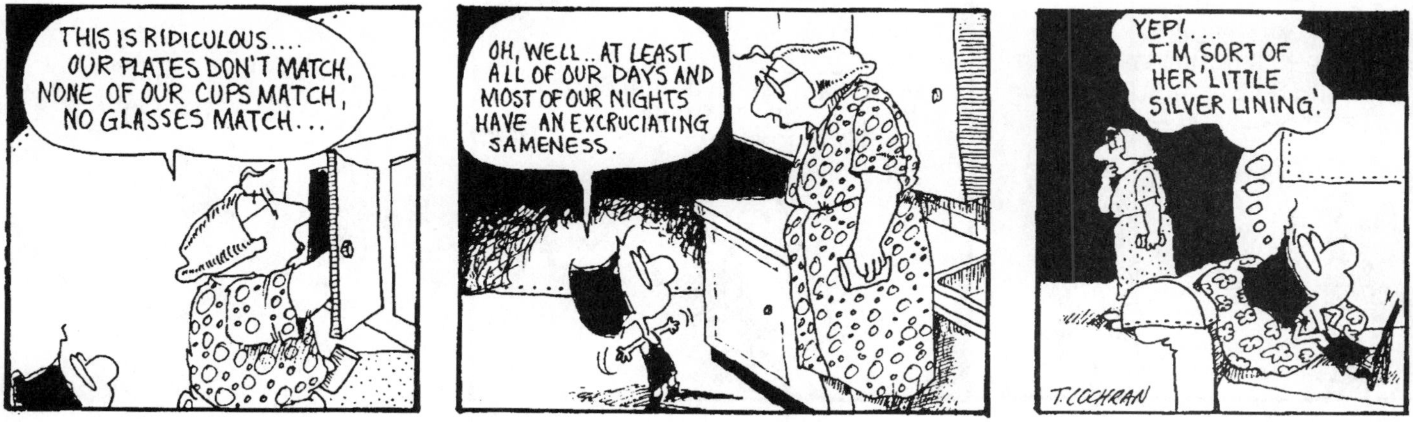
THIS IS RIDICULOUS.... OUR PLATES DON'T MATCH, NONE OF OUR CUPS MATCH, NO GLASSES MATCH...
OH, WELL.. AT LEAST ALL OF OUR DAYS AND MOST OF OUR NIGHTS HAVE AN EXCRUCIATING SAMENESS.
YEP!... I'M SORT OF HER 'LITTLE SILVER LINING'.
T. COCHRAN

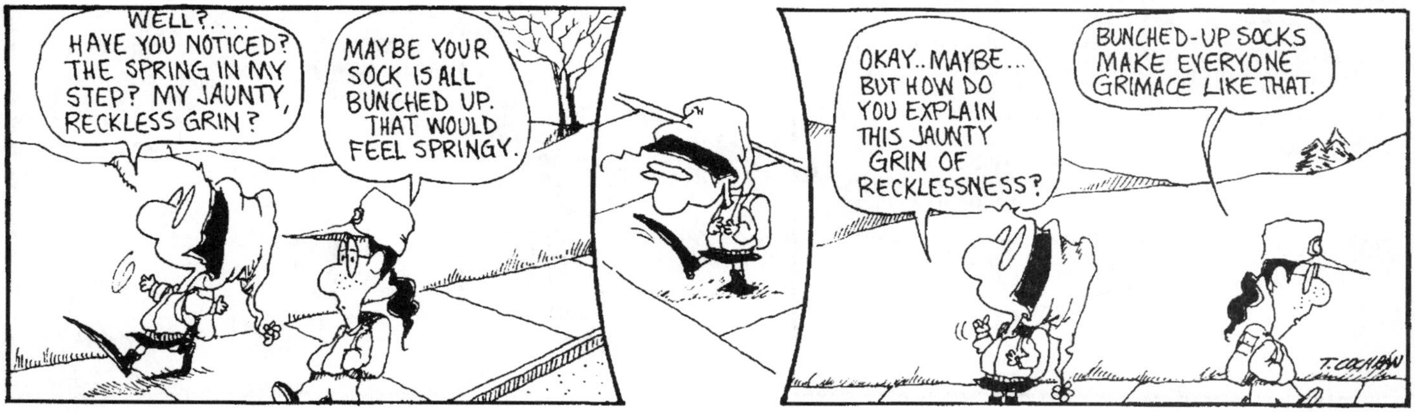
WELL?.... HAVE YOU NOTICED? THE SPRING IN MY STEP? MY JAUNTY, RECKLESS GRIN?
MAYBE YOUR SOCK IS ALL BUNCHED UP. THAT WOULD FEEL SPRINGY.
OKAY.. MAYBE... BUT HOW DO YOU EXPLAIN THIS JAUNTY GRIN OF RECKLESSNESS?
BUNCHED-UP SOCKS MAKE EVERYONE GRIMACE LIKE THAT.
T. COCHRAN

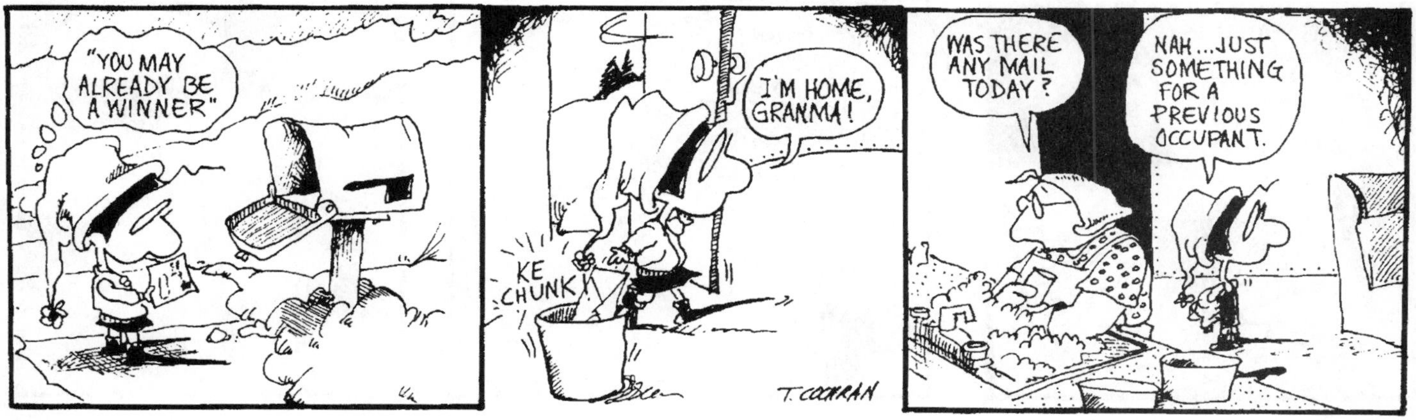
"YOU MAY ALREADY BE A WINNER"
I'M HOME, GRANMA!
KE CHUNK
T. COCHRAN
WAS THERE ANY MAIL TODAY?
NAH... JUST SOMETHING FOR A PREVIOUS OCCUPANT.

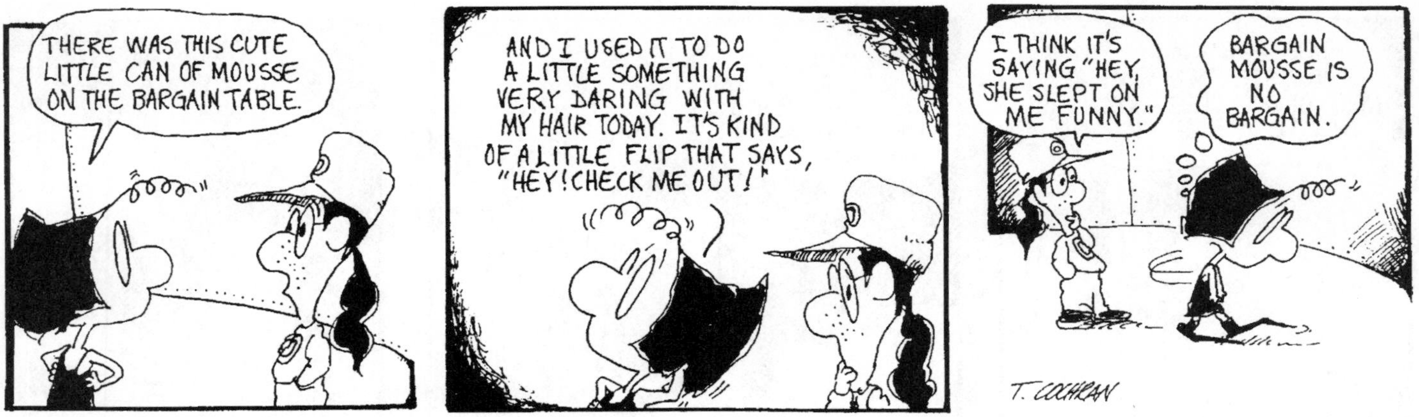
THERE WAS THIS CUTE LITTLE CAN OF MOUSSE ON THE BARGAIN TABLE.
AND I USED IT TO DO A LITTLE SOMETHING VERY DARING WITH MY HAIR TODAY. IT'S KIND OF A LITTLE FLIP THAT SAYS, "HEY! CHECK ME OUT!"
I THINK IT'S SAYING "HEY, SHE SLEPT ON ME FUNNY."
BARGAIN MOUSSE IS NO BARGAIN.
T. COCHRAN

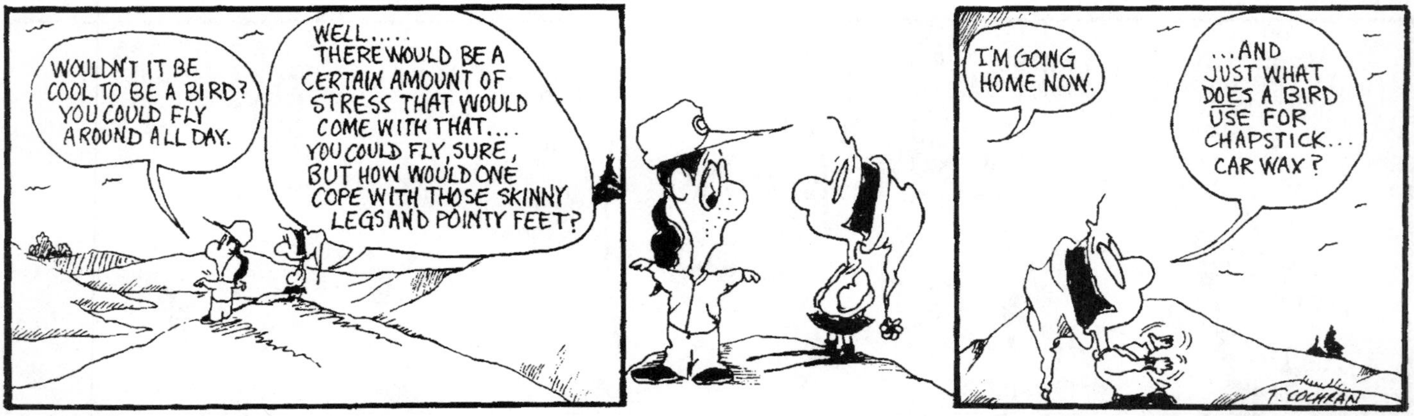
WOULDN'T IT BE COOL TO BE A BIRD? YOU COULD FLY AROUND ALL DAY.
WELL..... THERE WOULD BE A CERTAIN AMOUNT OF STRESS THAT WOULD COME WITH THAT.... YOU COULD FLY, SURE, BUT HOW WOULD ONE COPE WITH THOSE SKINNY LEGS AND POINTY FEET?
I'M GOING HOME NOW.
...AND JUST WHAT DOES A BIRD USE FOR CHAPSTICK... CAR WAX?
T. COCHRAN

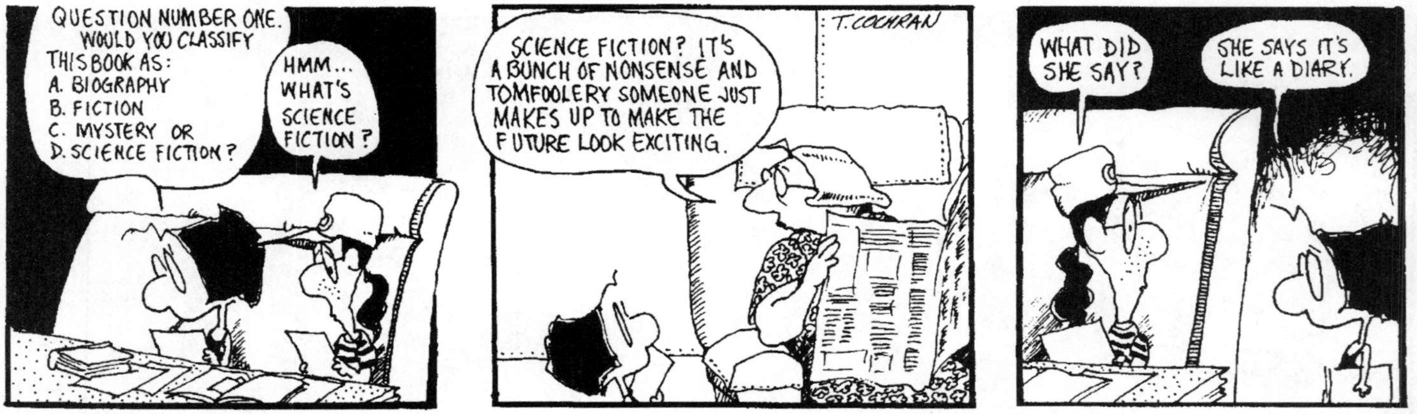
QUESTION NUMBER ONE. WOULD YOU CLASSIFY THIS BOOK AS:
A. BIOGRAPHY
B. FICTION
C. MYSTERY OR
D. SCIENCE FICTION?
HMM... WHAT'S SCIENCE FICTION?
T. COCHRAN
SCIENCE FICTION? IT'S A BUNCH OF NONSENSE AND TOMFOOLERY SOMEONE JUST MAKES UP TO MAKE THE FUTURE LOOK EXCITING.
WHAT DID SHE SAY?
SHE SAYS IT'S LIKE A DIARY.

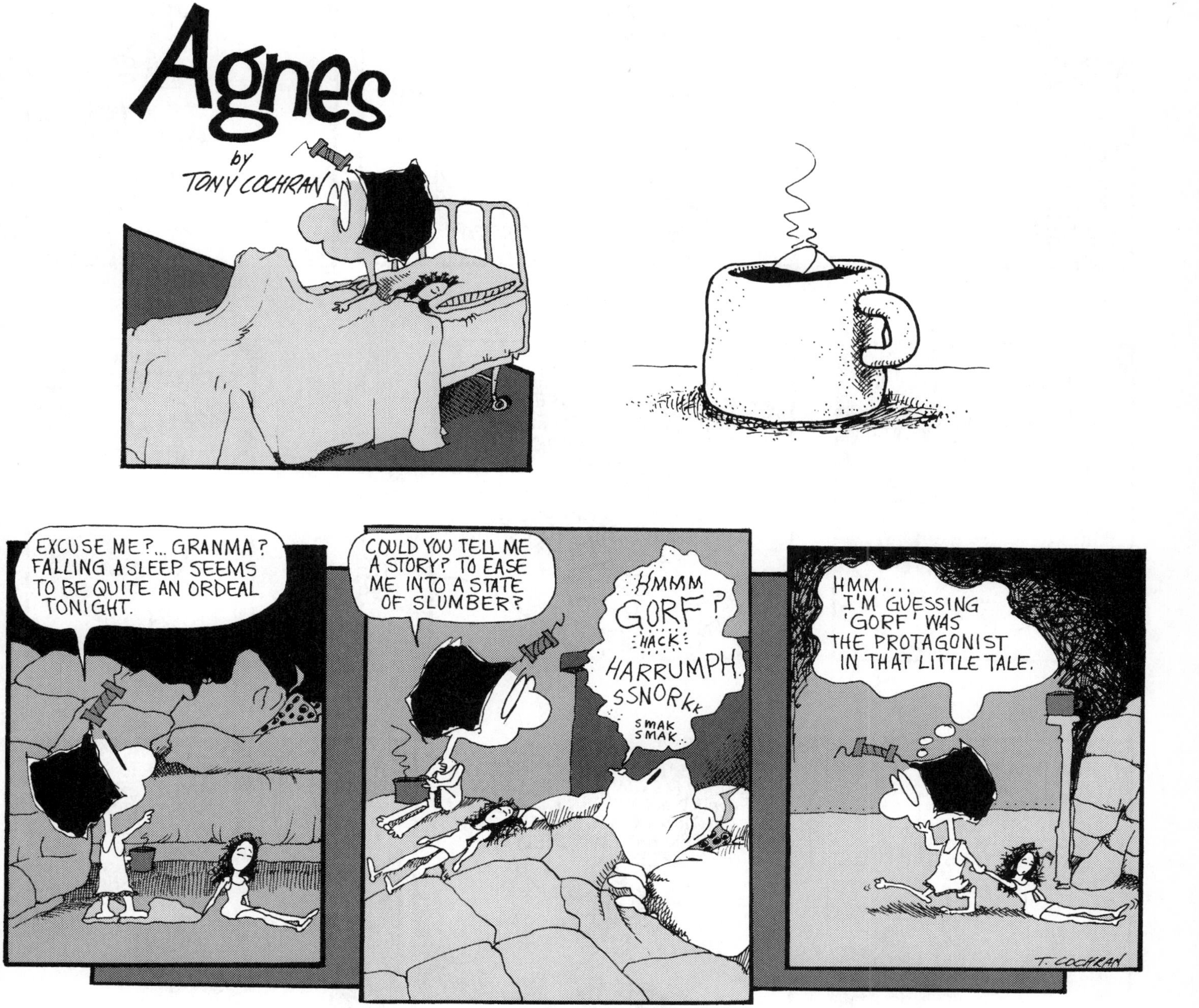
Agnes
by
TONY COCHRAN
EXCUSE ME?... GRANMA? FALLING ASLEEP SEEMS TO BE QUITE AN ORDEAL TONIGHT.
COULD YOU TELL ME A STORY? TO EASE ME INTO A STATE OF SLUMBER?
HMMM
GORF?
HACK
HARRUMPH
SSNORKk
SMAK SMAK
HMM.... I'M GUESSING 'GORF' WAS THE PROTAGONIST IN THAT LITTLE TALE.
T. COCHRAN

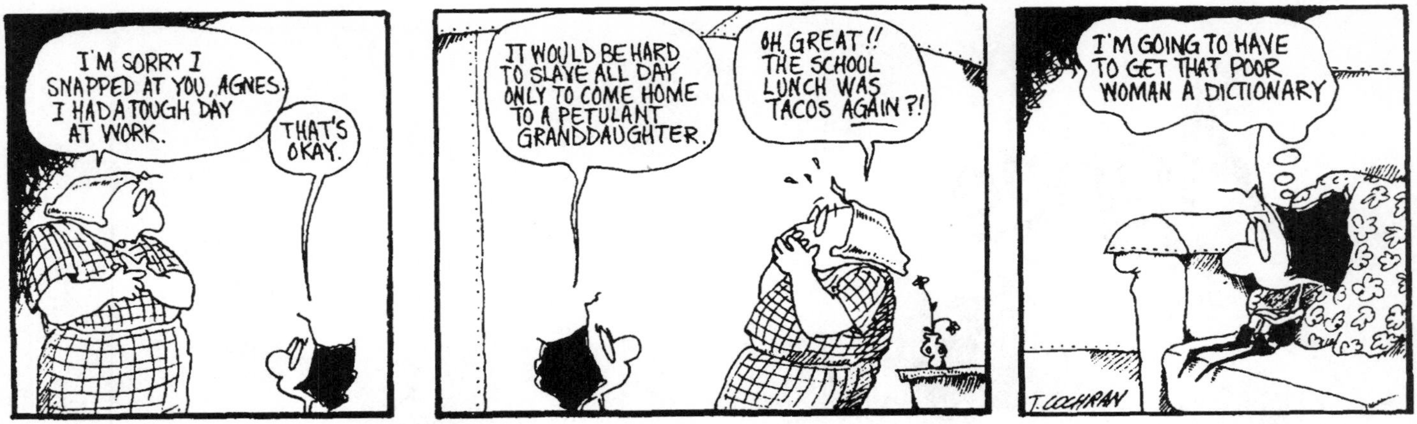
I'M SORRY I SNAPPED AT YOU, AGNES. I HAD A TOUGH DAY AT WORK.
THAT'S OKAY.
IT WOULD BE HARD TO SLAVE ALL DAY ONLY TO COME HOME TO A PETULANT GRANDDAUGHTER.
OH, GREAT!! THE SCHOOL LUNCH WAS TACOS AGAIN?!
I'M GOING TO HAVE TO GET THAT POOR WOMAN A DICTIONARY
T. COCHRAN

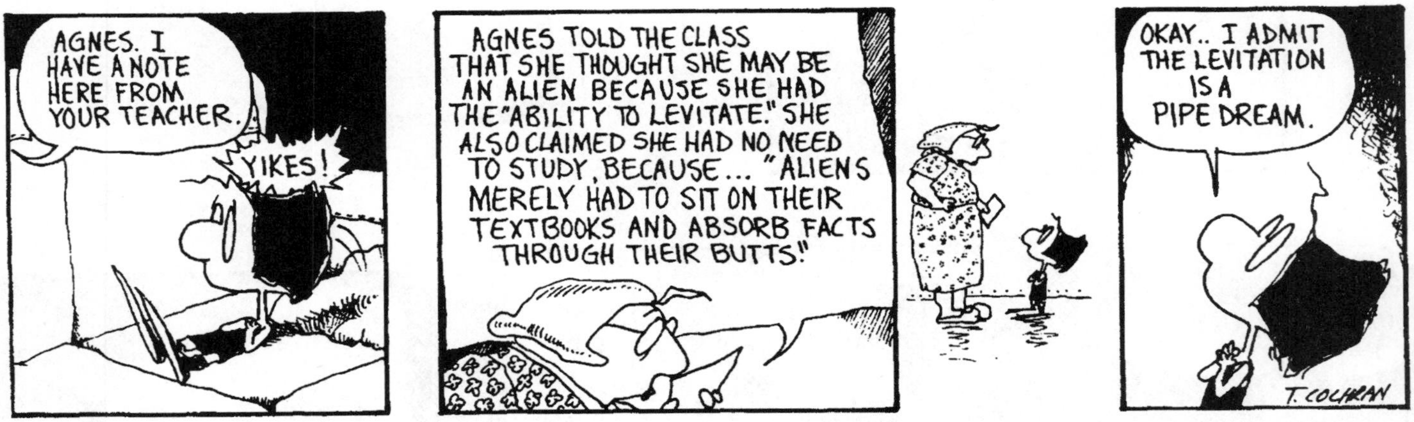
AGNES. I HAVE A NOTE HERE FROM YOUR TEACHER.
YIKES!
AGNES TOLD THE CLASS THAT SHE THOUGHT SHE MAY BE AN ALIEN BECAUSE SHE HAD THE "ABILITY TO LEVITATE." SHE ALSO CLAIMED SHE HAD NO NEED TO STUDY, BECAUSE... "ALIENS MERELY HAD TO SIT ON THEIR TEXTBOOKS AND ABSORB FACTS THROUGH THEIR BUTTS."
OKAY.. I ADMIT THE LEVITATION IS A PIPE DREAM.
T. COCHRAN

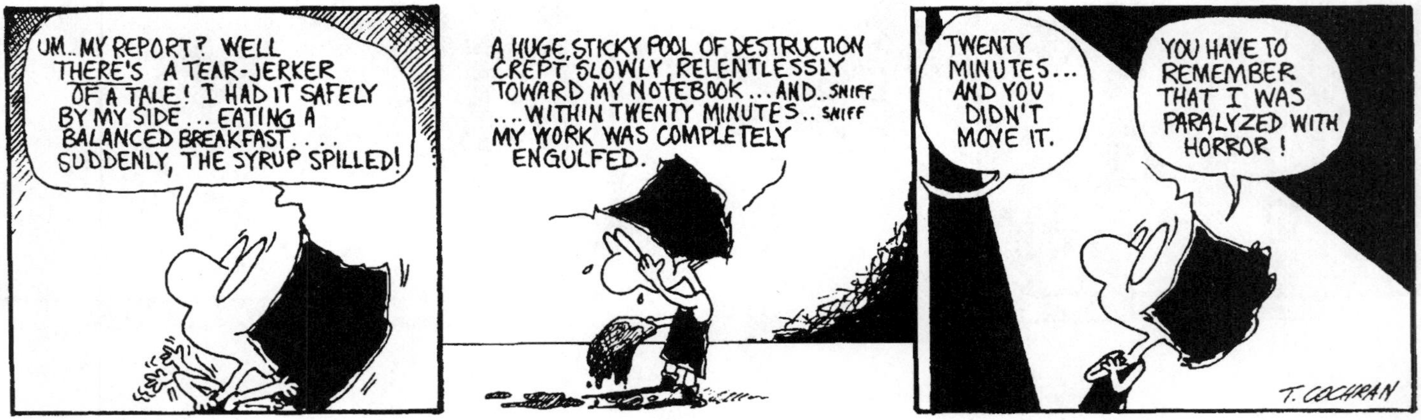
UM.. MY REPORT? WELL THERE'S A TEAR-JERKER OF A TALE! I HAD IT SAFELY BY MY SIDE... EATING A BALANCED BREAKFAST..... SUDDENLY, THE SYRUP SPILLED!
A HUGE, STICKY POOL OF DESTRUCTION CREPT SLOWLY, RELENTLESSLY TOWARD MY NOTEBOOK... AND.. SNIFF ....WITHIN TWENTY MINUTES.. SNIFF MY WORK WAS COMPLETELY ENGULFED.
TWENTY MINUTES... AND YOU DIDN'T MOVE IT.
YOU HAVE TO REMEMBER THAT I WAS PARALYZED WITH HORROR!
T. COCHRAN

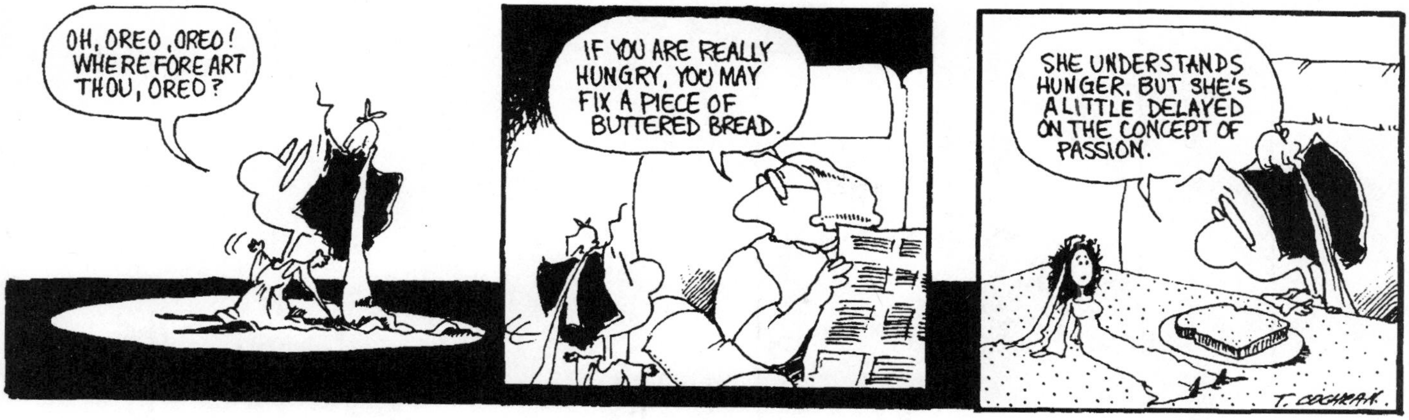
OH, OREO, OREO! WHEREFORE ART THOU, OREO?
IF YOU ARE REALLY HUNGRY, YOU MAY FIX A PIECE OF BUTTERED BREAD.
SHE UNDERSTANDS HUNGER, BUT SHE'S A LITTLE DELAYED ON THE CONCEPT OF PASSION.
T. COCHRAN

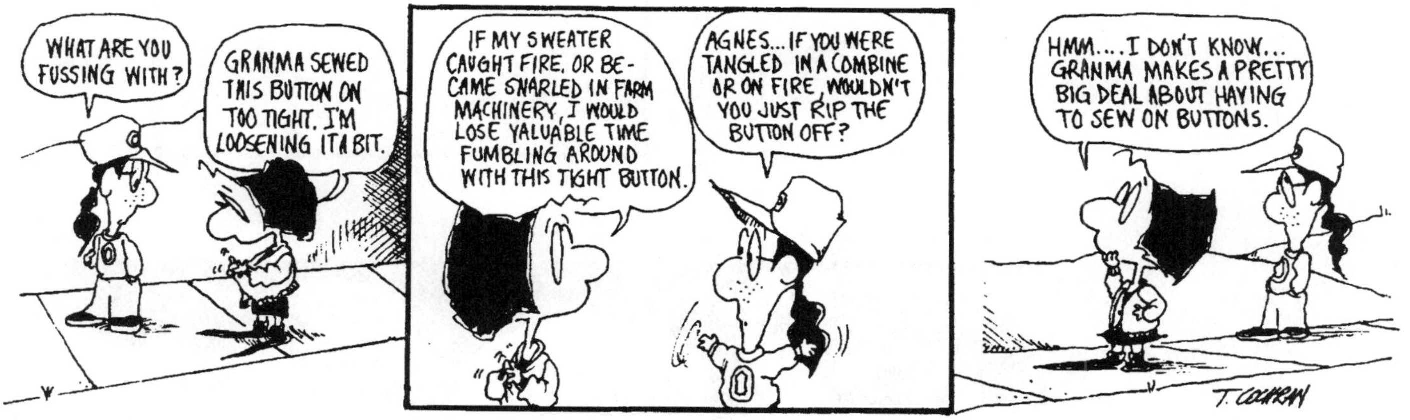
WHAT ARE YOU FUSSING WITH?
GRANMA SEWED THIS BUTTON ON TOO TIGHT. I'M LOOSENING IT A BIT.
IF MY SWEATER CAUGHT FIRE, OR BECAME SNARLED IN FARM MACHINERY, I WOULD LOSE VALUABLE TIME FUMBLING AROUND WITH THIS TIGHT BUTTON.
AGNES... IF YOU WERE TANGLED IN A COMBINE OR ON FIRE, WOULDN'T YOU JUST RIP THE BUTTON OFF?
HMM.... I DON'T KNOW... GRANMA MAKES A PRETTY BIG DEAL ABOUT HAVING TO SEW ON BUTTONS.
T. COCHRAN

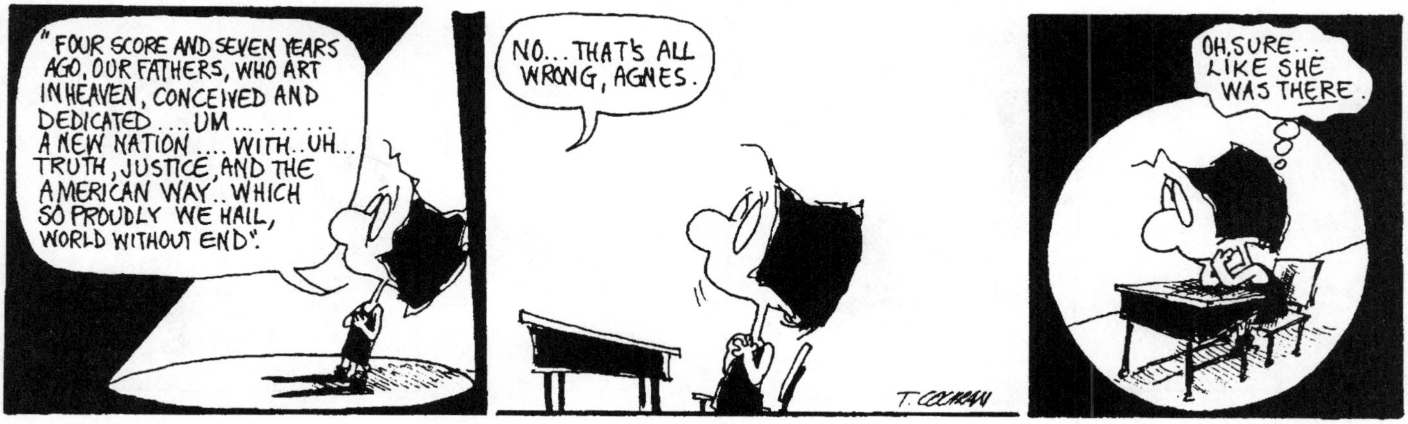
"FOUR SCORE AND SEVEN YEARS AGO, OUR FATHERS, WHO ART IN HEAVEN, CONCEIVED AND DEDICATED ....UM .... A NEW NATION .... WITH..UH... TRUTH, JUSTICE, AND THE AMERICAN WAY.. WHICH SO PROUDLY WE HAIL, WORLD WITHOUT END".
NO... THAT'S ALL WRONG, AGNES.
T. COCHRAN
OH, SURE... LIKE SHE WAS THERE.

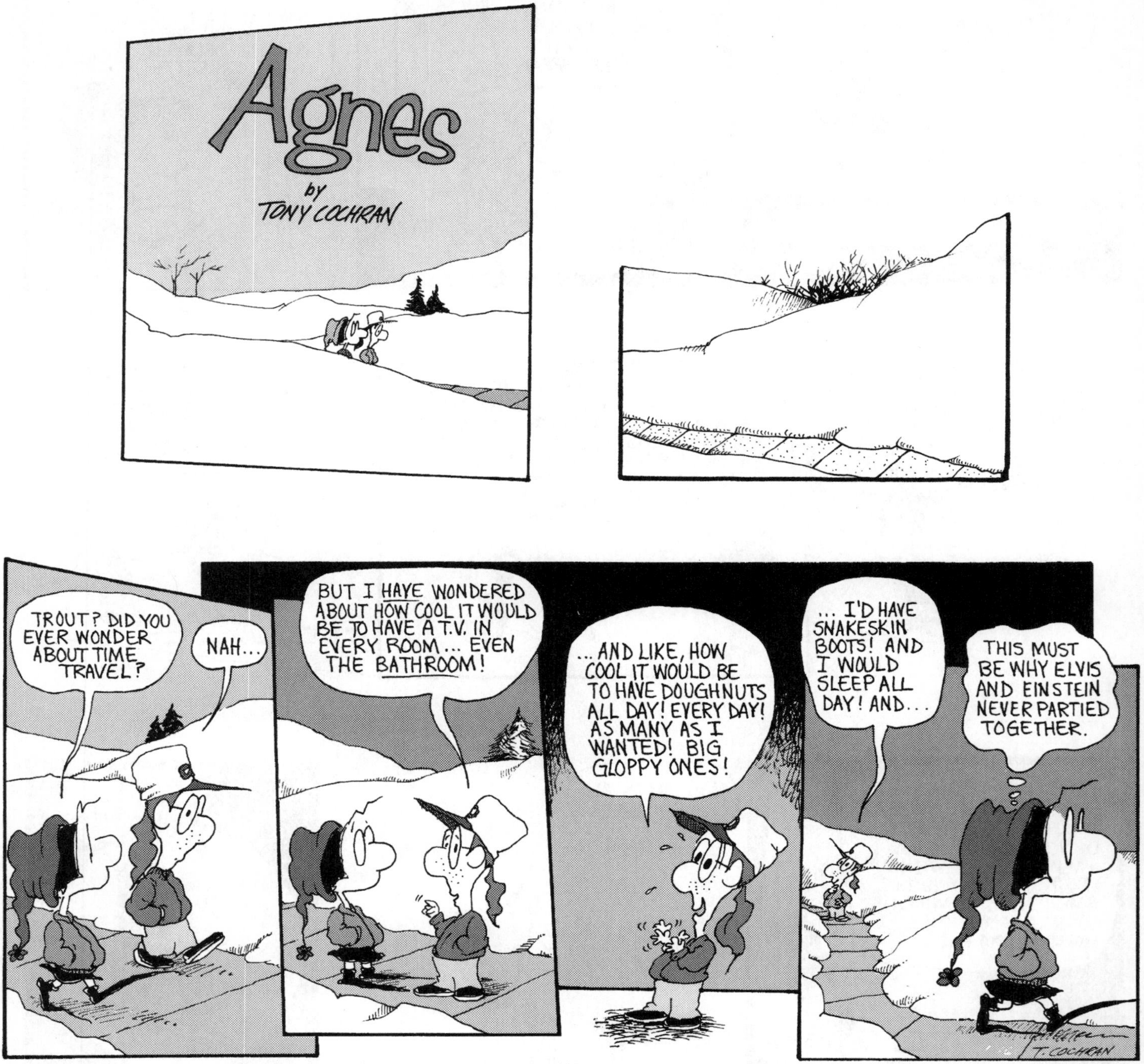
Agnes
by
TONY COCHRAN
TROUT? DID YOU EVER WONDER ABOUT TIME TRAVEL?
NAH...
BUT I HAVE WONDERED ABOUT HOW COOL IT WOULD BE TO HAVE A T.V. IN EVERY ROOM... EVEN THE BATHROOM!
...AND LIKE, HOW COOL IT WOULD BE TO HAVE DOUGHNUTS ALL DAY! EVERY DAY! AS MANY AS I WANTED! BIG GLOPPY ONES!
... I'D HAVE SNAKESKIN BOOTS! AND I WOULD SLEEP ALL DAY! AND...
THIS MUST BE WHY ELVIS AND EINSTEIN NEVER PARTIED TOGETHER.
T. COCHRAN

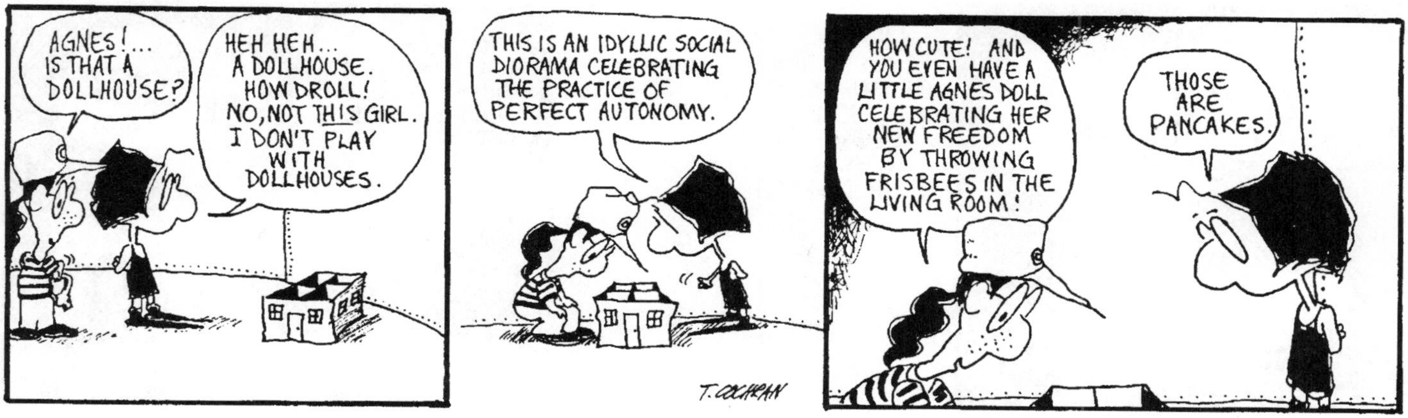
AGNES!... IS THAT A DOLLHOUSE?
HEH HEH... A DOLLHOUSE. HOW DROLL! NO, NOT THIS GIRL. I DON'T PLAY WITH DOLLHOUSES.
THIS IS AN IDYLLIC SOCIAL DIORAMA CELEBRATING THE PRACTICE OF PERFECT AUTONOMY.
T. COCHRAN
HOW CUTE! AND YOU EVEN HAVE A LITTLE AGNES DOLL CELEBRATING HER NEW FREEDOM BY THROWING FRISBEES IN THE LIVING ROOM!
THOSE ARE PANCAKES.

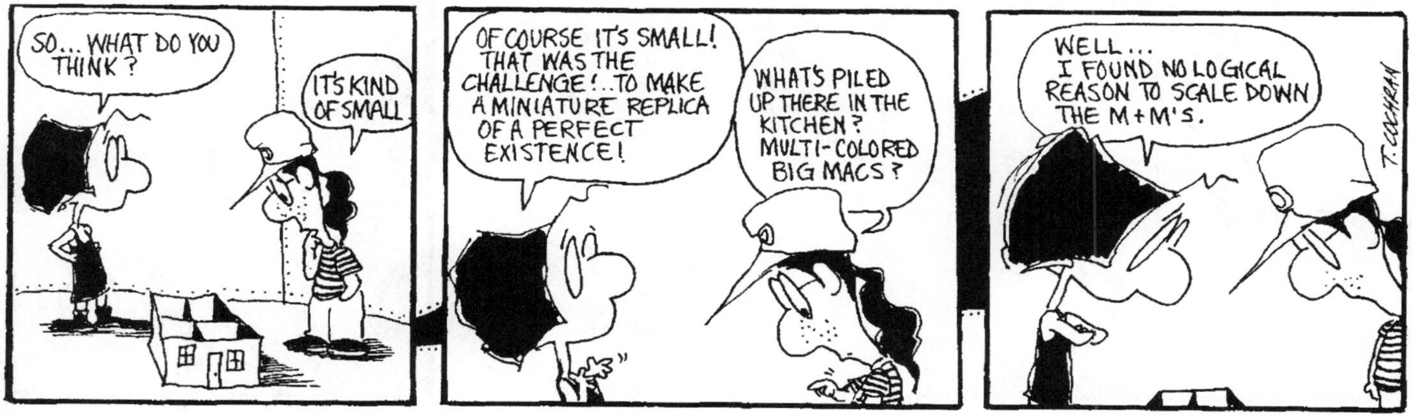
SO... WHAT DO YOU THINK?
IT'S KIND OF SMALL
OF COURSE IT'S SMALL! THAT WAS THE CHALLENGE!...TO MAKE A MINIATURE REPLICA OF A PERFECT EXISTENCE!
WHAT'S PILED UP THERE IN THE KITCHEN? MULTI-COLORED BIG MACS?
WELL... I FOUND NO LOGICAL REASON TO SCALE DOWN THE M+M'S.
T. COCHRAN

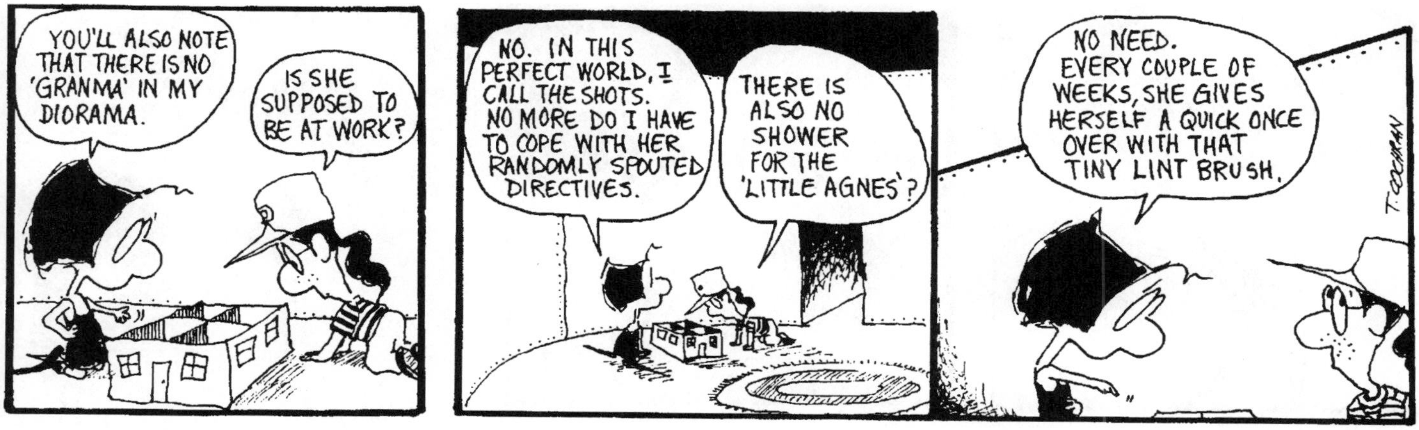
YOU'LL ALSO NOTE THAT THERE IS NO 'GRANMA' IN MY DIORAMA.
IS SHE SUPPOSED TO BE AT WORK?
NO. IN THIS PERFECT WORLD, I CALL THE SHOTS. NO MORE DO I HAVE TO COPE WITH HER RANDOMLY SPOUTED DIRECTIVES.
THERE IS ALSO NO SHOWER FOR THE 'LITTLE AGNES'?
NO NEED. EVERY COUPLE OF WEEKS, SHE GIVES HERSELF A QUICK ONCE OVER WITH THAT TINY LINT BRUSH.
T. COCHRAN

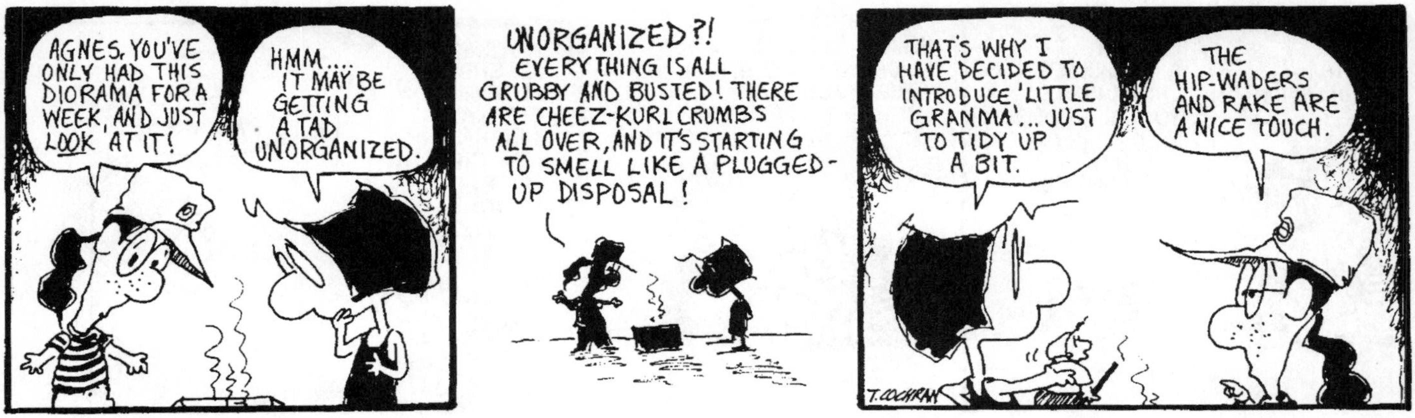
AGNES, YOU'VE ONLY HAD THIS DIORAMA FOR A WEEK, AND JUST LOOK AT IT!
HMM.... IT MAY BE GETTING A TAD UNORGANIZED.
UNORGANIZED?! EVERYTHING IS ALL GRUBBY AND BUSTED! THERE ARE CHEEZ-KURL CRUMBS ALL OVER, AND IT'S STARTING TO SMELL LIKE A PLUGGED-UP DISPOSAL!
THAT'S WHY I HAVE DECIDED TO INTRODUCE 'LITTLE GRANMA'... JUST TO TIDY UP A BIT.
THE HIP-WADERS AND RAKE ARE A NICE TOUCH.
T. COCHRAN

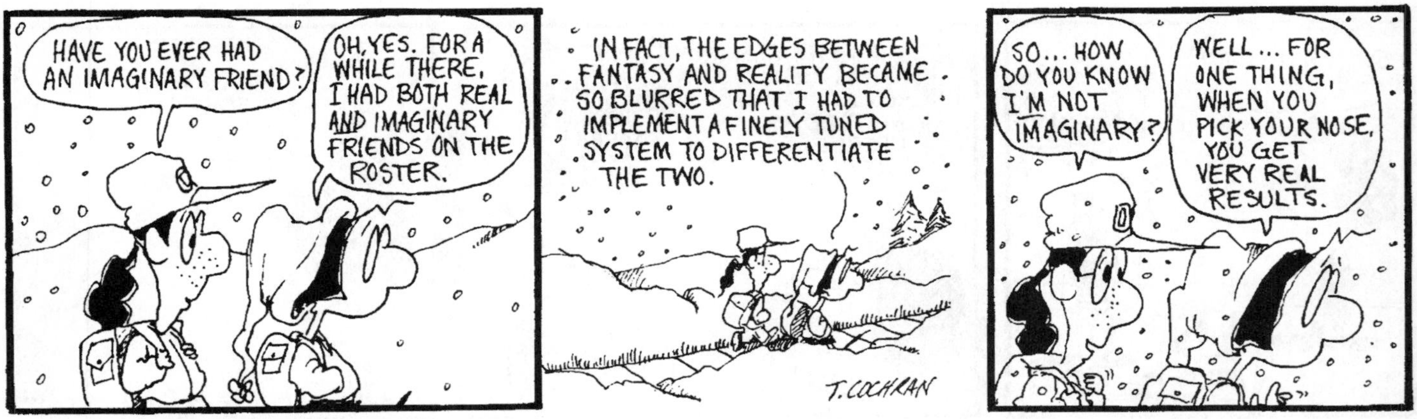
HAVE YOU EVER HAD AN IMAGINARY FRIEND?
OH, YES. FOR A WHILE THERE, I HAD BOTH REAL AND IMAGINARY FRIENDS ON THE ROSTER.
IN FACT, THE EDGES BETWEEN FANTASY AND REALITY BECAME SO BLURRED THAT I HAD TO IMPLEMENT A FINELY TUNED SYSTEM TO DIFFERENTIATE THE TWO.
T. COCHRAN
SO... HOW DO YOU KNOW I'M NOT IMAGINARY?
WELL... FOR ONE THING, WHEN YOU PICK YOUR NOSE, YOU GET VERY REAL RESULTS.

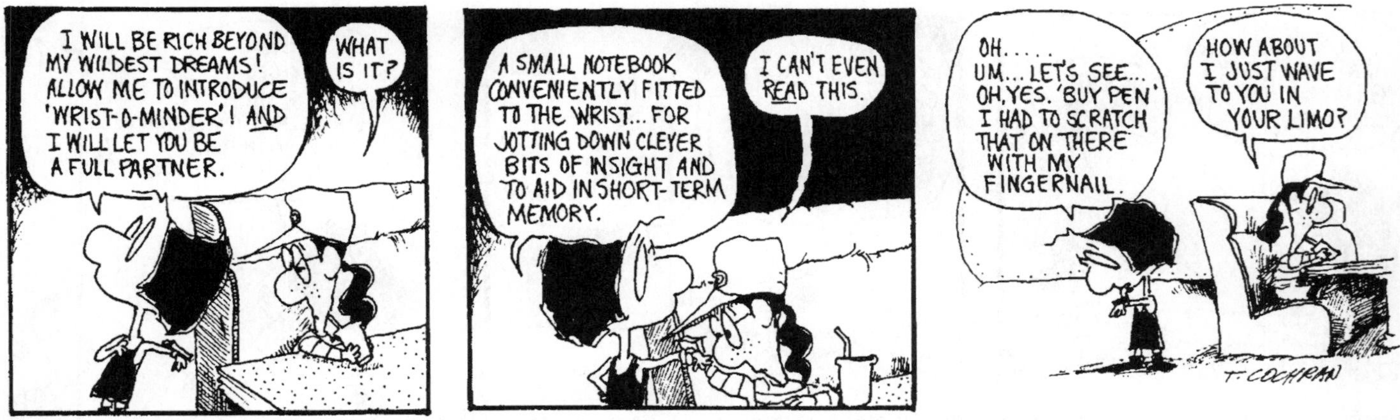
I WILL BE RICH BEYOND MY WILDEST DREAMS! ALLOW ME TO INTRODUCE 'WRIST-O-MINDER'! AND I WILL LET YOU BE A FULL PARTNER.
WHAT IS IT?
A SMALL NOTEBOOK CONVENIENTLY FITTED TO THE WRIST... FOR JOTTING DOWN CLEVER BITS OF INSIGHT AND TO AID IN SHORT-TERM MEMORY.
I CAN'T EVEN READ THIS.
OH..... UM... LET'S SEE... OH, YES. 'BUY PEN' I HAD TO SCRATCH THAT ON THERE WITH MY FINGERNAIL.
HOW ABOUT I JUST WAVE TO YOU IN YOUR LIMO?
T. COCHRAN

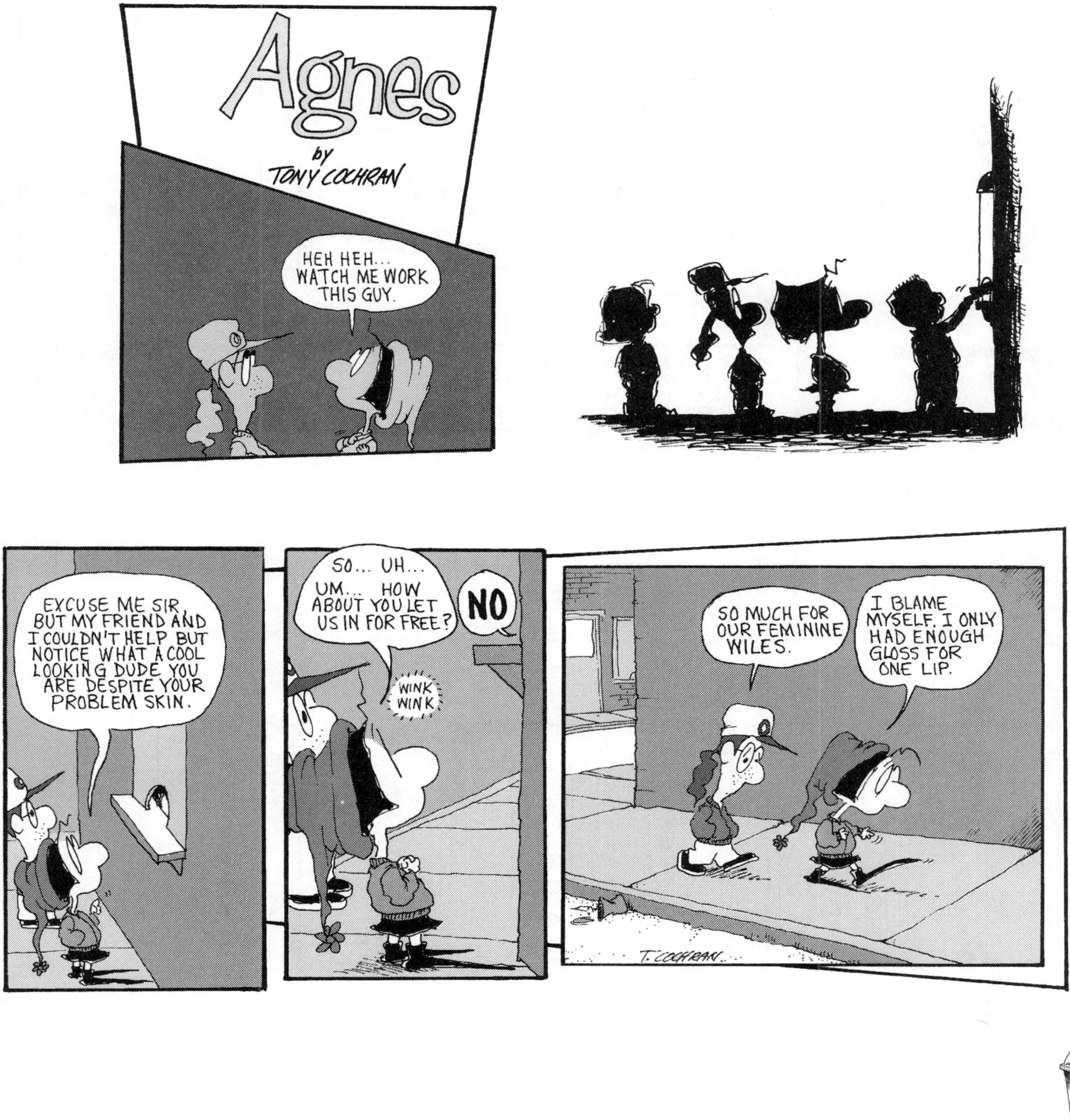
Agnes
by TONY COCHRAN
HEH HEH... WATCH ME WORK THIS GUY.
EXCUSE ME SIR, BUT MY FRIEND AND I COULDN'T HELP BUT NOTICE WHAT A COOL LOOKING DUDE YOU ARE DESPITE YOUR PROBLEM SKIN.
SO... UH... UM... HOW ABOUT YOU LET US IN FOR FREE?
WINK WINK
NO
SO MUCH FOR OUR FEMININE WILES.
I BLAME MYSELF. I ONLY HAD ENOUGH GLOSS FOR ONE LIP.
T. COCHRAN

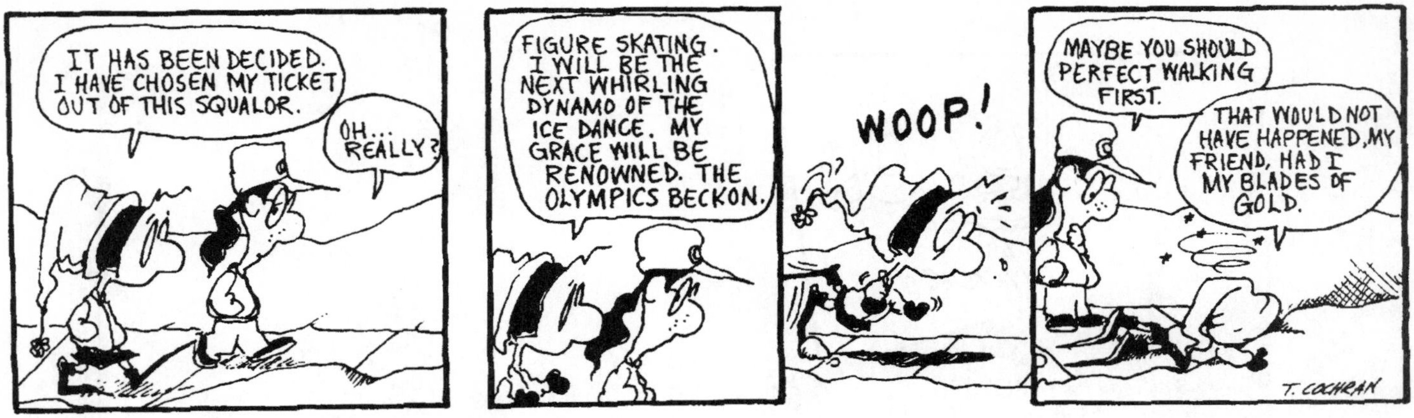
IT HAS BEEN DECIDED. I HAVE CHOSEN MY TICKET OUT OF THIS SQUALOR.
OH... REALLY?
FIGURE SKATING. I WILL BE THE NEXT WHIRLING DYNAMO OF THE ICE DANCE. MY GRACE WILL BE RENOWNED. THE OLYMPICS BECKON.
WOOP!
MAYBE YOU SHOULD PERFECT WALKING FIRST.
THAT WOULD NOT HAVE HAPPENED, MY FRIEND, HAD I MY BLADES OF GOLD.
T. COCHRAN

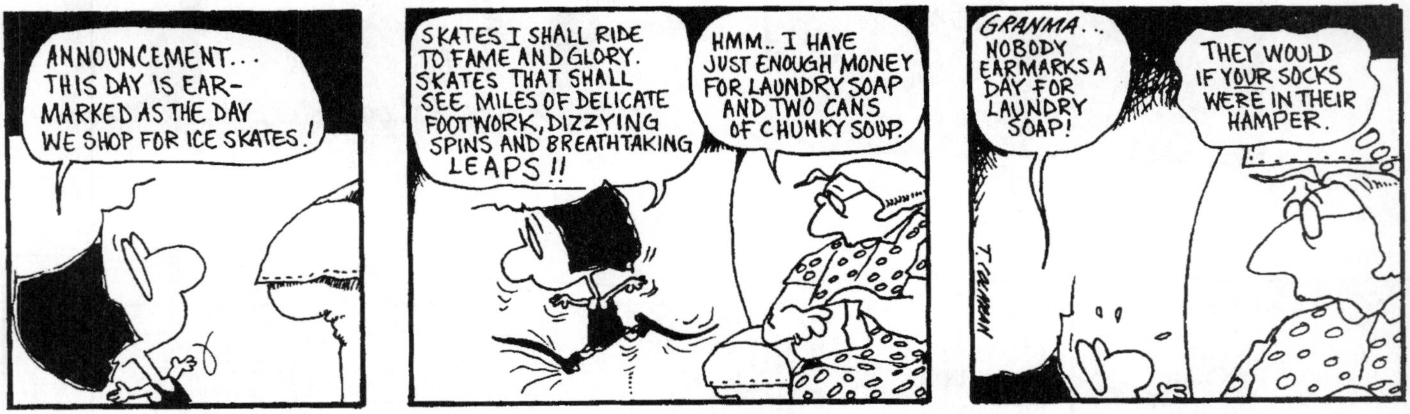
ANNOUNCEMENT... THIS DAY IS EAR-MARKED AS THE DAY WE SHOP FOR ICE SKATES!
SKATES I SHALL RIDE TO FAME AND GLORY. SKATES THAT SHALL SEE MILES OF DELICATE FOOTWORK, DIZZYING SPINS AND BREATHTAKING LEAPS!!
HMM.. I HAVE JUST ENOUGH MONEY FOR LAUNDRY SOAP AND TWO CANS OF CHUNKY SOUP.
GRANMA... NOBODY EARMARKS A DAY FOR LAUNDRY SOAP!
THEY WOULD IF YOUR SOCKS WERE IN THEIR HAMPER.
T. COCHRAN

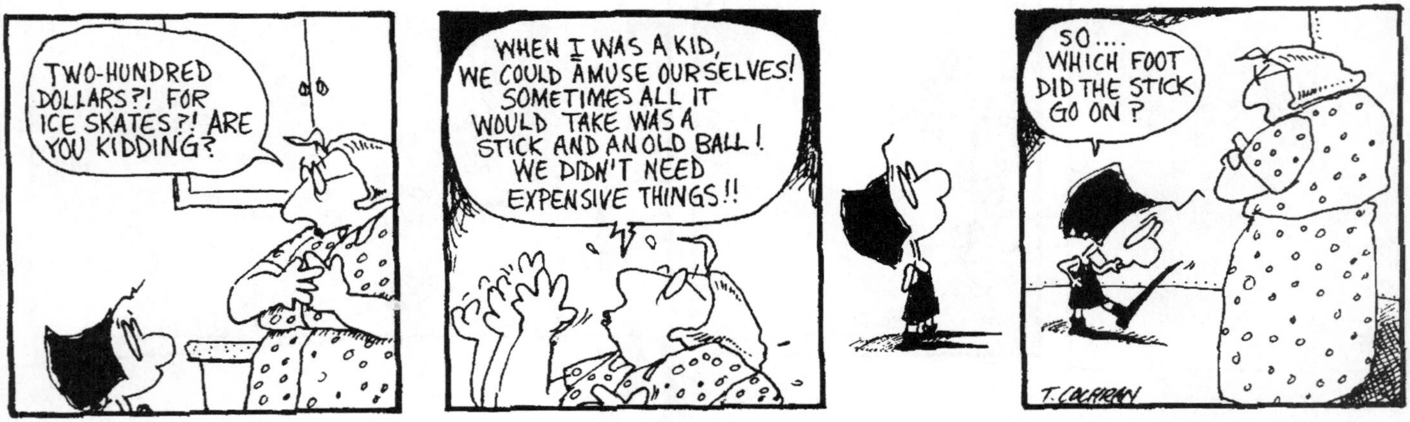
TWO-HUNDRED DOLLARS?! FOR ICE SKATES?! ARE YOU KIDDING?
WHEN I WAS A KID, WE COULD AMUSE OURSELVES! SOMETIMES ALL IT WOULD TAKE WAS A STICK AND AN OLD BALL! WE DIDN'T NEED EXPENSIVE THINGS!!
SO.... WHICH FOOT DID THE STICK GO ON?
T. COCHRAN

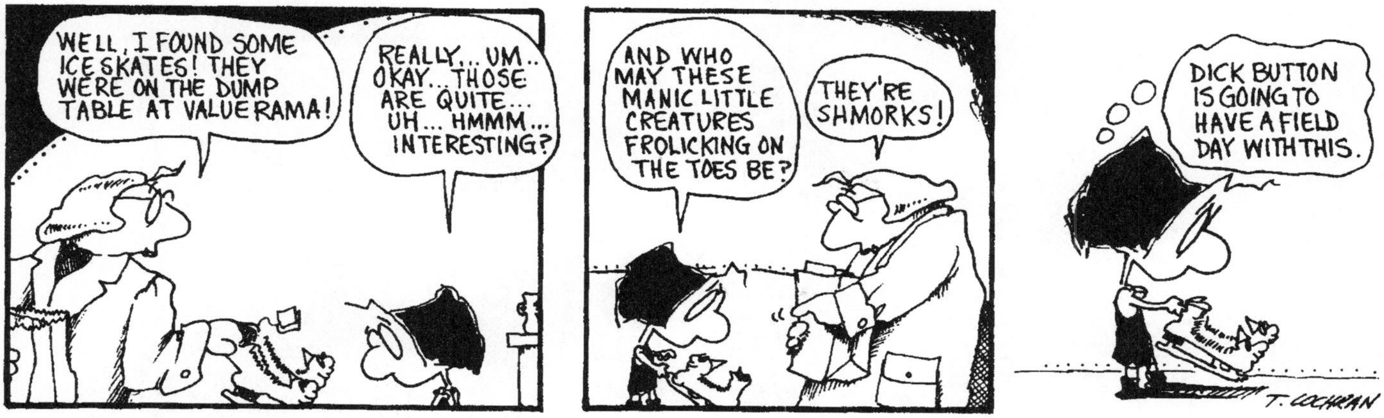
WELL, I FOUND SOME ICE SKATES! THEY WERE ON THE DUMP TABLE AT VALUERAMA!
REALLY... UM.. OKAY... THOSE ARE QUITE... UH... HMMM... INTERESTING?
AND WHO MAY THESE MANIC LITTLE CREATURES FROLICKING ON THE TOES BE?
THEY'RE SHMORKS!
DICK BUTTON IS GOING TO HAVE A FIELD DAY WITH THIS.
T. COCHRAN

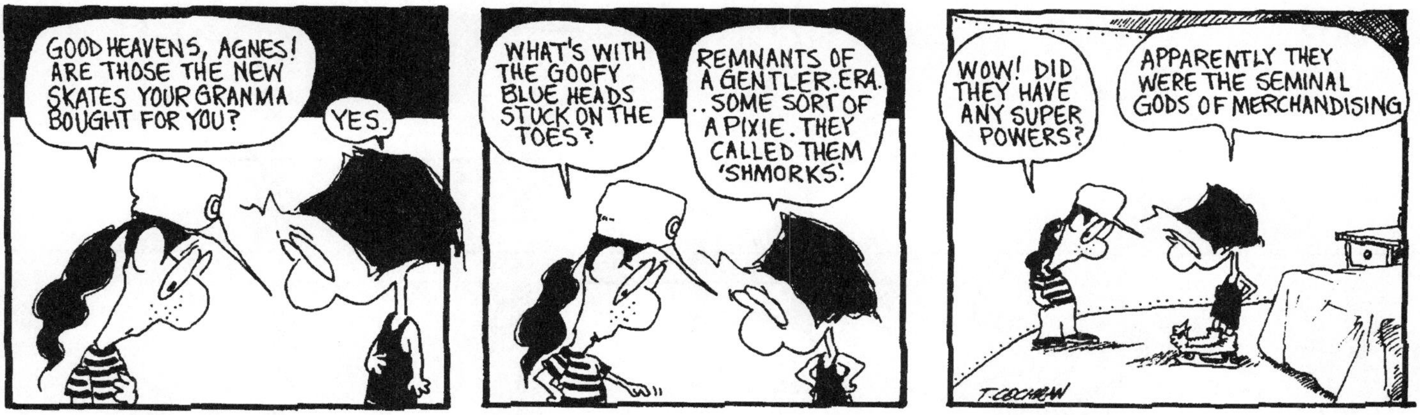
GOOD HEAVENS, AGNES! ARE THOSE THE NEW SKATES YOUR GRANMA BOUGHT FOR YOU?
YES.
WHAT'S WITH THE GOOFY BLUE HEADS STUCK ON THE TOES?
REMNANTS OF A GENTLER ERA. ..SOME SORT OF A PIXIE. THEY CALLED THEM 'SHMORKS'.
WOW! DID THEY HAVE ANY SUPER POWERS?
APPARENTLY THEY WERE THE SEMINAL GODS OF MERCHANDISING.
T. COCHRAN

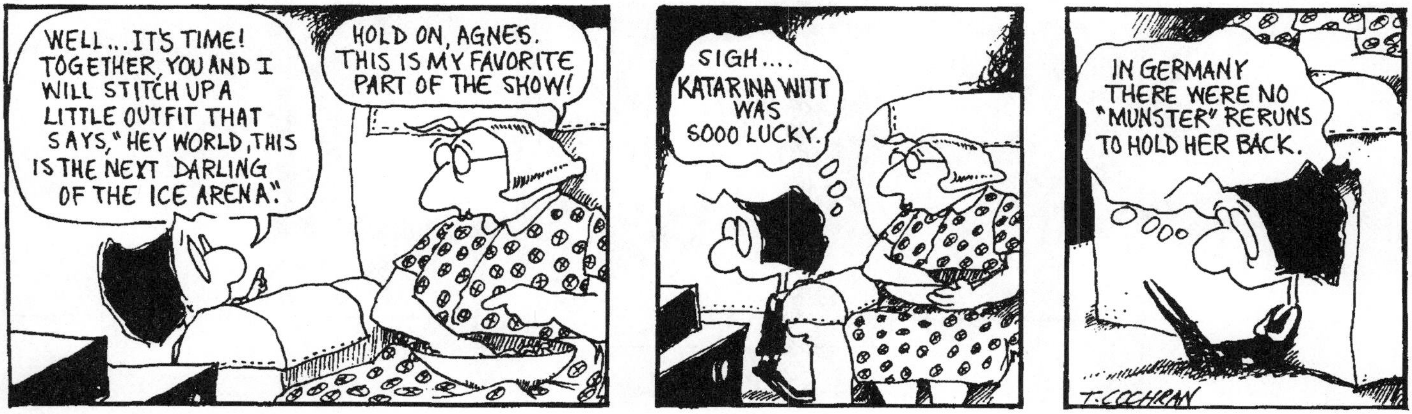
WELL... IT'S TIME! TOGETHER, YOU AND I WILL STITCH UP A LITTLE OUTFIT THAT SAYS, "HEY WORLD, THIS IS THE NEXT DARLING OF THE ICE ARENA".
HOLD ON, AGNES. THIS IS MY FAVORITE PART OF THE SHOW!
SIGH.... KATARINA WITT WAS SOOO LUCKY.
IN GERMANY THERE WERE NO "MUNSTER" RERUNS TO HOLD HER BACK.
T. COCHRAN

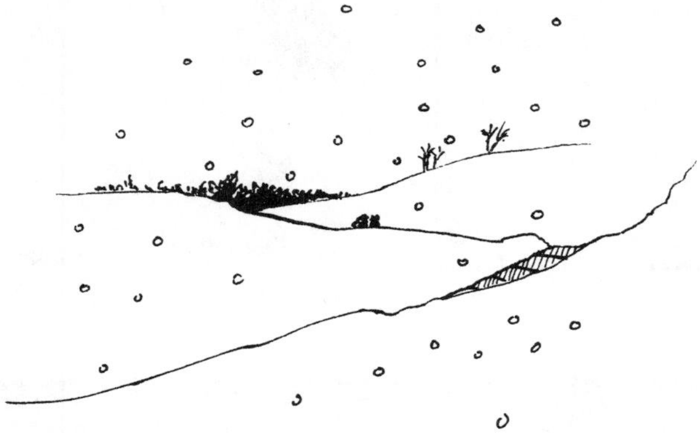

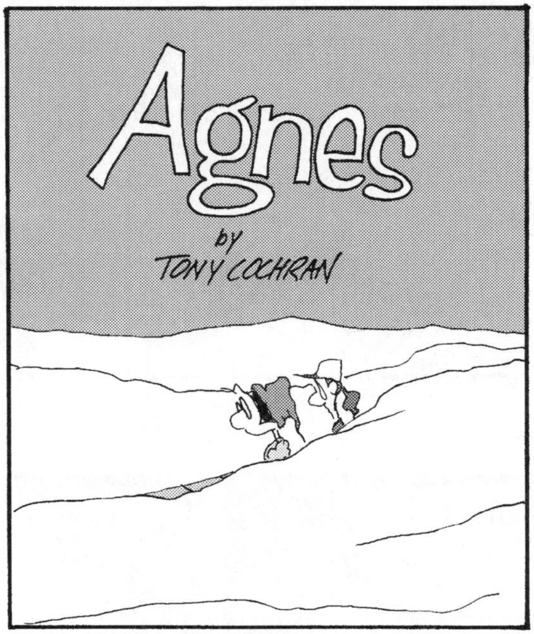
Agnes
by
TONY COCHRAN

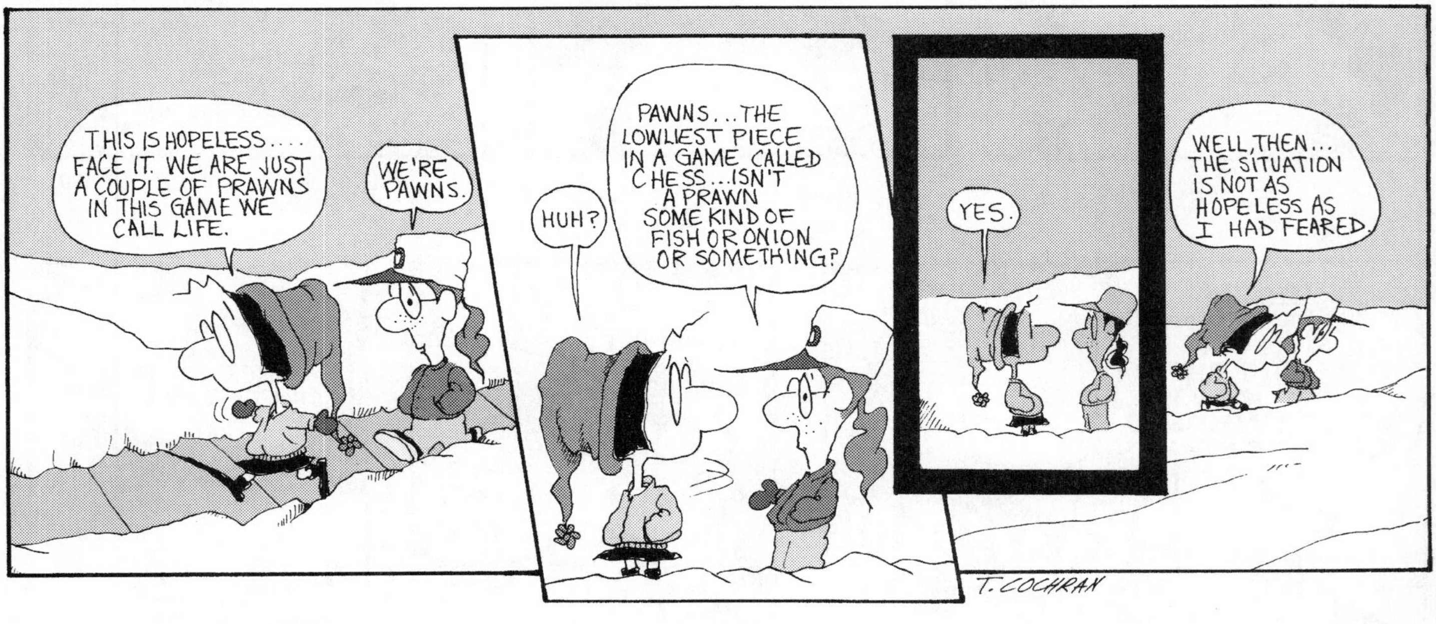
THIS IS HOPELESS.... FACE IT. WE ARE JUST A COUPLE OF PRAWNS IN THIS GAME WE CALL LIFE.
WE'RE PAWNS.
HUH?
PAWNS...THE LOWLIEST PIECE IN A GAME CALLED CHESS...ISN'T A PRAWN SOME KIND OF FISH OR ONION OR SOMETHING?
YES.
WELL, THEN... THE SITUATION IS NOT AS HOPELESS AS I HAD FEARED.
T. COCHRAN

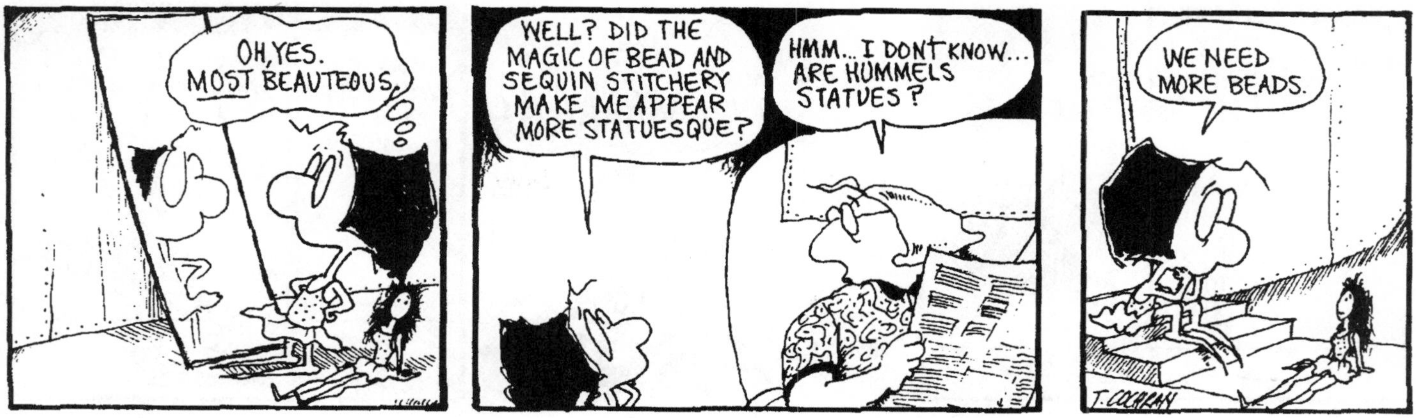
OH, YES. MOST BEAUTEOUS.
WELL? DID THE MAGIC OF BEAD AND SEQUIN STITCHERY MAKE ME APPEAR MORE STATUESQUE?
HMM... I DON'T KNOW... ARE HUMMELS STATUES?
WE NEED MORE BEADS.
T. COCHRAN

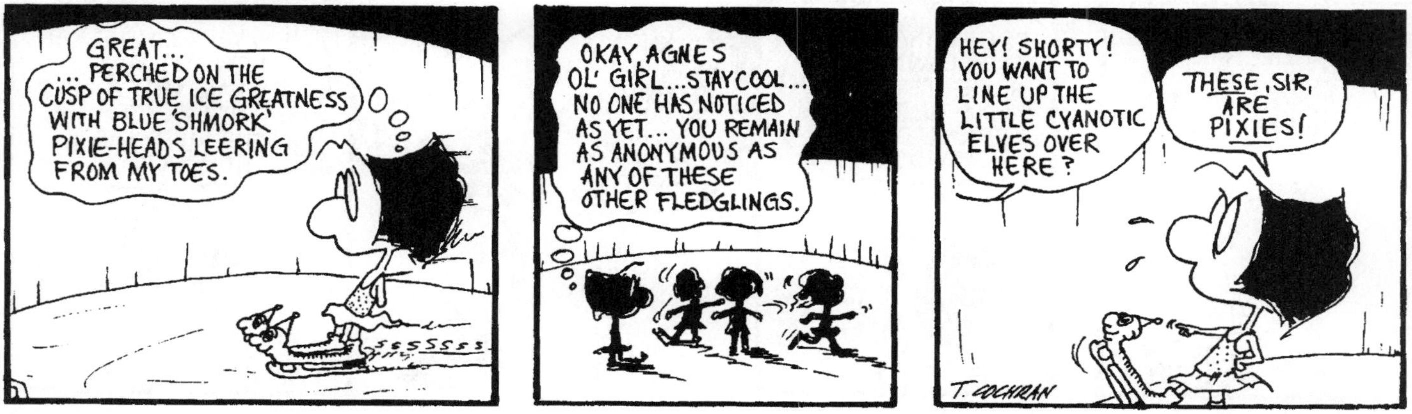
GREAT... ...PERCHED ON THE CUSP OF TRUE ICE GREATNESS WITH BLUE 'SHMORK' PIXIE-HEADS LEERING FROM MY TOES.
SSSSSSS
OKAY, AGNES OL' GIRL... STAY COOL... NO ONE HAS NOTICED AS YET... YOU REMAIN AS ANONYMOUS AS ANY OF THESE OTHER FLEDGLINGS.
HEY! SHORTY! YOU WANT TO LINE UP THE LITTLE CYANOTIC ELVES OVER HERE?
THESE, SIR, ARE PIXIES!
T. COCHRAN

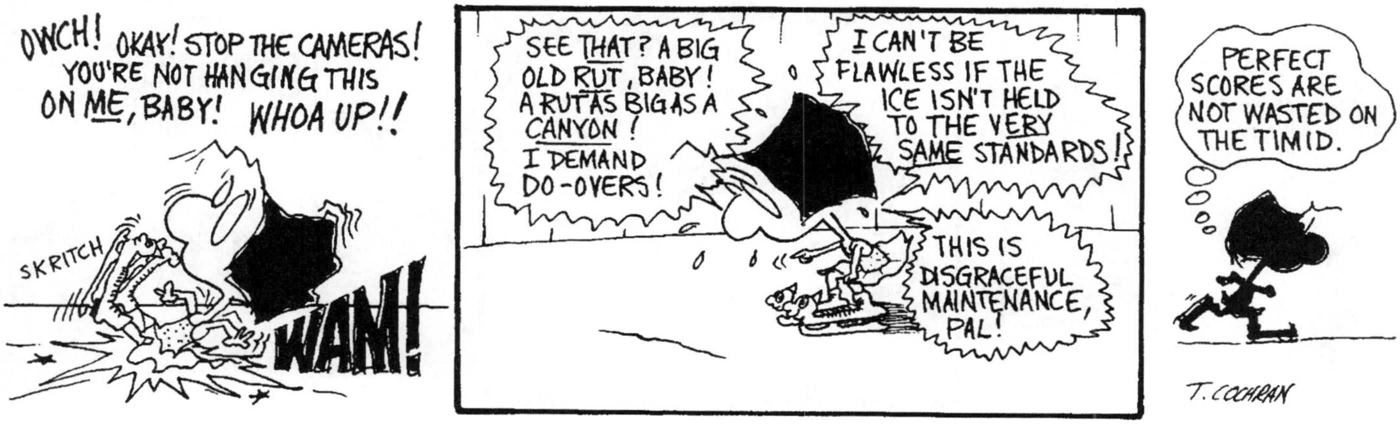
OWCH! OKAY! STOP THE CAMERAS! YOU'RE NOT HANGING THIS ON ME, BABY! WHOA UP!!
SKRITCH
WAM!
SEE THAT? A BIG OLD RUT, BABY! A RUT AS BIG AS A CANYON! I DEMAND DO-OVERS!
I CAN'T BE FLAWLESS IF THE ICE ISN'T HELD TO THE VERY SAME STANDARDS!
THIS IS DISGRACEFUL MAINTENANCE, PAL!
PERFECT SCORES ARE NOT WASTED ON THE TIMID.
T. COCHRAN

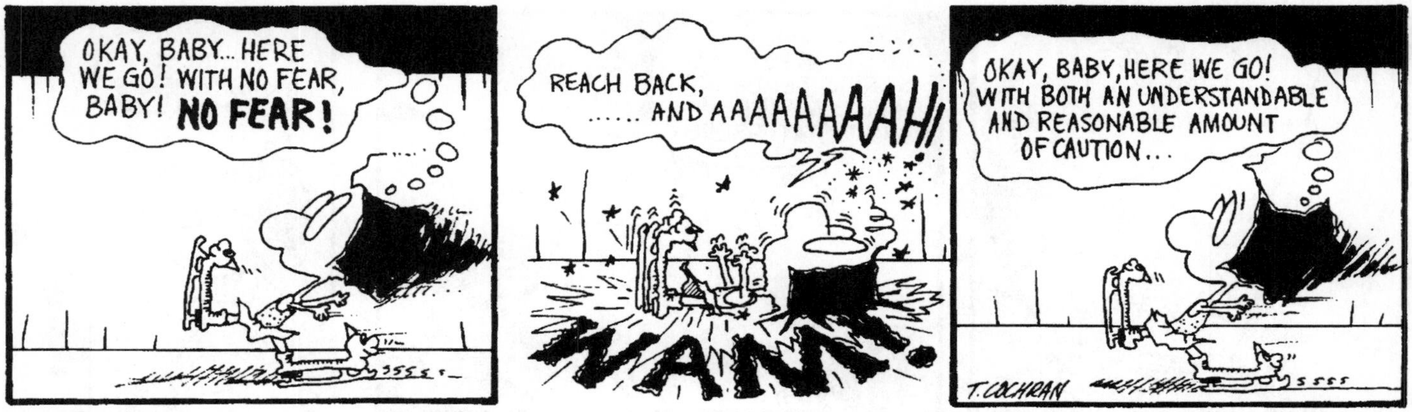
OKAY, BABY... HERE WE GO! WITH NO FEAR, BABY! **NO FEAR!**
REACH BACK, ... AND AAAAAAAAAH!
WAM!
OKAY, BABY, HERE WE GO! WITH BOTH AN UNDERSTANDABLE AND REASONABLE AMOUNT OF CAUTION...
T. COCHRAN

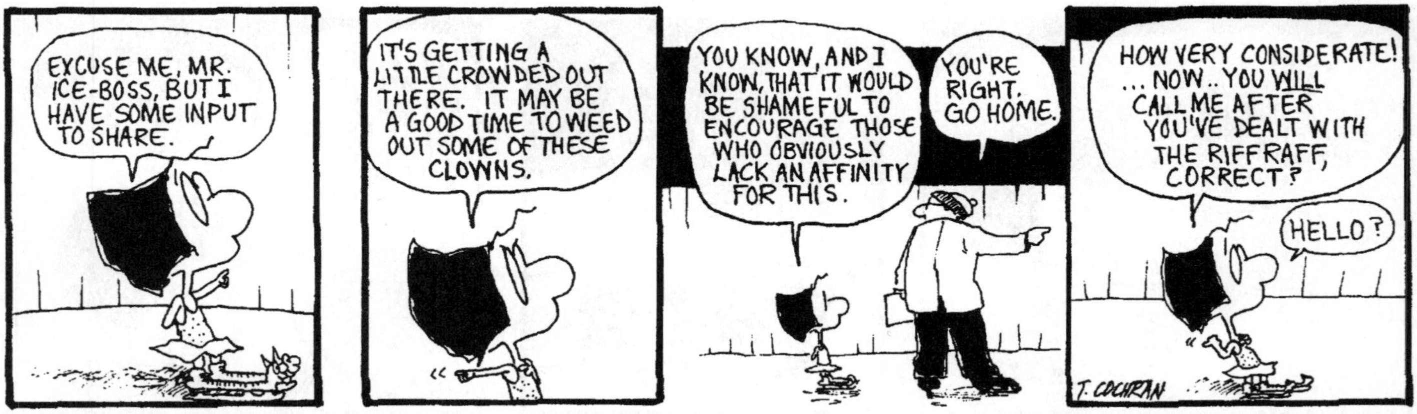
EXCUSE ME, MR. ICE-BOSS, BUT I HAVE SOME INPUT TO SHARE.
IT'S GETTING A LITTLE CROWDED OUT THERE. IT MAY BE A GOOD TIME TO WEED OUT SOME OF THESE CLOWNS.
YOU KNOW, AND I KNOW, THAT IT WOULD BE SHAMEFUL TO ENCOURAGE THOSE WHO OBVIOUSLY LACK AN AFFINITY FOR THIS.
YOU'RE RIGHT. GO HOME.
HOW VERY CONSIDERATE! ... NOW.. YOU WILL CALL ME AFTER YOU'VE DEALT WITH THE RIFFRAFF, CORRECT?
HELLO?
T. COCHRAN

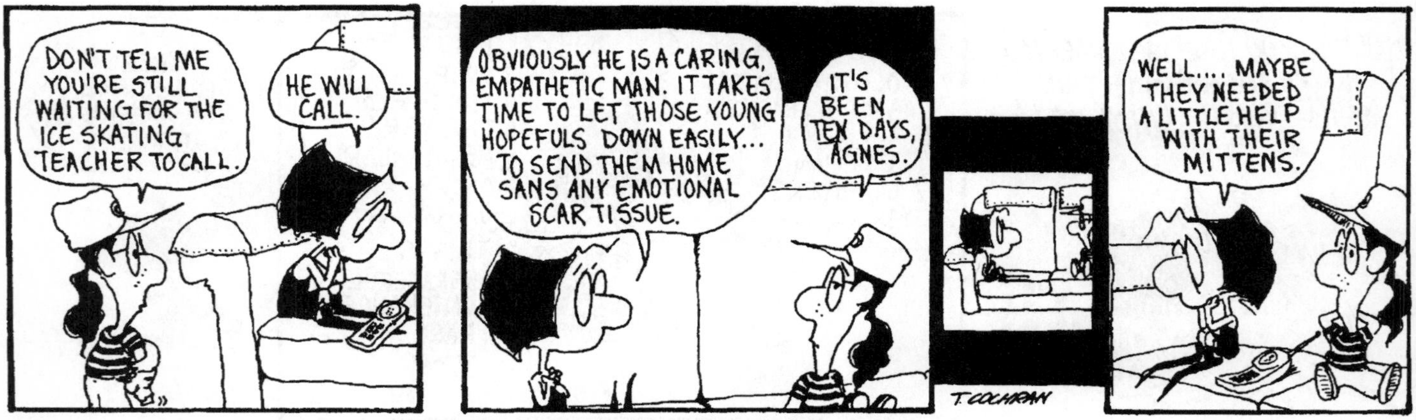
DON'T TELL ME YOU'RE STILL WAITING FOR THE ICE SKATING TEACHER TO CALL.
HE WILL CALL.
OBVIOUSLY HE IS A CARING, EMPATHETIC MAN. IT TAKES TIME TO LET THOSE YOUNG HOPEFULS DOWN EASILY... TO SEND THEM HOME SANS ANY EMOTIONAL SCAR TISSUE.
IT'S BEEN TEN DAYS, AGNES.
WELL.... MAYBE THEY NEEDED A LITTLE HELP WITH THEIR MITTENS.
T. COCHRAN

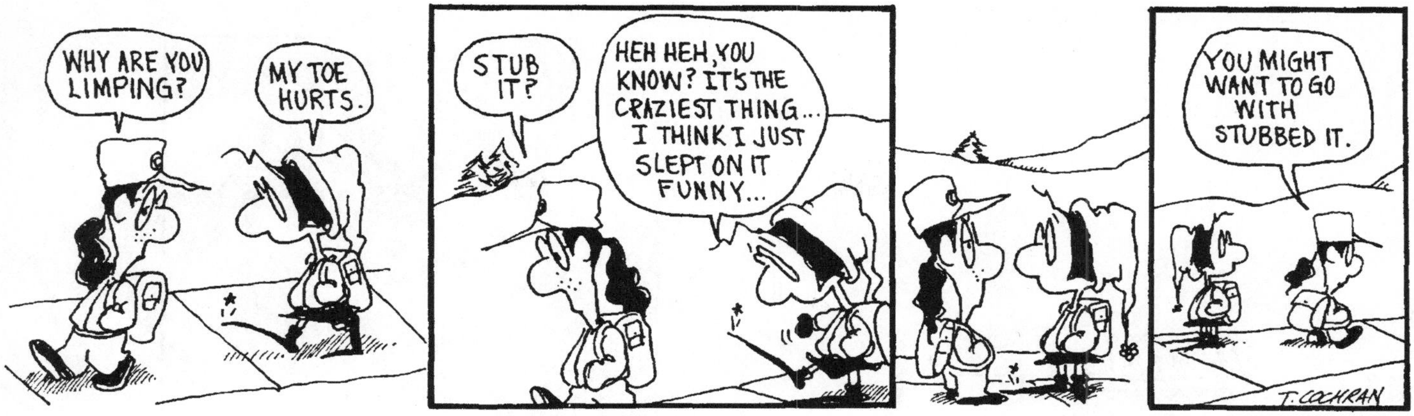
WHY ARE YOU LIMPING?
MY TOE HURTS.
STUB IT?
HEH HEH, YOU KNOW? IT'S THE CRAZIEST THING... I THINK I JUST SLEPT ON IT FUNNY...
YOU MIGHT WANT TO GO WITH STUBBED IT.
T. COCHRAN

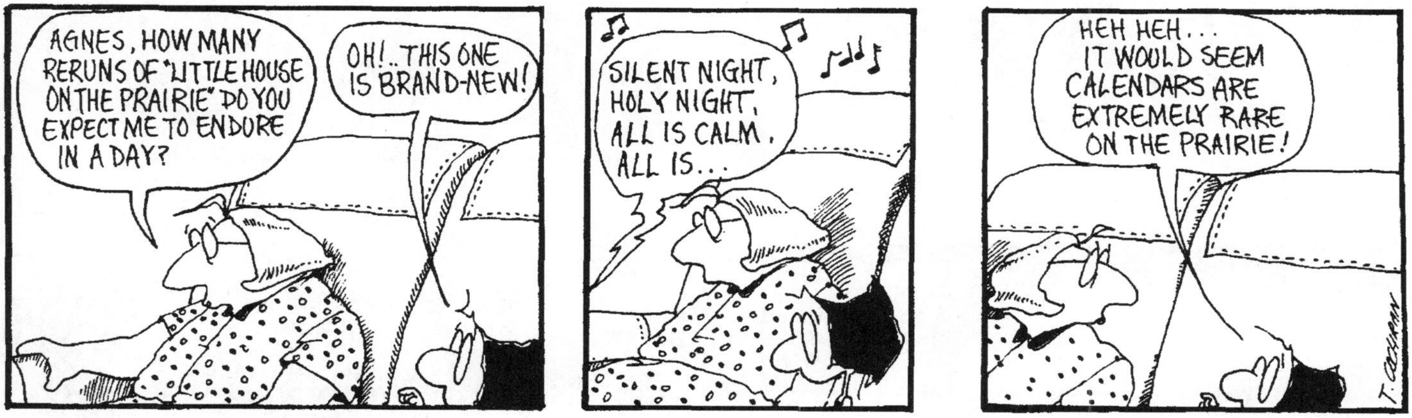
AGNES, HOW MANY RERUNS OF "LITTLE HOUSE ON THE PRAIRIE" DO YOU EXPECT ME TO ENDURE IN A DAY?
OH!..THIS ONE IS BRAND-NEW!
SILENT NIGHT, HOLY NIGHT, ALL IS CALM, ALL IS...
HEH HEH... IT WOULD SEEM CALENDARS ARE EXTREMELY RARE ON THE PRAIRIE!
T. COCHRAN

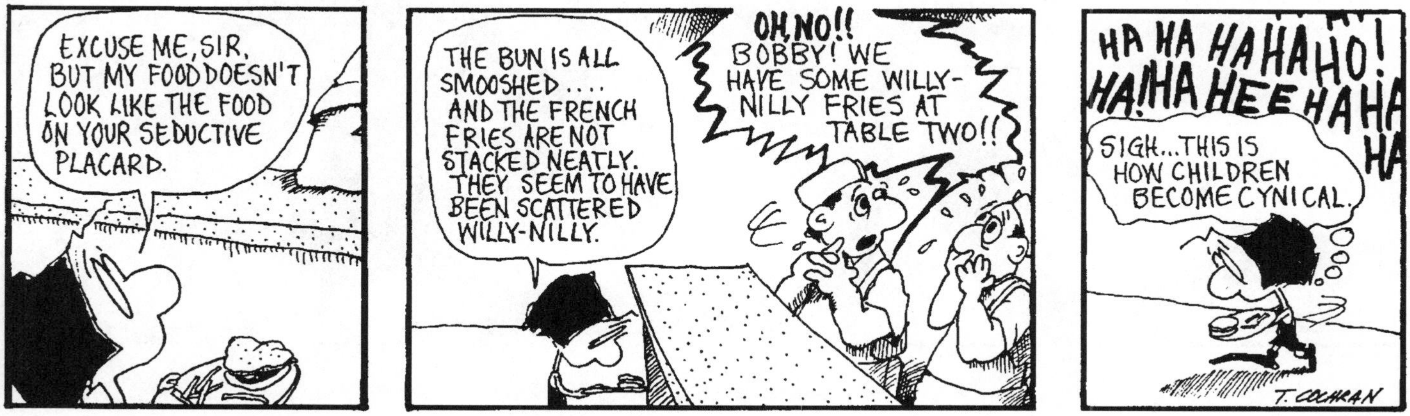
EXCUSE ME, SIR, BUT MY FOOD DOESN'T LOOK LIKE THE FOOD ON YOUR SEDUCTIVE PLACARD.
THE BUN IS ALL SMOOSHED.... AND THE FRENCH FRIES ARE NOT STACKED NEATLY. THEY SEEM TO HAVE BEEN SCATTERED WILLY-NILLY.
OH, NO!! BOBBY! WE HAVE SOME WILLY-NILLY FRIES AT TABLE TWO!!
HA HA HAHA HO! HA! HA HEE HA HA HA HA
SIGH...THIS IS HOW CHILDREN BECOME CYNICAL.
T. COCHRAN

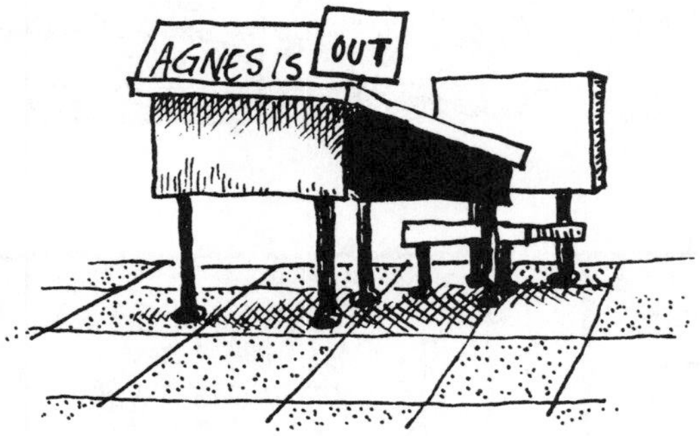
AGNES IS OUT

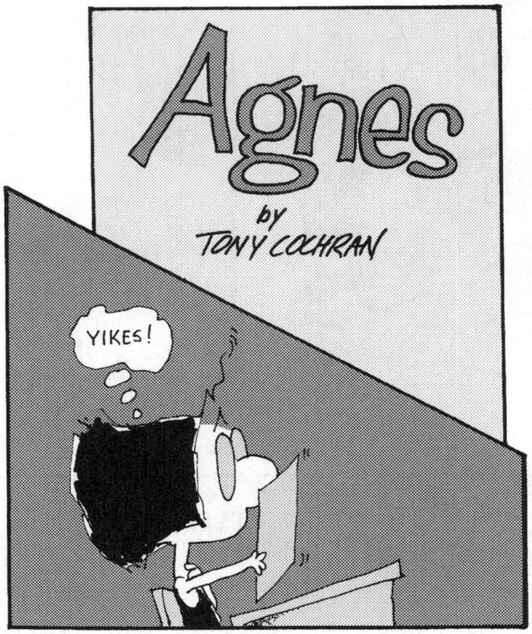
Agnes
by
TONY COCHRAN
YIKES!

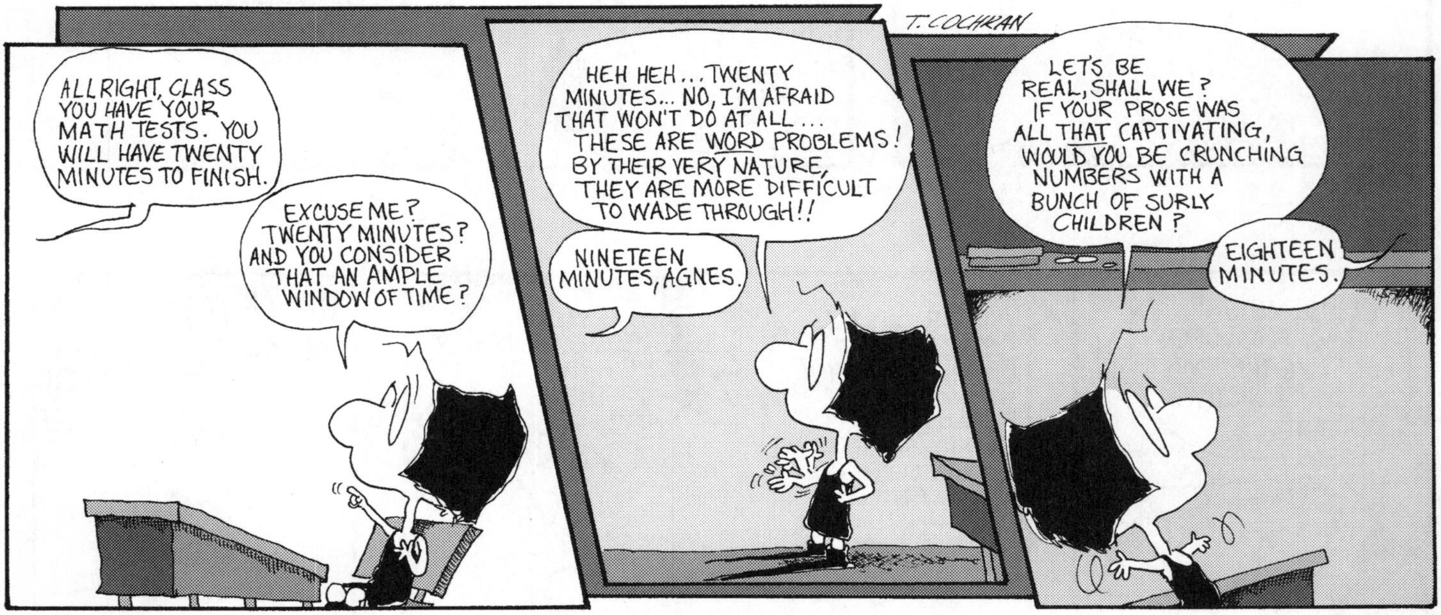
T. COCHRAN
ALL RIGHT, CLASS YOU HAVE YOUR MATH TESTS. YOU WILL HAVE TWENTY MINUTES TO FINISH.
EXCUSE ME? TWENTY MINUTES? AND YOU CONSIDER THAT AN AMPLE WINDOW OF TIME?
NINETEEN MINUTES, AGNES.
HEH HEH... TWENTY MINUTES... NO, I'M AFRAID THAT WON'T DO AT ALL... THESE ARE WORD PROBLEMS! BY THEIR VERY NATURE, THEY ARE MORE DIFFICULT TO WADE THROUGH!!
EIGHTEEN MINUTES.
LET'S BE REAL, SHALL WE? IF YOUR PROSE WAS ALL THAT CAPTIVATING, WOULD YOU BE CRUNCHING NUMBERS WITH A BUNCH OF SURLY CHILDREN?

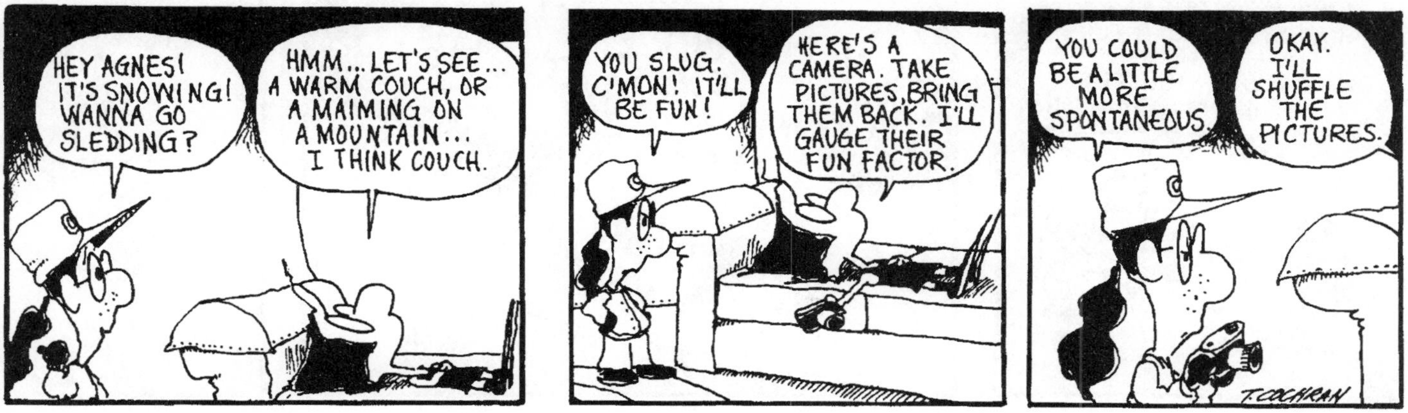
HEY AGNES! IT'S SNOWING! WANNA GO SLEDDING?
HMM... LET'S SEE... A WARM COUCH, OR A MAIMING ON A MOUNTAIN... I THINK COUCH.
YOU SLUG. C'MON! IT'LL BE FUN!
HERE'S A CAMERA. TAKE PICTURES, BRING THEM BACK. I'LL GAUGE THEIR FUN FACTOR.
YOU COULD BE A LITTLE MORE SPONTANEOUS.
OKAY. I'LL SHUFFLE THE PICTURES.
T. COCHRAN

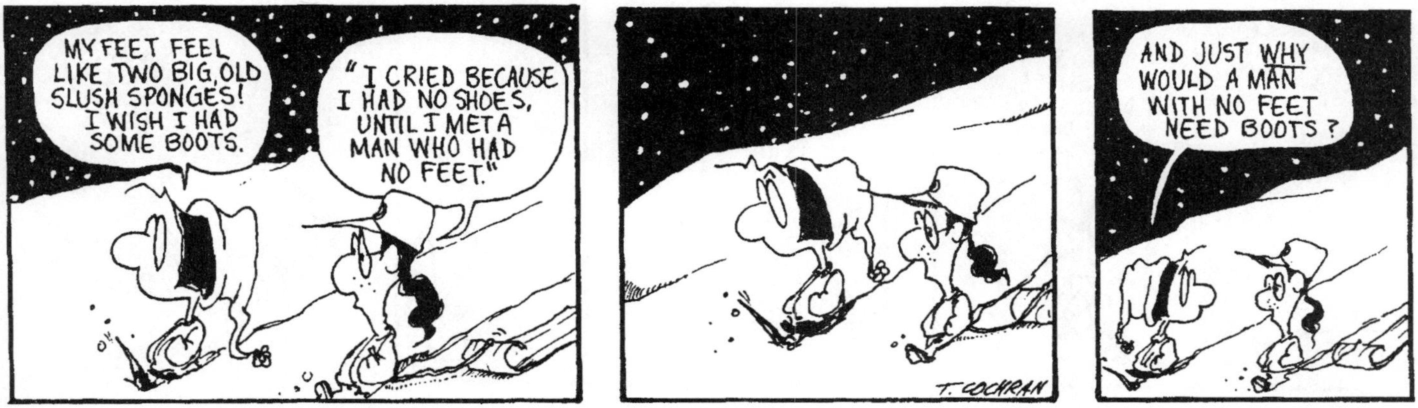
MY FEET FEEL LIKE TWO BIG, OLD SLUSH SPONGES! I WISH I HAD SOME BOOTS.
"I CRIED BECAUSE I HAD NO SHOES, UNTIL I MET A MAN WHO HAD NO FEET."
T. COCHRAN
AND JUST WHY WOULD A MAN WITH NO FEET NEED BOOTS?

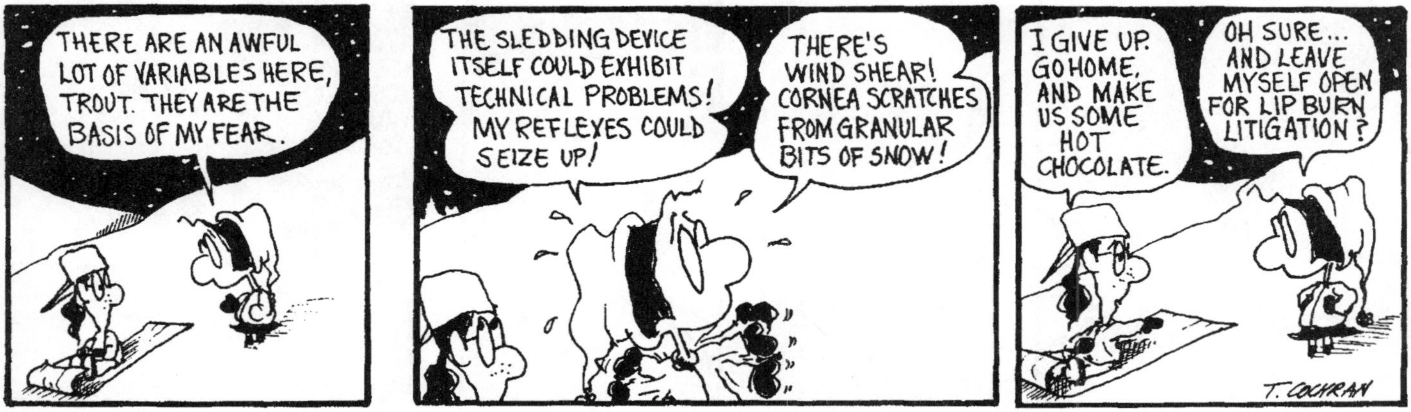
THERE ARE AN AWFUL LOT OF VARIABLES HERE, TROUT. THEY ARE THE BASIS OF MY FEAR.
THE SLEDDING DEVICE ITSELF COULD EXHIBIT TECHNICAL PROBLEMS! MY REFLEXES COULD SEIZE UP!
THERE'S WIND SHEAR! CORNEA SCRATCHES FROM GRANULAR BITS OF SNOW!
I GIVE UP. GO HOME, AND MAKE US SOME HOT CHOCOLATE.
OH SURE... AND LEAVE MYSELF OPEN FOR LIP BURN LITIGATION?
T. COCHRAN

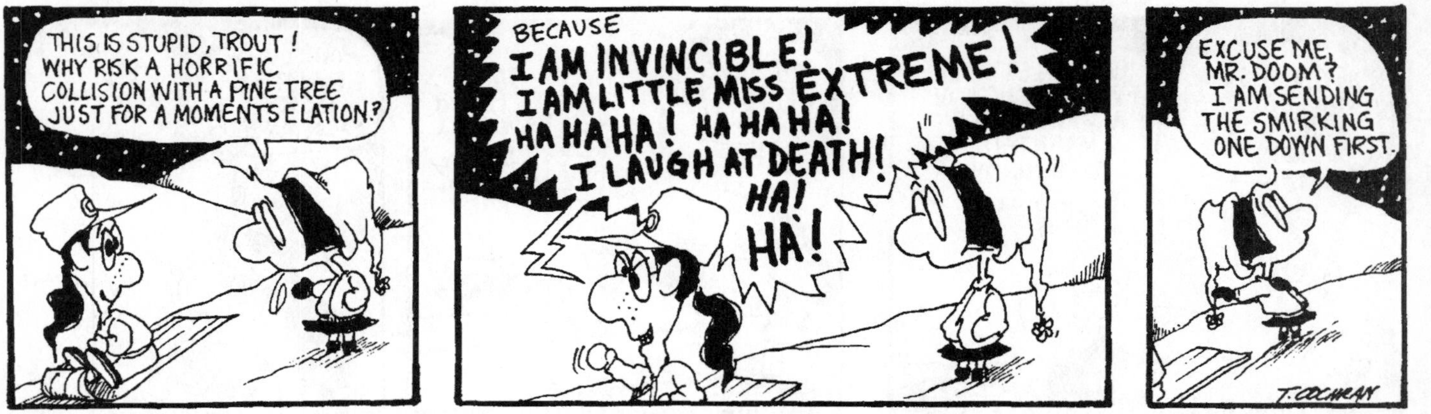
THIS IS STUPID, TROUT! WHY RISK A HORRIFIC COLLISION WITH A PINE TREE JUST FOR A MOMENT'S ELATION?
BECAUSE I AM INVINCIBLE! I AM LITTLE MISS EXTREME! HA HA HA! HA HA HA! I LAUGH AT DEATH! HA! HA!
EXCUSE ME, MR. DOOM? I AM SENDING THE SMIRKING ONE DOWN FIRST.
T. COCHRAN

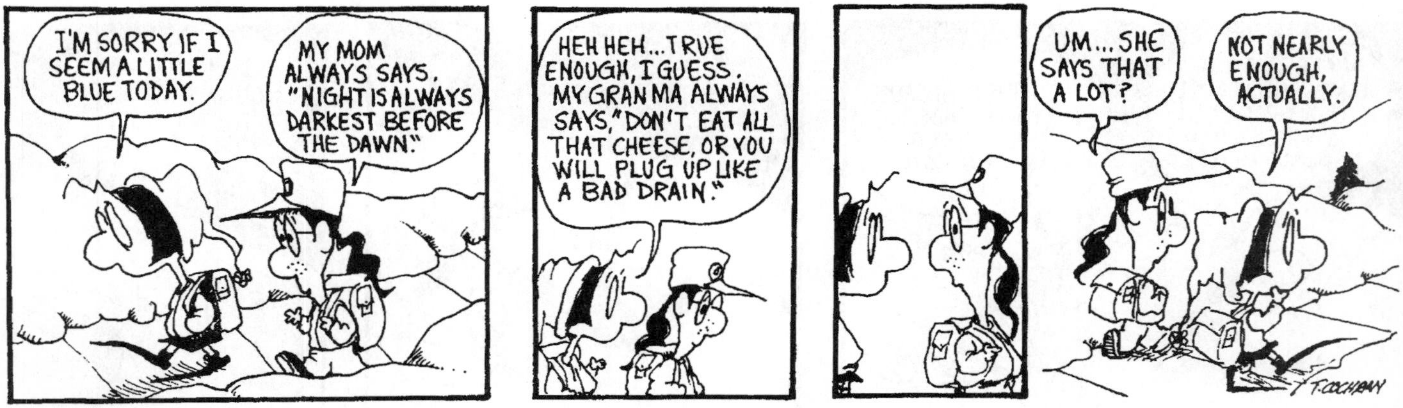
I'M SORRY IF I SEEM A LITTLE BLUE TODAY.
MY MOM ALWAYS SAYS, "NIGHT IS ALWAYS DARKEST BEFORE THE DAWN."
HEH HEH... TRUE ENOUGH, I GUESS. MY GRANMA ALWAYS SAYS, "DON'T EAT ALL THAT CHEESE, OR YOU WILL PLUG UP LIKE A BAD DRAIN."
UM... SHE SAYS THAT A LOT?
NOT NEARLY ENOUGH, ACTUALLY.
T. COCHRAN

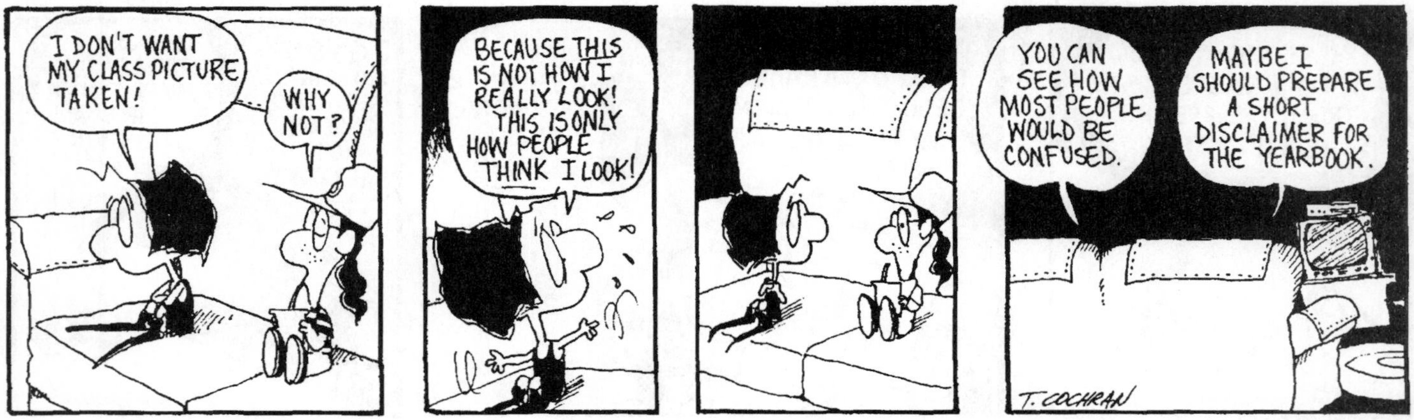
I DON'T WANT MY CLASS PICTURE TAKEN!
WHY NOT?
BECAUSE THIS IS NOT HOW I REALLY LOOK! THIS IS ONLY HOW PEOPLE THINK I LOOK!
YOU CAN SEE HOW MOST PEOPLE WOULD BE CONFUSED.
MAYBE I SHOULD PREPARE A SHORT DISCLAIMER FOR THE YEARBOOK.
T. COCHRAN

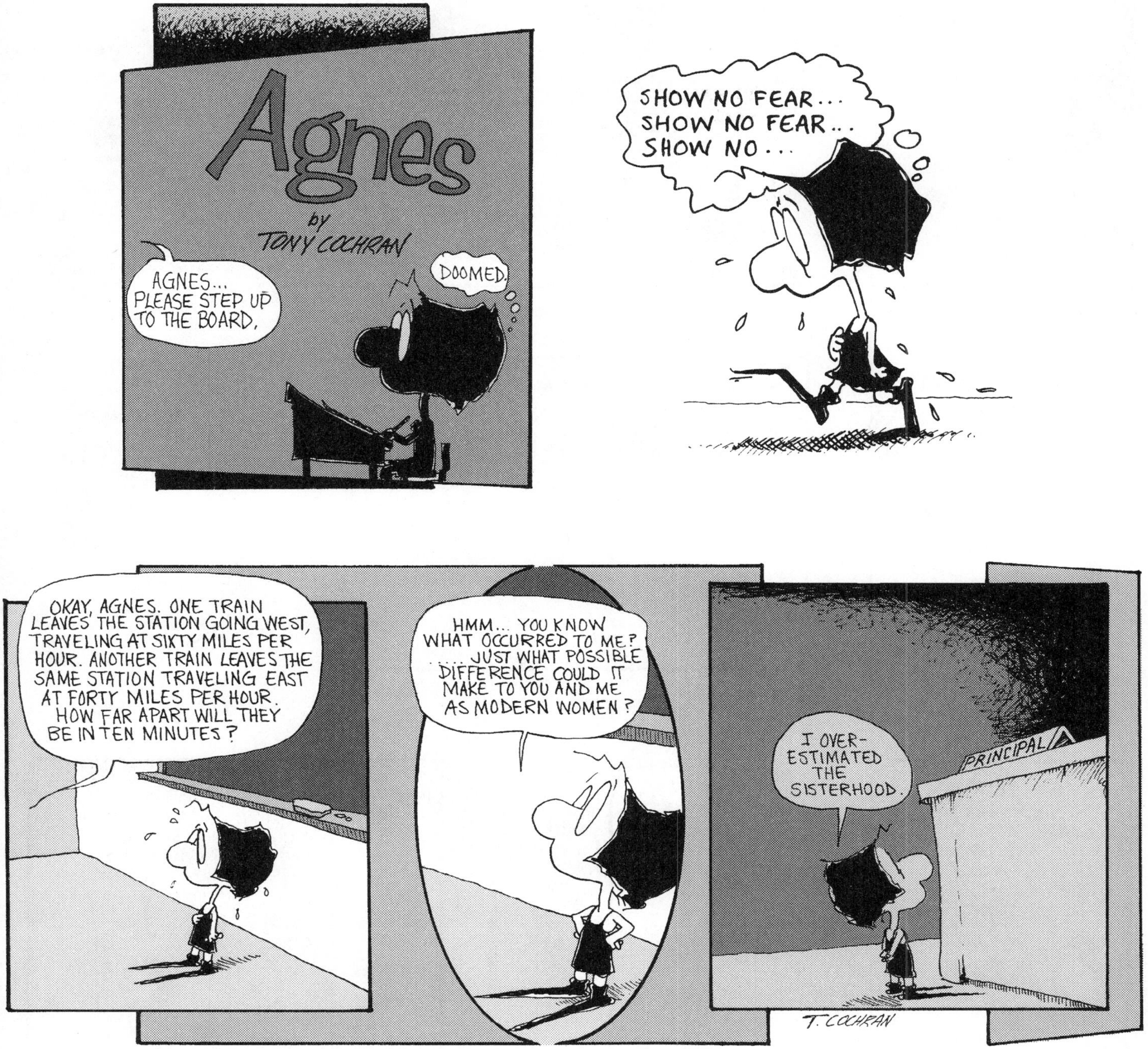
Agnes
by TONY COCHRAN
AGNES... PLEASE STEP UP TO THE BOARD.
DOOMED.
SHOW NO FEAR... SHOW NO FEAR... SHOW NO...
OKAY, AGNES. ONE TRAIN LEAVES THE STATION GOING WEST, TRAVELING AT SIXTY MILES PER HOUR. ANOTHER TRAIN LEAVES THE SAME STATION TRAVELING EAST AT FORTY MILES PER HOUR. HOW FAR APART WILL THEY BE IN TEN MINUTES?
HMM... YOU KNOW WHAT OCCURRED TO ME? ..... JUST WHAT POSSIBLE DIFFERENCE COULD IT MAKE TO YOU AND ME AS MODERN WOMEN?
I OVER-ESTIMATED THE SISTERHOOD.
PRINCIPAL
T. COCHRAN

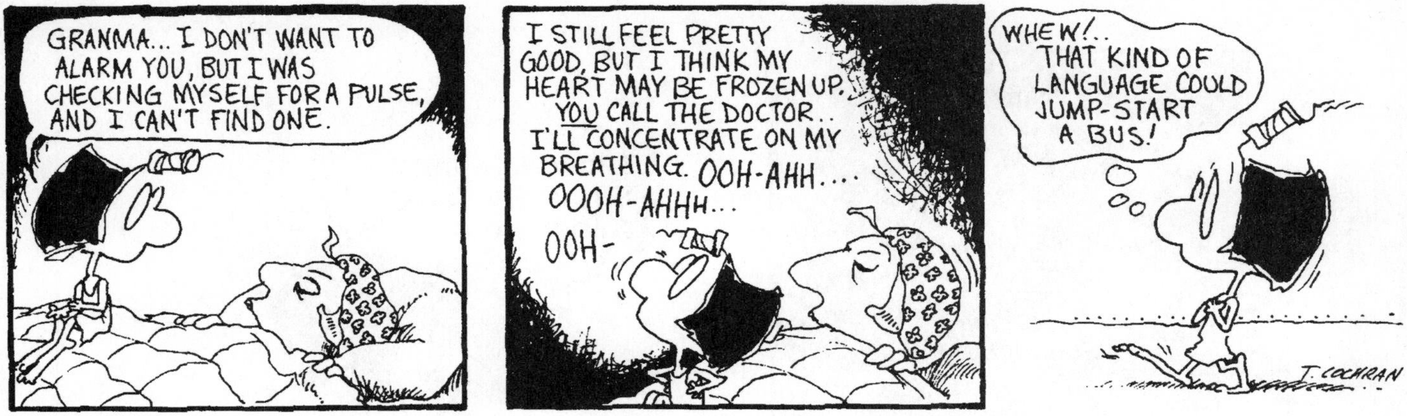
GRANMA... I DON'T WANT TO ALARM YOU, BUT I WAS CHECKING MYSELF FOR A PULSE, AND I CAN'T FIND ONE.
I STILL FEEL PRETTY GOOD, BUT I THINK MY HEART MAY BE FROZEN UP. YOU CALL THE DOCTOR.. I'LL CONCENTRATE ON MY BREATHING. OOH-AHH....
OOOH-AHHH...
OOH-
WHEW!.. THAT KIND OF LANGUAGE COULD JUMP-START A BUS!
T. COCHRAN

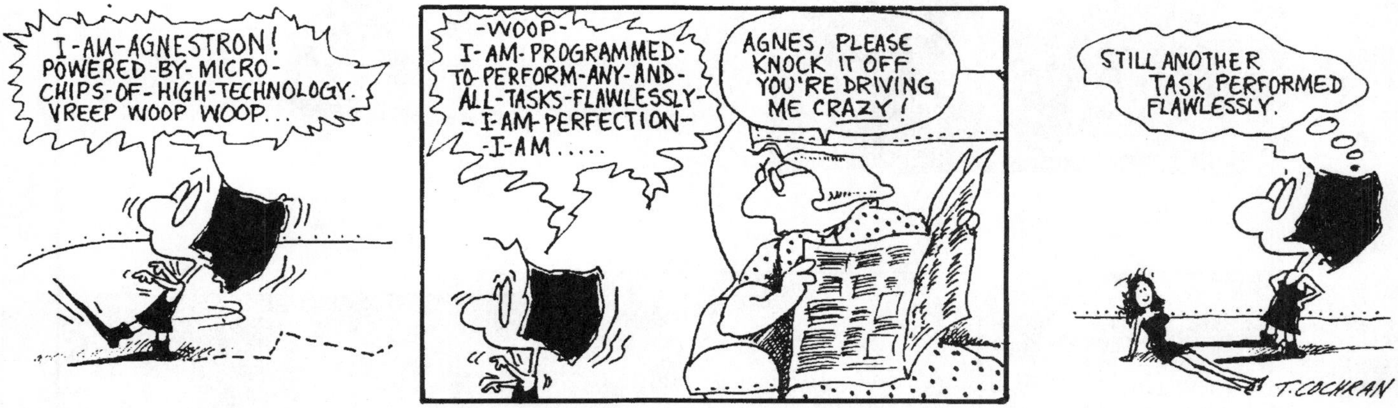
I-AM-AGNESTRON! POWERED-BY-MICRO-CHIPS-OF-HIGH-TECHNOLOGY. VREEP WOOP WOOP...
-WOOP- I-AM-PROGRAMMED-TO-PERFORM-ANY-AND-ALL-TASKS-FLAWLESSLY- -I-AM-PERFECTION- -I-AM.....
AGNES, PLEASE KNOCK IT OFF. YOU'RE DRIVING ME CRAZY!
STILL ANOTHER TASK PERFORMED FLAWLESSLY.
T. COCHRAN

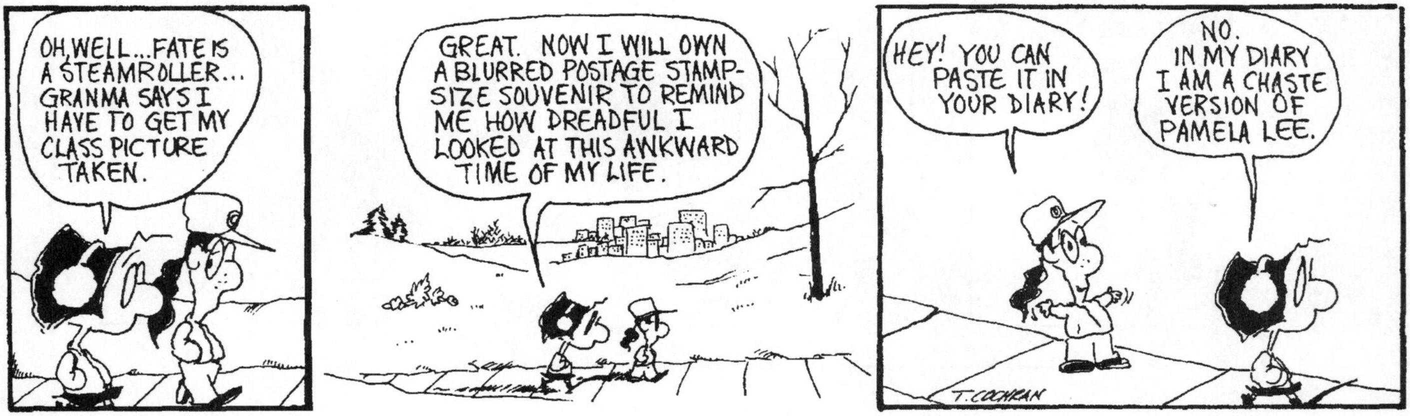
OH, WELL...FATE IS A STEAMROLLER... GRANMA SAYS I HAVE TO GET MY CLASS PICTURE TAKEN.
GREAT. NOW I WILL OWN A BLURRED POSTAGE STAMP-SIZE SOUVENIR TO REMIND ME HOW DREADFUL I LOOKED AT THIS AWKWARD TIME OF MY LIFE.
HEY! YOU CAN PASTE IT IN YOUR DIARY!
NO. IN MY DIARY I AM A CHASTE VERSION OF PAMELA LEE.
T. COCHRAN